Emile and Isaac Pereire

Manchester University Press

Studies in
Modern French History

Edited by
Mark Greengrass and Pamela Pilbeam

This series is published in collaboration with the UK Society for the Study of French History. It aims to showcase innovative short monographs relating to the history of the French, in France and in the world since *c.*1750. Each volume speaks to a theme in the history of France with broader resonances to other discourses about the past. Authors demonstrate how the sources and interpretations of modern French history are being opened to historical investigation in new and interesting ways, and how unfamiliar subjects have the capacity to tell us more about the role of France within the European continent. The series is particularly open to interdisciplinary studies that break down the traditional boundaries and conventional disciplinary divisions.

Titles already published in this series

Catholicism and children's literature in France:
The comtesse de Ségur (1799–1874)
Sophie Heywood

Aristocratic families in republican France, 1870–1940
Elizabeth C. Macknight

The routes to exile: France and the Spanish Civil War refugees, 1939–2009
Scott Soo

The Society for the
Study of French History

Emile and Isaac Pereire

Bankers, Socialists and Sephardic Jews
in nineteenth-century France

HELEN M. DAVIES

Manchester University Press

Copyright © Helen M. Davies 2015

The right of Helen M. Davies to be identified as the author of this work has been asserted by her in accordance with the Copyright, Designs and Patents Act 1988.

Published by Manchester University Press
Altrincham Street, Manchester M1 7JA, UK
www.manchesteruniversitypress.co.uk

British Library Cataloguing-in-Publication Data
A catalogue record for this book is available from the British Library

Library of Congress Cataloging-in-Publication Data applied for

ISBN 978 1 7849 9356 6 *paperback*

First published 2015

This paperback edition first published 2016

The publisher has no responsibility for the persistence or accuracy of URLs for any external or third-party internet websites referred to in this book, and does not guarantee that any content on such websites is, or will remain, accurate or appropriate.

Typeset in Minion by
Koinonia, Manchester
Printed and Bound in Great Britain by
Lightning Source

To the memory of Renee, Bob, and Jeffrey
and for John

Contents

List of figures	*page* ix
Acknowledgements	xi
List of abbreviations	xiii
Introduction	1
1 Bordeaux: a Sephardic childhood	9
2 The new society	33
3 The new entrepreneurs	61
4 The adventure of rail	87
5 Capitalism and the State	112
6 The family business	139
7 Private lives of public men	162
8 Boom and bust	194
9 Epilogue	221
10 Conclusion	233
Appendix: Pereire companies	242
Select bibliography	244
Index	257

Figures

1 Emile Pereire (1855). Photograph Nadar, Bibliothèque nationale de France, Estampes et Photographie *page* 34
2 Isaac Pereire (1850s). Photograph Nadar, Archives de la famille Pereire 35
3 James de Rothschild. Photograph Robert Jefferson Bingham, Reproduced with permission of The Rothschild Archive 77
4 Maquette locomotive Paris-St-Germain. Archives de la famille Pereire 79
5 Napoléon III (1860). Photograph Mayer & Pierson, Wikimedia Commons. George Eastman House, Rochester, NY 104
6 Eugène Pereire (1890s). Photographer unknown, Photo © Musée d'art et d'histoire du Judaïsme 148
7 Emile Pereire II (1898). Photograph Grands Magasins du Louvre, Private collection 150
8 Henry Pereire (1890s). Photograph Paul Boyer, Archives de la famille Pereire 152
9 Gustave Pereire (1880s). Photograph Fritz Luckhardt, Archives de la famille Pereire 153
10 Rachel Herminie Rodrigues Henriques (Herminie), Mme Emile Pereire. C. Brun after Alexandre Cabanel, Private collection 168
11 Fanny Rebecca Rodrigues Pereire, Mme Isaac Pereire, with her daughters Jeanne and Henriette. Photograph Robert Jefferson Bingham, Photo © Musée d'art et d'histoire du Judaïsme 171
12 Cécile Rodrigues Pereire, Mme Charles Rhoné. Photograph Bayard and Bertall, Photo © Musée d'art et d'histoire du Judaïsme 172

13	Suzanne Chevalier, Mme Emile Pereire II. Photographer unknown, Private collection	175
14	Juliette Betzi Fould, Mme Eugène Pereire. Photograph P. Frois, Photo © Musée d'art et d'histoire du Judaïsme	176
15	Château Palmer. Archives de la famille Pereire	177
16	Amélie Emerique, Mme Gustave Pereire. Photographer unknown, Photo © Musée d'art et d'histoire du Judaïsme	183
17	Léontine de Stoppani, Mme Henry Pereire. Photographer unknown, Archives de la famille Pereire	184
18	Emile Pereire (1863). Photograph Robert Jefferson Bingham, Collection Serge Kakou, Paris	195
19	Isaac Pereire (1860s). Photograph L. Angerer, Collection of the author	199
20	Commencement of construction, rue Impériale, Marseille. Photograph A. Terris, Archives de la famille Pereire	211

Acknowledgements

A rich story emerges from the Pereire family archive, one in which warmth and generosity to strangers were the hallmark of a very particular Parisian family. These attributes have not skipped the generations. For her spontaneous welcome into her home, her readiness to open many doors and her continuing interest, I thank Géraldine Pereire Henochsberg, custodian of the Archives de la famille Pereire and great-great-granddaughter of Emile and Herminie Pereire. The existence of the Archives owes everything to the determination and perseverance of her mother, Colette Pereire, and I record our debt to her on my account and on that of other historians. I thank Anita Pereire, widow of François Pereire, a great-grandson of Isaac and Fanny Pereire, who provided me at the outset with much kindness and a memorable space in Wiltshire in which to engage with the works in her possession. She has now generously consigned these to the family archives in Paris. Anita Pereire's daughter, Laure Pereire, has shown a continuing interest in my work and extended great hospitality for which I am grateful.

Many mentors, friends, and colleagues have eased my path in the evolution of this book. I thank Peter McPhee for his continuing support of my work from its origins as a dissertation. It would be immeasurably the poorer without his wisdom, insights, counsel and excellent judgement. Franck Yonnet epitomises for me the collegiality of the historical fraternity and I am grateful for his sharing his work so willingly with another Pereire scholar. I thank the series editors, Mark Greengrass and Pamela Pilbeam, whose guidance and critiquing added so much to the final product. For their help at various times I thank Robert Aldrich, Melanie Aspey, Hubert Bonin, Ian Coller, Marc Desti, Paola Ferruta,

Susan Foley, Gilles Jacoud, Julie Kalman, Hervé Le Bret, John Merriman, Kerry Murphy, Gérard Nahon, Jean-Marc Olivier, the late Alain Plessis, Pauline Prévost-Marcilhacy, Philippe Régnier, Gideon Reuveni, Sylvia Sagona, Charles Sowerwine and Fiorenza Taricone.

I am especially indebted to Tony Kelly of Archiva Lucida and Fay Woodhouse who performed miracles in transforming manuscript into book. Catherine de Saint Phalle helped me enormously in translation from the French. For their help in specific ways I am grateful to Jacques Béjot, Christian Bourdeille, Michel Cardoze, Clara Dicharry, Sherrel Djoneff, Nicolas Feuillie, Christophe Fouin, James Hargrave, Jean-Claude Laumet and Michael Sibalis.

I thank the many staff of archives and libraries across France, from provincial towns to large cities, who conscientiously and professionally went to great lengths to ensure a scholar from the Antipodes received every assistance. And I record my gratitude to the staff of Manchester University Press who have dealt with me at all times with unfailing courtesy, encouragement and commitment.

Finally, none of this would have been possible without the support and affection of my husband, John Nicholson, who has been there at every step. I thank him for his constancy, his understanding and our wonderful life together. This book is dedicated to my late parents and brother, all gone before they could share my pleasure in its completion, and to John.

The reader should not hold any of those whom I have mentioned here responsible for errors or inaccuracies. I am solely responsible for any and all inadequacies.

Abbreviations

ACB	Archives communales de Bayonne
ACCP	Archives du Consistoire Central de Paris
ADG	Archives départementales de la Gironde (Bordeaux)
ADP-A	Archives départementales des Pyrénées-Atlantiques (Pau)
ADP-O	Archives départementales des Pyrénées-Orientales (Perpignan)
AFP	Archives de la famille Pereire
AMBx	Archives municipales de Bordeaux
AN	Archives nationales de France
AN/MC	Minutier central des notaires de Paris
ANMT	Archives nationales du monde du travail, Roubaix
AN/AP	Archives nationales/Archives privées
AP	Archives de Paris
BMBx	Bibliothèque municipale de Bordeaux
BNF	Bibliothèque nationale de France
BNF-A	Bibliothèque nationale Arsenal
BNF-F-M	Bibliothèque nationale François-Mitterrand
BNF-R	Bibliothèque nationale Richelieu
BNF/NAF	Bibliothèque nationale Nouvelles Acquisitions Françaises
BT	Bibliothèque Thiers-Dosne
Écrits	*Écrits de Emile et Isaac Pereire*
GL	Goldsmiths' Library of Economic Literature (University of London)
Oeuvres	*Oeuvres de Emile et Isaac Pereire*
OSSE	*Oeuvres de Saint-Simon & d'Enfantin*
PLM	Chemin de fer de Paris à Lyon et à la Méditerranée
PSG	Chemin de fer de Paris à Saint-Germain-en-Laye
CGM	Compagnie Générale Maritime
Transat	Compagnie Générale Transatlantique

Introduction

In November 2012, the then Spanish Justice Minister Alberto Ruiz-Gallardon made an extraordinary announcement, rescinding the 500-year-old edict of expulsion ordered by King Ferdinand and Queen Isabella of Spain in 1492 in which they had decreed that their Jewish subjects convert to Catholicism or face expulsion. The Spanish government will now invite descendants of the Sephardic Jews of Spain – that is, those who had not converted to Catholicism – to return, offering them full Spanish citizenship.[1] The Portuguese government is also enacting legislation conferring Portuguese nationality automatically on descendants of those who suffered during the Inquisition. These much delayed apologies, admission of error and wrongdoing against the Jews, and the implicit recognition of cultural, social and economic loss to the two countries, has provided an unexpected context for this book.

As a result of the 1492 edict, several hundred thousand Jews had fled to the port cities of the Mediterranean and Atlantic seaboards. Large numbers sailed directly for North Africa, others went to the Levant, eventually settling in Constantinople, Thessaloniki and Sofia. Some went to Livorno, Venice and Trieste. Many took shelter in Portugal where their financial and commercial skills and their networks elicited initial enthusiasm from King Manuel I, a welcome which lasted a mere five years. Some achieved relative safety in a few northerly European cities, congregating in urban areas of Amsterdam and London. By the middle of the sixteenth century, a number had also settled in small groups in France, in Bordeaux and in what is now a suburb of Bayonne, St Esprit-lès-Bayonne. This market town, which quickly became the largest Jewish settlement in the southwest, some 2,500 by the end of the eighteenth century, was a centre for other small towns further afield where Sephardim made their homes, in Bidache, Dax, Labastide-Clairence and Peyrehorade.

Many Jews also took the path to conversion, thus disappearing forever into the protective anonymity of Spanish society. Others who stayed in Spain or Portugal did so under suspicion of the authorities, coming to be known as *conversos*, crypto-Jews, a term frequently applied indiscriminately but carrying life or death consequences. Still others did indeed continue to practice their religion covertly, living a clandestine existence in fear. The fruits of this complex history of population movement and religious upheaval are crystallised for us in the Sephardic diasporas around the Atlantic seaboard where Jews, crypto-Jews and *conversos* alike formed a complex pattern of trading networks in the New World.

The brothers Emile and Isaac Pereire were among the descendants of these Spanish *conversos* and Portuguese refugees from *auto da fe*.[2] They were to become pivotal and sensational figures in nineteenth-century France, their lives and careers a lens through which to re-examine its history. They were born in extraordinary times: Emile in 1800 during the Consulate of Napoléon Bonaparte; Isaac in 1806, after Napoléon had crowned himself Emperor. They were children of Bordeaux, an eighteenth-century trading power-house brought to its knees by the demise of the slave trade and incessant war against Britain and other European enemies. They were also beneficiaries of the French Revolution, among the first Jewish citizens of France born free and equal amid a cohort described as 'the French generation of 1820'.[3] Gifted men born into poverty at a time of economic depression, the Pereires were brilliant, idealistic and ambitious, determined to achieve great things in post-revolutionary France. Leaving Bordeaux in the early 1820s for the opportunities promised in the capital, the brothers were thus part of a wave of young people who surged to Paris from the provinces. The legacy they took with them was to be crucial in shaping their perceptions and their future actions.

Fascinated by the teachings of the economist and philosopher Claude-Henri de Rouvroy, comte de Saint-Simon, they contributed significantly to Saint-Simonianism, the evolving philosophy of social, economic and financial reform which emerged after the death of Saint-Simon. Drawing on the ideas, skills and networks with which Saint-Simonianism provided them, and added to an acquaintance with the industrial and technological innovations transforming Britain, they were among the first to implement the new rail technology in France. It was to be Emile, a financial wizard and not a scientist or engineer at all, whose capacity nevertheless to comprehend and implement complex scientific and engineering ideas led to the first passenger railway in France, from Paris to St Germain-en-Laye, the industrial and commercial significance of which, as is often said, far exceeded its nineteen kilometres. Isaac, a genius with figures, contributed to their partnership in financial matters in critical ways. More innovations and a plethora of business enterprises were to flow from the remarkable and complementary talents and personalities of the two brothers.

Their Saint-Simonian understanding that major railway development required investment capital on an unprecedented scale saw them launch the first investment bank of any size in Europe, the Crédit Mobilier. Through innovative organisation structure the bank became the holding company for enterprises in which it had major investments. They initiated the first regular passenger shipping service between Le Havre and New York and the first regular postal service between France and North America; they founded one of the first department stores in Paris, Les Grands Magasins du Louvre; they were among the first to use the new telegraph; they financed the photographer Nadar; and funded construction of the main sewerage line in the capital. They operated companies distributing gas lighting and water heating throughout Paris; providing horse-drawn public transport and taxi services, as well as industrial laundries to the metropolis; and La Ceinture, the forerunner to the Métro, owes much to the Pereires. Their hotels, the Grand Hôtel du Louvre and the Grand Hôtel, were probably the first purpose-built elements of Paris' tourism infrastructure. They purchased and developed Château Palmer, a splendid *vignoble* in the Médoc and developed Arcachon on the Atlantic seaboard as one of the first seaside resorts. They redeveloped great swathes of Paris' right bank, and attempted to do the same for Marseille. Indeed, Paris' seventeenth *arrondissement* is in large part a Pereire creation and so are chunks of the eighth and ninth. Nor were their activities confined to France, for they stood behind banks and railways in Spain, Germany, Italy, the Netherlands, Russia, Switzerland and the Austro-Hungarian and Ottoman Empires. The nature of every one of their enterprises bespoke modernity, and the verve with which they implemented their ventures demonstrated a new mentality. Emile and Isaac Pereire were thus major players in the industrialisation of France and in the modernisation of French banking, critical figures in implementing domestic and foreign-policy initiatives of government.

For these reasons alone – the sheer scope, significance and spectacular nature of their achievements, their fascination with technology, their capacity to grasp its potential – the Pereires should interest us. But there are further explanations, for their story casts light more broadly on the richness, complexity and pivotal nature of the world into which they were born.

As Jews empowered for the first time in European history to make their own way, their story is one of enormous self-confidence and bravura. Sephardic Jews, they were born into a religious culture which regarded its members as part of the Jewish nobility, different from and superior to their co-religionists, the Ashkenazim. For the Sephardim claimed descent from the royal house of Judah and, throughout most of their history, had accommodated to the host communities within which they lived and worked. Before their expulsion from Spain they had reached positions of power and influence there, achieved great wealth, and produced important philosophers, poets and musicians. Over several centuries during the period of the three religions, they had learned to co-exist with Christianity and Islam without losing their faith but, with the order to leave or to convert to Catholicism, many chose the latter course. In the wake of the edict of expulsion the small number who sought refuge in France integrated as Jews within the Catholic majority, becoming a vital part of the booming mercantile economy in eighteenth-century Bordeaux. Successive monarchs accorded them increasingly liberal civic and economic rights so that by the time of the French Revolution they were able to argue, rightly or wrongly, that they were in no need of emancipation since they had achieved it already.

Emancipation which broke down the legal barriers to progress and gave them equality also confronted them with dilemmas, of reconciling their new citizenship with their religion. Nor was this equality unquestioned as anti-Jewish activity and anti-Semitism gathered strength over the century, challenging the very basis on which Jewish equality had been accorded. The Pereires as Jewish success stories and members of France's *grande bourgeoisie* are thus persons of interest in the historiography of assimilation and acculturation.

In post-revolutionary France, theories of political, social and economic reform proliferated. As Saint-Simonians the Pereires were in the vanguard of two apparently contradictory philosophies: of capitalism, which Saint-Simonianism encouraged through its emphasis on banking and credit, industry and technology; and of socialism, which was implicit in the Saint-Simonians' doctrine of social reform and explicit in its application to 'the poorest and most numerous class'. That these ideologies could be reconciled at an early stage in the development of each bears witness to the integrating character of Saint-Simonianism as well as to the capacity of the Pereire brothers to distil what they needed and make the result work. While the early socialism of which the Pereires had been proponents gave way to militancy as the French industrial working class increased in number and sophistication, becoming more vocal and better organised, the Pereires retained what now seems a rather naïve faith in the power of business to avert through job-creation the violence which became a hallmark of later nineteenth-century socialism. But their Saint-Simonian education did not let them down when we consider how many of their spectacular commercial and industrial achievements (and some of their failures also) can be laid at the door of Saint-Simonianism.

Political regimes changed like a series of revolving doors in nineteenth-century France, yet it was a period of surging economic growth. The Bourbon Restoration which was in many respects repressive and backward-looking unleashed a ferment of ideas which were to be exploited during the succeeding government of Louis-Philippe. The July Monarchy, which ended in revolution, saw the triumph of the bourgeoisie and the beginning of the railway age. The Second Republic, which also ended in regime change, placed opportunity into the hands of Saint-Simonians who created new banking initiatives to expand the new industries. The Second Empire, oppressive and unstable as it was towards the end, was a period of concerted efforts to expand the economy and revive commercial and industrial growth. The Pereires' story is a commentary on this history.

For each of them, then, Saint-Simonianism was the logical expression of the values and attitudes instilled from an early time and the instrument through which they transformed, albeit differently, their experiences as Jews: the religious acculturation; the sense of responsibility for others inherited from the Sephardic communities of the southwest; an impoverished childhood; and the lessons inherent in the depressed economy of Bordeaux. While their exploits were frequently reported in contemporary nineteenth-century journals in Britain and North America, the lives and careers of Emile and Isaac Pereire are scarcely known in the English-speaking world today. Where they have been addressed at all, and frequently this is no more than a mention, the Pereires are often typecast as villains or as *parvenus*, lackeys to Napoléon III; foils to the infinitely more clever and ultimately triumphant James de Rothschild; or corrupt business figures intent on enriching themselves at the expense of the life savings of thousands of small investors. The ideas they developed from Saint-Simonianism have largely been ignored; their roots in the provincial centre of Bordeaux treated cursorily; their cultural formation as Sephardic Jews at a time of Jewish emancipation neglected.

They have been better served in their native country, both in monuments and in literature. In Paris, there is a Métro station and a suburban (RER) railway station named after them, and the bifurcated boulevard Pereire Nord and Pereire Sud. At one time these boulevards issued into and out of a handsome place Pereire now, and only after opposition from residents, re-named place Maréchal-Juin.⁴ Plaques commemorating their activities are to be found at various significant places in the capital. The penumbra of their renown has spread to other members of their family as well, for in Bordeaux a street recalls their grandfather, Jacob Rodrigues Pereire, and in Bayonne a plaque inside the railway station notes that their mother, Rebecca Henriette Lopès Fonseca, was a Bayonnaise. There are reminders in other towns of their significance to France. And in each of the past two centuries and the present one, biographies of the Pereire have appeared.⁵

A biography of Emile and Isaac Pereire must be construed from many different archival sources. While these are summarised in the Select bibliography, the private Archives de la famille Pereire in Paris particularly require comment. Consisting of letters, manuscripts, company documents, privately published articles, a complete set of Pereire publications, this is an important collection but one which has suffered some depredation over the years. What has survived is thus largely incomplete and tends to be concentrated on certain subjects, a random collection thrown together by the hazards of time. Despite this imbalance the surviving material nevertheless covers a long period, from 1715 to 1900, and has been more than sufficient to allow this portrait to emerge when supplemented with other archival documents.

The historian is indebted to Emile Pereire himself: his habit of retaining drafts of much of his written correspondence as well as many of the responses to it is something of a godsend. Similarly, submissions the Pereires drafted for government on matters associated with their businesses frequently survived. One other element of the Archives demands special comment, that is, the volumes of Pereire journal articles and other writings, twenty-seven in all, gathered together early in the twentieth century by Isaac's son Gustave.⁶ While most of this material was published at some time or other and is thus theoretically accessible, it remains largely unknown. The complete writings of Emile Pereire for the journal the *National* in the 1830s, and Isaac's for the *Journal des débats* in the 1840s among others, are readily accessible only through Gustave Pereire's efforts on behalf of the two brothers.

While writing is a solitary occupation, historians do not write in a vacuum. Our work inevitably rides on the shoulders of previous scholars and is influenced for good or ill by our peers. France's economy and financial institutions in the nineteenth century have been particularly blessed with the quality of historical analysis and meticulous attention of past historians: Louis Bergeron, Jean Bouvier, Bertrand Gille, Louis Girard, Maurice Lévy-Leboyer and Alain Plessis, all of whom in one way or another have dwelt on the impact of the Pereires' ideas, vision, energy and skills, and all have contributed in important ways to this book. The fine work of Rondo Cameron and David S. Landes, writing over a long period in English, must also be recorded here. More recent economic historians, especially Hubert Bonin, Michael Stephen Smith and Nicolas Stoskopf, have shed light on individual institutions and individuals and their work has been stimulating and similarly invaluable.

This book is not a work of economic history, however. It engages more broadly, using the lives of two remarkable individuals to re-examine the history of France in the nineteenth century. It is concerned with their experiences as Jews, as Saint-Simonians, as provincials arriving in a metropolis and as capitalists close to the seat of power, as well as with the impact and significance of the enterprises they founded. The historiography in which they figure is thus wide-ranging. Previous biographical works on the Pereires, all written in French, entertained differing intentions depending, as biographies often do, on the interests of the author. The work of Jean Autin, who worked through the same family archives as I have, is the most comprehensive of these but his biography showed less interest in the Pereires' context than in their accomplishments. Autin's work remains a valued reference, nevertheless. I must also acknowledge and pay particular respect to the significance of Barrie M. Ratcliffe's articles on several aspects of the Pereire brothers' early lives and careers, written in the 1960s and 1970s and drawing also on the Archives de la famille Pereire. Finally, Saint-Simonian historiography, the life of which started on the movement's demise with Henri Fournel in 1832, now profits from the painstaking research and publication programme of scholars associated with the Société des études saint-simoniennes at the Bibliothèque de l'Arsenal in Paris. I am indebted to many of my predecessors and continue to learn from my contemporaries.

Notes

1 Gerry Hadden, 'Sephardic Jews invited back to Spain after 500 years', *BBC News Magazine*, 6 March 2013.
2 Richard L. Kagan and Philip D. Morgan (eds), *Atlantic Diasporas: Jews, Conversos, and Crypto-Jews in the Age of Mercantilism, 1500–1800* (Baltimore, 2009).
3 Alan B. Spitzer, *The French Generation of 1820* (Princeton, 1987).
4 Restaurants, pharmacies and a florist continue to use the name 'Pereire'.
5 Hippolyte Castille, *Les Frères Pereire* (Paris, 1861); Jean Autin, *Les Frères Pereire: le bonheur d'entreprendre* (Paris, 1984); Guy Fargette, *Émile et Isaac*

Pereire: l'esprit d'entreprise au XIXe siècle (Paris, 2001); Maurice-Edouard Berthon, *Emile et Isaac Pereire: la passion d'entreprendre* (Paris, 2007).

6 Emile et Isaac Pereire, *Écrits de Emile et Isaac Pereire* (Paris, 1900–9), 8 volumes further divided into at least 27 'Fascicules' and 'Parties'.

1

Bordeaux: a Sephardic childhood

Jacob Rodrigues Pereire and Miriam Lopès Dias were married in a synagogue in Bordeaux in 1766. Both Sephardic Jews, he had negotiated a circuitous path from Spain, to Bordeaux and then to Paris, she a simpler one from St Esprit-lès-Bayonne, a town across the River Adour from Bayonne. The groom was 51 years of age, his bride thirty years younger. He had come to matrimony late although there had been no lack of desire to find a partner, simply absorption in his vocation, that of teaching deaf-mute children how to speak.[1] For this he had received accolades and honours from the King and his court, the nobility and the academy. Influential members of the French Académie des Sciences had successfully proposed his membership to The Royal Society of London. A year before the marriage Louis XV appointed him secretary and interpreter in Spanish and Portuguese, an honorific but not particularly taxing position awarded in acknowledgement both of Rodrigues Pereire's skill and of his comparative penury.

Miriam Lopès Dias was unlikely to have been well-acquainted with Jacob Rodrigues Pereire before their wedding for this was an arranged marriage and the bridegroom had lived in Paris for some fifteen years. They were, however, distantly related, for there is evidence of a marriage between the Rodrigues Pereire and Lopès Dias families in the seventeenth century.[2] The match clearly would have delighted her family, for Jacob was highly regarded as a teacher in a difficult and worthy field. Aside from his eminence in Paris, he also held an official position at court as representative of the Sephardic communities of Bordeaux and St Esprit. The Lopès Dias family, for its part, was prominent and well-to-do in the Sephardic world of southwest France, the bride bringing a dowry of 10,000 *livres* with her.³ This is the extent of what is known about Miriam, however, a young woman who remains a shadowy figure and whose place in the literature serves only to confirm her role as the bearer of Jacob's heirs.

This chapter deals with the 'making' of their grandsons, two Jewish boys born after the Revolution into the close-knit Sephardic community of Bordeaux, a community confronted with the revolutionary decision of emancipation, bringing equality of citizenship and opportunity. Opportunity was, however, difficult to identify in a city afflicted by economic disaster brought on by the loss of the slave trade, constant war and British naval blockades. The effects of all these different elements – religious, social, economic and political – were to shape significantly the direction the Pereires took, the life choices they made or which were made for them, and the manner in which they confronted the opportunities when eventually they arose.

What is known of the early lives of Jacob's and Miriam's grandchildren Emile and Isaac Pereire must be reconstructed – from certain comparatively rare documents of the period, from documents relating to other Sephardic Jews, from archival material relating to the place where they lived, and from clues emerging from their later lives. Teasing out the significant moments as well as the trivia of daily life is thus a hazardous undertaking.

Despite the lack of material which might give greater solidity to an account of their early lives, however, some elements can be outlined with confidence. Bordeaux and its Sephardic community are crucial to an understanding of Emile and Isaac Pereire. For three centuries the port city had sheltered and supported Jewish refugees from Spain and Portugal, in the course of which the Sephardim had established their own community, carving out a valued role within the mercantile infrastructure. Before the French Revolution a mix of circumstances had determined their favourable situation: their financial acumen, their financial resources built up judiciously over a century or more, their commercial networks throughout the Sephardic diasporas, their utility to the Bordeaux economy in providing financial and banking services, and their stable community structure. From 1550, a series of letters patent signed by the monarch assured their legal status in France.⁴

A measure of the Jews' confidence and successful integration within the structures of Bordeaux can be seen in the organisation of their own community. Writing at the beginning of the nineteenth century, the Jewish historian and lawyer Francia de Beaufleury noted that in 1699 the Sephardim instituted for the first time a voluntary tax to support their own needs, including sustenance for their poor, *sedaca*, to which forty families contributed.[5] From a very early time, then, the provision of *sedaca* was at the heart of the organised life of the Jews of Bordeaux.

The rapid expansion of the Bordeaux economy in the eighteenth century brought advantages to its Jewish population as well, and great wealth to certain of them. There were stock brokers, *négociants*, maritime insurers and bankers, and some even became ship-builders and merchants themselves, the Furtados and the Rabas particularly becoming immensely wealthy through Sephardic networks in the Caribbean.[6] Another, David Gradis, in 1763 alone exported goods to Canada valued at nine million *livres*.[7] When in 1741 Jacob Rodrigues Pereire, his mother and his siblings arrived in Bordeaux from Spain, they found themselves in a Catholic city which welcomed their contribution to its economic strength and well-being and, in turn, had begun to tolerate Jewish religious observance. Numbering about 2,000 by the end of the eighteenth century, the Jews were an integral part, financially and legally, of this mercantile success. In 1760 the Bordeaux Sephardim were granted the status of a corporation, charged with regulating their own religious and commercial affairs, and directed by an oligarchy which stipulated the personal qualities and financial stability of its leaders. The oligarchy governed efficiently and well virtually every aspect of the lives of its people.[8]

Another town in France's southwest and another marriage also contributed to the social and cultural formation of Emile and Isaac Pereire. In April 1775, again in a synagogue, one of many in St Esprit-lès-Bayonne, the 27-year-old Mardochée Lopès Fonseca wed Esther de Daniel Delvaille. The groom, described as 'Master of laws', was of a well-established Sephardic family. The bride, with a similar background, brought a dowry of 10,800 *livres*, most of it in silver. Their respective families had escaped from Portugal early in the eighteenth century, taking refuge in St Esprit where individual members eventually became figures in the organisational life of the Sephardim.[9] They were the maternal grandparents of Emile and Isaac Pereire.

Despite constraints on their participation in the economic life of Bayonne and enforced anti-Jewish prohibitions concerning their living arrangements, the circumstance of living side by side in a small town helped the Jews of St Esprit to emerge from their status as pseudo-Christians and crypto-Jews earlier than their co-religionists in Bordeaux, asserting their identity as Jews from the seventeenth century. They were encouraged by the crusading mission of the financially ascendant Jews of Amsterdam, determined to revive Judaism in those centres where conversion to Christianity had proved overwhelmingly seductive. Spanish books of devotion printed in Amsterdam found a ready underground market in

St Esprit. The liturgy of St Esprit conformed to that of Amsterdam and rabbis were drawn from the northern congregation.[10]

Recognition of the usefulness of the Sephardic Jews to the French economy culminated in letters patent of 1776, signed by Louis XVI. Significant on two counts, they were the result of negotiation between the then Controller-General Jacques Turgot and Jacob Rodrigues Pereire as official representative at court of the Jews of the southwest of France, and they were written in terms which advanced the situation of the Jews considerably compared with those promulgated earlier.[11] Permitted to live and work where they chose in France even before the French Revolution and the decree of the Assemblée Nationale in January 1790 which granted them emancipation, the Sephardic Jews of the southwest had already been extended considerable liberties in recognition of their commercial and financial skills, their utility and, in the case of the Bordeaux Jews, their effective integration with the city's merchant community.[12] When the question of their admissibility as citizens was first posed before the new Assemblée late in 1789, the Sephardim were able to argue their own case with confidence.

The debate on Jewish emancipation during 1789–91 was not without rancour, however, hinging as it did on the particularity of Jewish communities, whether, by the nature of their religion and the demands it placed on communal life, Jews were capable of entering fully as citizens into the affairs of the nation – capable, that is, of being both Jews and Frenchmen. This perceived conundrum was most clearly expressed in the often-quoted statement of the deputy from Paris and member of the nobility Stanislas, comte de Clermont-Tonnerre: 'We must refuse everything to the Jews as a nation and accord everything to the Jews as individuals.'[13] A fiery debate was finally decided on 28 January 1790 by 374 votes in favour of emancipating the Sephardic and Avignon Jews and 224 against, but the kernel of Clermont-Tonnerre's dictum was not dissipated by this decision. It remained a predicament.[14]

In contrast, the Ashkenazi Jews of France waited a further twenty months before achieving emancipation in September 1791, during which time they had been subjected to repeated attacks of anti-Jewish violence. Numbering some 40,000 comparatively poor people at the Revolution the Ashkenazim, originally from central Europe, lived in small rural towns and villages in France's northeast, in Alsace-Lorraine, observing traditional Jewish customs and ways of life. The degree of integration with business achieved in Bordeaux by the Sephardim was missing in Ashkenazic communities. Indeed, many French regarded the Ashkenazim as unassimilable. This disparity was played on shamelessly throughout the eighteenth century by the Sephardim who went to great lengths to distance themselves from their co-religionists in the northeast, particularly in the face of anti-Jewish attack from Voltaire and Rousseau among others, which they countered with claims of superiority over the Ashkenazim in their own communal and religious practices. Jacob Rodrigues Pereire had commissioned one polemic from the Sephardic philosopher from Amsterdam, Isaac de Pinto, in which de Pinto was at pains to distinguish between Sephardim and Ashkenazim, to counter the 'disadvantageous and unjust prejudices that one has against … the Portuguese and Spanish Jews'.[15] This antipathy remained an irritant well into the nineteenth century.

Jacob Rodrigues Pereire did not live to see the Revolution, dying nine years before the fall of the Bastille. His sole surviving son Isaac, the father of Emile and Isaac, was nine years old at Jacob's death and a younger daughter Abigail was the only other living child of the marriage with Miriam Lopès Dias.[16] Remaining family members returned to Bordeaux where eventually Isaac trained as a *négociant*, his path to maturity eased by the social standing of his parentage. By August 1789 he had found a promising commercial position.[17] But with the coming of the Revolution, Bordeaux's continuing economic success, and Isaac's, depended on peace and the slave trade, neither of which was assured. The Declaration of the Rights of Man and the Citizen, which Mirabeau and the Abbé Grégoire among others supported strongly for its implicit inclusion of the black slaves in the Caribbean, of whom there were half a million in St Domingue alone, thus met a contradictory response from the Bordelais. The Sephardim were no better disposed towards emancipation of the slaves than the Catholic merchants.

After initial enthusiasm for the Revolution the city of Bordeaux experienced increasing difficulty in reconciling its own interests with those of a dominant and centralising Paris and the principles of 1789. The rebellion of the slaves in St Domingue in 1791, a situation which rapidly deteriorated into chaos and, later, the British blockade of the port, contributed to a notable loss of economic dynamism.[18] Radical changes in the administrative arrangements which governed France saw civic prestige and influence ebbing away as well when even the Bordeaux Parlement was abolished.[19] Bordeaux became the administrative capital of the department of the Gironde, rather than the provincial metropolis of the sprawling region of the Guyenne. War in April 1792 was to change everything. In mid-1793, the loose coalition of deputies opposed to the Jacobins, known as the Girondins and based in part in Bordeaux, attempted to mount a revolt against the inexorable power of Paris and the Jacobins, but the failure of their Federalist revolt proved disastrous for the once vibrant city. This coupled with the merchants' dependence on the slave economy and the English naval blockade exposed them to further distress. When, in July 1793, British and Spanish troops intervened in St Domingue, victory was assured for the rebelling slaves. To retain the colony within the Republic the French legislature had little choice but to ratify emancipation, which it did in February 1794. Bordeaux was in crisis.[20]

Chaos and fear prevailed, its citizens facing financial ruin and political disaster. The British blockade coupled with emancipation of the slaves had a profound effect on the city. The blockade had completely severed the mercantile community's transatlantic links and emancipation of the slaves exposed its dependence on the slave trade and the lucrative crops of sugar and coffee. The merchants of Bordeaux were under political threat as well, the majority having supported the moderate Girondins and thus now the target of reprisals initiated by the Convention's *envoi en mission*, Garnier de Saintes. More than 200 *négociants* were brought before a specially convened Commission Militaire designed to eliminate 'egoism'.[21]

As partners in the Bordeaux business community the Sephardim suffered equally; hundreds of them were engaged in the city's commercial world. While none faced the guillotine, Sephardic *négociants* were subjected to huge fines nevertheless.[22] As supporters of the Girondin cause many were also hunted down, the wealthy merchant and ship owner Abraham Furtado forced into hiding and his house ransacked.[23]

Somewhat before this turmoil, Isaac Pereire at the age of twenty-one had been appointed one of four official administrators of the Jewish welfare organisation, the Société de Bienfaisance. Among his colleagues were two young men who remained friends for the rest of his life and who were to play a significant role in the lives of his children: Isaac Rodrigues Henriques, known as Rodrigues *fils* ['son'], and Samuel Alexandre, or Alexandre *fils*. Another who had preceded Isaac Pereire as an administrator of the Société was the older man, Mardochée Lopès Fonseca, also more widely known as Fonseca *neveu* ['nephew'].[24] All would have been acquainted with each other already but in 1793, Fonseca, Pereire and Rodrigues became in some senses business associates. In the absence of one or other from Bordeaux through the exigencies of war they corresponded, their letters shedding light on the situation of the Sephardim over five years during which they attempted to do business as well as come to grips with the more personal demands being placed on them as Frenchmen and Jews. The correspondence is also a testament to friendship forged at a time of fear and uncertainty.

The three did not move exclusively in Sephardic circles; as commercial men in an important trading city they could scarcely avoid the Catholic merchant majority. But their business dealings and associations were solidly embedded within the Sephardic network. At the same time, while all three had welcomed the Revolution for the liberty and opportunity it afforded, the terms of the decree of emancipation confronted them with serious questions about their religious affiliation. Early in the letters we find them wrestling with their religious and social acculturation in an effort to reconcile Judaism with a new civic identity. One particular move signalled their intentions well: with the Revolution Isaac Pereire ceased to employ the name 'Rodrigues' and Isaac Rodrigues that of 'Henriques', names which had emphasised their Portuguese origins.

Each of them was influenced significantly by the literature of the Enlightenment, Fonseca in particular possessing a library of surprising sophistication for his time and milieu including the complete *oeuvres* of Voltaire, many volumes of Rousseau, as well as of Hume, Raynal, Condillac, Condorcet, Mably, Fontenelle and Buffon. The letters they themselves wrote were sometimes embellished with reference to the *philosophes* and were in the main well constructed, well expressed and lucid, despite the sometimes erratic punctuation and spelling. They also seem to have been active in contemporary intellectual circles. While in Paris in 1797, Fonseca made the acquaintance of the geographer Alexander Von Humboldt and requested Pereire to extend hospitality when Humboldt visited Bordeaux.[25]

Religion was a point of differentiation between the three, however. Rodrigues' position was probably the most radical for, he wrote to Isaac Pereire, it was not to 'the accomplishment of the prophecies that one must look for inspiration: it is in the progress of philosophy and, by consequence, that of public reason which have overthrown Despotism, founded the Republic and reminded man of the exercise of the inalienable rights he owes to nature'.[26] Rodrigues had absorbed well the lessons of the Enlightenment and the principles of the Revolution. Mardochée Lopès Fonseca and Isaac Pereire, in contrast, attempted to integrate Judaism with the evolving revolutionary discourse, and on several occasions while the two were in St Esprit their behaviour was at least ambivalent when confronted with political demands which might involve a compromise with their religious values.[27] Thus they remained practicing Jews while endorsing revolutionary principles and the delights of Enlightenment literature.

Louis XVI's execution provoked the Spanish Bourbons into war against France, and in response the Convention in August 1793 launched a mass conscription. Isaac Pereire was conscripted into the Armée des Pyrénées-Occidentales headquartered in Bayonne.[28] There he also became secretary to a revolutionary club, the Société Montagnarde et Régénérée des Amis de la Constitution de 1793, founded by Fonseca. Remarkably, in contrast with the Bordelais, the Sephardic Jews of St Esprit gave their total support to the Jacobins, even re-naming the town 'Jean-Jacques Rousseau'.[29] Members of the Société complained to the Jacobins in Bayonne about decoration on the façade of the cathedral Ste Marie, resulting in destruction of the offending ornamentation by a team of masons.[30] On the celebration of the Festival of the Supreme Being in May 1794, Fonseca wrote a revolutionary prayer which integrated elements of the Torah, receiving wide circulation and praise in Sephardic Jewish circles.[31]

The fall of Robespierre saw the demise of the Société, and Fonseca was forced to make a precipitate return to Bordeaux, taking refuge in the home of Rodrigues *fils*. It was only a few months later, in October 1794, that Rodrigues married Fonseca's daughter, Sara-Sophie.[32] This union, like many Jewish marriages, was probably arranged, a complement to the business arrangement between the groom and his father-in-law, although what is known of it testifies only to satisfaction with what was to be a long and happy marriage. The couple's first child, a son, Benjamin Olinde, was born the following year.

The end of the Terror and of warfare on French soil facilitated greater economic activity under the Directory, despite rampant inflation.[33] When, from early 1795, neutral shipping from the United States began to reinvigorate transatlantic trade with Bordeaux, Fonseca, Pereire and Rodrigues were thus able to mix their illicit commerce – they had been dealing illegally in foreign currencies – with more legitimate activities, for their letters include accounts for buying and selling candles and cotton piece goods like handkerchiefs, and references to small-scale marine assurance or trading on the bourse.[34] Rodrigues was not to remain in Bordeaux for much longer, however. On his formal discharge from the Army in 1796, he and Sara-Sophie left for Paris at the behest of the Bordeaux shipowner, manufacturer and financier Boyer-Fonfrède,[35] who had opened an office in Paris where Rodrigues was to be employed.[36] Rodrigues *fils* was in the vanguard of thousands of Jewish men and women from the provinces who made that journey in the next century.

On the successful conclusion of the war against Spain in July 1795, Isaac Pereire too was discharged from the Armée des Pyrénées-Occidentales, though he joined the staff of General François Antoine Desnoyers in Toulouse as his secretary soon after in 1796.[37] It is unclear what this role amounted to although his proficiency in Spanish would have proved useful to a grateful employer dealing with a myriad of problems requiring just that skill in the aftermath of war. Isaac did not remain long in Toulouse, however, returning to Bordeaux where he resumed the business association with his two friends, both then in Paris. Rodrigues, a skilled bookkeeper, accountant and *négociant*, had found another position, this time with the Parisian bank of Berr Léon Fould, of a Jewish family from Lorraine settled in Paris from 1787.[38] For his part, Fonseca having found no joy in the capital, by the dawn of the new century returned to Bordeaux.

Isaac Pereire's family had scarcely weathered the revolutionary years with ease. His mother, Miriam Lopès Dias, and his aunt had died within months of each other in 1791, and his uncle David Rodrigues Pereire only a couple of years later. By 1800 his sister Abigail was his only immediate family, and she had become traumatised by events to the point of mental breakdown.[39] Now in partnership in a marine insurance business with Fonseca *neveu*, in February, Isaac Pereire at 29 years of age took a wife also, the 22-year-old Rebecca Henriette Lopès Fonseca, second daughter of Fonseca *neveu* and Esther de Daniel Delvaille, who brought a dowry of 10,000 francs to the marriage.[40] While Isaac claimed to have followed his own inclination in his choice of a bride, confiding to a friend his hope to be a father before the end of the year, here also there was more than likely some pressure exerted by his friend and father-in-law, keen to cement an alliance through marriage with his daughter.[41]

Rebecca Henriette, who was known as Henriette, was a product of St Esprit, a young practicing orthodox Jewish girl, unaccustomed to any society other than Jewish. Her early life contained few references to the Catholic stronghold across the River Adour in Bayonne. In 1788, the Lopès Fonseca family moved permanently to the much larger city of Bordeaux, followed there by revolution and war. While Bordeaux was home to a certain anti-Jewish sentiment and behaviour, nevertheless, its closely-integrated Jewish quarter provided her family with considerable security. Henriette thus remained cocooned within the Sephardic world, uncomprehending of and unreceptive to any influences other than those she already knew. This was to have a lasting and disquieting influence on her children.

Isaac's hopes were realised at the end of the year with the birth on 3 December 1800 of the couple's first child, a son. The birth certificate was witnessed by both Rodrigues *fils* and Alexandre *fils*, testimony to the devoted mentors the newborn could count on as he grew older. The child was given two names: Jacob for his paternal grandfather, as was the custom, and Emile, possibly in recognition of Rousseau's innocent.[42] The choice of name evoked the presence of non-Jewish influences in the life of the father and the literary tastes of the child's maternal grandfather, and it was as Emile that the child became known.[43]

While striving to earn a living with his father-in-law and to support his new family, Isaac Pereire also harboured ambitions to revive the memory of his late father, and even that he himself might one day take on the same vocation, teaching deaf mutes to speak. But the vision of restoring his father to a special place in French history was incompatible with both his personal (he spoke of possessing too much 'vivacity' for the task) and his financial capacities. 'All these motives lead me to renounce the art of my late father, but not the possession of his secret', he wrote.[44] With the pressures on the family business he was thus forced to reassure Fonseca *neveu* that he would not depart from the prudent behaviour upon which his father-in-law had recently congratulated him. He would do nothing rash.

The Bordeaux economy began to show signs of recovery, buoyed by a series of excellent vintages of wine. By May 1802, after the First Consul Napoléon Bonaparte had announced the re-introduction of slavery and the Code Noir which regulated it, and heartened by the Peace of Amiens, a large fleet of 208 ships was fitted out in Bordeaux for the colonial trade. But the next year war broke out again and the British captured over sixty of the Bordeaux fleet. At the same time, the former slaves in St Domingue, who had been instrumental in beating off the Spanish troops there during the Revolution, were finally and definitively victorious against Napoléon's expeditionary army, on New Year's Day 1804, declaring themselves the independent republic of Haiti.[45] Bordeaux would never recover its pre-revolutionary place in Atlantic trade: the world had changed forever.

Isaac's new family had grown in 1803 with the birth of another son, Mardochée Télèphe, named, again according to custom, for the infant's maternal grandfather who witnessed the certificate. The infant's second name might tell us something more of the literary tastes of grandfather and father, recalling the mythological son of Hercules and the central character in a utopian novel of 1784 dealing with the bonds of male friendship.[46]

Paradoxically, however, the years 1803–7 which were for Bordeaux the best of the entire revolutionary and Napoléonic period were the very ones in which the marine insurance business carried on by Pereire and Fonseca went from bad to worse, as indebtedness among members of the Sephardic community had spiralled out of control.[47] These were difficult times: at the very moment of his new son's birth the marine insurance business was close to bankruptcy. By May, Isaac's business affairs were in such a parlous state he voiced great fears about the rupture of the Peace of

Amiens, in late March, triggering disastrous consequences for his father-in-law and himself. He prayed that they would not be overwhelmed by this adversity.[48]

A run on the banks in 1805 shuddered throughout the major cities in France and when, late that year, Mardochée Lopès Fonseca died, Isaac was placed under even greater pressure. He suspended payment, forced to come to an arrangement with his creditors.[49] His bankruptcy, flowing on from more widespread financial disarray within the Sephardic community, brought him to the edge of despair, letters written at the time seeming almost to threaten suicide. Isaac was an overly emotional man in any case, prone to exaggeration and to feelings of rejection, one might even say paranoia. But his death at the age of thirty-five in November 1806 was probably the result of typhoid, the years 1805–6 having seen 'a cruel epidemic' brought on over a particularly hot summer by some well-intentioned but ineffectual efforts to drain a polluted stream close to the Sephardic quarter.[50]

That day Isaac's creditors caused the apartment to be sealed to ensure none of his effects were spirited away, allowing it to be opened only at certain times. Drawing together the inventory, which itself makes unhappy reading, took nine visits by the Bordeaux notary Mathieu and the faithful Alexandre *fils*, named guardian to Isaac's sons.[51] The apartment on the second and third floors of number 12 rue des Fossés des Carmes was tiny: two bedrooms, a kitchen, a 'vestibule' and two corridors. The condition of its furnishings was so lamentable as to draw comment. Aside from bedding and dining pieces, chairs, an old brass clock and a pier-glass, there was a miscellaneous collection of framed family pictures, two infants' chairs, an infant's bath, a sabre, and a brass Sabbath lamp, their total value estimated to be just over one thousand francs. There were also goods on consignment including lace, handkerchiefs of printed muslin and Madras, satin shawls, pieces of taffeta and seven dozen pairs of buckskin gloves.

Isaac Pereire also left a substantial library, impressive for its eclectic subject matter: a Bible, together with an accompanying dictionary, a history of the Old Testament, a copy of the New Testament in Greek and Latin, and *L'Histoire des juifs* by Flavius Josephus – even a history of the Council of Trent – sat beside essays by Montaigne and by Locke. More significant, however, was the large number of books about Spain or things Spanish, all probably in turn the legacy of his own father. The total value of the library was reckoned at about four hundred and twenty three francs.[52]

Aside from Isaac's literary estate, however, his executors found a dispiriting collection of documents indicative of commercial failure: the agreement between Isaac and his creditors of January 1806; tally sheets detailing negotiations with members of the Sephardic community aimed to reduce his debts; promissory notes also, and letters of exchange, mostly issued by companies themselves insolvent or bankrupt. There were legal judgements in Isaac Pereire's favour and against other Sephardim but these were of dubious worth since, the executors found, the debtors were themselves insolvent.

The tragic circumstances of Isaac's bankruptcy and death reverberated through the family for years. Compounding the melancholy was the birth, only five days after his death, of his third son. The infant was named simply Isaac without further embellishment, underscoring the father's loss and the mother's grief.[53] Henriette was thus left to raise three small boys alone and in considerable hardship. Aside from her financial problems as the widow of a bankrupt, her child was born in times of high infant mortality. Indeed, over 20 per cent of his contemporaries did not survive beyond five years of age.[54]

The year following Isaac's birth was one of great danger for the city, the British embargo on neutral shipping effectively sealing Bordeaux to the outside world. Bad times continued and bankruptcies, even among the larger firms trading in wine and cognac, took their toll.[55] Nowhere was this disaster more graphically illustrated than in Bordeaux's demography: between 1791 and 1808, years of the Revolution, Directory, Consulate and Empire, the population fell from 110,000 to 92,500, the penalty for dependence on the Atlantic sea-trade and colonial produce.[56] France's economic life was concentrating inexorably around Paris and the north, a trend apparent from the Revolution.

The Emperor Napoléon visited Bordeaux for the first time in April 1808. He was on his way to Bayonne (where he succeeded in obtaining the abdication of the Spanish Bourbons), returning the following August. His arrival back in Bordeaux was as memorable for the Sephardim as for the rest of the Bordelais, the Empress Josephine honouring the wealthy Raba *frères* with a visit to their mansion at Talence, a suburb of Bordeaux, and bestowing praise on what she found there.[57] This visit to what had once been the premier mercantile city shocked the Emperor, however, prompting him perhaps to over-compensate for his previous neglect: following the visit he contributed a new town hall, a prefecture, a hospital, an almshouse, an amphitheatre and a riding school.[58] But none of these could offset the paucity of jobs which would support family life, much less stimulate ambition in three young boys, the price paid by Bordeaux for the loss of France's colonies and constant war. Paris began to siphon away the new generation born during the Revolution and Consulate, and though the memories of Bordeaux's golden era remained sufficiently vivid among the populace to feed the imagination of the Pereire boys, the causes underlying the city's decline became salutary lessons to be absorbed. The benefits of free trade and of an economy unfettered by unnecessary taxes became axiomatic in this environment. So too did the need for adequate transport linkages and a banking system which gave more flexible access to credit, supported crucially by the absence of war and political unrest. All these elements were taken up by Bordeaux's economic and political theorists, becoming fundamental to the Pereires' economic philosophy also.[59]

More immediately relevant to the Bordeaux Jews, however, was the programme Napoléon had instituted two years earlier to encourage them to renounce any vestige of 'particularism' in their move towards complete assimilation, prompted by allegations of usurious practices against the Ashkenazim of the east by certain Strasbourgeois. This programme of regulation placed the Jews in an ambiguous situation, compromising the rights and privileges gained with the granting of emancipation by the Revolution. Their civic status and religious activities henceforth were to be prescribed by imperial decree, thus differentiating them from other citizens. These decisions were guided by an Assemblée des Notables nominated by the prefects of those regions where there were numerically significant Jewish communities, and the Sephardim were elected by their peers to the most powerful positions in that Assemblée: Abraham Furtado as President and Rodrigues *fils* as Secretary. In July 1808, Napoléon instituted a system of consistories throughout the major cities of France to regulate and manage Jewish religious and communal life.[60] He also issued a decree requiring all Jews to register their names with the municipal authorities. This census of 1808, despite the problems of its covert agenda, contained an unintended benefit for later historians, providing rare insights into the lives of the Bordeaux Sephardim.[61]

To meet the education expenses of her sons, Henriette and her brother Jacob Lopès Fonseca had opened a modest shop, 'Au Juste Prix', a shop for 'haberdashery, linen-drapery and other articles wholesale and retail', at number 2 rue Bouhaut, a densely-populated section of the Sephardic quarter well-known for its small, dark shops selling second-hand clothing.[62] This street, which effectively extended the road from Spain into Bordeaux and now forms the southern section of the rue Sainte-Catherine, was a short distance from the rue des Fossés des Carmes where the family had previously lived.[63] A dozen people shared the same address. Aside from the 'widow Pereire née Lopès Fonseca' and her three sons, there were seven members of the 'Pereyre-Soares' family, closely linked for many decades with the organisational life of the Jews in St Esprit. Indeed, one of them, Gabriel Pereire-Soares, had become the first Jewish mayor in French history. Living nearby were other families whose names recur in Bordeaux's Sephardic history: the Vaz, Raba, Dalmeyda, Mendès and Avigdor families, together with Avignon Jews the Astrucs.[64]

In the census year 1808 there were more than 2,000 Jews living in Bordeaux, over 2 per cent of the total population, and at its epicentre was this street, the rue Bouhaut.[65] The Pereire boys thus grew up in an extended family household within a community of families similarly placed, many having been former residents of St Esprit. These were busy, noisy places, crowded with relatives and friends. Close-knit relationships developed which for reasons either of affection or commerce frequently led to marriage. Friendships, like that between Emile and the young Adolphe Mirès and Télèphe Astruc, lasted a lifetime. Family members lived in adjacent houses, retaining closeness and affinity. Neighbours helped each other, with work, with money and by sharing, to ward off the effects of poverty and the great anxiety among those poorer members who lived from day to day. But the quality of this society is best exemplified in the relationship between the Pereire family and Alexandre *fils*. The loyalty he had displayed towards their father extended subsequently to Isaac's widow and her boys who became a continuing commitment. For the remainder of his life, Alexandre, a successful banker whose own grandmother had been a member of the Gradis family, stood *in loco parentis* to the Pereire brothers. The two families rarely lived far apart in Bordeaux and even in the census of 1822, by which time Alexandre and his family had moved to the rue Ste Eulalie, we find 'Widow Rodrigues Pereire' living in a neighbouring property.[66]

Nevertheless, the Pereire family was in financial difficulty throughout the period which close friends and kin could scarcely alleviate, and the brothers were, from their earliest years, beneficiaries of Sephardic welfare.[67] Henriette's situation was far from uncommon, for widows headed nearly one in four Sephardic households.[68] On 23 November 1811, the Bordeaux Chambre de Commerce reported altogether 10,000 citizens in receipt of assistance, and many were Sephardim. The greater part of the Bordeaux Consistoire budget of 1809, a pool of money made up of contributions on a fixed scale according to means, was allocated largely to care of the sick and the poor.[69]

The Bordeaux Consistoire was central not only to the economic life of its members but to their religious lives as well. In 1809, and not without some misgivings, it appointed Abraham Andrade, the former revolutionary and sometime President of the Jean-Jacques Rousseau Comité de Surveillance, as Chief Rabbi.⁷⁰ Andrade had been an ally and close friend of both Fonseca and Isaac Pereire in St Esprit during the Revolution. The new Consistoire soon after received imperial approval to build the first public synagogue in France, in the rue Causserouge within the Jewish quarter.⁷¹ Perhaps this was an overly ambitious project for the community, for the Consistoire was forced to write to the Prefect of the Gironde in December 1810 advising that their funds were entirely exhausted, and even with approval to raise a loan there were likely to be problems completing the structure on time.⁷² Eventually, however, in May 1812, the synagogue was completed and inaugurated with great ceremony – culminating in a performance of works by Haydn and pieces especially composed for a choir of men and boys.⁷³ The Consistoire informed head office in Paris:

> A new temple is going to present itself soon to our eyes ... The signal is given, Israelites. Share our joy. After having long camped under tents, we direct ourselves towards the place the Lord has destined for us. May your voices unite with ours to intone the divine canticles which are the eternal exhortation and consolation of the faithful servants of God.⁷⁴

The significance of this grand occasion was two-fold, demonstrating the special place the Bordeaux Sephardim held within the nation's Jewry and, reciprocally, the place which France was assuming in the collective Sephardic consciousness. The rhetorical question in Rabbi Andrade's inaugural sermon – 'Is this a new Jerusalem which emerges with us from the night of the tomb?' – was apt.⁷⁵ The synagogue quickly became a significant element in Pereire family life, for it was here they now worshipped regularly as part of a wider community, and all three boys celebrated their bar mitzvah within the new temple. Henriette's youngest, Isaac, sang in the choir.

The impact of poverty on the Pereires' educational attainment was considerable, and yet they displayed in later life an apparently high level of education, erudition and an excellent grasp of the French language. This is puzzling under the circumstances, since schooling was problematic for all Sephardic children in Bordeaux during the first decade of the nineteenth century. Jules Mirès, brother of Emile's close friend Adolphe, was to write that in his youth he had learned only a few elements of French.⁷⁶ But Jewish children were permitted to attend both the *lycée* and Catholic schools in Bordeaux and, at the suggestion of their uncle Rodrigues, Henriette appealed to the Grand Maître de l'Université Impérial in Bordeaux to enrol Emile and Télèphe, using as her bargaining tool the important part the boys' grandfather had played in the affairs of the Sephardic community. But Henriette's appeal came to nothing.[77] As an alternative, Emile and Télèphe may have attended the 'house of education' founded by David Mendès in 1810, about which little is known save that it employed both Jewish and non-Jewish teachers.[78] When, twenty years later, Isaac described himself in a letter to a friend as 'a Jew by birth and almost by education', he may have been referring to this schooling as much as to his upbringing.[79]

The failure of Henriette's haberdashery in 1813 brought an end to school days for the older boys. Télèphe was already living with her brother in Bordeaux and Rodrigues *fils* immediately offered to take Emile to Paris. But Henriette would not entertain the idea of a lengthy separation from any of her children even under the difficult circumstances in which she found herself.[80] She was particularly concerned for the future of her youngest son Isaac, now 7 years old, whose opportunities for a sound education seemed even more remote than they had been for Emile and Télèphe. Henriette's own level of education was not high. Her handwriting was imperfect, her spelling inaccurate. But she was by no means illiterate. She had a fair grasp of the French language and was able to put sentences together on paper. More significantly, she put a high value on education. The Pereires must have profited as well from the legacy of books and ideas to be found on both sides of the family, providing a substantial resource to intelligent children. That Henriette did, nevertheless, manage to provide a solid and varied education for her sons was recalled by them with gratitude in later life. Isaac as an old man extolled her virtues: a pious, enlightened and truly superior woman who did not shrink from any sacrifice, from any privation, to ensure her children received an education worthy of their grandfather, passionate to do good for her boys.[81] Henriette's attitude towards education as the lever to social advancement and self-improvement, well-engrained in Jewish culture, was also sparked by her vision of the boys as true descendants of their grandfather Jacob.

For Emile, however, the age of 13 and the bar mitzvah at the Bordeaux synagogue ushered in his adult life; his mother's business having collapsed, he was forced to leave school behind and become a breadwinner. This was by no means an unusual age for boys to seek their first employment: only six years previously, the 13-year-old James de Rothschild had joined the family business in Frankfurt following haphazard tutelage.[82] But Emile's cousin Olinde Rodrigues, who was five years older, had been educated at the Lycée Impérial in Paris, and the young Pereire, who was clearly talented, may well have hoped for a similar education. What learning Emile had was put to good use early, however. From the age of fifteen he earned money writing for publication, using any spare moment in the evenings and during other leisure hours, motivated by his great capacity for work and by family responsibility.[83] His late hours, however, owed as much to a malady which had started early and from which he suffered throughout his life: he was a chronic asthmatic, frequently deprived of sleep and thus habituated to working when he could do nothing else.

Emile's entry into the workforce preceded by one year Napoléon's fall, which saw the restoration of the Bourbons in 1814, proclaimed first in Bordeaux to the evident joy of citizens now totally exhausted by the effects on their economy and society of more than two decades of war. The city warmly welcomed the duc d'Angoulême, youngest son of the comte d'Artois (later to become Charles X), who stayed for several months. The Bordeaux Chambre de Commerce early in 1816 was able to report a higher level of commercial activity which continued into the next year, but with the loss of French colonies and of overseas trading activity, the slave trade having been finally abolished during 1815–18, the economy was moving only painfully.[84] The patterns of trade which had seen the port increasingly bypassed during the long years of war became entrenched with the Restoration. This period did witness the rise of a certain style of entrepreneurial business in the city, however, exemplified by the Samazeuilhs and Balguérie-Stuttembergs particularly, the former with their network of credit banks and the latter with their interests in banking and shipbuilding, family businesses which operated in ways similar to those created later by the Pereires and possibly providing models for them.[85]

As a result of these depressed circumstances, however, the older Pereire brothers were forced initially to work in low-level clerical positions for a kind of estate agent, a situation which Emile found unchallenging and offering minimal financial reward.[86] He drafted a letter of complaint and threatened to resign, arguing that the salary offered was insufficient for him to support his mother after the sacrifices she had made for the education of her children. It did not even begin to meet her expenses.[87] In 1815 he commenced work with Nunès and Hardel as a trainee *négociant*, a position he appears to have found more congenial, for many years later he reflected on the responsibility he had been called upon to exercise from a very early age, effectively as the head of the family. Having been in business since 1817 he wrote of how: 'I found through my own work, without the support of any capital, sufficient means for my existence and for those of many others.'[88] The next year Isaac, celebrating his bar mitzvah in December 1819 with the administration of the Bordeaux Consistoire and the synagogue choir in attendance, also took his first paid position as a ledger clerk for David Gradis.[89]

In that year, a winter of bitter cold and frosts, their brother Mardochée Télèphe died. He was 17 years of age. The second of the Pereire brothers, Télèphe had known his father Isaac and his maternal grandfather after whom he was named, which the young Isaac had not. His death provided a different perspective on sibling relations between the two he left behind. Old enough to challenge Emile as the leader and with sufficient distance in years between himself and his younger brother to be accepted in this role, Télèphe was both elder brother to Isaac and Emile's deputy, as well as the mediator between them. His loss placed a different, spectral, cast on relations between those who survived him, one in which the difference in their ages suddenly assumed a large gulf to be bridged in different ways. Evidently a young man of great talent and qualities, Emile especially was struck with great force by his brother's death. A grief-stricken letter to friends makes this clear, for Télèphe was 'his only friend from infancy, his only companion in study, the only company and to distract him from pain he has only the presence of his inconsolable mother to whom he can give neither relief nor calm'. Suffering a severe attack of asthma, Emile was bedridden for seventeen days.[90] Henriette's own grief may thus have been the spur for Rodrigues *fils* to encourage her once more to move to Paris with her sons. She continued to have doubts about the desirability of this course, nevertheless, and it took some time before she finally agreed that Emile at least should leave Bordeaux. The decision once made, however, from that point Paris became the centre, though not always the focus, of their lives.

By 1822, Emile and Isaac were about to turn 22 and 16 years of age respectively; they had been shaped by the complex events and influences of time, place and religion into which they were born. Their world was in turmoil in the wake of revolution, incessant war and economic recession. The Consulate, followed by Empire and then the Bourbon Restoration, created an unstable and uncertain political life and a political culture in ferment. Concepts of equality and citizenship, the legacy of the French Revolution, were constantly renegotiated, nowhere more evidently than with the Jews of France. Yet this period also saw ideas of nationalism crystallise, attracting especially those groups previously excluded from citizenship, and the Sephardim were among many for whom the prospect of full participation in French national life was immensely attractive.

The collective memory of Bordeaux's past instilled patterns of working which endured. Bordeaux was a city where young Sephardic boys learned the language of business from an early age, knowing their future lay somewhere within the repertoire of trade and commerce. A boy was likely to find his first job either within the family business or, as with the Pereires, with others in the Sephardic community, serving to explain their preoccupation with business, their breadth of interest and capacity to master detail of the most arcane nature. Striking too was the preponderance of *brothers* who made their way in business together, a fraternal association which the Pereires were to emulate.[91] And in their case, through sometimes extreme deprivation, there was at the core a propensity for hard, sustained work which excluded all diversion.

Bordeaux as a port city also gave a particular perspective on the outside world. Sephardic 'diasporas' throughout the Mediterranean, the Atlantic and major cities in northern Europe all had played a role in the entrepreneurial expansion of trade and commerce in remote and exotic places. The growth of mercantilism in the seventeenth century owed much to Jewish exiles from the Iberian peninsula who settled in Amsterdam. And while the vitality of these communities had been sapped by the early nineteenth century, vestiges of the networks themselves were still extant and their history intact.[92] In their earliest employment, with Nunès and Hardel and with David Gradis, both trading within the Sephardic network, Emile and Isaac Pereire gained experience and familiarity on which they were to build in their later working lives.

Domestically, the Sephardic community, while not without its antagonists, did give additional immunity from the social impact of economic catastrophe. Family and neighbours looked after their own. There was structure and cohesion also in the face of chaos, the Bordeaux Consistoire in many ways mirroring the eighteenth-century *Mahamad*, the council of Sephardic businessmen which had governed the community wisely, using their financial muscle and business acumen. The Consistoire literally kept its flock alive, with medicines, food and household goods. The religious character of the Sephardic community in Bordeaux, influenced by the presence of refugees from St Esprit, should also be recalled here, some commentators having cast the community as shallow and devoid of spiritual commitment.[93] Yet the Sephardim fashioned over centuries a unique form of Judaism, one which had sustained the faithful through loss and expulsion from Jerusalem and from Spain, through continuing oppression and through death, and which had been kept alive largely by devout Sephardic women. With a rich and historically important liturgy and the use of the arts to ornament ritual, the Sephardim were to exert considerable influence over Judaism during the century which lay ahead.

As through osmosis, then, the two young Sephardic Bordelais were able to distil the lessons learned in this particular city, within this singular community, from the complex circumstances and the adversity experienced by their family, preparing themselves thus for the ideas that were to confront them and the opportunities they were to grasp in later life.

Leaving Bordeaux for Paris was neither painless nor was it without its challenges, however. Emile's departure especially was precipitate, engineered swiftly in response to circumstances. He was the first of the family to go, filled with apprehension, scarcely finding time to take leave of his family and the small circle of close friends being left behind – Adolphe Mirès, and Téléphe and Aristée Astruc. Even the first hint of youthful romance, captured in a song for which he wrote the words, 'L'Olympe transporté dans la rue Bouhaut', had to be terminated abruptly.[94] We do not know to whom this was addressed although there were several Bordelaises with whom he continued to correspond for the rest of his life.[95] Perhaps it was a youthful passion which served to crystallise the affection he carried for Bordeaux from the moment he left. What lay before him and, later, Isaac, was unknown and foreign.

Notes

1 Works on Jacob Rodrigues Pereire begin with nineteenth-century texts: Edouard Séguin, *Jacob-Rodrigues Pereire ... Notice sur sa Vie et ses Travaux, Précédées de l'Éloge de Cette Méthode par Buffon* (Paris, 1847); Ernest La Rochelle, *Jacob Rodrigues Pereire: premier instituteur des sourds-muets ... sa vie et ses travaux* (Paris, 1882); Renée Neher-Bernheim, 'Un Pionnier dans l'art de faire parler les sourds-muets: Jacob Rodrigues Pereire', *Dix-Huitième siècle: juifs et judaïsme* 13, Revue Annuelle (1981). For an alternative view see Karine Lasne, 'Jacob Rodrigues Pereire et l'abbé de l'Épée: Perspectives croisées sur l'enseignement des enfants sourds', *Reliance* 15 (2005).
2 According to a family tree in the Archives de la famille Pereire (hereafter AFP).
3 La Rochelle, *Jacob Rodrigues Pereire*, pp. 281, 456.
4 Gérard Nahon (ed.), *Les 'Nations'juives portugaises du sud-ouest de la France (1684–1791)* (Paris, 1981), p. 21.
5 Louis Francia de Beaufleury, *L'Établissement des juifs à Bordeaux et à Bayonne, depuis 1530* (reprint 1800, Bayonne, 1985), p. 29.
6 Gérard Nahon, *Juifs et judaïsme à Bordeaux* (Bordeaux, 2003), pp. 76–82.
7 Zosa Szajkowski, *Jews and the French Revolutions of 1789, 1830 and 1848* (New York, 1970), p. 255.
8 Frances Malino, *The Sephardic Jews of Bordeaux: Assimilation and Emancipation in Revolutionary and Napoleonic France* (Tuscaloosa, 1978), pp. 12–13.
9 AFP, 'Certificat de mariage', 13 April 1775.
10 Gérard Nahon, *Métropoles et périphéries: séfarades d'occident* (Paris, 1993), p. 259.
11 Nahon, *'Nations' juives portugaises*, pp. 41–4; 'Lettres Patentes portant confirmation des privilèges des Juifs Portugais', June 1776, Versailles. Anne Robert Jacques Turgot, Baron de Laune, a theorist of economic liberalism, occupied a

number of economic ministerial posts during the reign of Louis XVI.
12 Ibid., pp. 45–6, XV, '1790, Paris: Lettres Patentes du Roi, sur un décret de l'Assemblée Nationale, portant que les Juifs ... y jouiront des droits de citoyen actif'.
13 M. le comte Stanislas de Clermont-Tonnerre, député de Paris, *Opinion de ...* (Paris, 1789), p.13.
14 Esther Benbassa, *The Jews of France: A History from Antiquity to the Present* (Princeton, 1999), pp. 81–2.
15 [Isaac de Pinto], *Apologie pour la nation juive ou Réflexions critiques sur le premier chapitre du VIIe des oeuvres de Monsieur de Voltaire, au sujet des juifs* (Amsterdam, 1762), p. 4.
16 The family grave in Montmartre cemetery, Paris, indicates Isaac's birth as 1767. Records of the Paroisse de Saint Eustache show that he was born 9 February 1771. Records of the Société Pereire note the date of his circumcision as 16 February 1771. I thank Colette Pereire for this information.
17 La Rochelle, *Jacob Rodrigues Pereire*, p. 466.
18 Alan Forrest, *Society and Politics in Revolutionary Bordeaux* (London, 1975), pp. 52–3.
19 Ibid., p. 25; and Alan Forrest, *The Revolution in Provincial France: Aquitaine 1789–1799* (Oxford, 1996), pp. 183–4, 247.
20 Carolyn Fick, *The Making of Haiti: The Saint Domingue Revolution from Below* (Knoxville, 1990), ch. 5.
21 Helen M. Davies, 'Friendship in the Revolution: A Sephardic Correspondence (1794–1799)', *French History and Civilization: Papers from the George Rudé Seminar* 4 (2011), 65–80. See also Philippe Gardey, *Négociants et marchands de Bordeaux: de la guerre d'Amérique à la Restauration (1780–1830)* (Paris, 2009), pp. 195, 203.
22 Davies, 'Friendship', 58–9. Of all fines handed down, 30 per cent were levied against the Sephardim who comprised a comparatively small percentage of the business community. The only Jew guillotined was Joseph Mendès, a Catholic convert. See Nahon, *Juifs et judaïsme*, p. 172.
23 Abraham Furtado, 'Mémoire d'un Patriote proscrit', in *Bibliothèque de Bordeaux* [hereafter BMBx], *Fonds Patrimoniaux* (Bordeaux, no date).
24 Archives municipales de Bordeaux [hereafter AMBx], GG 845, 'Culte Israélite: Naissances, Mariages, Décès, 1706–1792', pp. 71, 78–9.
25 AFP, Fonseca, Paris, to Pereire, Bordeaux, 7 September 1797.
26 Ibid., Rodrigues, Bordeaux, to 'I. de J. Pereyre chez l'héritier d'Ic. Levy à J. J. Rousseau Lez-Bayonne', 11 June 1794.
27 See for instance Pierre Hourmat, *Histoire de Bayonne*, Vol. 2: *La Révolution 1789–1799* (Bayonne, 1992), pp. 61, 71, 226.
28 Peter McPhee, *Living the French Revolution, 1789–99* (London, 2006), pp. 131–8.
29 Albert Darricau, *Scènes de la Terreur à Bayonne et aux Environs 1793–1794* (Bayonne-Biarritz, 1903), pp. 23–5; Ernest Ginsburger, Grand Rabbin, *Le Comitë de Surveillance de Jean-Jacques Rousseau Saint-Esprit-Lès-Bayonne:*

procès-verbaux et correspondance II octobre 1793–30 fructidor an II (Paris, 1934), p. 43.
30 Ginsburger, *Comité de Surveillance*, p. 26, fn. (1).
31 Henri Léon, *Histoire des juifs de Bayonne* (1893; reprint Marseille: 1976), p. 164. The event is reminiscent of an earlier celebration by the Jews of Metz who sang a Hebrew version of the Marseillaise in the Metz synagogue to celebrate an important military victory at Thionville. See Ronald Schechter, 'Translating the "Marseillaise": Biblical republicanism and the emancipation of Jews in revolutionary France', *Past and Present* 143 (1994), 108–35.
32 AFP, 'Acte de mariage Isaac Rodrigues Henriques et Sara-Sophie Lopès Fonseca'.
33 Characterised as the 'Commercial Republic' in James Livesey, *Making Democracy in the French Revolution* (Cambridge, MA, 2001).
34 Silvia Marzagalli, 'Establishing Transatlantic Trade Networks in Time of War: Bordeaux and the United States, 1793–1815', *Business History Review* 79 (2005), 811–44.
35 J.-J. Hemardinquer, 'Affaires et politique sous la monarchie censitaire. Un libéral: F.-B. Boyer-Fonfrède (1767–1845)', *Annales du Midi* 73 (1961). François-Bernard was the brother of Jean-Baptiste Boyer-Fonfrède, a Girondin guillotined in 1793.
36 AFP. Writing from Bordeaux, Rodrigues *fils* addressed a letter to Pereire there, 21 August 1796.
37 Frédéric Barbier, 'Les Origines de la maison Fould: Berr Léon et Bénédict Fould (vers 1740–1864)', *Revue historique* 1 (1989).
38 La Rochelle, *Jacob Rodrigues Pereire*, p. 482. In a letter to a pupil of Jacob Rodrigues Pereire, 17 May 1800, he wrote of 'the state of alienation in which this poor child has fallen.' Abigail died in May 1802.
39 Archives départementales de la Gironde [hereafter ADG], 3E 24127, notaire Mathieu, 'Inventaire, Isaac Rodrigues Pereire', 10 December 1806.
40 La Rochelle, *Jacob Rodrigues Pereire*, p. 482, letter to Marie-Magdaleine Marois, 17 May 1800.
41 See AMBx, IE 27, notaire Mathieu, 'Acte de naissance 361, Jacob Emile Rodrigues Pereire'. Emile Pereire's name was written without an accent on the capital 'E'.
42 For an account of the naming of Sephardic children at this period see Anne Bénard-Oukhemanou, *La communauté juive de Bayonne au XIXe siècle* (Anglet, 2001).
43 La Rochelle, *Jacob Rodrigues Pereire*, p. 474.
44 Ibid., p. 485, to Fonseca, 13 January 1801.
45 Fick, *Making of Haiti*, p. 236.
46 Jean Cavignac, *Dictionnaire du judaïsme bordelais aux XVIIIe et XIXe siècles: biographies, généalogies, professions, institutions* (Bordeaux, 1987), p. 192. See also AMBx, IE 33 (microfiche), notaire Mathieu, 'Acte de naissance 952, Mardochee Telephe Rodrigues Pereyre' [sic], 26 April 1803. Télèphe was the central character in the twelve-volume novel, *Télèphe* (1784) by Jean de Pechméja.

47 Jean Tulard (ed.), *Dictionnaire Napoléon* (Paris, 1989), p. 267.
48 La Rochelle, *Jacob Rodrigues Pereire*, 7 May 1803, p. 508.
49 Noted in ADG, 3E 24127, notaire Mathieu, 'Inventaire Isaac Rodrigues Pereire', 10 December 1806.
50 M. Capelle, 'Observations sur les mouvemens [sic] de la population de Bordeaux depuis le 1er jour de l'an XI (23 septembre 1802) jusqu'au 31 décembre 1820', *Académie des Sciences, Belles Lettres et Arts de Bordeaux du 27 aôut 1821* (Bordeaux, 1821), 156.
51 ADG, 3E 24127, notaire Mathieu: 'Inventaire Isaac Rodrigues Pereire'.
52 Ibid. This sum was only slightly less than the estimated value of the library of Mardochée Lopès Fonseca. See ibid., 3E 24125.
53 ADG, 1E 45, 'Acte de naissance, 1717, Pereire Isaac Rodrigues', 28 November 1806.
54 Capelle, 'Observations', 141.
55 Albert Soboul, 'La Reprise économique et la stabilisation sociale 1797–1815', in Fernand Braudel and Ernest Labrousse (eds), *Histoire économique et sociale de la France, tome III: L'avènement de l'ère industrielle (1789–années 1880)* (Paris, 1976), p. 103.
56 François Crouzet, 'Bordeaux: An Eighteenth Century *Wirtschaftswunder*', in François Crouzet (ed.), *Britain, France and International Commerce: from Louis XIV to Victoria* (Aldershot, 1996), p. 42.
57 Nahon, *Juifs et judaïsme*, pp. 188–9.
58 de Pelleport-Burête, *Les Oeuvres de la Paroisse Ste-Eulalie de Bordeaux – Conférence* (Bordeaux, 1895), p. 13.
59 David Todd, *L'Identité économique de la France. Libre-échange et protectionnisme (1814–1851)* (Paris, 2008).
60 Nahon, *Juifs et judaïsme*, pp. 174–80.
61 AMBx, 30E 1, 'Déclaration d'adoption des noms des personnes de culte hébraïque [décret du 20 juillet 1808] (15 octobre 1808–1er juin 1810)'. Confusion had arisen from the use of patronymics and place-names, and a lack of clarity in identifying individuals. The decree was also intended to encourage the Jews to Frenchify their names.
62 AFP, 'Ve. Pereire et Frère, Rue Bouhaut, no. 2', Bordeaux, to Rodrigues *fils*, Paris [late 1813]. 'Au Juste Prix' translates roughly as 'The Right Price'.
63 Jean Cavignac, *Les Israélites bordelais de 1780 à 1850: autour de l'émancipation* (Paris, 1991), p. 303.
64 AMBx, 30E 1, 'Déclaration d'adoption des noms'.
65 Cavignac, *Israélites bordelais*, pp. 302–6.
66 At no. 10 and no. 11 rue Ste Eulalie. AMBx, IF 4 (microfilm), 'Recensement 1822', p. 396.
67 Autin, *Frères Pereire*, p. 22.
68 Cavignac, *Israélites bordelais*, pp. 320–6, 294, Tableau LXXIX, and p. 257.
69 Cavignac, *Dictionnaire*, p. 248. Of the budget, 22 per cent was contributed by the Raba family.
70 Nahon, *Juifs et judaïsme*, pp. 179–80.

71 ADG, 7V 14 'Culte des Israélites: Construction des Synagogues'.
72 Ibid., 7V 19, 'Culte des Israélites: Comptabilité, Budgets, indemnités et traitements du personnel, secours, correspondance', 25 December 1810.
73 Nahon, *Juifs et judaïsme*, p. 183.
74 Ibid., p. 182, in which Nahon is quoting from the Archives du Consistoire Central de Paris [hereafter ACCP], ICC 21.
75 Ibid., p. 202.
76 Jules Mirès, *À mes juges: ma vie et mes affaires* (Paris, 1861), pp. 8–9.
77 ADG, 7V 19, Bordeaux Consistoire to the Prefect of the Gironde, 10 avril 1807. See also La Rochelle, *Jacob Rodrigues Pereire*, p. 514.
78 Cavignac, *Israélites bordelais*, p. 334.
79 Bibliothèque nationale de France, Arsenal [hereafter BNF-A], Fonds d'Eichthal, 14804/13, Isaac to Euryale Cazeaux, 3 November 1832.
80 AFP, Henriette, Bordeaux, to Rodrigues *fils*, Paris, undated, but probably late 1813.
81 La Rochelle, *Jacob Rodrigues Pereire*, p. 513.
82 Anka Muhlstein, *Baron James: The Rise of the French Rothschilds* (New York, 1984), p. 27.
83 BMBx, 'Les manuscrits récolements: inventaire complementaire, Per-Pay'. This was noted in an undated piece by J. Gourraigne about Emile Pereire published in the *Gazette de Beaux Arts*, and quoting the Pereires' contemporary Jules Mirès.
84 ADG, 8M 1, fo. 47, reports to the Prefect of the Gironde.
85 Hubert Bonin, 'La Splendeur des Samazeuilh, banquiers de Bordeaux (1810–1913)', *Revue historique*, no. 584 (1993), 349–89; Bertrand Gille, *La Banque et le crédit en France de 1815 à 1848* (Paris, 1959), pp. 126–7.
86 Autin, *Frères Pereire*, p. 22.
87 AFP, undated letter Emile, Bordeaux, to his unnamed employer.
88 Ibid., Emile Pereire to the Minister of Finance, 9 June 1858.
89 Autin, *Frères Pereire*, p. 22. See also AFP, letter in Emile Pereire's hand to 'Mr. Julian', 10 December 1819, foreshadowing that Isaac was about to 'faire sa prière dans le temple'.
90 AFP, undated letter Emile, Bordeaux, to unknown friends informing them of the death of Télèphe.
91 Cavignac, *Israélites bordelais*, pp. 267 ff.
92 Kagan and Morgan, *Atlantic Diasporas*, p. xi and passim. The use of the plural, 'diasporas', reflects the diversity of Jewish communities around the Atlantic seaboard.
93 See for instance Malino, *Jews of Bordeaux*.
94 AFP, undated but found among early documents, to be sung to the air 'Pegase est un cheval'.
95 Ibid., correspondence with Anaïs Jullian of Bordeaux, who later became Anaïs Oxeda. Amélie and Félicie Jullian were also friends of Emile Pereire.

2

The new society

Like their literary counterparts Lucien Rubempré and Julien Sorel, Emile and Isaac Pereire set out with high ambitions and equally slender resources, Emile arriving in Paris late in 1822 and Isaac joining him a year later in November 1823, on the eve of his seventeenth birthday.[1] The journey by coach had been interminable, Emile describing in a letter home 'a brusque jolting which transported me to Paris' and the stupefaction on his arrival. With each kilometre traversed the warmth and sociability of the rue Bouhaut receded. A revolution had been wrought in him, he wrote, 'I am transplanted to a new world.'[2]

Emile's memorable description encapsulates the shock experienced by young provincial men and women on arriving in the huge metropolis, but it was simply the first of many challenges to be confronted by the Pereires in this 'new world'. These challenges were to be intensified by their encounter with Claude-Henri de Rouvroy, the comte de Saint-Simon, whose political and economic philosophy encompassed nothing less than a new society. This chapter will explore how these two young men responded to the 'new world', the dramatically new physical environment in which they found themselves; what impact the new ideas of Saint-Simon had on them and their existing beliefs; and how and what they in turn contributed to conceptualising a radically 'new society'.

On their arrival in Paris they were both young adults. What did these young men look like? How would one characterise them? Their appearance must be judged from later photographs, portraiture and oral descriptions, but these show little resemblance between them. Emile was diminutive, rather wiry indeed, a face with fine features, intense dark eyes, a confident full mouth, and the whole crowned by a shock of uncon-

1 Emile Pereire (1855). Bibliothèque nationale de France, Estampes et Photographie

trollable dark hair. His great-grandson Alfred Pereire was to muse: 'how such a fire could burn in such a body without consuming him'.[3] Isaac, in contrast, was the larger man, 'strong and cheerful', according to Alfred, his face rounder, skin tone 'yellow but fleshy', his mouth thinner, hair curly and fine.[4] In all likelihood one resembled Henriette and the other their father Isaac. They may have spoken Spanish as did other Sephardim from Bordeaux.[5] Certainly, it seems they spoke French with strong Gascon

2 Isaac Pereire (1850s). Archives de la famille Pereire

accents, for Ernest Feydeau, who had an axe to grind in relation to the Pereires, later castigated 'their atrocious meridional gibberish'.[6]

In assuming responsibility at an early age as the male head of the Pereire family, however, Emile began to betray an unattractive trait of character, one which recalled that of his late father. He could become headstrong, intransigent, reacting angrily when his authority was questioned and refusing to acknowledge alternative courses to his own, that another's point of view might be more reasonable or be preferred. This belief in his own personal infallibility could also lead to critical and thoughtless behaviour: directed towards his rivals it was a formidable weapon but towards his friends it was hurtful and cruel, an impediment to friendship. But nowhere was this more evident in these early years than in his relationship with Isaac, some of whose late adolescent behaviour Emile could scarcely tolerate. Isaac, much-loved in his adult life, was nevertheless a rebellious adolescent who grew into a rebellious young man.

For his part, Isaac was the child of a father dead before his time, the loss of whom may have remained problematic. The more romantic of the two, at least in the way he experienced and responded to life, Alfred Pereire for one considered him to have been the 'director' ['réalisateur'] and his brother the 'idealist', for Isaac certainly did not lack practical skills, as he was later to demonstrate.[7] Isaac as the youngest son was closest to his mother, perhaps even the more favoured, carrying as he did his father's name and given the circumstances of his birth. His relations with his brother at this early period were complex, a mix of brotherly affection and sibling rivalry which Emile recognised.[8] Speculation may suggest that Isaac also sought the missing father in his elder brother, a role which placed Emile inevitably in an ambiguous position. Emile himself had also spent the greater part of his life without a father in a family which, however extensive, had been deprived of a most significant figure. Cast in the role of father to his younger brother, he was preparing himself for future difficulties.

Both Emile and Isaac had also been brought up to revere the memory of their grandfather, Jacob Rodrigues Pereire, whose eminence as an innovator in treating deaf mutes, whose official position at court and significance in the history of Sephardic Jews of the southwest, all rendered him a towering figure in their lives. As grandsons of the fabled Jacob they were heirs to a tradition in which close proximity to the seat of power, public visibility and monetary reward went hand in hand with service to the disadvantaged. A less encouraging and unwelcome note, at odds with the success of their grandfather, was the very real evidence of their father's failure. They were to be reminded of these equally as the years passed.

While Emile and Isaac were both accustomed to urban life – Bordeaux, despite its travails, remained a large provincial city and they had lived and worked at its centre – Paris, with a population approaching 800,000, overwhelmed them.[9] The city's boundaries had been extended outwards in 1784 with construction of the wall for the Fermiers-généraux, the tax collectors, releasing land for dwellings to accommodate the burgeoning population. Nevertheless, the capital city they were to discover was becoming fouler than it had been for centuries, for Paris remained a medieval city, its streets narrow, dark, and stinking.[10] Population increased daily and, with it, congestion, housing density stretched to capacity, filth and squalor, open drains and sewers, effluent coursing down the centre of narrow streets. Louis Chevalier, who famously characterised and equated Paris' increasing population density with its increased crime rate, as *classes labourieuses et classes dangereuses*, aptly quoted Claude Lachaise's *Topographie médicale de Paris* of 1822:

> The sun shines for a short time only in some of the streets, hardly at all in others and never in most of them, and … the people living on the ground floor are still in the dark when the sun is far up the horizon. This lack of sunlight may be regarded as one of the true causes of the city's humidity and of the prodigious amount of mud that carpets its streets.[11]

Waiting on the arrival of Henriette and Isaac, Emile wrote often from Paris to family members, friends and former neighbours. He was lonely in the capital and there were people and places he missed. Business was conducted differently and he was forced to learn new ways of doing things.[12] In the meantime, Henriette's situation in Bordeaux had become ever more precarious, and even meeting the rent led to recurring crises.[13] Nevertheless, she needed Emile's urging to leave and to bring Isaac with her. In Paris, the brothers would be in good hands, Emile reminded her. When he fell ill, his aunt Sara-Sophie cared for as him as Henriette would herself.[14] Sara-Sophie's family of eight children had made the young Pereire instantly at home in a noisy, sociable, disputatious environment. The Rodrigues were not well-off; rather, they lived a 'modest and sober life', economies made in her daughters' *toilettes* and in what was not indispensable to their diet providing Sara-Sophie with the means to pay for music and other lessons.[15] The family lived in the rue des Petites-Écuries in what was then Paris' third *arrondissement* (and is now the tenth). The *quartier*, known as the faubourg Poissonière, was to the south of the 1784 Fermiers-généraux wall and a comparatively recent residential area undergoing rapid change.[16] Their apartment was a salon for financiers, bankers and economists, Jews and Christians alike, for although Isaac Rodrigues had retained a professional association with the Paris Consistoire as secretary until 1825, he was far more tolerant of non-Jews than was his sister-in-law in Bordeaux. Among the *habitués* was a Bayonnais, Jacques Laffitte, a former governor of the Banque de France who held an ambition to establish a bank providing investment capital to industry. Benoît Fould, in whose bank Isaac Rodrigues was employed, was another regular guest. The economist, Vital-Roux, who was also a regent of the Banque de France and had recently published a treatise arguing for greater availability of credit to industry, was yet another. The Protestant Hottinguer brothers were frequent visitors, as were the bankers Jacques Ardoin and Salomon Halphen.[17] It appears that the Pereires thus found themselves in stimulating company with an early opportunity to meet on terms of comparative intimacy significant figures in Paris' financial and commercial world, individuals who were in a position to assist them when needed.

When they arrived in Paris, then, Emile and Isaac Pereire lived in the midst of a Jewish family which, although its members associated with non-Jews, gave some continuity to their experience of daily life in Bordeaux. Nevertheless, there were also profound differences. The Jewish population in Paris had increased considerably over the first two decades of the nineteenth century. The Pereires were just two among some 7,000 Jews living there in the 1820s, a remarkable growth when compared with the numbers recorded by the Paris Consistoire in 1809, when there were fewer than half that number.[18] By the end of their first ten years in the capital there would be well over 8,500 Jews, by far the greatest number Ashkenazim from northeastern France.[19] Their visibility had increased with their numbers. Throughout the 1820s, Emile and Isaac Pereire thus remarked not only a huge metropolis but an entirely different religious and cultural environment from the one they had left, in which Catholic dominance would be reinforced by the succession of Charles X to the Bourbon throne.[20] Here they must make their way, the world all before them. Its prospect was daunting.

The household in which the Pereires found themselves was itself in the process of transformation. While the Rodrigues still associated principally with Jews, they had ceased to practice Judaism to any degree, grasping the possibilities opened to them through emancipation including entry to an appealing secular intellectual culture. Olinde Rodrigues reflected on this a few years later: 'I was born a Jew', he wrote, 'and yet my father wanted to make of me a man for the future and not of the past; I never practised the rites of judaism'.[21] Nevertheless, the stance adopted under the Restoration by the prevailing Catholicism, which questioned the Jews' fitness for equality of citizenship, added at least some ambiguity to their acceptance into the non-Jewish community. The Charte Constitutionnelle of Louis XVIII, which stipulated freedom of religion, also declared the Catholic Church the state religion. The Bourbon Restoration was marked throughout by extraordinary Catholic missionary activity, designed to reinvigorate and convert people to Catholicism: 1,500 missions drew crowds of up to 20,000 souls at a time.²² Soon after the Pereires arrived in Paris, essay competitions were held in Rouen (1823) and in Strasbourg (1824) to determine whether Jews were capable of entering fully into French society.²³ In response Jewish writers had begun to address the 'regeneration' of Jewish religious practices, to render them more acceptable to non-Jews.

It is not surprising then to find Emile Pereire reflecting on his own faith. Within months of his arrival in Paris, writing to his mother of friendly arguments with members of the Rodrigues household, he reassured her that he made no concessions even though his cousins rarely agreed with him. He wrote with approval of a book which had just appeared, *Loi de Moïse ou système religieux et politique des Hébreux*, by a Sephardic writer, Joseph Salvador.²⁴ Emile later told a friend in St Esprit that it placed Judaism in 'the rank that it deserved among civilised people', the law of Moses the sole point of departure for 'all existing laws', worthy of respect and study, the equal of any of the other major religions and particularly of Catholicism.²⁵ Salvador's argument was ambitious for he proposed Judaic law as the model for constitutional government at a time when political legitimacy was increasingly contested: Louis XVIII's 'ultras', supported by the Catholic missions, sought vigorously to re-establish the Divine Right of Kings.²⁶ Salvador's book had already been translated into Spanish and Emile endeavoured to acquaint Sephardic audiences in Bordeaux and St Esprit with its merits.²⁷ Nevertheless, the differences on points of religion between the Pereire and the Rodrigues families weighed heavily on Emile from the beginning, as various letters to family members confirm.²⁸

Rodrigues *fils*' helpfulness towards his young charges extended to their livelihoods, and his extensive network and reputation were invaluable to them in finding employment. At the beginning Emile worked for his uncle at the Fould Bank. In January 1823, he wrote to Adolphe Mirès of a career offering every opportunity for his ambition, to which his loyal friend replied that he expected to see Emile engaged in the 'whirlwind of big business' once he had settled.²⁹ Isaac, who was to become highly proficient in bookkeeping and accounting with his uncle's expert tuition, was barely twenty years of age when appointed head of accounting for Vital-Roux & Cie.³⁰

The Rodrigues family was important in the education of the Pereires in even more directly personal ways, however. Olinde, the eldest child, was aged twenty-seven in 1822 and he and Emile became close friends immediately. Eugène was slightly younger than Isaac Pereire, but they also quickly formed an attachment. These ties were strengthened when Emile resolved to marry his cousin Rachel Herminie, one of six daughters. This love match, as letters attest, was brought to a head by Emile's fear that he had a rival for her affections. But the Rodrigues couple was delighted with the prospect. In April 1824 his friends in Bordeaux wished Emile and Herminie well on the occasion of their wedding and on Emile's union forever with 'the one who raised in you the first sentiments of love'.[31] In spite of her parents' estrangement from Judaism, and probably because of her groom's continuing religious attachment, Herminie's marriage took place at the synagogue in the rue Notre-Dame-de-Nazareth, Rodrigues *fils* providing under the circumstances (of his financial position and of his six daughters) a generous dowry of 4,000 francs. A trousseau valued at 2,000 francs including silver was an additional sign of the Rodrigues family's generosity.[32] If Paris was to be the centre of Emile's life and career it helped that there existed already extensive kinship relationships which would anchor him there.

Emile's attraction towards, and intimate knowledge of, the increasingly secular Rodrigues family was, however, the cause of a painful confrontation between his mother and her sister's family, one which marked a turning point in his own religious inclinations. When she finally arrived in Paris, Henriette had found a household considerably different in its religious and cultural habits from those of Bordeaux. The comportment of the Rodrigues women, with their lack of reverence for the Sabbath, affronted her.[33] She returned to Bordeaux in high dudgeon with Isaac in tow.[34] Emile was filled with misgivings for Isaac had become the pawn in a power struggle between himself and his mother. He confided in Alexandre *fils* a strong conviction that Isaac and he were destined to be partners: 'he was by nature called to be my partner', he wrote, a belief placed in jeopardy by his mother's behaviour. Only assurances made to her by both her sons concerning their religious commitment seemed to restore the peace, but the need to make these assurances amounted to a concession which distanced Emile a little further from Judaism.[35]

This was not the only instance of dissension over religious questions. While Rodrigues *fils* was combative in his espousal of reason as the one true basis of philosophy, which may have contributed to his resignation as secretary of the Paris Consistoire in 1825, this philosophical stance was at odds with the decision taken by his daughter Sophronie, with his moral support, to have her children baptised in the Catholic Church. Sophronie's husband was the son of Abraham Andrade, the Chief Rabbi of Bordeaux, adding further frisson to the dilemma. The couple's actions thus reverberated well beyond Paris. Emile now found himself in an unenviable position: he had married into a family about which his mother entertained grave doubts and whose attitude towards the practice of her religion caused her pain. His own disquiet about the baptisms was considerable, writing to his uncle Jacob Lopès Fonseca in Bordeaux: 'Andrade has not spoken to me of it at all. I have thus not made known to him how much I disapprove of his conduct. But he knows my opinion in this regard because I have expressed it to the whole family'.[36]

Religious issues had come to dominate. In 1824, Louis XVIII's brother, the comte d'Artois, ascended the throne as Charles X. He also inherited his brother's Prime Minister, the comte de Villèle. Charles X was determined to reinstate even more reactionary measures than had his predecessor, attempting to restore the unity of Church and State through the King, and symbolised by his elaborate coronation at Rheims Cathedral in May 1825.[37] A Sacrilege Act was passed which punished sacrilegious acts with severe penalties, including death. Relatively generous provisions of the Charte, which had at least enshrined freedom of religion, were replaced with restrictions on Jewish life including access to education. Jews were prohibited from teaching and from being taught in the universities. This intolerance rendered the Pereires more than ever mindful of their own Jewish identity. Their cousin Olinde, a brilliant mathematician educated at the Lycée Impérial and the Université de Paris, had been prevented from teaching at the École Normale, the school founded in 1793 during the Revolution and designed to train teachers imbued with Enlightenment attributes. He was forced through anti-Jewish pressure to abandon his ambition to work as a mathematician.[38] The Ministry of Education systematically placed impediments in the way of Jewish candidates among Olinde's contemporaries aspiring to teaching posts in higher institutions.[39] Olinde turned to banking in which there were no such prohibitions. The sentiment underlying these restrictions against employing Jews in higher education, however, had filtered through into popular literature whose authors, alarmed at the rate of Jewish migration to Paris, were quick to identify 'the Jewish problem'.

Both the ideas in circulation and the circumstances of the Andrade marriage influenced Emile Pereire considerably, the position he had now reached captured in a forthright letter to his uncle, Fonseca, to whom he wrote in 1826: 'I am not religious, you know, I was born in the Jewish faith and there I stay. Not that I believe it perfect but because I do not know a better and I have the personal conviction that to change one must be either a sincere believer or a hypocrite.' Judaism was inseparable from his identity. He had been born into the Jewish faith and that was the end of it. Moreover, since religious affiliation of some sort was 'obligatory' in French society, 'my children will be [brought up as] Jews, the unjust prejudices which strike this religion will not deter me from this resolution'.[40]

While Emile's religious doubts would not lead to any abandonment of his identification with Judaism, at the time he was entertaining them he and Isaac became absorbed by the teachings of a contemporary philosopher, an engagement which was as momentous as it was eventually disruptive. At the time of their arrival in Paris, Olinde Rodrigues had become secretary to the comte de Saint-Simon (1760–1825) to whom Olinde introduced the Pereires at the home of the banker Jacques Ardoin, possibly as early as 1824.[41] This meeting with Saint-Simon and a closer acquaintance with his thought was to unleash, as Isaac's son Gustave Pereire vividly described much later, 'a whole series of young and beautiful intellects', anxious to give solid form to their aspirations.[42]

Saint-Simon had begun writing about contemporary problems in the early years of the new century, but during the Restoration, in penury, he began a stream of studies dealing with ideas of social progress. He developed concepts in his works which his disciples were to use later as the springboard for elaboration. He thought in broad terms about the world, government, society and religion. He envisaged a united and peaceful Europe in the wake of Napoléon's military conquests and the brittle peace of France's Bourbon Restoration. His theories of industrial society gave primacy to science, and industrialists, scientists and artists would together bring about the fusion of government, work and religion. The basis of society since the French Revolution exacerbated poverty through the precedence accorded to landed gentry and those living off investment whom he described as 'l'oisif' (literally 'idle' or lazy), as against those who worked productively for their living, 'l'industriel'. He began to attract disciples, some of whom acted at various times as his secretary: Auguste Thierry, Auguste Comte and Léon Halévy had all preceded Olinde Rodrigues in this role.[43] Several journals, among them the *Organisateur*, emerged with the assistance of these young men. In a well-known article in this publication Saint-Simon had weighed up the comparative cost to France should it lose 3,000 of its aristocrats, clergy, judiciary, land owners and public servants, as against losing the same number of scientists, engineers, artists and artisans, an article which appeared shortly before the assassination of the duc de Berri.[44] This unfortunate coincidence saw him tried for complicity in the assassination, a trial which he survived but which gave fright to those whose support he needed most, the lawyers and bankers who would finance his work. He attempted suicide.

Early in 1825, with Olinde Rodrigues's assistance, what turned out to be Saint-Simon's last work appeared, *Le Nouveau christianisme*, a work of which Olinde was to write several years later that it led to 'the association of the universal family; from this day was made possible the reunion of

Jews and Christians at the heart of a New Christianity, the universal religion'.⁴⁵ On his death-bed, Saint-Simon counselled Olinde that 'to do great things one must be passionate'. Olinde, who was scarcely in need of such advice, closed the dead philosopher's eyes.⁴⁶

Le Nouveau christianisme posited a belief that Christianity as it had been practised had failed, that the basic tenet of Christ's teaching, to love one's neighbour as oneself, had been ignored. To re-assert and to live by this fundamental principle, society would need to move beyond present-day Christianity in order to improve the conditions of the poorest and most numerous class. The 'new Christianity' would thus lay the foundation for a new society. This view was entirely agreeable to Jews who sat at Saint-Simon's feet, for the Christian text at the core of Saint-Simon's essay had its genesis in the Old Testament and was itself, in the form of *sedaca*, central to Jewish life.

Upon Saint-Simon's death in May 1825 a small number accompanied the cortège to Père Lachaise cemetery where he was buried in a modest grave, one on which the head-stone marked the resting place of 'Claude-Henri Rouvroy Saint-Simon Economiste'. The next day Olinde Rodrigues took steps to ensure that this economist was not forgotten. With several distinguished business figures as shareholders – among whom were those Saint-Simon had at times alienated, such as the bankers Laffitte and Ardoin – Olinde Rodrigues and another disciple, Prosper Enfantin, established a journal, the *Producteur*.⁴⁷ Emile wrote a short piece for it on a report to the Chambre de Commerce concerning the provision of coal to the capital, appearing among the 'Mélanges' in May 1826.⁴⁸ Isaac also assisted with production and, with Emile's encouragement, Adolphe Mirès distributed the *Producteur* in Bordeaux.⁴⁹ The Pereires were thus early evangelisers.

By 1825, Isaac Pereire too had cause to reflect on his position in relation to Judaism, sparked by an episode involving another of the Rodrigues daughters. He became enamoured of the young (16-year-old) Mélanie Rodrigues, provoking strong opposition from Emile, their mother and the girl's parents. Henriette attached impossible conditions to the alliance, effectively dashing any possibility of marriage, demanding, as Isaac wrote to Alexandre *fils*, 'that my uncle renounce any union with Christians'. Isaac retorted that it was impossible to sacrifice his love, absorbing as it did his every thought and consuming his 'temperament'.

The affair appalled Emile. In his letters to Isaac, who had returned to Bordeaux yet again, he emphasised his brother's youth – Isaac was still only 19. He wrote of the painful conflict he had experienced between the rules which had been his mainstay in childhood and adolescence, those of his mother, and those of his wife's family. Out of all this Henriette managed to extract some kind of confession of faith from Isaac for he noted in a letter that: 'Mother is sure of me as to religion, I have written to her on this subject, so there will be no more discussion', echoing what Emile had written two years previously, that she had demanded reassurance of her boys' religious devotion in the midst of the alien Rodrigues family.[50] The Pereires' faith, already challenged by the domestic circumstances within which they struggled and by the prevailing Catholicism outside, seemed thus to have become further muddled with filial duty.

It would have pleased their mother, however, that Emile and Isaac attempted to revive interest in the significance of their grandfather, Jacob Rodrigues Pereire, a task they had inherited from their parents and which they had accepted with as much devotion. Now that both lived in the city where their grandfather had principally made his mark it became clear that Paris had forgotten him. With the help of a former pupil, Marie-Magdeleine Marois, they compiled a dossier on Jacob Rodrigues Pereire's methods of teaching deaf mutes to speak which in 1825 they deposited with the Institut National des Sourds-Muets (National Institute of Deaf Mutes) in the rue Saint-Jacques. There for the time being the documents remained. Any further effort in that quarter was placed on hold although not the Pereires' hopes of seeing their grandfather accorded the honours they had come to believe were his due. Fifty years would pass before his contribution would be the subject of public discussion once more.[51]

Isaac's late adolescence may have proved difficult, but he drew consolation from his friendship with Eugène Rodrigues. Both younger brothers of forceful elder siblings, they were drawn together from the outset of Isaac's move to Paris, becoming inseparable as part of the group which was forming around the *Producteur* and, a little later, out of the phoenix which became Saint-Simonianism. Olinde Rodrigues had also introduced both young men to the charismatic Prosper Enfantin, now a leader of the Saint-Simonian movement, a meeting which was to have considerable impact on them.

Prosper Enfantin was the son of a bankrupt which circumstance, in a story not uncommon among the Saint-Simonians and as is often said, had prevented him from pursuing his chosen career in the army, instead attending the École Polytechnique where his tutor was Olinde Rodrigues. Finding a position in St Petersburg with a French bank, he was introduced to several young graduates of his former École who had some familiarity with the ideas of Saint-Simon. On his return to Paris in 1824 he once more encountered Olinde Rodrigues and was introduced to Saint-Simon himself and to his circle.[52] After Saint-Simon's death, he and Olinde were joined by St-Amand Bazard, a former member of the Carbonari (the secret society which had aimed to overthrow the Bourbon Restoration), as the three leaders in what evolved, after the demise of the *Producteur*, into a new movement, appealing particularly to talented young men and women searching for spiritual and intellectual sustenance after the calamity of Empire and the prohibitions of the Restoration. Bazard was not the only former adherent of a different cause: Philippe Buchez and Pierre Dugied had been Carbonari also. Hippolyte Carnot and Michel Chevalier had belonged to the Knights' Templars, a quasi-masonic group which emphasised military order and looked back to a historic past. Others were drawn directly from Freemasonry. They were joined by a host of disaffected youth united by 'the anomie of the self, a sense of being outsiders'.[53] The Pereire brothers were not alone.

Before the *Producteur* ceased publication Saint-Simonianism *per se* could not be said to have existed; certainly the bankers and financiers who had financed the journal would not have described themselves thus. But articles on issues which captured the attention of the emergent generation had led to a coalescing of interests around certain key themes: aspects of industry, technology and banking; political economy; transport, including canals; religion; and the writings of Saint-Simon himself. These subjects were to lay the foundations for wider discussion among Saint-Simon's followers: Saint-Simonians were starting to develop the themes which their namesake had laid out. They began from the premise that society demanded new direction, that only a rejuvenated and redirected economy would address the problems induced by war, poverty and social dislocation. They saw in the application of technology the way forward for this new society. They spoke of 'association' rather than competition as a new approach to industry and society, one in which people joined together voluntarily for the public good. Saint-Simon had given little attention to the bank as an instrument of change, but his followers saw a new banking system as crucial to the new economy and hence to society, 'facilitat[ing] the transfer of capital from the idle who possess it but who do not know how to use it to those of the workers who wish to use it'.[54] The banker would have a central role in this new society.

The radical ideas which preoccupied the Pereires were cast aside, however, when, in August 1827 at the age of forty-nine, their mother died at Auteuil near Paris. She had been ill for some time, seeking relief from what Emile described as agonising chest pain and which was probably heart disease, resorting to the application of leeches. But as her condition grew worse, Emile and Isaac stayed at her bedside until the end, holding her hand and reciting with her the Jewish prayer, the *Shema Israel*: 'Hear,

O Israel: the Lord our God is one'.[55] Death came eventually, affecting them profoundly, Emile reflecting on more than one occasion that she had been both mother *and* father to her two sons, that her life had been one of pain and emotional suffering. Just as she might have started to enjoy the benefits of their success her life was taken. Moreover, Henriette was the constant link with Bordeaux and St Esprit, the Sephardic circle of family and friends built up over two centuries. To her they owed their history, their identity as Jews, their very survival from an early age and the hopeful fulfilment of their aspirations. They never forgot this, remaining profoundly grateful and indebted to her. But while her influence remained palpable, her death also released them finally from any outward constraints on their freedom to explore and to express differing approaches to religion. Henriette's end thus coincided with the period when the Pereires became actively involved in Saint-Simonianism.[56]

The Pereires, who had been on the fringes of the *Producteur*'s editorial group and had already participated in informal discussions became more closely involved with the leadership.[57] Indeed, the wider Pereire-Rodrigues family had become a pillar of Saint-Simonianism, for Charles Sarchi, who married Félicie Rodrigues, a sister of Olinde, and Henri Baud, who eventually married Mélanie, and were therefore brothers-in-law of Emile Pereire, also became devotees.

Olinde Rodrigues was now deputy director in the new mortgage bank, the Caisse Hypothécaire, which advanced finance raised through debentures. He had arranged a position there for Enfantin and it was in the bank's offices that the Saint-Simonians as a group first began to meet regularly. The political tenor of the *Producteur* was in conflict with the increasingly liberal views of figures prominent in Parisian political and intellectual life, however, including Constant, Lamennais and Stendahl, and of another political journal, the *Globe*. This opposition to the *Producteur* contributed in the end to a fall in circulation which rendered the journal unsustainable, and publication ceased altogether in December 1826 when it was forced on the editors that it was not paying its way.[58]

The reign of Charles X became increasingly unpopular within the country at large. His chief minister, Villèle, was in open conflict with the writer François-René, vicomte de Chateaubriand, on the issue of freedom of the fourth estate, Chateaubriand having launched a society in defense of the press. In the election of 1827 this led to Villèle's resounding defeat by a group which included liberals as well as royalists. Charles X appointed the inexperienced vicomte de Martignac to replace Villèle in a bid to shore up the conservative cause, but Martignac's team was no better prepared to deal with this volatile political scene than the predecessor. With protracted economic crisis the next few years were to be unstable.⁵⁹

Saint-Simon's followers continued to meet, gaining disciples from outside of Paris. To the young Isaac, Enfantin delegated the task of keeping Jacques Rességuier from Castelnaudary in Languedoc informed of doctrinal developments so that Rességuier in turn might be well-armed as an apostle. These are among the most significant examples of Saint-Simonian writings during what was a fallow period of consolidation and reflection. Over eighteen months from January 1828, Isaac's letters revealed a growing confidence in his own literary capacity, and demonstrate something of the contribution he made to the shaping of Saint-Simonian thought on financial and economic matters.

Private property had been in the public mind since 1826 when Charles X had introduced a bill to the Chambre des Députés intended to revise the provision which dealt with inheritance in the Code Civil. He aimed to make it simpler for the first-born male in a family to inherit property, making this the default position in a will rather than equality of inheritance as introduced in 1791. The bill was thus directed towards shoring up the landed aristocracy. Public opinion was vocally opposed to this proposition, however, seeing it as a return to primogeniture and thus to a reinstatement of inequality.⁶⁰ While the bill was defeated, public concerns remained.

Isaac's exposition of the subject to Rességuier drew praise from Enfantin, who described it as rigorous and scientific:

> The whole globe is the *property* [sic] of mankind [Isaac wrote]. It is a vast workshop in which all men, united in a great association, must combine and divide their work … *The slavery of the workers*, there is the real basis of the right to property, through conquest, a right that the progress of the sciences, of industry and of morality will make disappear, in bringing about the emancipation of the entire working class, and in organising society according to the idea of the ownership of work.⁶¹

Economic and social reform would depend on the bank which would provide direction to industrial development. The bank would also fund the costs of culture, education, philosophic works and the fine arts; it would repay society's debt to retired workers, widows and orphans; and finally and foremost, promote improvement in the moral and physical existence of the poorest class.⁶² The 21-year-old Isaac now signed his name 'Pereire jeune', thus distinguishing himself from his brother.⁶³ And Enfantin was to recall ten years later how in 1827 and 1828 he had gathered around him a group which he called 'the little church', the young Eugène

Rodrigues, Charles Sarchi and Isaac Pereire, all of an age, all now related in some way, and a group to whom Enfantin truly was 'father'.[64]

Emile Pereire for his part was now a married man with a small family for his first child, Fanny Rebecca, was born in February 1825. It has been said that his competence impressed the banker James de Rothschild and that Rothschild provided him with an office at the Bourse as a broker of foreign commercial paper.[65] Certainly he was working assiduously and making a name for himself, but the bright prospects which seemed assured at the outset of his move to Paris were compromised by a faltering economy. While his commitment to Saint-Simonianism was strong, his responsibilities as a father and breadwinner prevented him from contributing to the cause as ardently as his brother. His contacts with other Saint-Simonians, Olinde Rodrigues being an exception, were thus less intimate than those enjoyed by Isaac.

Isaac Pereire and the younger Rodrigues started to work together more closely when Eugène commenced an essay expounding the religious basis of Saint-Simonianism. Enfantin had encouraged Eugène to correspond with Rességuier as Isaac had done and it was these letters which laid the foundation for what became a Saint-Simonian theology.[66] The movement was thus being transmogrified from a 'doctrine' into a 'religion'. Eugène had been prepared for this turn as much by his own brother, for Olinde Rodrigues and the Saint-Simonian hierarchy had begun to see in religion a means of drawing together strands of the evolving doctrine, in particular that of an increasing emphasis on the working class, grasping the need to move beyond Christianity, the current practice of which was inconsistent with the gospel.[67]

The young Jewish Saint-Simonians found this point of departure especially appealing. Believing Judaism to be replete with practices inconsistent and inharmonious with the society in which they were now citizens, they sensed that the majority in French society was averse to Jews and to Judaism. At the same time, Saint-Simonianism shared particular characteristics with Judaism: there was a messianic quality to the doctrine, a sense of a special mission and a special people.[68] To move beyond Christianity to a new religion, while paying respect to Judaism as a forerunner of *Le Nouveau christianisme*, was thus a position which may have helped many Jews resolve the disparity they faced, between religious intolerance on the one hand and their own sense of a significant identity on the other.

Eugène's correspondence with Rességuier during 1828 and 1829, later published as *Lettres sur la religion et la politique*, is remarkable both for the way in which the writer demonstrated continuity between Judaism and Christianity and for its intention to endow the Saint-Simonian movement with a religious base.[69] The Jews had made of Israel a productive place and with their dispersal their ideas about industry had extended over the entire globe. But the religion of the future, Eugène wrote, whatever it was to be called, 'will be the social and religious principle applied to all humankind'. He called for tolerance: 'Christians, hold out your hand to the Jews, God commands you to cease to hate them, and to learn to love him first of all by loving them.'[70]

The number of Jews associated with Saint-Simonianism and their impact upon it has been mildly controversial.[71] At the beginning, their presence within the movement was seized upon by its detractors and, much later, a view of their influence as perfidious was caught up in the tide of anti-Semitism crystallised by the Dreyfus Affair. In fact the number of Jewish Saint-Simonians was not large accounting, as I estimate, for one in twelve of those close to the inner circle, though this was wildly disproportionate to their number in the wider community.[72] More significantly, they formed a critical mass within the movement and thus influenced the doctrine in important ways. Most were Sephardim introduced by Olinde Rodrigues whose brother Eugène, the Pereires and his brother-in-law Charles Sarchi became prominent. Léon Halévy and Gustave d'Eichthal, whose Ashkenazi family had converted to Catholicism in 1817, were others. Several women associated with the Rodrigues family, including Emile's wife Herminie and her sisters Félicie and Mélanie, also attended meetings and contributed financially. They owed their commitment both to the welcome and social ease they found and to the respect for Judaism apparent in Saint-Simonian doctrine, which they in turn had been able to influence.

The Rodrigues women were not unique for there was a larger number of women attracted to the movement, brought there not only through accidents of birth or through marriage ties but by a growing understanding among men in the Saint-Simonian movement that gender placed unfair contraints on the talents and aspirations of women. Henri Fournel's wife Cécile had joined together with Claire Bazard, wife of St-Amand Bazard, and Olinde's wife Euphrasie Rodrigues. Annette Flachat, Eugénie Niboyet, Pauline Roland and Suzanne Voilquin all brought a feminist perspective to Saint-Simonianism.[73]

A second level of collaboration had formed around the leadership, the primary group having become known as 'the college'.[74] Aside from the Jewish Saint-Simonians, those describing themselves as Saint-Simonians included the Talabot brothers Paulin, Léon, Edmond and Jules, originally of Limoges; another Limogeois, the young mining engineer Michel

Chevalier and his brother Auguste; Henri Fournel, formerly a director of Le Creusot iron works; and Enfantin's closest friend, the Lyonnais businessman François Arlès-Dufour. All of these men remained, for good or ill, intimately linked with the Pereires' fortunes. Most of them were polytechnicians, engineers educated at the École Polytechnique, Émile Clapeyron, Stéphane and Eugène Flachat and Gabriel Lamé being some of a larger number. By 1830 there were to be as many as 130 polytechnicians among the Saint-Simonians whose leadership had deliberately set out to promote its philosophy in this quarter.[75] Some were also graduates of the École des Mines. What attracted these young men was Saint-Simonianism's intuitive grasp of the relationship between technology and society, an understanding of the impact technology would come to exert on economic and social life.

The Saint-Simonians had become sufficiently confident during 1827-28 to promote the cause through a series of public meetings. It was St-Amand Bazard who delivered the lectures, seventeen in all, for the most part at 12 rue de Taranne in Paris.[76] Their significance to the Pereires' history lies in the themes and ideas which resonated thereafter in the Pereires' life work.

Bazard painted a grim picture, beginning with 'the painful situation in which European society finds itself at present'.[77] He spoke of the liberal doctrines currently in vogue in which unfettered competition in industry sacrificed its victims, creating fraud and bad faith. An exploited proletarian class had emerged akin to slavery. Women too were in a state of 'subalternity'. The times thus cried out for a new doctrine and direction, one which focused the effort of society around the physical and intellectual improvement of the poorest and most numerous class.

The new doctrine was full of promise. Universal association would replace competition and proprietors would cede their powers to leaders who would love, nurture and develop the skills and well-being of their work force. Education would be accessible to all, enabling workers to fulfil their vocational capacities. Depending fundamentally as it did on industry and the application of technology, this new Saint-Simonian society required a centralised system of banks at the core to regulate and fuel the needs of industry through the judicious provision of, and more liberal access to, credit. While Bazard proposed radical change in society as a necessity, he stopped short of revolution: for the doctrine of Saint-Simon 'has for its objective to change profoundly, radically the system of sentiments, of ideas and of interest; ... it does not want to wreak havoc on society'.[78]

The final meeting, which dealt with the 'religious development of humanity', restated the positive features of Judaism and of Christianity as the direct inheritor of the revelation of Moses. Judaism was credited as the model for one of the Saint-Simonians' central ideas, the primacy of 'association', for monotheistic Judaism invited virtually all humanity to form a 'universal association'; at the heart of the Jewish 'nation', religious belief, common to all classes, was the bond which attached them to society.[79]

With the Exposition at an end, however, Isaac Pereire, now nearly 23 years old, suffered a sort of breakdown.[80] He described to Enfantin the deep state of lethargy into which he had fallen, attributing this to the change in direction of the movement, towards its religious denouement. Perhaps Isaac had only just come to realise how profoundly different was this new direction in which Enfantin determined to take the Saint-Simonians, how much at odds with Isaac's religious life hitherto. While there is much talk of God in the letter he wrote, it also tells of the relationship which had developed between Isaac, the young fatherless man, and Prosper Enfantin, the adored 'father'. All three of the leaders – Enfantin, Rodrigues and Bazard – were now addressed as 'father', but none courted this form of address as ardently as Enfantin who bore a particular affection for the younger Pereire.

September 1829 also witnessed a deepening political crisis in France. Charles X dismissed his prime minister, Martignac, and made way for an old supporter, the archconservative prince de Polignac whose Cabinet would be made up of similarly reactionary figures. Spurred on by a feared return to ultra-conservatism, the opposition political parties mobilised around the republicans and the house of Orléans, for which the rallying point became Jacques Laffitte's newspaper, the *National*.[81] The Saint-Simonians played no direct role in this turn of events but having been on the receiving end individually of a number of adverse royal decisions and having made their position as opponents of certain royal policies clear, they could not help but gain enthusiastic support from among the young. They were entering the most exhilarating, productive, testing and confused time in their short history. The Pereires would find it equally so.

An acute shortage of food was causing misery throughout the countryside.[82] The impact of high tariff protection against basic raw materials, wool, silk and coal, coupled with prohibitive costs in importing sophisticated machinery and skilled labour from England, impeded the rate of industrial growth. Finance was inaccessible. The Banque de France defined its role narrowly and investment in industry was within neither its comprehension nor its repertoire. Besides, with its activities focused on Paris, in many cases the factory owner in the larger town or city relied for funding solely on the usurious practices of the notaries.

The urban workforce was the immediate casualty. Between 1815 and

1830, wages had declined by nearly 30 per cent while food prices rose by 66 per cent. In the department of the Nord alone, 163,000 factory workers in 1828 were in receipt of welfare.[83] The Le Chapelier law of 1791 was still in force, prohibiting strikes and denying tradespeople the right of association, despite which as many as thirty strikes occurred in Paris in 1830 alone.[84] And while the number of industrial workers in France was still relatively small (about two million in 1820 within a total population of just over 30 million) they crowded together increasingly in the larger urban areas in squalid, unhygienic conditions, which contributed to a growing social unrest.[85]

The years 1829–30 were thus a watershed in the development of class consciousness in France. In the process, the Saint-Simonians became crucial to the formulation of ideas about the situation of the working population and the vocabulary which expressed those ideas. Workers' conditions would not be addressed politically since the vast majority of the country was effectively disenfranchised, especially the young and the less well-endowed, age and property-ownership being prerequisites for the electorate as well as the candidates. Nor was the prevailing political philosophy of the liberal opposition with its emphasis on unrestrained domestic competition and high tariff protection against imported goods likely to ameliorate the situation. Saint-Simonians sought to address and respond to these issues through their doctrine.

The building in the rue Monsigny where Enfantin lived with several other Saint-Simonians had become the movement's headquarters. The *Globe* happened to be located there also, and while its editors had been opposed to Saint-Simonianism, financial difficulties had forced a change of ownership and, to varying degrees, a change of heart.[86] Thus Pierre Leroux, Charles-Augustin Sainte-Beuve and Eugène L'Herminier sold the journal to the Saint-Simonians and made the decision for the time being to follow Enfantin. Together with the *Organisateur*, a journal acquired in 1829, the movement now had two journals at its disposal, located in the same building and managed by Michel Chevalier.[87]

The Pereires began to publish widely in the Saint-Simonian press, publishing in the *Globe* alone some seventy-five articles.[88] Indeed Emile Pereire took up journalism full-time. Each responded through his writing to contemporary economic circumstances, comprehending and interpreting the conditions of city workers through the prism of their youthful experience in Bordeaux, empathetic with the victims of economic crises. There is much similarity in their writings, for both saw solutions to France's difficulties in economic and financial terms, consistent with Saint-Simonian discourse. But there were also differences. Emile had a particularly national perspective, concerned with the interplay of economic and social forces on all of France, on Bordeaux and the Gironde as much as on Paris and the Île-de-France. Their styles differed too: whereas Emile's was almost identifiably analytical, examining current political and economic events coolly, Isaac's was emotive and the more didactic. He wrote unashamedly to persuade and to convert. But whatever the subject or the individual style, both obviously enjoyed writing and had a penchant for it, using language with great flair. The value of the education which, by whatever means, Henriette had been able to provide for them is nowhere more evident than in these articles. Intelligence combined with lucidity and erudition in their writing. At the same time, they grasped the utility of journalism, becoming adept in identifying issues and presenting them in accessible, compelling form to their readers.

Their intimate involvement in the Saint-Simonian movement and an understanding of how public opinion can be shaped through adroit commentary was the beginning of a manner of working which they were to use for many different purposes over the years, including garnering support for their own projects. Newspaper editors especially were to be courted. And their journalism called on a network who alerted them to new stories and who could be called upon to supply detailed information. The capacity to identify people who could forward their plans and projects and to persuade them it was in their interests to do so was a trait in evidence from this time. The developing Saint-Simonian doctrine had been a collaborative effort and the content of these journalistic pieces shows how thoroughly a part of the movement the brothers had become. While the foundation of much of the doctrine was clear enough by the time of Bazard's Exposition late in 1828, the economic and political ideas now became sharper, more focused and more radical. The Pereires' journalism thus characterised Saint-Simonianism in all its permutations.[89]

Crucially, in the months which followed the last of the lectures in the rue de Taranne, Eugène Rodrigues' theological explorations had encouraged Enfantin and Bazard to the view that the doctrine was moving inexorably beyond Christianity as its basis, making of Saint-Simonianism itself a new religion. This was contrary to the path pursued by the former Carbonaro Philippe Buchez, however, whose own position tended towards pantheism. On Christmas Day 1829, Buchez and his supporters left the Saint-Simonian movement. What happened in the Saint-Simonian hierarchy then was thus as shocking as it was ultimately destructive: Olinde Rodrigues voluntarily resigned from what had been a triumvirate of 'supreme fathers', leaving the leadership to Bazard and Enfantin. His reasoning is difficult to interpret for he did not volunteer his position without misgiving: as he reminded his colleagues, he was the sole remaining link with Saint-Simon.[90]

The New Year, 1830, began as badly for Olinde as for the Pereires, with Eugène Rodrigues' death at the age of 23. Inexperienced in relations with the opposite sex, he had fallen in love with a young woman from Grenoble, Mlle de Roissy, whom he had been sent to convert. This emotion seems to have been too much for the young man, and indeed Pereire family legend tells of Eugène's death as a result of unrequited love. Long after, Charles Sarchi confirmed this version of events, blaming Sara-Sophie and Eugène's sisters for their imprudent talk, lighting 'in the heart of my brother-in-law, Eugène, an absurd passion, which made him unhappy, and drove him very young to the tomb'.[91] He lingered for eight days, according to Enfantin, and was buried in a grave immediately behind that of Saint-Simon at Père Lachaise cemetery where he rests still.

The premature loss of Eugène Rodrigues robbed Isaac of 'a great spirit, a well-loved friend, with whom our youth glided away in an intimate community of study and work'.[92] He resolved to take up the work his cousin had started, turning his attention towards the religious element of Saint-Simonian doctrine.

The Saint-Simonians found the year 1830 momentous in other, more political ways. While they cannot be said to have encouraged either the abdication of Charles X or the ascendancy of Louis-Philippe, as the Restoration Government of Polignac reeled from crisis to crisis, meetings held by the Saint-Simonians were packed with men and women, a thousand at a time. And despite the Saint-Simonians' abstention from the political skirmishing of the various groups, in effect the movement offered an alternative to the Bourbon regime in office.[93]

Forays into foreign policy by Polignac, notably the recent taking of Algiers, had the appearance of glory about them but they did not translate into victory at home. Fresh elections held over June and July 1830 in an effort to reinstall the ultras once again failed their purpose, for the opposition liberals and Orléanists won easily.[94] The political situation became perilous when the Assemblée Nationale moved a vote of no confidence in Polignac's Government. Refusing to accept the decision of the electorate and work with a hostile government, Charles X and Polignac prorogued Parliament, introducing a gag on the liberal press, dismissing the Assemblée and preparing to issue writs for fresh elections based on a sharply-reduced electorate. Ignoring the gag, Laffitte's *National* and other journals called for Polignac's resignation. But it was the rioting of Paris' artisans which triggered the more drastic solution to the impasse, rapidly escalating into the July Revolution. Barricades were erected for the first time in centuries. As Armand Carrel, the editor of the *National* was to reflect: 'There was not the slightest suspicion of what was going on below us in the class deprived of political rights.'[95] After three days of bloodshed, during which 2,000 people were killed, a coalition of Orléanists and liberals saw Louis-Philippe, duc d'Orléans, installed as France's first avowedly constitutional monarch, 'the citizen king'.[96]

Saint-Simonian responses to the July Revolution were not notably coherent. Violent political action was not something which they found explicable and it was certainly not an approach they endorsed. While Olinde Rodrigues for one was eager and ready for the fray, his cousins' immediate reactions to the July Revolution are less clear.[97] Alfred Pereire wrote much later that they remained 'faithful to their principles', staying at home, studying and working and certainly going nowhere near the barricades.[98] Whatever the truth of this assessment, however, there is no evidence to connect the Pereires directly with the revolutionary events happening around them: the profound effect wrought on them by the 'Trois Glorieuses' found its voice in their journalism.

The ultimate success of the Orléanist cause saw Laffitte's brief rise to power as President of the Chambre des Députés in August 1830 and Chief Minister in Louis-Philippe's government two months later. This circumstance provided the brothers with an opportunity to develop a business plan together, one which may well have been encouraged by Laffitte whom they had known since their arrival in Paris. Argout, the new Minister of Finance, had set up a commission of inquiry to look into causes underlying the general malaise in industry and commerce, distress which was voiced first in Bordeaux (as the Pereires later recalled) but which spread rapidly to other cities in France.[99] It was this commission the Pereires approached in September 1830 with a proposal to establish a bank, having among other objectives investment in commerce and industry against solid guarantees, and based on principles of mutuality and on the issuing of interest-bearing bank notes. Government was to provide guarantees to the extent of fifty million francs, thus ensuring stability in times of downturn; a council of bankers, merchants, significant manufacturers and members of government would provide wisdom and experience in assessing the credit-worthiness of borrowers; and interest would be paid on bank notes at the fixed rate of one centime per 100 francs per day. In the Pereires' words: 'an entirely new order is to be established, founded on liberty; an order which must give each day a greater importance to work'.

This proposal, based on the inter-dependence of industry, finance and labour, reflected ideas which Enfantin, Olinde Rodrigues, Bazard, Carnot and others had elaborated over the previous four years and which Isaac

Pereire had used in his letters to Rességuier. But while some have been tempted inaccurately to see in the proposal a precursor to the Crédit Mobilier, it did take the Pereires a stage further into the realm of the practical.[100] The commissioners' task was already drawing to a conclusion when the project was submitted, however, and while a small group of prominent bankers, Ardoin, Mallet and Benoît Fould among them, made further investigations ultimately an alternative proposal was preferred to that of the Pereires.

It was to be Laffitte, whose ministerial tenure lasted only until March 1831, who took the initiative several years later in starting the first investment bank in France, in 1837.[101] More significantly for the Pereires, however, it was their first effort to define a workable banking structure and a compelling example of their capacity to distil concrete proposals from Saint-Simonian ideas. It was also their first essay as partners.

Notes

1 Rubempré, the hero of Balzac's *Les Illusions perdues*, from Angoulême in France's southwest and Sorel of Stendahl's *Le Rouge et le noir* from the fictional 'Verrières' in the department of Doubs.
2 AFP, undated letter to his former employer, Nunès.
3 Ibid., Alfred Pereire, 'Les fondateurs de la Compagnie Générale Transatlantique: Emile et Isaac Pereire 1800–1880' (unknown, undated publication).
4 Ibid.
5 Jules Mirès in *À mes juges*, pp. 8–9, noted that he spoke little French until aged 13.
6 Ernest Feydeau, *Mémoires d'un coulissier*, 2nd edn (Paris, 1873), p. 166.
7 A. Pereire, 'Les fondateurs'. Nicolas Stoskopf, *Banquiers et financiers parisiens* (Paris, 2002), p. 274, draws a similar conclusion, describing Emile in later life as the 'entrepreneur' and Isaac as the 'patron'.
8 AFP, Emile, Paris, to Isaac, Bordeaux, probably 1825. The only rivalry which could exist between two brothers lay in being 'a submissive and grateful son' to their mother, he counselled.
9 Louis Chevalier, *Labouring Classes and Dangerous Classes in Paris during the First Half of the Nineteenth Century*, trans. Frank Jellinek (London, 1973), pp. 182–3. In 1817 population in the twelve pre-1860 *arrondissements* was 713,966, an increase of 14.67 per cent on the figures of the previous census of 1811. A further 50,000 lived in the communes to be annexed in 1860 and which were included from the next census of 1831.
10 Eric Hazan, *The Invention of Paris: A History in Footsteps*, trans. David Fernbach (London, 2011), pp. 17–19.
11 Chevalier, *Labouring Classes*, p. 151. Chevalier's thesis has been challenged by Ratcliffe in 'Classes laborieuses et classes dangereuses à Paris pendant la

première moitié du XIXe siècle? The Chevalier Thesis Reexamined', *French Historical Studies* 17, 2, 542–75. Ratcliffe co-authored with Christine Piette a related study: *Vivre la ville: Les classes populaires à Paris (1er moitié du XIXe siècle)* (Paris, 2007).
12 AFP, Emile, Paris, to M. Nunès, Bordeaux, undated [late 1822].
13 Ibid., Henriette to B. Gradis, Bordeaux, 17 October 1823.
14 Ibid., Emile to Henriette, Bordeaux, 15 September 1822.
15 Charles et Félicie Sarchi, *Lettres à Hélène: Correspondance de Charles et Félicie Sarchi à leur fille Mme. Van Tieghem*, Louis Bachy (ed.) (Montpellier, 2006), Vol. 1 (1862–1868), 2 (1869–1875), 3 (1876–1878). Félicie to Hélène, Vol. 1, pp. 42–3, letter 21, September 1862.
16 Hazan, *Invention of Paris*, pp. 139–44. Cadastral data through the Archives de Paris (hereafter AP), 'Plans parcellaires de Paris et ses communes annexées (XIXe siècle)', F/31/77/13–20.
17 This *milieu* was described in Alfred Pereire, *Autour de Saint-Simon: documents originaux* (Paris, 1912), p. 101.
18 Jay Berkovitz, *The Shaping of Jewish Identity in Nineteenth-Century France* (Detroit, 1989), p. 112; Christine Piette, *Les Juifs de Paris (1808–1840): la marche vers l'assimilation* (Quebec, 1983), p. 50.
19 Piette, *Juifs de Paris*, p. 50; Benbassa, *Jews of France*, ch. 8.
20 Works consulted on the Restoration include André Jardin and Jean-André Tudesq, *Restoration and Reaction, 1815–1848*, trans. Elborg Forster (Cambridge, 1983); Sheryl Kroen, *Politics and Theater: The Crisis of Legitimacy in Restoration France, 1815–1830* (Berkeley, CA, 2000); Emmanuel de Waresquiel and Benoît Yvert, *Histoire de la Restauration 1814–1830: naissance de la France moderne* (Paris, 2002); Francis Démier, *La France de la restauration 1814–1830* (Paris, 2012).
21 Comte Henri de Saint-Simon et Prosper Enfantin, *Œuvres de Saint-Simon et d'Enfantin* (hereafter OSSE), 2nd edn (Paris, 1865–77), Vol. 11, p. 209, séance, 27 November 1831.
22 Kroen, *Politics and Theater*, pp. 83–90.
23 Berkovitz, *Shaping of Jewish Identity*, pp. 46–7; and Julie Kalman, *Rethinking Antisemitism in Nineteenth-Century France* (Cambridge, 2010), pp. 160–6.
24 AFP, Emile to Henriette, 15 November 1822.
25 Quoted in Léon, *Histoire*, p. 428, letter, January 1823.
26 Lisa Moses Leff, *Sacred Bonds of Solidarity: The Rise of Jewish Internationalism in Nineteenth-Century France* (Stanford, 2006), pp. 74–5.
27 AFP, Emile to Henriette, 15 November 1822. Ratcliffe addressed the ways in which the Pereires faced the prospect of assimilation in 'Some Jewish problems in the early careers of Emile and Isaac Pereire', *Jewish Social Studies* 34, 3 (1972), 189–206.
28 AFP. He wrote to his brother, his friends Mirès and Astruc, his Aunt Rosalie and his Uncle Fonseca about these difficulties.
29 Ibid., Adolphe Mirès to Emile, 5 January 1823.
30 A. Pereire, *Autour de Saint-Simon*, p. 101.

31 AFP, Adolphe Mirès to Emile on behalf of himself and Aristée and Telèphe Astruc, 25 April 1824.
32 ACCP, GGI, 'Mariages célébrés dans le temple de la rue Notre Dame de Nazareth à Paris', 4. See also AFP, Isaac Rodrigues, 'Avancement d'hoirie à mes enfants'.
33 AFP, Emile to Samuel Alexandre, Bordeaux, 14 June 1824.
34 Ibid., Adolphe Mirès, to Emile, 25 December 1823.
35 Ibid., Emile to Samuel Alexandre, Bordeaux, 24 June 1824. 'She is sure of my brother and me, our opinion is known to her, what more does she want?'
36 Ibid., Emile to Fonseca, Bordeaux, 5 February 1826.
37 Waresquiel and Yvert, *Histoire de la Restauration*, pp. 382–7.
38 Georges Weill, *L'École saint-simonienne: son histoire, son influence jusqu'à nos jours* (Paris, 1896), p. 18; Robert B. Carlisle, *The Proffered Crown: Saint-Simonianism and the Doctrine of Hope* (Baltimore, 1987), pp. 42–3.
39 Simon Altmann and Edouardo L Ortiz (eds), *Mathematics and Social Utopias in France: Olinde Rodrigues and His Times* (Providence, 2005), Chapter 3.
40 AFP, Emile, Paris, to Fonseca, Bordeaux, 4 August 1826.
41 Alfred Pereire, *Je suis dilettante* (Paris, 1955), p. 103.
42 *Écrits*, t.1 [fasc., 1], B1 [Introduction].
43 Henri Saint-Simon, *Oeuvres Complètes*, Introduction, notes et commentaires par Juliette Grange, Pierre Musso, Philippe Régnier and Franck Yonnet, 4 vols (Paris, 2013). See also Alfred Pereire, *Des premiers rapports entre Saint-Simon et Auguste Comte, d'après des documents originaux (1816–1819)* (Paris, 1906).
44 Frank E. Manuel, *The Prophets of Paris* (New York, 1965), p. 112.
45 James Bland Briscoe, 'Saint-Simonianism and the Origins of Socialism in France, 1816–1832' (PhD dissertation, Columbia University, 1980), p. viii.
46 *OSSE*, t. 1, pp. 121, 101.
47 Ibid., t. 2, p. 150.
48 Henri Fournel, *Bibliographie saint-simonienne* (Paris, 1833), p, 51.
49 Henri Lauzac, *Isaac Pereire* (Paris, 1864), p. 7.
50 AFP, Isaac to Alexandre *fils*, Bordeaux, 24 July 1826; Isaac to Henriette, Bordeaux, 25 September 1825; Emile to Isaac, Bordeaux, 2 October 1825.
51 La Rochelle, *Jacob Rodrigues Pereire*, pp. 526–30.
52 See especially Antoine Picon, *Les Saint-simoniens: raison, imaginaire et utopie* (Paris, 2002), pp. 53–7.
53 Pamela Pilbeam, *The Saint-Simonians in Nineteenth-Century France: From Free Love to Algeria* (Basingstoke, 2014), p. 12.
54 Prosper Enfantin, 'On discount banks (second article)', *Producteur*, Vol. 2, 16, 1826, 109–25, in Gilles Jacoud (ed.), *Political Economy and Industrialism: Banks in Saint-Simonian economic thought* (London, New York, 2010), p. 40.
55 From Deuteronomy 6:4.
56 AFP, Emile, Paris, to his aunt Reche, uncle Fonseca and Samuel Alexandre, Bordeaux, 31 August and 24 September 1827.
57 Carlisle, *Proffered Crown*, p. 48.
58 Ibid., p. 56. See also Picon, *Saint-simoniens*, pp. 53–7.
59 Waresquiel and Yvert, *Histoire de la Restauration*, pp. 331–405.

THE NEW SOCIETY 59

60 *Écrits*, t. 3: fasc.1, p. 33, Enfantin to Rességuier, May 1828.
61 Ibid., Isaac to Rességuier, 28 April 1828, pp. 9–11.
62 Ibid., Isaac to Rességuier, 28 July 1828, pp. 26–30.
63 BNF-A, Fonds Enfantin, 7643/185, 'Reprise du Producteur', 4 August 1828.
64 Ibid., 7628/11, Enfantin to Holstein, 22 August 1837.
65 Muhlstein, *Baron James*, pp. 108–9.
66 BNF-R, Fonds Alfred Pereire, NAF 24611/15 and /32 (micro 9894), Eugène Rodrigues to Rességuier, 21 October, 21 December 1828.
67 Carlisle, *Proffered Crown*, pp. 89–90.
68 William B. Cohen and Irvin M. Wall outline a coherent set of reasons why Jews became attracted to left-wing politics, in the course of which they deal with Saint-Simonianism. See their 'French Communism and the Jews', in Frances Malino and Bernard Wasserstein (eds), *The Jews in Modern France* (Hanover, NH, 1985), pp. 81–102.
69 Eugène Rodrigues, *Lettres sur la religion et la politique, 1829: suivies de l'éducation du genre humain de Lessing traduit de l'allemand* (Paris, 1831), pp. 34–6.
70 Ibid., pp. 40, 131–2.
71 Carlisle, *Proffered Crown*, especially pp. 63–6. Ratcliffe downplays both the numbers and the influence of Jews in 'Economic Influence of the Saint-Simonians: Myth or Reality', in Joyce Duncan Falk (ed.), *Proceedings of the Fifth Annual Meeting of the Western Society for French History* (Santa Barbara, 1978), p. 253.
72 BNF-A, Fonds Enfantin 7822/29, 'Classement des membres de la famille saint-simonienne par Fonctions'.
73 Ibid., 7822/28, 'Livre des Comptes de la Doctrine tenu par Isaac Pereire – Situations'. Michèle Riot-Sarcey (ed.), *De la liberté des femmes: 'lettres de dames' au Globe (1831–1832)* (Paris, 1992), pp. 99–104, includes a letter from Mélanie Rodrigues.
74 Picon, *Saint-simoniens*, Chapter 3, for an account of Saint-Simonian activists and their backgrounds.
75 Antoine Picon, *Les Polytechniciens au XIXe siècle* (Paris, 1994), p. 11.
76 Carlisle, *Proffered Crown*, pp. 89–112, for an extensive account of the Exposition.
77 *Doctrine de Saint Simon: première année, exposition 1829* (Paris, 1830), p. xxiv.
78 Ibid., pp. 128–33, 137.
79 Ibid., pp. 321–7.
80 BNF-R, Fonds Alfred Pereire, NAF 24610/225 (microfilm 9893), Isaac to Enfantin, September 1829.
81 Waresquiel and Yvert, *Histoire de la Restauration*, pp. 439, 465–7.
82 Pamela Pilbeam, *The 1830 Revolution in France* (London, 1991), Chapter 3.
83 Roger Magraw, *A History of the French Working Class*, Volume 1, *The Age of Artisan Revolution* (Oxford, 1992), pp. 48, 59; Guillaume de Bertier de Sauvigny, *The Bourbon Restoration*, trans. Lynn M. Case (Philadelphia, 1966), p. 255.
84 Magraw, *French Working Class*, p. 53. Roger Price examined the beginning of structural change in French industrial development and its impact on labour in *An Economic History of France, 1730–1914* (London, 1981), pp. 93–125.

85 François Caron, *An Economic History of France* (New York, 1979), p. 23. Caron accepted the figures of the economist, J. C. Toutain, in 'La population de la France de 1830 à 1965', *Cahiers de l'Institut de science économique appliquée*, ser. AF, 9 (1967). See also Price, *Economic History*, pp. 192–217, who deals with the related factors of food supply, disease and migration.
86 Carlisle, *Proffered Crown*, pp. 133–4.
87 Ibid.
88 Articles began to be signed only towards the end of the journal's life. See *Écrits*, t. 1 [fasc. 1], pp. v–vii, where Gustave explained his method of attribution, noting that this 'collaboration' commenced with the *Globe* later in 1830.
89 Briscoe, 'Saint-Simonism'. Picon in *Saint-simoniens*, pp. 79–87, deals with Saint-Simonian skills in the art of propaganda.
90 Carlisle, *Proffered Crown*, pp. 113–21.
91 Sarchi, *Lettres*, t. I, p. 343, letter 227, Charles to Hélène, 25 January 1867.
92 I. Pereire, *La Question religieuse* (Paris, 1878), p. 85.
93 *OSSE*, t. 2, p. 48.
94 The Orléanists were named after a branch of the Bourbons and supported a constitutional monarchy.
95 J. L. Talmon, *Romanticism and Revolt: Europe 1815–1848* (London, 1967), p. 41. The 'Trois Glorieuses' are covered fully in Pilbeam, *1830 Revolution*, Chapter 4. For an account of the downfall of Charles X see Sauvigny, *Restoration*, Chapter 23.
96 Pamela M. Pilbeam, *Republicanism in Nineteenth-Century France, 1814–1871* (London, 1995), p. 96.
97 *OSSE*, t. 2, p. 193.
98 A. Pereire, *Autour de Saint-Simon*, p. 124.
99 Christopher H. Johnson, 'The Revolution of 1830 in French economic history', in John M. Merriman (ed.), *1830 in France* (New York, 1975), pp. 148–55.
100 *Écrits*, t. 5, fasc. 2, Première Partie 1, 'Projet de Banque: Basé sur le principe de la Mutualité et sur l'Émission des Billets à Rente (Présenté le 4 Septembre 1830 par MM. Pereire)', pp. 1–18.
101 Rondo Cameron, Olga Crisp, Hugh T. Patrick and Richard Tilly (eds), *Banking in the Early Stages of Industrialization: A Comparative Study* (London, 1967), p. 106.

3

The new entrepreneurs

The last two years of the Saint-Simonian movement saw a painful schism develop between its leaders which affected the whole membership. Ideas about social justice and reform, of economic and financial innovation, were to be confounded by a competing agenda involving Saint-Simonianism as a religion, the position of women, divorce and free love. These different strands of doctrine sat together uneasily, causing disquiet, rarely capable of integration in any coherent way despite the best efforts of devotees. But while the tensions which thus flared were to contribute to the demise of the movement, the end also permitted individual Saint-Simonians to take advantage of opportunities in the wider world. Saint-Simonianism had armed them with ideas about the economic and social changes necessary to invigorate a new society and the scale of industrial development essential to take France into the modern age; with experience in publicity to convert a reluctant government and enthuse an eager public; and with useful networks to provide finance and skills essential to the tasks which lay ahead. It had also encouraged an entrepreneurial spirit. This chapter deals with this vitally important episode and shows how, through Saint-Simonianism, Emile and Isaac Pereire found their vocation as railway entrepreneurs.

Saint-Simonians had turned their attention increasingly towards the 'proletarian', a word they now used frequently to describe men and women of the industrial working class and whom they set out actively to convert and to draw into the 'family'. They created workers' associations organised around the *arrondissement*, each served by a doctor and a pharmacist.[1] Every Sunday at midday there was preaching in the Salle Taitbout in the street of the same name where up to 600 working people crammed into the lecture hall and many attended classes later that day.[2] Further lectures took place three or four times during the week, including at the Salle d'Athénée in the place de la Sorbonne.

It was at the Salle d'Athénée in the autumn that Isaac Pereire gave his four 'Lessons on Industry and Finance' which the *Globe* printed late in 1831.[3] In these lessons, Isaac undertook a comprehensive analysis of the class struggle between the 'workers' ('travailleurs') and the 'idle', and the means by which that struggle might be transformed. Isaac interpreted the term 'travailleur' broadly as all who earned their living from 'direct and personal labour', thus going beyond manual and trades occupations to include, for example, banking, among other income-producing activities. It was synonymous with Saint-Simon's 'industriel', a term his followers also used.[4] Not all of the ideas belonged to Isaac alone and the close collaboration between a number of Saint-Simonians who produced almost all the writing renders it difficult to identify individual authorship. But the 'Lessons' are an important contribution to that body of work which was produced by the Saint-Simonians over the last year or so of the movement's existence, demonstrating their author's capacity to synthesise, to develop and to articulate sophisticated economic and financial solutions to social inequity and disadvantage.

He addressed problems inherent in concepts of value, exchange and money, arguing against the idea of money as the sole signifier of value and in favour of alternatives, such as bills of exchange.[5] He foreshadowed the 'successive decrease of idleness, the progress towards universal association of the workers', all of whom would have at their disposal the instruments they needed.[6] His lesson 'On the progress of the workers and the decline of the idle' proposed a solution to the issue of property ownership through the bank (reminiscent of his letters to Rességuier) which would place the instruments of production – land, factories and machinery – into the hands of those best able to employ them. The right to property thus would not perish but would be transferred to the workers; instead of being the preserve of the 'idle' it would be transformed from something jealously guarded to something approaching 'the love of the worker for the object on which he will have concentrated all his activity'.[7] While the role of the bank was thus critical to the realisation of this Saint-Simonian objective, a metamorphosis in the ownership of property, most contemporary banks were unsuited to this purpose, founded as they were by and for the idle. The Banque de France was part of the problem, constituted in the interests of its shareholders rather than of small business or the workers. It was not a bank for the whole of France (its bills did not circulate outside Paris), it was opposed to lower interest rates and too focused on high dividends. To address its deficiencies he outlined the new system of banking, a 'savings and loans bank', issuing its own interest-bearing bank notes, non-redeemable bonds, and directed by captains of industry who would personally guarantee credit advanced to industry.[8]

In the rapid evolution of the idea of 'socialism' in Saint-Simonianism, the concept of the class struggle between the 'workers' and the 'idle' and of the right to property and inheritance came to take on greater importance from the beginning of the July Monarchy, especially as the government displayed little interest in addressing the issues.[9] Worker organisations themselves began to appropriate these concepts and the vocabulary in which they were framed. Isaac Pereire's 'Lessons' thus show how thoroughly he had mastered complex ideas to paint a broad picture of contemporary society and a vision for its future.

'Letter to a Jewish woman', which he published in the *Organisateur*, was a more personal statement, an exploration of his religious beliefs and his attitude towards Judaism during the Saint-Simonian period. It reveals the influence of the literature of regeneration in one young man's attempt to come to terms with being at once a Frenchman and a Jew. It is also redolent of Saint-Simonian new ideas about women.

The pretext Isaac claimed for the letter was the imminent marriage between a young woman who was a practising Jew and one of his close friends. She had accused him, he said, of outraging his mother's memory, of committing apostasy, claims which he denied vigorously. Isaac reminded the young woman of the numerous 'contradictions' into which Jews were forced, however, 'to make a vain alliance between the faith of their fathers and the exigencies of the times'. Judaism was far from ideal, consecrating woman absolutely in her subalternity: 'The wife is bought, the husband gives a piece of money in exchange for her purity, and it constitutes a contract.' For Isaac's ideal society, the Saint-Simonian heaven on earth, was one in which humanity formed a single family in which there would be neither masters nor slaves but solicitous fathers and devoted sons, where all social institutions would have as their goal the improvement of the lot of the poorest and most numerous class, where each individual would be classed according to his capacity and compensated according to his works.[10]

The letter may have been an essay in artistic licence, written in the context of his own marriage to his cousin from Bordeaux, Rachel Laurence Lopès Fonseca, which had taken place in August 1830. She was 18 years old.[11] Little is known of this marriage; indeed, two years before it took place there was not a hint that it would come about and while the bride's father, Henriette's brother Jacob Lopès Fonseca, may have had aspirations in this direction Emile for one was slow to recognise them. The financially-strapped Jacob had approached Emile to arrange a position for him in Paris, but Emile cautioned Jacob against such a move altogether. He was more likely to find husbands for his three daughters in Bordeaux, for he knew not a single eligible Jew in Paris.[12] But in the end marriage between Laurence and Isaac was arranged, albeit without a dowry, nor was there a marriage contract between them, nor a religious service, simply the civil marriage at the Mairie of the second *arrondissement*.[13]

At the beginning of her marriage Laurence was hesitant about Parisian ways and society, sensitive to what she considered to be slights or indifference on the part of Isaac's friends and acquaintances. She was lonely, forcing Isaac to remonstrate with an old acquaintance who had failed to visit her in Paris when that would have been an act of kindness. It is clear, however, that the time of their marriage and the birth of their first child coincided with Isaac's most passionate and public statements in support of women. While Saint-Simonianism was going through a period of soul-searching, if not turmoil, about the position of women, there is a profoundly emotive tone in Isaac's letter which suggests that he had only just begun to understand their condition personally. Late in 1831, barely two weeks after the birth of their first child, he was to declare publicly: 'I feel that, up to now, woman has not obtained in the doctrine the place that she must occupy one day; and that beyond us men, there is a whole world compromised, a world tortured by horrible suffering that we must overthrow.'[14]

By January 1831 both Emile and Isaac Pereire had taken rank in the movement, recorded by the *Globe* as in the 'second degree' of those around Enfantin and Bazard.[15] Emile, having a family to support and employed outside Saint-Simonianism, did not play a direct role in a day-to-day sense but, with his brother, he assisted Gustave d'Eichthal as director of 'matériel'.[16] Isaac on the other hand appears to have resigned from his position with Vital-Roux when he became director of correspondence for the *Globe*, a leap of faith also taken by Enfantin and Olinde Rodrigues who had similarly resigned their positions with the Caisse Hypothécaire.[17] Isaac's task with the *Globe* was onerous: as many as 1,200 letters flowed in monthly from the provinces, which found him working thirteen hours daily until the early hours of the morning. On the very day his first child was born he wrote to his colleague Alexis Petit, begging for help in answering letters which threatened to overwhelm him.[18]

Meanwhile, Buchez's departure had led to instability. Enfantin's increasing domination of the personal lives of Saint-Simonians exacerbated it, intruding into emotional and domestic situations in a manipulative manner. The religious direction which Saint-Simonianism was taking and advocated by Eugène Rodrigues led to questions of a Messiah. Enfantin, becoming convinced that God was asexual, made the connection that Saint-Simonianism should embrace the equality of women. This new turn introduced to the meetings of the inner circle much discussion of marriage and the family, of sex within marriage and of prostitution. Delicate relations between particular married couples became subject to wider speculation, leading to discord. The Bazards were not immune and when Enfantin, late in 1831, exposed difficulties even in their marriage, St-Amand Bazard suffered a stroke from which he never recovered.[19]

Prosper Enfantin began to gather the family together at the rue Monsigny in a series of Enseignements (Teachings) designed to consolidate his leadership. In these meetings Enfantin went even further than he had previously in pushing the boundaries of discussion. Morality and sexual fidelity, equality between the sexes and divorce were subjects addressed fairly freely. Enfantin invited confessions of faith and Isaac Pereire was one who responded, reaffirming his great love for, and debt to, Enfantin in an emotional outpouring:

> You have given me much; I owe you, in a way, all that I am. It is thanks to you that the power of love has been revealed in me. ... I love you more than ever, because I understand perfectly well the direction in which you are leading us. I sense that industry will receive a powerful impulse from us ... Be sure, my shoulders will not fail.[20]

Emile Pereire, on the other hand, did not attend the Enseignements and had not accompanied his brother down the path towards a Saint-Simonian religion. Nor did he evince any interest in the cause of women. He had begun to distance himself from the movement out of clear disquiet with the direction in which it was heading – towards quasi-mysticism, espousal of free love and, equally important, acknowledgement and reinforcement of Enfantin as leader. Isaac, with his dependence on Enfantin, was about to experience painfully divided loyalties, between Enfantin and his elder brother. As Emile Pereire was preparing to quit the Saint-Simonian movement, Isaac was ordering its uniform: a pair of grey trousers, a pair of blue trousers, and a 'blue costume of the 2nd degree', the whole costing 137 francs.[21]

Police interest in the public meetings was sparked initially by the attention given by the Saint-Simonians to the 'proletarian', particularly when the Lyon silk-workers rose in insurrection in November 1831.[22] But it was the new and shocking subject matter of free love and divorce which prompted them to take action. The beginning of the end came at midday on 22 January 1832 when the municipal guards arrived at the Salle Taitbout, ceremoniously locking up the meeting room and moving on to the rue Monsigny where they found Enfantin and Olinde Rodrigues, both of whom were called before a magistrate.[23] Subsequently, forty of the faithful, all men, followed Prosper Enfantin to his mother's home at Ménilmontant where for the next few months they attempted to lead a communal life for which few of them had been prepared. Isaac Pereire stayed behind to liquidate the business affairs of the movement at the rue Monsigny.

Olinde also resigned. His wife Euphrasie, who had confided in Enfantin details of her marital situation which then became common knowledge, had asked for a 'de facto "divorce"', causing Olinde considerable anguish.[24] Olinde's resignation thus triggered Emile Pereire's public break with the Saint-Simonians, demanding his letter of resignation be published in the *Globe*. He had ceased to be part of the Saint-Simonian movement because, he wrote: 'I have never shared your moral position and ... my cooperation in your journal has only ever been for the political and economic aspect.'[25]

He was more frank about his antagonism in a private letter to Enfantin. Nor had he hidden his opinion of Enfantin from those who were among the leader's most devoted supporters, including his own brother, exerting pressure on him to make a break.[26] Isaac returned to Bordeaux, having conceded to his brother's wishes that he do so. Emile meanwhile wrote to Georges Cazeaux in Bordeaux that Isaac had been forced to choose between Enfantin and himself, that the disagreement was a most serious one, a rupture in fact which could not easily be repaired.[27]

Concerns about the movement's finances had in any case begun to exacerbate difficulties in the relationship between Isaac Pereire and Enfantin. By August 1831 the number of subscribers to the *Globe* had fallen away to 500, and the print-run to a mere 2,500 copies. Isaac and Olinde Rodrigues had been instrumental in raising a loan through public advertisement against properties contributed to the cause by Saint-Simonian members.[28] The principal lenders – d'Eichthal, Fournel, Enfantin, Alexis Petit and his mother, Mme Petit – lost well over one million francs.[29] Charges of corrupt and unscrupulous dealings were hurled back and forth between the former Saint-Simonians, and Chabarnier, the liquidator appointed by Enfantin, was also to accuse Isaac Pereire of fraud.[30]

During this period Armand Carrel, another former Carbonaro associated loosely with the Saint-Simonians and editor of the liberal newspaper *National*, invited Emile Pereire to write for him, an invitation which may have been initiated by the journal's proprietor Jacques Laffitte. Emile commenced on his resignation from the Saint-Simonians in November 1831.[31] The content of many of his articles for the *National* was simply reportage on meetings of the Chambre des Députés and, less often, of the Chambre des Pairs, for both of which for a time he prepared the official reports. His longer pieces most frequently concerned the effects on the working class of financial and economic decisions taken by government, particularly on workers in the large cities outside Paris. In 1833 alone he wrote well over 200 articles, some of them brief news items it is true, but there were frequently more reflective items also.[32] He was thus one of only a handful of Saint-Simonians continuing to write for a large audience at that time, the former leaders being under a cloud and the former followers for the most part totally demoralised.

Late in 1832, Enfantin and Olinde Rodrigues, together with Chevalier, Emile Barrault and Charles Duveyrier, went on trial and were convicted on two counts: of outraging public morality and of breaking the law on public association. Henri Baud defended his brother-in-law Olinde who, at a second trial, was fined and exonerated, along with Barrault. But this was the end of Saint-Simonianism as a movement, with Enfantin and Chevalier imprisoned in Sainte-Pélagie prison in 1833.[33]

In 1832 the Pereires had been residents of Paris for almost a decade. Emile was now thirty-one years of age and Isaac twenty-five. Both married with young families, Emile's now included another daughter, Cécile, born in 1829, and Isaac and Laurence had their firstborn, a son Eugène, named for Eugène Rodrigues.[34] They had all moved from the rue des Petites-Écuries to the nearby rue Montholon (no. 26) where Léon Halévy and his brother Fromenthal, who was soon to achieve renown as composer of the opera *La Juive*, also shared an apartment.[35] Léon remembered the Pereires at this time as 'both young, full of ardour', Emile clearly under the inspiration of Saint-Simon and of his cousin Olinde Rodrigues: 'He was already dreaming of the absolute domination of man over nature and over matter (at the risk of being absorbed by it).'[36]

One of the most striking characteristics of both Pereires was their great self-confidence and ambition, forged of their mother's expectations and their grandfather's achievements. Both displayed exceptional intellectual gifts, the legacy of previous generations and of chance. And they also had in abundance particular personal qualities, nurtured in the singular circumstances of the rue Bouhaut in Bordeaux. From this time they brought to every business proposition they encountered great energy and vitality together with notable incisiveness, organisational skill and a talent for implementing multifaceted projects. Such personal gifts had gestated in the challenging environment of a single-parent family with the simple imperative to survive, demanding resourcefulness, hard work, a capacity for improvisation and the taking on of adult responsibilities from an early age. All of these would now come into play.

On Emile's part there was from the beginning an instinctive comprehension of the need for and the power of trust, an understanding which Isaac too came to share. Their own relationship demanded it and when that trust was endangered, as it had most recently with Isaac's overt, albeit temporary, allegiance to Enfantin, it was Emile's faith that it could be repaired which carried them through. On the practical side, the Pereires' experience of finance, once the only career open to Jews, was critical to the new industry and they brought high financial acumen to the task which lay ahead, a clear appreciation of the demand which would be required for credit on a scale hitherto unimagined.

The July Monarchy was a period of disenchantment for many, and the Pereires themselves were among those who, at the outset, had attacked the regime's inadequacies. But later it was also one of growing prosperity for them, a time when they contributed to – in some cases introduced – particular initiatives of the department of the Ponts et Chaussées (literally bridges and roads), which as much as anything accounted for economic growth of the 1830s and early 1840s. By now they had a highly developed set of ideas about what was required of the State to bring about economic and social well-being and Emile in particular became increasingly skilled in negotiations with well-placed individuals to achieve their aims. From Saint-Simonianism they carried an enthusiasm for the uses of technological innovation of all kinds, and they had a good eye for recognising the people who could help them implement these innovations. Above all, however, they found among the engineers of the Ponts et Chaussées officials who were not simply technologically competent but skilled in putting ideas to, and getting results from, an often sluggish and inward-looking government. And while the Pereires attacked the protectionist philosophy of the political majority, they did support limited forms of intervention by the State in industrial development, both views faithful to Saint-Simonianism. Within this fortuitous combination of technical brilliance and political skill in conjunction with nascent capitalism, there lies a partial explanation for the economic progress which marked the later July Monarchy. It has been usefully said that the growth experienced by France during 1832–48 owed much to the personal compatibility between the Saint-Simonian businessman Emile Pereire and the Director of the Ponts et Chaussées, Baptiste Alexis Victor Legrand.[37]

Michael Graetz offered another interpretation of the Pereires' success, crediting Saint-Simonianism with considerable ideological significance for French industry, 'an ideology that could inspire a new type of entrepreneur capable of staying ahead of the events', its potency comparable to that of nationalism in Germany and liberalism in England. The Pereires, for whom 'Saint-Simonian ideology instilled determination and constancy in their efforts', are an essential part of Graetz's thesis.[38] These complementary interpretations, giving weight both to the personal rapport and mutual usefulness between Emile and Legrand and to Saint-Simonianism's powerful legacy for the enterprising individual, highlight perceptively the significance of the Pereires to the era.

Karl Marx had a different perspective, though not a conflicting view, reminding his readers how Jacques Laffitte had declared to the duc d'Orléans before he was crowned King Louis-Philippe: 'From now on the bankers will rule', proclaiming an 'aristocracy of finance' – of bankers, financiers, railway owners and coal and iron miners – as the real rulers of France during the July Monarchy.[39] From the opposite end of the spectrum, Alexis de Tocqueville agreed, noting how in 1830 'the triumph of the middle class was decisive and so complete that the narrow limits of the bourgeoisie encompassed all political powers, franchises, prerogatives, indeed the whole government'.[40]

With the closure of the *Globe* in April 1832, Pierre Leroux and Jean Reynaud took on the *Revue encyclopédique* which published articles by some former Saint-Simonians, including Emile Pereire who made his name in a critique of the State budget of 1832 brought down by the government leader, the banker Casimir Périer.[41] In his forceful article he adopted ideas which flowed not solely from Saint-Simonianism but from some of the emerging radical workers' publications as well, the *Artisan* being one. 'Association', in the context of addressing workers' concerns and recognition of the exploitation of workers by 'the idle' was a critical element:

> The goal of every society is the improvement in the moral, physical and intellectual condition of all its members. It is the progressive increase in the circle of association which must reunite all workers in a community of interest, will and thought so that the last vestiges of exploitative work may progressively decrease the privileges of idleness.

The budget of 1832, like its predecessor, was merely a servile imitation of all the budgets of the Restoration. It rewarded the undeserving and ignored the working class.[42]

In similar vein he was to take up once more the Lyon silk-workers' cause after violent demonstrations broke out in the city in March 1833, the result of a massive decrease in wages. He next defended the coal miners of Anzin, seventeen of whom in May 1833 had been brought before the tribunal at Valenciennes in the north for public protests against the Anzin mining companies.[43]

By 1833, then, the analysis of society offered by each of the brothers was solidly based on Saint-Simonian principles and prescriptions. All human struggle must have as its objective improvement in the lot of the poorest and most numerous class. Inherited wealth and property were still the bases of society and the core impediment to progress, leading to a class struggle between the 'idle' and the 'workers'. The July Revolution had been for nothing. Tariffs and indirect taxes, the adverse effects of which flowed on to the working classes and the produce of provincial cities, were not the answer. Improvement could only be achieved through productive investment in science and industry, leading to employment. This would, in turn, require a major overhaul in banking through a centralised system providing credit to industry, thus creating innovative uses for 'lazy' money tied up in property. With their wise counsel and informed decision-making, bankers and industrialists would direct such a bank which would also have strong financial backing from government. This bank was evidently not the Banque de France.

Organised Saint-Simonianism no longer existed, its demise affecting Emile and Isaac Pereire in different ways. The elder emerged the more easily, relatively unscathed. With an undeniable passion in his writing, stoked by his perception of government inadequacy, he had distilled from the movement a concern about social justice for workers in the large provincial cities, for the poorest and most numerous class. And there also emerged in his writing a clear set of actions to attack poverty. A new approach to banking, credit and free trade were devices to be employed in its achievement. The younger, who had had the more emotionally challenging experience of Saint-Simonianism, was of one mind with his brother in his ideas of social justice achieved through economic means. He was the more radical in his exploration of novel solutions to poverty and unemployment, however, as his 'Lessons' demonstrate.

What distinguished one from the other was the place religion held in their minds. Neither rejected their Jewish heritage, continuing to acknowledge their birth-right as Jews, cherishing in their emotional lives the experiences absorbed as part of the Sephardic communities of the southwest. But Saint-Simonianism had wrought profound changes in their religious lives. Emile Pereire remained outwardly a practicing Jew, albeit one who no longer experienced in his religion or, indeed, in any other, deep solace or inspiration. Isaac Pereire, by contrast, found in Saint-Simonianism a set of beliefs which fulfilled his spiritual as well as his intellectual needs. Equally important, they had achieved a measure of stability in their own relationship. Isaac now acknowledged what Emile had always believed so firmly, that they were destined to be partners. Together they could realise projects of great utility to France.[44]

At this point it is useful to retrace our steps by a year or so. For while, as we have seen, the last days of the Saint-Simonian movement unravelled in spectacular fashion, there had been a number of solid advances in the evolution of practical ideas as well. These ideas – on urban development and transport particularly – came to form the basis for future action by Emile and Isaac Pereire and will repay exploration.

First, there had been few if any references in Saint-Simonian literature to bucolic colonies or establishments in the countryside like Fourier's *phalanstère* or Owen's New Harmony community in Indiana. In their concentration on the 'industrialist' and the 'proletarian', on the benefits of technology in employment and economic development, the Saint-Simonian utopia was urban, resembling simply a vastly improved Paris, the central node in a network of rail, canals and roads.[45] The Saint-Simonians did not take a serious interest in Paris itself until the summer of 1832, however, when a fierce epidemic of *cholera morbus* broke out in the capital where it remained concentrated for some time until spreading to the larger towns and cities.[46] Between March and October, 18,000 people of all classes succumbed to the disease, among them being Louis-Philippe's chief minister Casimir Périer and the King's republican rival General Lamarque. But cholera was more likely to take the slum-dweller than the wealthy, and the official map of its incidence in 1832 delineated a high concentration among those living around the Cité and the Hôtel de Ville of inner Paris.[47] This circumstance concerned the Saint-Simonians who, like everyone else, equated the disease with an idea of Paris itself as somehow a symbol of urban decay. They saw the cholera epidemic issuing from filthy and unhygienic living conditions among the poor in the capital and the resulting personal and domestic odours, the lack of air and sunshine; in short, all the outward signs of poverty itself.[48]

From early April 1832 there appeared in the *Globe* a series of articles advocating a thoroughgoing programme of purification and urban renewal of Paris, with improved sewerage and the distribution of clean water from the rue du Louvre to the Bastille.[49] The authors brought a technological perspective to bear on the problem. Emile Pereire's interest in a healthier city environment was triggered as much by personal as by public considerations, however. Cholera had attacked the Midi, as his friend Adolphe Mirès informed him, raising fears about the safety of friends and family.[50] Additionally, Emile's chronic asthma rendered 'the lungs of Parisians' a subject of personal concern in his articles in the *National*, adding his voice to the growing interest in air quality and pollution.[51]

He noted the haphazard building activity under way in Paris to house a population which had increased by more than 60 per cent in twenty years. Over-development in some quarters was accompanied by chronic over-crowding in the central city and certain of the inner *banlieues*. Yet other quarters were comparatively deserted.[52] He also began to consider the special nature of Paris and its department of the Seine, as the principal market place, the centre of a national network. He reflected on its administration, its finances and its governing structures, and these issues were to retain his interest, making him highly literate in urban matters at the same time as his attention was attracted to attendant business opportunities.[53]

Something else occurred as a result of the cholera epidemic, at once tragic and fortuitous: in July 1832, Paulin Talabot's brother Edmond died. His funeral, departing from Ménilmontant for Père Lachaise cemetery, brought Emile Pereire together with a group of young Saint-Simonian engineers from the Ponts et Chaussées: Emile Clapeyron, Gabriel Lamé and Stéphane and Eugène Flachat. It was Clapeyron and Lamé who had introduced Enfantin to the ideas of Saint-Simon when they were teaching at the École des Travaux Publics in St Petersburg. The steam-powered Liverpool and Manchester (LMR) rail-line had opened in England only two years previously and the group discussed the prospects for rail transport in France, the potential of which until then had been realised only in certain limited, and by no means sophisticated, ways. For the Ponts et Chaussées graduates, much was to be gained from constructing a steam-powered passenger rail line between Paris and the outlying town of Saint-Germain-en-Laye, not least as a demonstration project attracting public attention and as the beginning of a broader network.[54] To this effect they were in communication with George Stephenson and his son Robert, originators of the LMR line.

Lamé, Clapeyron and the Flachat brothers published their ideas in a seminal piece on the significance of public works, including the railways, to the future economy of France.[55] They differed with the Pereires on the issue of government involvement in infrastructure: while for the engineers this *was* the government's business, Emile Pereire argued for government subsidies to private railway developers where necessary. But as he was to write, any major development in the railway network, such as that between Paris and Bordeaux, would demand wholesale changes in the financial and banking systems then in place.[56]

Michel Chevalier's 'Mediterranean system' outlined in the *Globe* on 12 February 1832 also gripped the imagination of his colleagues and his readers.[57] The concept was daring – a vast, steam-powered rail link from the English Channel at Le Havre to the Mediterranean, via Paris and Lyon to Marseille, and thence to North Africa by sea, drawing in the large cities and towns of France as well as the rest of Europe, and thus creating a massive network to spread the benefits of industry and maintain the peace. France's 'civilising mission' was implicit in Chevalier's concept, but so too were the possibilities for extending English trade and harnessing its know-how, and for France in gaining ready access to the fruits of colonialism in North Africa. This was the first time the Saint-Simonians had shown any real interest in the Muslim world.[58]

In an article in the *Globe* Isaac Pereire immediately addressed the 'Mediterranean system' in the wider context of a languishing and depressed French industrial base, a manufacturing sector crushed by foreign competition, resulting chronic unemployment and the inability of the Minister for Commerce and Public Works in the new government, the comte d'Argout, to comprehend the problem, much less find a solution.[59]

Emile Pereire already had a clear idea of the role the railways could play in national life, combining utility and innovation with the capacity to render life easier for the poorest and most numerous class. Rail represented rapid communication; the transport of people and of goods to and from market, including across international borders; and lower prices for basic commodities. He thought broadly from the outset, Léon Halévy describing him as seeing:

> France transformed by railways and steam; he already saw this new Paris ... with its monuments, its boulevards and all the exuberance, all the expansion of sensual life; he wanted for all, and above all for men of intelligence, physical well-being, luxury even.[60]

Both Pereires thus crystallised the benefits of rail in terms of their economic and social impact in typically Saint-Simonian manner.

As Bordelais, however, they had a further consideration, cognisant of the disadvantages suffered by their home city as a result of its isolation from the capital, its economic decline exacerbated by distance and by poor transport and communications infrastructure. They knew this at first hand for they visited Bordeaux with relative frequency, suffering long, tedious, even dangerous, voyages by road, lasting at least three days at a stretch.[61] And so, while the focus of their first palpable business endeavour was to be the nation's capital, the potential for fast, more efficient connections to be made throughout France and beyond was not lost on them. Nor was the capacity of rail to make money.

Emile Pereire's active interest in building an *entrepôt* in Paris may have provided the germ of an idea for a rail line, as Ratcliffe has suggested.[62] The July government had introduced a law in February 1832 providing for such a facility and called for proposals for its location. Emile's articles for the *National*, based on the meetings of various government bodies, provided him with access to privileged information about potential sites. He was almost certainly working on behalf of one of the contending parties, conceivably Labrousse whose interest was in developing an *entrepôt* from Tivoli to St Ouen. A related issue was the vexed question of expropriation of the necessary land for which a bill was discussed in the Chambre des Députés during the early part of 1833. Emile well appreciated the benefits such a measure would attract to the city of Paris, making it the central market place for colonial products in France and elsewhere, the focal point for all rolling stock, bringing a large working population of tradesmen for the building activity which would inevitably follow. While his involvement in the company competing for the *entrepôt* did not bear fruit, the exercise was nevertheless useful. It gave him from an early stage considerable knowledge of available and desirable parcels of land in proximity to the city's centre which would serve a rail network. It afforded him experience in negotiating with land-owners as well.[63] Perhaps more telling and percipient (in the light of much later events), however, was his assessment of the significance of the plaine Monceau. As he wrote to Michel Chevalier:

> this quarter will become known as one of the most beautiful in Paris. The Boulevard Malesherbes ... will be the most beautiful of the capital. Moreover, the King possesses at the extremity of this Boulevard his attractive property of Monceaux [sic]. As soon as these quarters are built and inhabited the value of this property will be doubled or tripled.[64]

When in September 1832 Emile Pereire wrote the first of his two articles on 'Railways, canals and highways', he had already translated into action the discussion at Ménilmontant with his colleagues among the engineers: with great bravura he had submitted to the Prefects of the Seine and of the Seine-et-Oise a proposal to build a passenger rail line between Paris and St Germain-en-Laye, a distance of nineteen kilometres.[65] In October 1832, plans also went to Legrand, the Director of the Ponts et Chaussées. By March the following year their approvals were in place: all that was lacking was the necessary finance, calculated at five million francs.[66]

The construction of the Paris–St-Germain (PSG) line was an education for the two Pereires and they had much to learn. They were fortunate to be in the hands of the supremely talented Eugène Flachat and Clapeyron, visiting England several times to study railway innovation and management and discuss their own plans with British engineers.⁶⁷ In letters addressed to Emile Pereire during 1833, Flachat advised Emile on the best organisational strategy to make progress. Soon after, when they discussed presentations to the bankers, Flachat criticised his proposed handling of these. Apprehensive, fully aware of the importance of these meetings, Emile became nervous. Before a significant and potentially difficult presentation Flachat counselled him to calm down if they wished to be taken seriously. They began to meet daily to maintain control over the myriad emerging details.⁶⁸ This training in presentation and management of a large infrastructure project was time well spent, however: both Pereires learned from the engineers but they were excellent pupils.⁶⁹

In the search for finance the Saint-Simonian circle again proved invaluable, introducing the Pereires to financiers, some of whom remained lifelong friends. The PSG saw the commencement of a long, fruitful and loyal friendship between Emile and Adolphe d'Eichthal, Gustave's younger brother. Their father was of the Bavarian banking family Seligmann, sent to Paris during the Restoration when he changed his name and converted to Catholicism. Adolphe d'Eichthal's friendship would be resilient enough to withstand Emile's at times impossible obstinacy and to stand up to him when Emile's intransigence took his enterprises along paths d'Eichthal considered dangerous, foolhardy or compromising.⁷⁰

In 1834, he provided Emile Pereire with entrée to considerable banking figures in Auguste Thurneyssen, Sanson Davilliers and possibly James de Rothschild, although Emile Pereire was probably acquainted with Rothschild already.⁷¹ Each of these financiers, together with d'Eichthal himself, eventually contributed over one million francs to the six million needed – but as Isaac Pereire later pointed out, they did not finally come to the party until the project was approved by the Chambre des Députés.⁷² Emile Pereire himself invested 300,000 francs, a sum well beyond the means of both brothers combined; indeed, the purchase price of the land for the eventual Gare Saint-Lazare which was to take 30,000 francs was said by a contemporary to be all they had.⁷³ They did not even have the finance necessary as security for the concession and it was Adolphe d'Eichthal who, together with Auguste Thurneyssen, in 1834 extended Emile a loan.⁷⁴

If it was the Pereires' meeting with Saint-Simon in 1825 which instilled in them an abiding philosophy and a plan of action and which gave them a congenial circle of acquaintances, some of whom ultimately became business associates, it was their no less fateful introduction to James de Rothschild which gave them the wherewithal – the capital, the high-level contacts and the *savoir faire* – to begin to direct their talents towards the enterprises through which they are chiefly remembered.

The Rothschilds as an international family business were risk-averse and nervous of investing in rail, having had little experience in financing industrial undertakings and no desire to experiment. Their history as 'court Jews' gave them expertise in lending to governments and in commercial operations, and the Rothschild family in England had already turned its back on the LMR, a business decision which James came to recognise as a collective error of judgement by the family.[75] The change in the family's business policy, starting in the mid-1830s, was spurred on by government support for particular railways infrastructure and by expectations of financial gains resulting from the sale of railways shares to a receptive public.[76] But while Salomon Rothschild in Vienna was then considering investment in a rail link between Vienna and a city in Poland, Emile Pereire was the real influence on James, undoubtedly impressing him from the beginning with his capacity to mount a strong financial argument, his logic and his enthusiasm.[77] Flachat's training was paying off. Emile was eloquent and persuasive and he, too, was an outsider to Paris: James' laboured pronunciation of French betrayed Teutonic antecedents just as Emile's displayed his Gascon roots.[78] Isaac confirmed his brother's influence in his reminiscences of these early days, adding of Rothschild that 'one shouldn't be surprised that he hesitated to take responsibility for a work for which he had not been prepared either by the nature of his business or by the habits of his mind'.[79] Rothschild, the elder by eight years, dubbed Emile 'little Pereire' and a certain affection came to characterise their relationship.

Such backing gave Emile considerable advantages which he had hitherto lacked. James de Rothschild was banker to Louis-Philippe and his entourage and Emile thus gained access to members of the government and the court. He could influence a broader range of issues than had been his lot previously, thanks to the prestige associated with his proximity to Rothschild. When further railway ventures emerged, Rothschild could also provide access to the financial resources of the premier bank in Europe and Britain. Importantly, the Pereires' relationship with James de Rothschild aligned them with a figure at the centre of Jewish life in Paris. An Ashkenazim who was also orthodox, a native of Frankfurt where his father had originally made his money dealing in old coins, later becoming banker to the Elector of Hesse-Kassel, James also had brothers, but in London, Naples, Vienna and Frankfurt, where each had established a branch of the family banking empire. Rothschild's history could scarcely have provided a greater contrast with that of the Pereires.

3 James de Rothschild. Reproduced with permission of
The Rothschild Archive

In June 1835, the Chambre des Députés approved the establishment of the Compagnie du Chemin de Fer de Paris à St Germain in Emile Pereire's name as director and with a board made up of the four bankers.[80] Emile, conscious that conflict of interest might interfere with his plans, had just resigned from the *National* when the Chambre was preparing the bill concerning the concession.[81] His salary was to be 12,000 francs per year and Clapeyron, Stéphane Flachat and Lamé the project's engineers. From that time onwards, as Isaac himself remembered later, the lives of the Pereires and railways were indivisible.[82]

As to Isaac, the messy business of winding up the Saint-Simonians' finances had to be endured for several years, a final labour of love from him and Olinde Rodrigues which turned out to be thankless with the men and women who had once been colleagues turning upon each other. Léon Faucher wrote to Emile Pereire that 'in Lyon, in Marseille, in Toulouse, all the progressive men, such as Arlès Dufour ... are strangers and isolated'. Of Hoart at Grenoble he lamented: 'what a miserable employment of a high intelligence'.[83] Isaac Pereire continued to meet his former colleagues, however, and with Enfantin's release from prison with plans for an expedition to Egypt, despondency among the Saint-Simonians gradually began to lift.[84] According to Isaac in November 1832, after their experiences at Ménilmontant the followers – Duveyrier, Gustave d'Eichthal, Lambert and Simon in particular – began once more to exert their influence individually on the world at large.[85] Isaac, too, was now writing for both the *Temps* of Guizot and Jacques Coste and for Emile de Girardin's *Journal des connaissances utiles*.[86]

Prosper Enfantin was painfully short of money on his release from Sainte-Pélagie and dependent upon the goodwill of his former devotees. Isaac was one of those who supported him. Indeed, at Chevalier's request in 1837 he covered Enfantin's debts, coincidentally discovering further financial problems in the process.[87] But despite a certain bravado, Enfantin's reduced circumstances were unwelcome to him. With the growing status and influence of the Pereires he began to exhibit a different attitude towards them, an aggrieved tone creeping into his correspondence. If Pereire could find an honourable position for him, he wrote, 'a gift that I would be far from rejecting', it would be without prejudice, simply a mark of their past affection. But he was realistic, for 'I don't believe that my return in the world can be brought about directly [sic] by the men I have raised up in the world.'[88]

When he did eventually join his brother at the PSG, Isaac played a significant role in creating the administrative and management systems of the railway company. His experience in accounting gained in working for Vital-Roux and his skill in developing original approaches to finance found their natural habitat. The systems he developed for the PSG became the model for all subsequent Pereire ventures. Equally significant, in his first direct experience of industry he worked very closely with the workforce during the whole period 'with the most touching solicitude'.[89] Now responsible not only for the finances but also for managing staff, he was in a position to implement the ideas to which he had previously given much thought in his writing, and at a time when the government was employing increasingly repressive measures towards labour. Thus did the partnership of the Pereires begin in earnest, with the elder concentrated on the external tasks, the financing, negotiating, purchasing and overseeing of construction, and the younger on the internal questions, the systems needed to run a new business.

The first passenger rail line in France was immensely controversial and its construction innovative, Emile persuaded the government to use soldiers to undertake much of the work.[90] Adolphe Thiers, who was for part of the time Minister for the Interior and later Minister for Public Works, thought it would be at best a sort of rollercoaster destined for the amusement of the public.[91] Even their supporter Adolphe Blanqui, brother of the revolutionary Auguste, found its potential overrated, though he did note sardonically in one of a series of articles in the *Courrier français*: 'Thank God, while they talk about what purpose is served by the railways, the railways are happening.'[92]

4 Maquette locomotive Paris–St-Germain. Archives de la famille Pereire

On 24 August 1837, Queen Amélie, accompanied by the duchesse d'Orléans, the ducs de Montpensier and d'Aumale and the comte de Flahaut, formally inaugurated the Paris–Saint-Germain line. Six hundred dignitaries – ambassadors, government ministers, prefects, men of letters – attended the launch. Two days later the public had its first taste of rail travel, enjoying both the novelty and the utility. The journey took twenty minutes to Saint-Germain, twenty-seven on the return to Paris, and as Jules Janin was to write in the *Journal des débats*: 'Yesterday still, to go to Saint-Germain, it was a voyage; today it is no more than to leave your home.'[93] The public took the rail line to its heart, making a hit of the song 'Titi au chemin de fer au Saint-Germain'. A popular entertainment which personalised the confrontation between the city of Paris and the railway, 'Le chemin de fer de Saint-Germain' was a sell-out when it opened on 23 September 1837 at the Théâtre de la Porte Saint-Antoine.[94] By the end of that year the line had carried nearly 500,000 passengers and generated over 500,000 francs in revenue. The share price, which opened in 1836 at 540 francs, at one time doubled before the end of 1837.[95]

For Emile Pereire the inauguration of the PSG brought reward beyond the profits from his shares or the handsomely-paid position of considerable status: Louis-Philippe made him immediately a Chevalier of the Légion d'Honneur.[96] A still nervous James de Rothschild confessed to his 'dear nephews', however: 'at the moment, I am not hot for the railways'. But a year or so later, he was pleased to write to them: 'I think that in time the St Germain will prove to be a very good investment.'[97]

Not only did the Pereires achieve public recognition, the PSG was the corner-stone of their subsequent success, the foundation of their wealth. For Emile had put considerable effort into identifying and resolving the location of the first railway station in Paris, facilitated by his earlier work on the *entrepôt*. His ambition was to use the Paris node as the entry point for a number of rail lines, and his first preference was for an area around the Madeleine, opposed by well-to-do and aristocratic land-owners who got to the ear of the Paris municipal council.[98] He was forced to settle for a piece of land just to the north, between the place de l'Europe and the rue Saint-Lazare, in which his interest had been aroused already.[99] There he remained during the construction of the Saint-Lazare railway station, his office a small temporary structure of planks from which he managed business.[100]

The need to expropriate land for public works of this kind was under consideration at the same time as the question of the *entrepôt* was being adjudicated. Some of the complexities stemming from negotiations in the case of the PSG embroiled the Pereires with protagonists formerly engaged in developing a pleasure park on available land. In this case the resulting legal mess was fought over for decades, initially concerning three landowners, the banker Jonas Hagermann, Sylvain Mignon and the Conseiller-général of the Seine, Didier-Nicolas Riant. In succeeding years, their heirs took up the case.[101] It is likely that the Pereires made a handsome profit from the expropriation, nevertheless, since they had already acquired land in this expectation.

A further difficulty for the company, technical rather than commercial, was the gradient in the vicinity of Saint-Germain which initially prevented the train from entering the town itself, forcing it instead to terminate three kilometres short at nearby Le Pecq. Emile Pereire's intention was uncompromising: to ensure the line arrived in the town itself. He thus set Eugène Flachat to work developing an 'atmospheric' railway engine capable of mounting the distance, a feat not accomplished finally until ten years later when the Paris–Saint-Germain finally pulled in to its new station.[102] Developing locomotive technology eventually rendered this solution obsolete.

The concept of the network was a Saint-Simonian innovation and it was one the Pereires embraced, conceiving the PSG as the first stage extending from Rouen, Le Havre, from Nantes and Brest.[103] They had the 'Mediterranean system' in mind from the beginning. Their experience as provincials also reinforced their belief in the value of such a network in linking Bordeaux and the Gironde with the rest of France and beyond – indeed, the first locomotive constructed for them at Le Creusot was named *La Gironde*. But while the PSG was still far from completion, in 1835 the Séguin brothers who had been active in developing transportation of freight by rail submitted a proposal to Louis-Philippe's government to build a passenger and goods rail link between Paris and Versailles, thus competing directly with the Pereires' future plans. Emile, with Rothschild's support, was forced to counter with a rival proposal, in the name of the PSG and using the existing line with a branch at Asnières. In July 1836, a law was proclaimed authorising two rail lines between Paris and Versailles, one along the right bank of the Seine, the other along the left.[104] This compromise was so misguided and unworkable its problems were to resonate for years. The Pereires and Rothschild nevertheless took on the Paris à Versailles (Rive Droite) which opened in August 1839.

The end of Saint-Simonianism thus saw the Pereires lay the foundations for their business success. While their finances were inadequate for the tasks they undertook, their skills in dealing with the financiers were not. They convinced not only the bankers of their capacity to implement totally novel infrastructure projects and to deploy competently the necessary capital, but they had developed assurance in their dealings with government officials, politicians, engineers and industrialists, all of whom came to believe in their visionary plans. Emile and Isaac Pereire had made a great leap forward, achieved through what was becoming a formidable partnership, one based on an understanding of each other's weaknesses and confidence in each other's strengths. This as much as any other factor would be at the heart of their legendary business empire.

Notes

1. GL, Considérant, Vol. 8, 'Rapport de Henri Fournel sur le degré des ouvriers (1), mai 1831', pp. 27–8.
2. Carlisle, *Proffered Crown*, p. 138.
3. *Écrits*, t. 1 [fasc., 1], 'Leçons sur l'industrie et les finances', pp. 1–61.
4. Pierre Musso, *Le Vocabulaire de Saint-Simon* (Paris, 2005), pp. 41–4.
5. *Écrits*, t. 1 [fasc., 1], pp. 1–13, 'Leçons sur la valeur, l'échange et l'argent'.
6. Ibid., p. 14, 'Deuxième leçon: transformation de la valeur, de l'échange, de l'argent dans l'organisation matérielle de l'avenir'.
7. Ibid., pp. 30–1.
8. Ibid., pp. 36–7, 58.
9. Briscoe, 'Saint-Simonism', especially pp. 209–25.
10. *L'Organisateur, gazette des saint-simoniens* (New York, 1973), 32, t. II, 26 March 1831, 251., p. 246.
11. AN-Léonore LH/2096/55: Eugène Pereire, 13525.
12. AFP, Emile, Paris, to Fonseca, Bordeaux, 7 April 1828.
13. AN, Minutier central (hereafter MC), VIII/1595, notaire Fould, 'Inventaire ... Madm. Pereire, 9 novembre 1838'.
14. During an 'Enseignement', BNF-A, Fonds Enfantin, 7622/81-2, 14 October 1831.
15. *Écrits*, t. 1 [fasc., 1], p. 47, *Globe*, 11 January 1831; BNF-A, Fonds Enfantin, 7822/29, 'Classement des membres de la famille saint-simonienne par Fonctions (été 1831)'.
16. 'Communion générale de la famille saint-simonienne', *Organisateur*, 48, 8 July 1831, 375.
17. Enfantin in 1830 and Rodrigues the following year. OSSE, t. III, p. 68 and t. IV, p. 201.
18. *Écrits*, t. 3, p. 64; BNF-A, Fonds d'Eichthal, 15031/152, 'Pereire jeune' to Petit, 2 October 1831.
19. Carlisle, *Proffered Crown*, pp. 166–70.
20. BNF-A, Fonds Enfantin, 7622/81-2, 14 December 1831. Underlines as in the original.
21. Ibid., 7819/188, tailor's bill dated December 1831.
22. Carlisle, *Proffered Crown*, p. 138.
23. *Écrits*, t. 1 [fasc., 1], pp. 295–6, described in the *Globe*, 23, 24 January 1832.

24 Carlisle, *Proffered Crown*, p. 158.
25 *Écrits*, t. 1 [fasc., 1], p. 292–3, 28 February 1832.
26 BNF-A, Fonds Enfantin, 7606/47, Emile to Enfantin, 20 February 1832.
27 Ibid., Fonds d'Eichthal 14804, Emile to Georges Cazeaux, 15 June 1832.
28 The *Globe* cost the movement 120,000 francs from its acquisition in August 1830. See *Écrits*, t. 1 [fasc., 1], p. 69, *Globe*, 31 August 1831; and p. 229. The Pereires contributed 2,000 francs.
29 Henry-René d'Allemagne, *Les Saint-Simoniens 1827–1837* (Paris, 1930), p. 438.
30 BNF-A, Fonds Enfantin, 7769/101–7.
31 *Ecrits*, t. 3, fasc., 1, pp. 292–3.
32 *Oeuvres*, s. D, t. 2, 'Le crédit moderne et la politique française (1831–1835)'.
33 Carlisle, *Proffered Crown*, pp. 215–23.
34 AFP, Rodrigues, 'Établissement de mes enfants'.
35 Léon Halévy, *F. Halévy: sa vie et ses oeuvres*, 2nd edn (Paris, 1863), pp. 16–22. The Rodrigues couple also lived there, as did two relatives, the brothers Edouard and Henri Rodrigues.
36 Ibid., p. 17.
37 By Johnson, 'The Revolution of 1830', pp. 147–58.
38 Michael Graetz, *Jews in Nineteenth-Century France*, trans. Jane Marie Todd (Stanford, 1996), pp.160–1, 194–5.
39 Karl Marx, *The Class Struggles in France (1830–1848)* (New York, [1964]), p. 34.
40 Alexis de Tocqueville, *Recollections*, trans. George Lawrence (London, 1970), p. 5.
41 G. Cuchet, 'Utopie et religion au XIXe siècle: l'oeuvre de Jean Reynaud (1806–1863), théologien et saint-simonien', *Revue historique* 631, July 2004, 577–99; *Écrits*, t. 1, fasc., 2, pp. vi, 1–6, 'Examen du budget de 1832', in *Revue encyclopédique*.
42 *Écrits*, t. 1, fasc., 2, pp. 1–6.
43 *Oeuvres*, s. D, t. 2, *National*, 19 May 1833, pp. 760–4; and 24 May 1833, pp. 920–4, 'Le Salaire des mineurs d'Anzin'.
44 BNF-A, Fonds d'Eichthal, 14804, Isaac, Paris, to [Georges] Cazeaux, Bordeaux, 3 December 1832, written in the context of Isaac's contributions to Emile de Girardin's *Connaissances utiles*: 'It will be easy for us … to realise with him projects of great utility for France.'
45 Picon, *Saint-simoniens*, pp. 245–7.
46 This chapter profited from Karen Bowie, *La Modernité avant Haussmann: formes de l'espace urbain à Paris 1801–1853* (Paris, 2001); David Harvey, *Paris, Capital of Modernity* (New York, 2003); and Nicholas Papayanis, *Planning Paris before Haussmann* (Baltimore, 2004).
47 Catherine J. Kudlick, *Cholera in Post-Revolutionary Paris: A Cultural History* (Berkeley, 1996), pp. 2, 16, 36ff.
48 Alain Corbin, *The Foul and the Fragrant: Odour and the Social Imagination*, trans. Miriam Kochan, Dr Roy Porter, and Christopher Prendergast (London, 1996), pp. 157–60.
49 GL, Considérant, *Globe*, Vol. 6, 2 April, 9 April, 13 April, 16 April 1832.

50 AFP, Mirès to Emile, 9 April 1832.
51 Corbin, *The Foul*, pp. 133, 215–17; Peter McPhee, *A Social History of France 1789–1914* (Basingstoke, 2004), p. 140. Pulmonary disease was a major contributor to almost half the deaths in and around Paris in the 1820s.
52 *Oeuvres*, s. D, t. 2, pp. 995–8, 'Influence de l'octroi sur l'assainissement de la ville de Paris', *National*, 23 July 1833.
53 Ibid., pp. 1195–1201, 1225–32. Articles on Paris' finances, the department of the Seine, and the administration of hospices appeared in the *National*, 8 December 1833.
54 *OSSE*, t. XXII, pp. 176–8. See also Maurice Wallon, *Les Saint-simoniens et les chemins de fer* (Paris, 1908), pp. 60–3.
55 *Vues politiques et pratiques sur les travaux publics en France*, par Lamé et Clapeyron, ingénieurs des mines, et par Stéphane et Eugène Flachat, ingénieurs civils (Paris, 1832).
56 *Écrits*, t. 4, fasc. 3, 'Travaux publics: des chemins de fer en France et en Angleterre', *National de 1834*, 23 January 1834, p. 1361.
57 Michel Chevalier, *Système de la Méditerranée*, Extrait du *Globe* du 12 février 1832.
58 Carlisle, *Proffered Crown*, pp. 197–206.
59 *Oeuvres*, s. G, t. 1, pp. 4–6, *Globe*, 21 February 1832.
60 Halévy, F. *Halévy*, p. 17.
61 Fargette, *Émile et Isaac Pereire*, p. 37.
62 Barrie M. Ratcliffe, 'The Origins of the Paris–Saint-Germain Railway', *Journal of Transport History*, New Series, 1 (1972), pp. 197–219.
63 Emile Pereire wrote about the *entrepôt* in the *Journal de commerce*, 5 May 1832. See *Écrits*, t. 4, fasc., 4, pp. 2138–46.
64 AFP, Emile to Michel Chevalier, 19 June 1832.
65 *Oeuvres*, s. G, t. 1, pp. 10–20, *National*, 22 September, 21 October 1832.
66 Ibid., p. 42–3, provides a comprehensive account of this period. Ratcliffe's 'Origins of the Paris–Saint-Germain Railway', pp. 197–219, details the complex organisational task which faced Emile Pereire.
67 Fargette, *Émile et Isaac Pereire*, pp. 44, 46.
68 AFP, Eugène Flachat to Emile, 21 January, 2 March, 16 November 1833, another undated, and another of 1835.
69 Villedeuil wrote of it as 'a test, a school, a didactic example', in *Oeuvres*, s. G, t. 1, pp. 3–4.
70 Hervé Le Bret, *Les Frères d'Eichthal* (Paris, 2012).
71 Muhlstein, *Baron James*, pp. 108–9, as noted above in Chapter 2 'The new society'.
72 I. Pereire, *La Question des chemins de fer* (Paris, 1879), p. 69. See also AFP, Flachat to Emile 1835, from which it is clear that James de Rothschild was not in the fold until just before Louis-Philippe gave his assent.
73 Théophraste, *É. M. Péreire* (Paris, 1856), p. 23. Funding of the PSG initially was through 2,350 shares at 500 francs per share for each of the four directors. Emile Pereire purchased 600 shares.
74 AFP, memo handwritten by Adolphe d'Eichthal, undated.

75 Niall Ferguson, *The World's Banker, The History of the House of Rothschild* (London, 1998), Chapter 15.
76 Ibid., p. 432.
77 Richard Schofield, *Along Rothschild Lines: The Story of Rothschild & Railways Across the World* (London, 2002), pp. 7–8.
78 Feydeau, *Mémoires*, p.166.
79 I. Pereire, *Chemins de fer*, p. 93.
80 *Oeuvres*, s. G, t. 1, ch. 1, p. 43.
81 *Écrits*, t. 4, fasc., 4, p. xii. Emile's last article appeared 4 May 1835.
82 I. Pereire, *Chemins de fer*, p. 11.
83 AFP, Faucher to Emile, 6 September 1833.
84 Carlisle, *Proffered Crown*, p. 231.
85 BNF-A, Fonds d'Eichthal, 14804/13, Isaac to Georges Cazeaux, Bordeaux, 3 December 1832.
86 A. Pereire, *Autour de Saint-Simon*, p. 136.
87 Jean-Pierre Alem, *Enfantin: le prophète aux sept visages* [Paris, 1963], p. 172. On Enfantin's return from Algeria, Isaac Pereire assisted him with a *rente* of 5,000 francs per annum. See also Sébastien Charléty, *Histoire du Saint-Simonisme (1825–1864)*, rev. edn (Paris, 1931), p. 240, fn.1.
88 *OSSE*, t. XI [1873], Enfantin to Arlès-Dufour, 13 November 1837, pp. 134–5.
89 Lauzac, *Isaac Pereire*, p. 12.
90 *Oeuvres*, s. G, t. 1, ch. III, p. 172.
91 Autin, *Frères Pereire*, p. 59.
92 *Oeuvres*, s. G, t.1, ch. II, p. 88, *Courrier Français*, 9, 11 January 1836.
93 Ibid., p. 122.
94 François Boulet, 'Les Pereire et l'arrivée du chemin de fer au travers des débats Saint-Germanois', *Bulletin des Amis du Vieux Saint-Germain* 43 (2006), 33.
95 *Oeuvres*, s. G, t. 1, ch. 2, p. 157, 165.
96 Stéphane Flachat was honoured also with a Légion d'Honneur.
97 François Caron, *Histoire des chemins de fer en France* (Paris, 1997), p. 120. Also Rothschild Archive, London, AL, T35, 1/43, James de Rothschild to his nephews in other European capitals, 17 June 1840.
98 Georges Ribeill, 'Les fondateures stratégiques des grandes gares parisiennes', in Karen Bowie (ed.), *Les Grandes Gares parisiennes au XIXe siècle* (Paris, 1987), pp. 29–30.
99 Ibid., pp. 53–6, Karen Bowie, 'Les grandes gares parisiennes: historique'. Bowie describes at length the various temporary options leading to the first station finally coming into being in 1841, negotiations discussed also in Ratcliffe's 'Origins of the Paris–Saint-Germain', pp. 210–11.
100 Castille, *Frères Pereire*, p. 37.
101 Johnson, 'Revolution of 1830', pp. 174–5. Also see BNF-F-M [Factum. Mignon, Sylvain (héritiers) 1838], 'Note sur les terrains de MM. les héritiers Mignon [expropriés pour l'ouverture de la tranchée du chemin de fer Paris à Saint-Germain], Paris, 1838'; [Factum ...] 'Requête pour M. Riant et les héritiers Mignon, contre la Compagnie du chemin de fer de Paris à Saint Germain –

1839'; [Factum ...] 'A Messieurs les jurés chargés de fixer les indemnités dues aux héritiers Mignon et au sieur Hallot, Paris 20 Mars 1839'; [Factum ...] 'Note sommaire pour la Compagnie du chemin de fer de Paris à Saint-Germain contre les héritiers Mignon et le sieur Hallot – 1839.'
102 Boulet, 'L'arrivée', p. 40.
103 I. Pereire, *Chemins de fer*, p. 78.
104 Known respectively as the Paris–Versailles (Rive Droite) and the Paris–Versailles (Rive Gauche).

4

The adventure of rail

The economic and financial reforms advocated by Saint-Simon and his followers came to be realised with the coming of rail to France. Rail revolutionised the French economy. Lagging far behind Britain in industrial development during the previous century, the French became skilled imitators. They copied British ideas, British skills and British technology – all with British help. Technology transfer flowed on to French manufactures and mining and changed rapidly the pattern and speed of communications and circulation of goods. But the necessary soft infrastructure – government regulation and support, finance accessibility, training systems – took longer to set in place. Political instability during the latter part of the July Monarchy and its successor the Second Republic compounded the difficulties confronting early railway concessionaires. This chapter deals with the stage of railway development in France which followed the inauguration of the PSG, the hesitant administrative arrangements which accompanied the concessions as the State attempted to define its role, and the insufficiency of investment capital to finance railway development. This is seen through the actions of the Pereire brothers as partners and major players, and highlights their extraordinarily entrepreneurial spirit and modus operandi.

The Pereires' developing partnership was placed under great pressure from the start. Their satisfaction with the inauguration of the PSG rail line, which took place in June 1837, had been marred by the sudden death a month earlier of Isaac's wife Laurence at the age of twenty-five, leaving Isaac with two small sons, Eugène and Georges. In the context of his own personal circumstances, including the failure of Saint-Simonianism and the conflict with Enfantin, Laurence's death was a cruel blow. The news circulated quickly throughout France and his friends were equally devastated. Michel Chevalier wrote to Emile Pereire with feeling about the tragedy of one so young struck down at a time when she and Isaac should have looked forward to a long, fruitful life together. He noted that Emile was to a degree compensating for the loss, that Herminie was again pregnant. 'I hope that you are going to have a beautiful boy, for you must have one', he wrote to the father of three daughters (Herminie had given birth to their third daughter, Claire, in 1834), presumably attempting some consolation for the loss of Laurence. Herminie gave birth in August to another girl, Marie, who died in infancy.[1]

The inventory taken at the time of Laurence's death points to a considerable improvement in the material circumstance of the younger Pereire, for both brothers had started to come up in the world. Isaac and Laurence had taken an apartment at number 16 rue de Tivoli, as had Emile and Herminie. This apartment boasted four rooms and a kitchen; a mahogany dining table and twelve chairs upholstered in silk, together with a buffet; a bookcase in Isaac's study; wardrobes and other bedroom furniture. The tableware was silver and there were paintings and other pictures decorating the apartment. The wardrobes held garments of silk, toile, cotton and cashmere. While claiming to have only 6,500 francs in his possession at the time of Laurence's death and, what was undeniably true, that she had brought nothing to the marriage and he had acquired nothing by way of inheritance during it, Isaac had begun to live well, nevertheless.[2]

On the death of his wife Isaac Pereire immersed himself in work, becoming assistant director to Emile in the Paris–Versailles (Rive Droite) and starting in 1838 a review of activities on the Bourse for the *Journal des débats*. This review was a departure in French journalism, providing the first regular commentary on movement in stocks and shares and on financial matters associated with listed companies. Isaac not infrequently emphasised the strength in the shares of the PSG and the Rive Droite. A typical entry, this one from the 'Revue of the week' of October 1838, exemplifies how this worked:

> The fall in railway shares has perhaps reached its limit this week; it had never been as strong [he wrote] ... All these stocks and in particular those of Plateaux, of Saint-Germain and of the Rive Droite de Versailles, nevertheless have not delayed in proving a strong revival.[3]

As Isaac was a shareholder in these companies his approach would be considered questionable nowadays. For one, Emile de Girardin, in the rival journal the *Presse*, harboured suspicions that the *Journal des débats* was employing someone at the heart of the PSG.[4] Even while working for the *National*, Emile Pereire had taken the opportunity to amplify the benefits of rail, to make the case for his own interests and dampen enthusiasm for any competition. Isaac now did likewise, although there was something more than public opinion at stake here, for he was writing for an audience of financially literate people who would have some direct impact on the share price of the PSG and the Paris–Versailles (Rive Droite).

He endured three difficult years following the death of Laurence, seeking help from Emile's wife Herminie and daughter Fanny in raising two sons: Eugène was seven and Georges 2 years old at the time of their mother's death. Herminie herself was pregnant once more, giving birth in February 1840 to Isaac-Emile, who was to become known as Emile II, and thus leaving Isaac's children increasingly in the care of his niece. Isaac was still in his early thirties and could be expected to seek another wife but it seemed to come as a shock when, in 1841, he declared his attachment to Fanny, then only 16 years old.[5] She was beautiful and intelligent, and her warm-hearted concern for the two motherless boys had impressed Isaac in many ways. Initially she rejected his advances and so also it appears did Emile and Herminie on her behalf. While endogamy was not a new practice in the Pereire family – both brothers after all had married cousins, which was not uncommon among Sephardic Jews – it may well have been the example of James de Rothschild and his wife Betty which provided a precedent for Betty Rothschild was James' niece and endogamy was family policy.[6] Such sensitive negotiations were rendered more complicated by the infant Emile, and then with the birth of Herminie's sixth child, Henry, just over a year later in April 1841. Aside from Fanny's youthfulness and Henry's imminent arrival, Emile was probably also concerned that this marriage might be unacceptable to his peers of the Parisian bourgeoisie and judged it prudent to place impediments in its path. While marriage in France between uncle and niece or aunt and nephew was by no means unheard of, it was not commonplace. The Code Civil required permission of the sovereign.[7] Again, in view of Isaac's earlier passion for Mélanie Rodrigues, an infatuation which had presented Emile and his mother with many problems, this was yet another challenge to the brothers' relationship.

Emile, Herminie and, more importantly, Fanny, finally gave way before the strength of Isaac's affections. But the petition begging dispensation from Louis-Philippe which was required of Fanny and Isaac was argued on two grounds: first, that the brothers' many business interests and close working relationship could only be compromised by Isaac's marriage to someone outside the family and facilitated by someone within it, an argument which sounds remarkably similar to Rothschild family policy; and second, that since Laurence's death four years previously, Fanny had practically raised his two children, who loved her like a second mother. Their interests were of 'grave and serious concern'. Louis-Philippe granted his dispensation and the marriage took place in August 1841.[8] A civil ceremony at the Mairie in the first *arrondissement*, was followed the next month by a wedding party at Emile and Herminie's house at Saint-Cloud, where they had moved in 1837. This celebration was described by one of the guests, Ismayl Urbain, as 'an event for the Saint-Simonians'.[9] It has been said, however, that subsequent relations between Isaac and Emile were frosty and it was only their mutual business interests that forced them to work together.[10]

While the Pereires' domestic drama was unfolding, the brothers were caught up in equally taxing circumstances concerning their businesses. The situation for rail in France, other than for those lines which the Pereires were directing, had become troubled quite rapidly. Nearly 1,100 kilometres of track for which concessions had been granted in 1838 had by December 1841 reduced to less than a thousand. The paucity of skill in implementation had forced a number of companies to declare bankruptcy and forfeit their concessions.[11] Experience gained by Emile and Isaac in building the PSG was thus of enormous value to them, one that few other would-be railway entrepreneurs had been fortunate to acquire. Despite the problems, profits to be made from rail in France began to seize the imagination of capitalists in England as well as in France and there was no shortage of proposals for concessions, from Anglo-French consortia and others.[12]

At this critical point the government made a significant decision. Already involved in supporting railways through expropriating land on which they would operate, after a false start in 1838, Victor Legrand imposed order on the situation if not his will on the government. Through *la grande charte* he introduced a dichotomy in responsibilities between providing railways infrastructure, land acquisition, the construction of stations, warehouses and workshops, guaranteed investment and setting freight and passenger charges – all of which became the responsibility of the State – and the exploitation of the line, the provision of material and equipment and the laying of track, which the private sector took on under time-limited leases.[13]

Ten main routes were distinguished and the Pereires had an interest in virtually all, particularly in the concession for the Orléans–Bordeaux which they contested vigorously.[14] They were Bordelais and could scarcely overlook the possibilities of linking the north with the southwest, 'the two centres of commercial exchange, and especially between Spain and the rest of the world', as Isaac later recalled.[15] In the contest for the concession, the Pereires had Rothschild's support and, significantly, the encouragement of the Bordeaux Chambre de Commerce. There was much argument about this particular line in the Chambre des Députés and in the press. Anti-Jewish sentiment was rising, fed by a conviction that rail interests were devouring the land on which they were so rapidly being developed, dispossessing the agricultural labouring classes in the process.[16] With this railway as with others sectional interests also played a large part: alternative transport operators, other concessionaires and pressure groups lobbied the deputies endlessly, reminding them how fickle their local power bases were.

A contribution to the Pereires' undoing may have been Emile's desire to integrate a line from Orléans to Bordeaux with that of Versailles which, in view of the two competing lines from Paris to that city, via the right bank and the left bank, would have raised additional complications unwelcome to an uncertain administration. In the event, the combined interests of the Pereires, Rothschild and the Bordeaux Chambre de Commerce were all defeated by the decision to go to public adjudication. The Pereire team, regarded as the officially sanctioned candidate for the concession, lost it to the Genevan François Bartholony, to their everlasting chagrin.[17]

They did not lose the Chemin de Fer du Nord, the fate of which was being decided almost concurrently with that of the Orléans-Bordeaux. An enormous undertaking, a rail line effectively from Paris to Brussels and with branches to the Channel ports, the Nord was an enterprise in which Emile Pereire had tried unsuccessfully to interest James de Rothschild even before the launch of the PSG.[18] Various explanations have been offered for his initial lack of success, but Isaac Pereire pointed to Rothschild's reluctance to invest in industrial enterprises, verified by letters exchanged between members of the Rothschild family and Emile Pereire in the early 1840s. Aside from James, his nephew Anselm was clearly dubious about Pereire's assessment of the Nord's potential profitability, writing to Emile in 1842: 'The picture that you paint is very seductive, I believe however that you have overloaded your palette with colours which are too brilliant.'[19] He demanded to be kept up to date with information on fluctuations in the market for rail stocks, chiding Emile for costing the family money. In view of Emile's temperament, this challenge to his authority and competence from within the Rothschild family must have been particularly galling.

James de Rothschild (and presumably Anselm) later repented his nervousness when in 1844 the concession was forced into competitive tender, regretting that he had not taken Emile's advice sooner.[20] By this time, however, leaving aside any sins of omission of which he may have been guilty, Emile's own irritation had become palpable. In August 1845, soon after the Rothschild consortium of French and English bankers won the concession, a consortium which he had engineered, he wrote to Rothschild.[21] Strongly worded and direct, surprisingly bitter, his letter betrayed his explosive temperament. He had been preoccupied by the Nord for nine years as Rothschild was all too aware, he wrote, but: 'I was wrong to want this railway six or seven years before everybody else and not to have been able to share my conviction with you at the moment when nobody else was thinking about it.' Claiming his position in relation to the Rothschilds to have been 'neglected too much', his treatment by Rothschild as one of 'aide de camp', he had been, nevertheless, after Rothschild himself, the second 'personification of the Nord railway', its public face with ministers, peers and deputies, with the press, and in the *salons*. He had remained faithful to the flag at times of desertion, refusing the temptation offered to join the boards of Anglo-French companies, invitations which would have been plentiful.[22] This letter, the last recourse open to him, bore all the signs of an angry and distressed man. For his part, presumably out of mischief, James de Rothschild was wont to play the Pereires off against Enfantin and others, being, as Enfantin himself was to note, 'charming towards me while speaking ill of the Pereires'.[23]

While Emile Pereire's aggrieved tone owed much to a perceived lack of appreciation by his chief and mentor, there was also irritation with their respective roles – James representing the whole board, responsible for deploying all its capital resources, with Emile far behind in second place as Director. Given his prescience in relation to the Nord and his hard work on behalf of Rothschild *frères*, both now fully justified by the result, Emile Pereire believed he had cause for complaint. Perhaps the elder Pereire, unequivocally the head of the family and controlling its interests, had struck turbulence in his conflicting role as 'little Pereire'. As the incident makes clear, a rift had occurred in relations between Emile Pereire, the clever, ambitious, aggressive implementer and Rothschild, the cautious, mocking holder of the purse strings.

For Jules Mirès, a brother of Emile's friend Adolphe and later a well-known adversary, the Pereires and the Rothschilds exemplified Sephardim and Ashkenazim, and he described their antagonism thus: the former as children of the Midi and citizens of France, contributing to the country which had granted them equality; the latter, Jews from the east, cold and methodical, concerned to conserve their own wealth at all costs.[24] This means of differentiation had been an element of Sephardic propaganda over a long period as we know, and as the Rothschilds were all too aware. It would have been at least an aggravation in the relationship between the two families. While it is unclear how this particular confrontation was resolved, Enfantin did note soon after, with considerable annoyance, that at a time when shares in the Nord were at a premium, Emile Pereire had been allocated 3,000 of them while he had received a mere two hundred.[25]

Only nine months after the concession was granted in April 1846, the Chemin de Fer du Nord line from Paris to Lille opened, giving the Pereires just cause for self-congratulation. The achievement was remarkable. Their team of 40,000 workers had completed all the construction works; the stations and workshops had appeared 'as if by magic', the track was laid, the engines and carriages built; the administrative and technical staff were in place, and a comprehensive system of accounting embracing the general and the specific applied 'with no fumbling'.[26] Emile Pereire was 45 years of age and Isaac 39. Now public figures, the *frères* Pereire were readily identifiable, their ambitions, characteristics and convictions crystallised. Already renowned as doers, having in abundance the practical skills to realise their plans, even their readiness for risk-taking was evident.

Despite his evident success while labouring on behalf of Rothschild *frères*, Emile Pereire frequently bridled at government decisions and those of the Chambre des Députés more generally. His continuing indignation with the hand the Rive Droite had been dealt was a case in point. There had been no ambiguity in his position when, in 1842, he stood as a candidate for a seat in the department of Eure-et-Loir to represent the market town of Nogent-le-Rotrou. He acted on the Saint-Simonian belief that the direct involvement of business people in France's highest decision-making body was necessary for good government. Indeed, Michel Chevalier had pressed him unequivocally: 'You must become a deputy', he wrote.[27] That this step could only be beneficial to his business interests also spurred him on. Placed strategically, north of Tours and between Chartres and Le Mans, Nogent-le-Rotrou was an ideal place from which to influence railway developments in the west and southwest regions and, according to his grandson Gustave Pereire, Emile stood in order to influence the outcome of the extension of the Paris–Versailles.

That he should decide to stand for election as a deputy is significant in itself, but so too was the manner in which he promoted his claims. Necessarily tailored to a conservative audience, one described as in the 'legitimist belt', as a personal summation of the man in his early forties, his political ideas, his views about his place in the world, it is revealing.[28] He made no secret of his self-interest: 'a powerful interest unites me with you: you know my energetic participation in the efforts of the most significant people of the departments of the west ... to endow these regions with a railway', he wrote.[29] Thus, if the electors were to invest their confidence in him he would place at their disposal the special knowledge and skill he had acquired in these pursuits. He did not seek to frighten the electorate. It was in the name of work that he presented himself for, he wrote, in his eyes work was the very life of modern societies: it constituted their power and their glory, intimately linked to the principles of order, of progress and of liberty. This description was not untypical of the rhetoric of the July Monarchy, with its emphasis on progress, order and stability and peace, Emile Pereire calling for the maintenance of existing institutions for 'nobody knows the price [of instability] better than I'. He only hinted at electoral reform, arguing that 'improvements' should be introduced when they were most generally appreciated and when they could be accepted without disturbance or concern for existing, legitimate rights. The goal of enlightened government must be improvement in the lot of all classes of society through the development of work, of education and morality. Personally, he owed to his industry alone an honourable and independent existence; he expected no favours. From 1835, in establishing the two railways he now directed he had presided over the execution of public works worth thirty-five million francs. Achieved entirely without cooperation from the government, they were now among the most important enterprises in France. From the outset, he had been occupied with a staff of 1,200 and with associated enterprises.[30]

Thus did Emile Pereire define a point of view from which his electorate might draw comfort but which was at the same time still solidly Saint-Simonian. He was not a republican, although we may read in this 'profession of faith' ideas which the republicans too had by now taken on board, such as improvement in conditions of the poorest and most numerous class. That government should be concerned pre-eminently with opportunities for the working class was scarcely a widely held point of view.[31] The emphasis on industrial development leading to employment and thence to economic and social benefit for the working class was Saint-Simonian to the core. His description of his own life reflected Saint-Simonian virtues: thought, work and independence.

This election, which Guizot had called to shore up support for his government and which was instead something of a disaster for him, saw two republicans returned to the Chambre, Alexandre-Thomas Marie and the former Saint-Simonian Hippolyte Carnot.[32] But Emile Pereire was not among the successful candidates, defeated by the well-known liberal and long-serving deputy (for Gers), General Jacques-Gervais Subervie.

Emile stood once more for Nogent-le-Rotrou in the election of 1846 and his declaration was this time little different from the earlier attempt, except perhaps for its brevity and its candour. In contrast with his writings for the *National* over a decade previously, he now believed the rights gained through two revolutions to be secure. Representative of no political party, free of engagement, he supported the July Monarchy at a time when, as one historian has commented, 'even the radical Ledru-Rollin seemed to have accepted ... its legitimacy'.[33] He had cause also to remind his readers how, in his writings and in his actions, his goal was to improve the lot of the 'working classes'. But this attempt to join the Chambre des Députés fared no better than the first and Emile Pereire lost narrowly to the 70-year-old incumbent Subervie by 151 votes to 163.[34]

Saint-Simonian Paulin Talabot had been pursuing Chevalier's 'Mediterranean system' as actively as the Pereires, though from a different direction. The Paris–Lyon rail line was bound to be central to this project and when the concession was awarded in 1845 Rothschild *frères* again played a significant role in its financing. This time it was Isaac Pereire who, having acquired formidable experience in establishing railway companies and in their operations, took his seat on the board alongside Rothschild. Unhappily, the board was divided from the outset, eventually forcing Isaac to resign. Finances of the company reached a parlous state and it finally conceded to the government.[35] This was neither a satisfying experience for Isaac nor a successful foray into the 'Mediterranean system'.

While Emile and Isaac remained in contact to a greater or lesser extent with most of their former colleagues, some of these relationships were becoming increasingly strained. Enfantin, now clearly envious of the Pereires' success, summed up a certain feeling when he wrote to René Holstein:

> I have received many letters from Paris and other places, they have addressed me with verbal demands begging me to exercise my influence over the P. [Pereires], my great influence! poor people who imagined that a friendship, a devotion of 30 years can count for something![36]

In June 1845, Enfantin wrote with glee to his friend Arlès-Dufour that he had been invited to ride in the same carriage with Rothschild to discuss the possibilities of a 'great line north-south', when 'I did as Satan did to Jesus, but the King of the Jews did not say to me "Get thee behind me Satan!"' Rothschild had begun to taunt the Pereires, hinting that the Nord might become part of a Paris–Lyon–Mediterranean equation. Later, Enfantin wrote that the idea he had put to Rothschild was in the process of being realised:

> I pass my days in the midst of these big businessmen, going from one to the other, well seen by all, dealing with them ... In a word treaties of 200 million are going to be signed by Messrs Rothschild, Hottinguer, [Charles] Laffitte and ME [sic].[37]

Enfantin's correspondence with Arlès-Dufour and others was written at the same time as renewed anti-Jewish literature appeared in France, focused in part also on the Pereires as financiers and capitalists. His letters reflected the influence of this literature even on former Saint-Simonians who had been on friendly terms with the Pereires, marking a gathering hostility in relationships which was to lead to cutthroat commercial rivalry and competition. Mathieu-Dairnvaell's *Histoire édifiante et curieuse de Rotschild* [sic] *Ier, roi des juifs* appeared in 1846 and in the same year Pierre Leroux published *Les Juifs, roi de l'époque*. They wrote intentionally to stir up public hatred against figures they portrayed as outsiders, 'the other', bent on taking economic and political power from true French. In these works, targeted primarily at the immense power and influence exerted by Rothschild, the Pereires were inextricably linked by reason of their mutually profitable business association and because they were also Jews. 'Mr Isaac has some securities,' wrote Mathieu-Dairnvaell of the younger Pereire: 'first of all he is a Jew, then he won 3 million in the intrigues of the bourse and of the railways; further, he is the accomplice of Mr Rothschild'.[38]

A rail disaster suffered by the Nord at Fampoux in 1846 in which fourteen people died, a figure disputed as an under-estimate by some of these detractors, provided the pretext for some of this literature.[39] There had been an earlier and indeed more disastrous rail accident, the catastrophic derailment on its approach to Meudon of a train of the Paris–Versailles (Rive Gauche) line in May 1842 in which fifty-five passengers had been killed, most of them burned to death and many unidentifiable.[40] Prominent Jewish business figures Benoît Fould of the bank Fould-Oppenheim and Auguste Léo, who headed the company, had also become targets of abuse. These two accidents generated such popular hysteria that fear of rail travel became widespread.[41] Even François Arago, the eminent scientist and deputy for the Pyrénées-Orientales, was moved to warn his fellows of the danger that steam trains might explode on entering a tunnel.[42] But the dominance in the railways business of Rothschild, whose investment then accounted for 38 per cent of all capital subscribed, prepared the ground for the virulence of the attacks.[43] Writers from all corners of the political spectrum thus found an audience primed for scapegoats. The presence within the Chambre des Députés of Achille Fould (a convert to Protestantism), Max Cerfberr and Adolphe Crémieux, all of whom had been elected deputies in 1842 when coincidentally *la grande charte* for the French rail network was introduced, added fuel to the fire. Their election lent credence to the claims of anti-Jewish writers that the influence of Jews on the government was sinister and pervasive and that it was growing beyond control.

What did the Pereires feel about these attacks? They were after all the butt of several. Unlike Gustave d'Eichthal, a convert to Catholicism who had written a little earlier of having 'kept an indelible memory of the pain caused me in my childhood by the reprobation attached to the name Jew', the Pereires did not at any time voice misgivings about their birthright and, despite their differing approaches to the practice of Judaism, identified publicly as Jews.[44] This was evident from 1840 when the Damascus Affair had burst upon the public consciousness, claiming the alleged ritual murder by Jews of a Franciscan friar and his servant in the Middle East. Emile Pereire was one of eight 'chosen from among the most distinguished' who met under the auspices of the Consistoire Central at Rothschild's home to form a 'special subcommittee' in support of an Anglo-French delegation to the Holy Land, illustrating Emile Pereire's readiness to play a role within Paris' Jewish community. Others in this group included Anselm Halphen, Max Cerfberr and, ironically, Anselm von Rothschild.[45]

By the time of the Nord's opening in 1846 many of the Pereires' personal and business characteristics had crystallised. The relationship between the two brothers was now settled. With the coming of children to Isaac and Fanny the brothers seem finally to have negotiated the problems raised by Isaac's second marriage. Theirs was a partnership, although it was not entirely one of equals. Emile was still indisputably the leader, the visionary, the one who negotiated with significant figures, who made strategic decisions often involving complex matters of technology, the dealmaker, the chief. Isaac was the loyal deputy, the sound manager of money and resources, a brilliant financier who, through the intellectual hot-bed of the Saint-Simonian years, developed innovative ways of managing the finances of the business, and of raising capital – interest-bearing banknotes, debenture bonds, annuities – these were all ideas gestating in Isaac's fertile mind.[46]

Already in their partnership the family circle was a powerful weapon, and family members were among their most intimate friends. The brothers-in-law Baud and Sarchi working with the PSG; their cousin Olinde Rodrigues providing welcome counsel; Olinde's parents Sara-Sophie and Isaac Rodrigues, until their deaths in February and September 1846 respectively, remaining among their close supporters together with the Rodrigues women, especially Félicie, Mélanie and Olinde's wife Euphrasie.

The Pereires' world view was settled. They were Jews which, as one historian observed, they 'refused to regard as a badge of shame and, on the whole, [they] persisted in taking pride in what they were and what they had become'.[47] While Emile remained more conscientious in this respect, attending the synagogue from time to time and directing some of his increasing wealth towards the Jewish community, he was no longer a believer. Isaac on the other hand, having been the more devoted to Saint-Simonianism in all its manifestations, and having lost his Jewish faith, remained committed to a God he saw in Saint-Simonian terms. He, too, nevertheless, gave alms to the Sephardim in Bordeaux at Yom Kippur.[48] The decision of the new Assemblée Nationale in 1790 granting citizenship to the Sephardim of Bordeaux and St Esprit also made the Pereires Frenchmen from birth. Their identity as both citizens of France *and* Jews inspired them, for they articulated more than once a sense of pride that this should have been so.[49] But it also drove them hard. There was much to achieve and to prove, captured in their prodigious capacity for hard work sustained day after day.

In 1844 alone, while collaborating on the two companies of which Emile Pereire was Director and Isaac his deputy, the PSG and the Rive Droite, they engaged in what an adversary was to call a 'civil war' with the Compagnie de Rouen, and endeavoured to rationalise competition with the Paris–Versailles (Rive Gauche). They battled for concessions extending the Versailles line as far as Rennes, from Orléans to Bordeaux, and from Paris to the Belgian frontier; and, at the same time, actively pursued the lines from Paris to Lyon and from Paris to Strasbourg. This was, indeed, 'a period of great intensity of spirit and of fertile activity'.[50] It was not, however, unusual.

By 1846, the Pereires' effort was being rewarded. They had some form of financial involvement in four of the railways then in existence. Emile's shareholdings at par value (500 francs) included 600 shares in the PSG; 600 in the Rive Droite; 2,760 in the Nord; and 500 in the Chemin de Fer de Creil à St Quentin (which merged with the Nord). With share-price increases these were valued (by 1845) at close to 3,500,000 francs: a profit of 57 per cent.[51] Isaac, who was an employee in three of the major companies, as well as earning a living as a journalist, probably held shares on his own account also, though the evidence is lacking. When Dairnvaell asserted that Isaac had engaged in shady dealings on the Bourse and had profited to the tune of three million francs, he had probably confused him with Emile who was also a closer 'accomplice of Mr. Rothschild'. If this is the case, it is scarcely tenable that Emile gained his shares fraudulently since he was a director of each of the companies in which he held a stake.

That the profits from these probably supported his dealings in expropriated land is another story.

But Emile and Isaac Pereire did not fully control their own destinies, despite their many successful projects, the material comfort and position they had already acquired, the opportunities afforded to implement the ideas debated a decade or more previously. And while this may have been endurable at a time of sustained economic growth and unlimited access to capital, in 1846 the economy faltered. At the same time, the opposition they had begun to encounter from former colleagues and even from some of their own business associates made it vital that they become independent, to strike out on their own.

The last years of the 1840s were beset by a downturn caused on the one hand by a poor grain harvest in 1846 and on the other by financial constraints placed on the availability of credit facilities at a time of overproduction. The result was industrial upheaval.[52] The government of Louis-Philippe, which had appeared so durable despite its increasing conservatism, was forced to compromise. In February 1848, after the banning of a political banquet in Paris, one of many held around the country, an impromptu coalition of workers, students and others opposed to the government demonstrated against this infringement on their liberties. The troops who came out briefly lost their resolve in the face of the barricades. Louis-Philippe abdicated and a provisional government, formed around republican opponents to the monarchy, proclaimed the Second Republic in France.[53]

The Pereires' response to the Revolution of 1848 was typical of Saint-Simonians more generally and this was as uneven as it had been in 1830. Sympathetic to the situation of the 'proletarian' as they were, they also had many reservations about the turn of events. Railways were among the most immediate of the public infrastructure attacked by the workers, and while the Pereires' railway interests survived the riots and fires which followed, they lost heavily. Railway stations were looted and vandalised. The burning of a railway bridge at Asnières in February interrupted the service of the PSG for several months, losing the company 15,000 francs a day and requiring 400,000 francs to install a temporary solution.[54] Both Emile and Isaac Pereire appear to have engaged personally in some of the violent events when, taking control of a company of mobile guards put at their disposal by Adolphe Crémieux, Minister for Justice in the provisional government, they seized back the workshops and the goods station at La Chapelle which workers of the Nord had commandeered.[55]

What can we say about the Pereires' attitude to the events of February 1848? They themselves were probably honest in contending much later that they had been neither royalists, nor imperialists nor republicans, and certainly they were not revolutionaries.⁵⁶ Their position is reminiscent of that described by Charles Lemonnier when in 1832 he had written of the Saint-Simonians: 'We love all the parties (republican, legitimist, *juste-milieu* ...) [ital. sic] but we are not with any party.'⁵⁷ In Gustave's words, 'they never renounced the principles of practical socialism, from the point of view of their purely progressive aspect, of which they had been the interpreters'. The emphasis was on the practical. The excesses of socialism could be tempered by 'a good organisation of credit ... the best, the only means of assuring work'.⁵⁸

Certain Saint-Simonians, however, the Pereires' cousin Olinde Rodrigues among them, had moved increasingly to the left after the demise of Saint-Simonianism, identifying publicly with the workers' cause.⁵⁹ This had not interfered with Olinde's relations with his cousins and his influence on them was still in many respects crucial, one particular incident bearing this out. Inviting many of his former colleagues, though not Enfantin, to meet at his home soon after the February uprising, he attempted to rally the Saint-Simonians towards 'a great political and religious movement embracing all the socialist parties'. The artisan Jules Vinçard, infuriated by the lacklustre responses of his friends of earlier days, noted how much they had changed in the intervening years. Personal interests now dominated 'or completely annihilated the principal which had once united them'. Vinçard challenged them to mount posters around Paris carrying a declaration of Saint-Simonian principles: 'the association of all the producers, remuneration according to work, and the radical abolition of all the privileges of birth, whatever they may be'. Only Isaac Pereire agreed to the proposal, swearing that he would sign it in his blood, a memory treasured by Vinçard 'of this generous outburst of love of the people, and I record it here as evidence of gratitude for its author'.⁶⁰ In 1848, Isaac at least had evidently not relinquished his allegiance to Saint-Simonian philosophy or to any of his ideals.

In fact, the Pereires worked actively with what was a largely middle-class republican government throughout this early period. They knew members of the provisional government well, including Crémieux and Michel Goudchaux (the latter was briefly Minister for Finance), both among a small number of Jews seeking public office nationally. Former colleagues at the *National* had become key figures, and former Saint-Simonians Léon Faucher, Pierre Leroux and Philippe Buchez were elected members of the Assemblée Nationale. Hippolyte Carnot was briefly Minister for Education in Lamartine's provisional government.

Indeed, at a time of economic crisis and financial ruin for many,

Jacques Laffitte's bank being among the casualties, the Pereires proved extremely useful to the new government. They advised on the creation of the Comptoir National d'Escompte de Paris, for example, which by 1849 was replicated in sixty-seven provincial cities. Emile Pereire with the deputy Achille Fould devised the Comptoir's statutes which provided relief to merchants in Paris and elsewhere by discounting commercial paper bearing two signatures and by advancing credit.[61] The capital required was advanced one-third each by the government, by the municipality and by subscription. Bonds were issued to soak up the pool of savings which existed in the community.[62] Both Pereires also served on a commission of Louis-Antoine Garnier-Pagès, Goudchaux's successor, to prepare a blueprint for the organisation and development of railways by the State, their intention covertly to ward off the government's proposed redemption of its investment in rail.[63]

Isaac's earlier unrewarding experience of the aborted Paris-Lyon rail inspired a group of prominent business leaders, including the duc de Galliera and Ernest André (who were to become figures in several of the Pereires' later companies), Jacques Ardoin and Benjamin Delessert, to encourage him to work on a plan to rescue the railway system. Conceiving a revival of the Paris–Lyon, but with an extension to Avignon and thence to Marseille, his project as it was outlined was debated at length and heatedly in both chambers. With the Talabots, other rail concessionaires, the canal operators, even the iron manufacturers, all contributing to a chorus of dissent, however, the proposal in this ambitious form was defeated: Isaac was preparing audaciously to seize complete control in the development of Michel Chevalier's 'Mediterranean system'. The stakes were too high to allow him to succeed.[64] This defeat in their pursuit of the grand plan in rail was both a rehearsal for the Pereires of things to come and an unwanted compromising of their future options.

Towards the middle of 1848 the open confrontation between capital and labour came to appal them. Together with most Saint-Simonians they were unnerved by violence. And, as they put it, nothing was to be gained in representing labour as the victim of an exploitative capitalism, 'a pitiless master as the common enemy, whom we must rid ourselves of soon'.[65] In June 1848, with Louis Blanc's national workshops closed and public meetings banned, the resulting violence lost them any faith they might have had in the capacity of the Republic to engineer longer-term solutions to the economic and political crisis. The insurrection, concentrating around Paris' east – Saint-Marcel, Saint-Antoine and Saint-Jacques – was put down brutally by troops led by the Minister for War, General Louis-Eugène Cavaignac, confirming the Pereires' fear that the situation was now critical.⁶⁶ They were primed for another significant intervention in their lives.

Prince Louis-Napoléon Bonaparte reappeared on the scene after several incompetent attempts before 1848 to re-insert himself into French political life as a serious figure. His ancestry was ambiguous, his Bonapartist credentials questionable.⁶⁷ Nevertheless, with the death of Napoléon's only son, the duc de Reichstadt, in 1832, Louis-Napoléon was undisputed leader of the Bonapartist cause, attempting a coup in Strasbourg and another in 1840 in Boulogne which resulted in his incarceration in the fortress of Ham in the Somme where he remained prisoner for six years. Initially, therefore, there remained as much doubt about his capacities as of his legitimacy. But his sense of timing, previously so lacking, was now impeccable. Standing for election as President on 10 December 1848 for a fixed term of four years, he won over 5.4 million votes (74 per cent) to General Cavaignac's 1.5 million. The radical Ledru-Rollin received 370,119 votes, while Lamartine, who had also contested the election, received only 17,910.⁶⁸ Léon Faucher became Minister of the Interior in the new government of Prime Minister Odilon Barrot.

A mix of desperation and wishful thinking motivated the Pereires' initial response to Louis-Napoléon. How did they first meet? It seems that by 1846 Louis-Napoléon was at least aware of Emile Pereire for he requested James de Rothschild to send Emile to the prison at Ham to discuss with him the financing of a canal in Nicaragua. Whether this meeting took place is not certain but it suggests that Emile was known and as a confidant of Rothschild.⁶⁹ They were also acquainted through Auguste de Morny, the Prince-President's half-brother, when he and Emile's friend Adolphe Blanqui were elected to the Assemblée in 1846. For their part, the Pereires began to see some benefit in the newcomer and to firm in their support.⁷⁰ This was not as aberrant as it may seem: so too for a time had Louis Blanc. Neither of them was inherently Bonapartist nor convinced by the newcomer's claims as successor to Napoléon I. The Pereires shared the same mixed feelings as many others over the political leadership.⁷¹

They rapidly came to believe Louis-Napoléon was at heart susceptible to Saint-Simonianism, however, and indeed a teacher and mentor, Narcisse Vieillard, a former Saint-Simonian, had familiarised him with the writings of Saint-Simon during the incarceration in Ham.⁷² A book published in 1844, *Extinction du paupérisme*, stamped Louis-Napoléon as having an ideology close enough to the Pereires' own. In it he expressed a genuine concern to improve the condition of the working class, even though his belief in agricultural colonies as the solution to their misery was fanciful. He was prepared to commit the resources of the State to generate benefits for commerce and industry and his ideas about taxes and the State's budget were reasonably compatible with Saint-Simonianism.[73] In another of his books, *Des idées napoléoniennes*, which by 1848 had sold half a million copies, he sought overtly to place the mantle of his uncle more firmly around his own shoulders. Finally, among Louis-Napoléon's ideas we also find a generally sympathetic attitude towards Jews.[74] The Pereires' political beliefs remained in the mould of Saint-Simon's: oligarchical, advocating government run by successful business men whose sound economic and financial policies would result in social benefits for all and who, while maintaining internal peace and stability, were yet concerned with the welfare of the poorest and most numerous class. Nevertheless, the difficult financial situation in which the Pereires found themselves at this period also shaped their behaviour. On the brink of losing the gains carefully amassed over the past decade, for railway share values had collapsed, they saw in Louis-Napoléon the figure who might restore the country to order and with it, their investments.

One particular meeting with the Prince-President, in February 1849, proved fortuitous. A branch line of the Nord between Créteil and St Quentin was to be inaugurated, stopping first at Compiègne where the officiating Prince-President was to board. Compiègne was significant in the Bonaparte mythology, but the occasion also gave Louis-Napoléon his first opportunity for exposure outside the capital.[75] It was a public relations coup. Scarcely had the train arrived at its destination than a great cry arose, 'Vive Napoléon!', and his speech on that occasion was correspondingly rousing:

> The hopes that my election have bred in the country will not be deceived; I share these wishes for the strengthening of the Republic. I hope that all the parties which have divided the country for forty years will find a neutral ground where they will be able to stand by each other for the grandeur and the prosperity of France.[76]

Recurring themes which underpinned his regime – prosperity, unity, the greatness of France – were spelled out publicly for the first time.[77] The Pereires had proved their usefulness, providing Louis-Napoléon with a platform for the kind of public display which he developed into the fine art of propaganda, allowing him to fashion an image as the true successor to his uncle and to garner support for his regime.[78]

The Pereires now had an advantage over James de Rothschild, whose former intimacy with the July Monarchy placed him at a disadvantage with the Bonapartists. Louis-Napoléon could scarcely ignore the foremost

5 Napoléon III (1860). Wikimedia Commons. George Eastman House, Rochester, NY

banker in Europe, and indeed they had had dealings from earlier times. But nor could Rothschild afford to display his deep antipathy for the newcomer. The whole family found Louis-Napoléon's lifestyle dishonourable and immoral (he arrived in Paris with his English mistress Mrs Howard) but, aside from questions of morality, they also feared he would take an overly interventionist approach to foreign engagement. While James loaned him a sum of money early in the piece, 20,000 francs, once the State budget was passed there was to be no more, he told his nephew, Anthony.[79]

Louis-Napoléon's term as Prince-President was marked by political turbulence throughout much of France. A divided Royalist opposition formed of Orléanists and legitimists, and the *démoc-socs*, a left-wing party which emerged from the former republicans, fought them and the Bonapartists for control.[80] The presidential term was to come to an end in 1852 and the Assemblée Nationale refused to vote in favour of a constitutional revision to extend it. In December 1851, with the support of the army and orchestrated by Morny, Louis-Napoléon staged a coup, brutally crushing the opposition which had broken out in Paris and the countryside. Twenty-seven thousand rebels were subsequently arrested. Following a plebiscite, Louis-Napoléon gained a ten-year term as President.[81]

The morning of the coup, Emile Pereire walked to James de Rothschild's home in the rue Laffitte. Some of the principal bankers of Paris who were also there peppered him with questions of what he had seen on the way, to which he was reported to have replied: 'the good humour of the officers, the vigour of the soldiers, the large deployment of the military forces, the indifference of the people reading the notices, the tranquility of Paris, in spite of the surprises of its awakening.'[82] None of this suggests any alarm about the dramatic event and apparently Emile Pereire exhibited no qualms about it. It was a reaction common among the people of Paris where there was general acquiescence to the coup despite the 400 dead, all killed by the army.[83] The bankers assembled at the Rothschild home greeted the news with relief, but the *coup d'état* cast the Second Empire forever as corrupt and illegitimate, a pariah regime rising from the ashes of the Second Republic. In the history of republicanism it remained a shameful and violent event, its antagonists 'obscure heroes who suffered in silence for the Republic'.[84]

What did the Pereires know of the coup? That it would occur was no secret in Paris: members of the Assemblée who had rejected the Prince-President's demand for more time were aware that it would happen. It is inconceivable that Emile and Isaac Pereire were in the dark. Louis-Napoléon's new secretary, Jean-François Mocquard, a member of the inner sanctum, knew them both, as did the banker Benoît Fould, who loaned money for the coup, and Morny, the 'maître d'oeuvre'.[85] Nor is there anything in the Pereires' writings to indicate that either harboured misgivings or doubts about the coup or the legitimacy of the regime it brought into being. Even towards the end of his life, Isaac could only see in the Second Republic 'the state of stagnation into which the railways industry fell', the final years notable only for their 'sterile agitations, for the unremitting struggles of the parties who disputed power'.[86] What mattered was the effect of politics on the railways, on business. The Pereires did not dwell on the replacement of a legitimate government by violence, the slaughter of men justly defending it.

In the aftermath of the *coup d'état*, however, one particular event which affected them both keenly was the death in December 1851 of Olinde Rodrigues, the result of what has been described as a tragic accident but about which nothing more appears to be known. He had exerted a considerable intellectual and moral influence on his cousins and a (rare) moderating influence on Emile. The Pereires were executors of Olinde's will in which he instructed his readers never to forget that, as sons of his father's best friend, Emile and Isaac had extended 'the heartfelt friendship of the best of brothers, that their purses have been mine'.[87] Unlike their politics, his had moved in a different direction since the breakdown of Saint-Simonianism as he concentrated his efforts increasingly towards projects for the working class. He would have continued to play a significant role in their lives had he survived and one can only speculate on the influence he may have wielded in the ventures which were about to unfold. Olinde Rodrigues' death, coming as it did when the Pereires were on the verge of their greatest entrepreneurial success, marked a turning point of sorts for the entire extended Pereire-Rodrigues family whose lives began to revolve inexorably around the Pereires.

Their early support for Louis-Napoléon was rewarded with a growing influence, enabling the Pereires to begin to implement business ventures which once they had only imagined. One of these innovations was the Crédit Foncier de France (known briefly as the Banque Foncière de France), created in February 1852 to provide for the orderly management of mortgage finance in France and to extend mortgages to farmers. Emile had taken up the idea during the Second Republic and he was to sit on the Crédit Foncier board.[88] Projects which gave advantage to Bordeaux also featured in discussions with Louis-Napoléon. The Pereires' motivation was a wish to be useful, to improve the prospects of the city and bring about progress, having, as Isaac described it: 'always nourished the desire to … give back to their native city, to Bordeaux, the splendeur it had once enjoyed before the fall of Saint-Domingue, the pearl of the Antilles, which was for a long time our principal colony'.[89]

The Pereires' quest for a Bordeaux railway concession had in August 1852 finally been successful. Named collectively the Compagnie des Chemins de Fer du Midi, the line was to run from Bordeaux to Bayonne and thence to Sète [then known as Cette], with a concession of ninety-nine years, and from Narbonne to Perpignan. The company, which would also assume management of the Canal Latéral de la Garonne, was conceded the line from Bordeaux to La Teste near Arcachon as well. The initial concession had been granted previously to a consortium principally of Bordeaux businessmen and to these were added Pereire associates either already engaged in the PSG or who were to become directors of the Crédit Mobilier: Ernest André, Jacques Ardoin, Bischoffsheim et Cie, Adolphe d'Eichthal, Léon Faucher, Vincent Cibiel, the duc de Galliera and, of course, both Pereires. Even Rothschild *frères* subscribed to this concession over which Emile presided.[90] With capital of 67 million francs divided into 134,000 shares of 500 francs, the Midi reserved the right to raise money through loans and issuing bonds. Each of the Pereires held 6,000 shares.[91] The coming of the railway to Bordeaux was to have immense implications for the region, providing a tremendous fillip to the distribution of its produce within France and to exports throughout Europe. From 1852 until 1878 the proceeds of the Mediterranean trade increased from nine million francs to forty-two million. The Bayonne rail produced a ten-fold increase.[92] But one considerable impediment to the growth of wine exports, to Great Britain in particular, remained the high tariffs.

Louis-Napoléon addressed the Bordeaux Chambre de Commerce in October 1852, proclaiming 'the Empire means peace', stating his imperialist intentions from the outset. He spoke of the immense uncultivated territories France must clear, the roads to build, the ports to dredge, rivers to make navigable, canals to finish, a railway network to complete. Facing Marseille was a vast kingdom to assimilate with France, he said, and, warming the hearts of the Bordelais, the west coast was home to all the great ports through which France could approach America. He repeated the substance of this speech about Empire soon after in Paris: 'It is order, work, credit, expansion imprinted on all the great public and private enterprises; it is well-being filtering into all classes of society.'[93] The congruence between the ideas laid out in both speeches and the Pereires' Saint-Simonianism might lead to speculation that they contributed to their writing. Perhaps it was fortuitous that the President's secretary Auguste Chevalier was a former Saint-Simonian and Pereire intimate. Thus not only had they ready access to Louis-Napoléon from early in his presidency, the Prince-

President had chosen their home town to make a major statement of his political economy, to which they may well have contributed.

But it was their success in finally persuading Louis-Napoléon of the worth of their ideas on central banking which defined from this time onwards the *frères* Pereire. The Rothschilds had provided a central source of finance in the development of the PSG and more importantly in that of the Nord. But the Pereires' relationship with James de Rothschild deteriorated during the last years of the decade. There is no evidence of a split, but while Emile remained on the board of the Nord he clearly found his role in relation to Rothschild irksome. For his part, the banker, who had been hit hard by the 1848 revolution, cautious in his investments and also inclined to play the Pereires off against Enfantin and the Talabots, focused more of his attention on the Nord and less on his other rail interests. He had resigned from the board of the PSG in 1849.[94] Having attempted fruitlessly for a number of years to persuade Rothschild to make an increasing commitment to industrial investments, the Pereires thus required an independent source of significant finance for their own new enterprises. It was about to be granted to them.

Notes

1 AFP, Chevalier to Emile, 28 July 1837.
2 AN, MC, VIII/1595, notaire Fould, 'Inventaire', 9 November 1838.
3 *Écrits*, t. 2, fasc. 1, Avant-Propos, p. 2 where Gustave Pereire also suggests he may have commenced these articles anonymously in 1834–35; ibid., pp. 285–6, 22 October 1838.
4 Ibid., p. 2.
5 Autin, *Frères Pereire*, p. 214.
6 Ferguson, *World's Banker*, pp. 195–6, 199. 'The most important reason for the strategy of intermarriage was precisely to prevent the five houses drifting apart. Related to this was a desire to ensure that outsiders did not acquire a share in the five brothers' immense fortune.' Betty was the daughter of Salomon who represented the family in Vienna.
7 AN, BB/15/322–333, 'Demandes de dispensations pour mariages (1832–60) sous l'article 164 du Code Civil'. There were some ninety such requests in 1841.
8 Ibid., BB/15/329, August 1841.
9 Michel Levallois, 'La Genèse de l'Algérie Franco-Musulmane d'Ismayl Urbain 1837–1848' (PhD dissertation, Institut National des Langues et des Cultures Orientales, Paris, 1999), p. 327.
10 Autin, *Frères Pereire*, p. 214.
11 *Oeuvres*, s. G, t. 1, ch. V, p. 356.
12 David S. Landes, *Bankers and Pashas: International Finance and Economic Imperialism in Egypt* (London, 1958), pp. 44–5.

13 Johnson, 'Revolution of 1830', p. 176.
14 I. Pereire, *Chemins de fer*, p. 85.
15 *Oeuvres*, s. G, t. 1, ch. VI, p. 584–7.
16 Kalman, *Rethinking Antisemitism*, ch. 5.
17 *Oeuvres*, s. G, t. 1, ch. VI, pp. 585–7.
18 'Théophraste', É.M. Péreire, p. 24.
19 AFP, Anselm von Rothschild, Frankfurt, to Emile, Paris, 22 January 1842.
20 I. Pereire, *Chemins de fer*, p. 95.
21 *Oeuvres*, s. G, t. 1, pp. 877, 914. The consortium consisted of Rothschild *frères* (Paris), Nathaniel Rothschild and Sons (London), Hottinguer et Cie, Charles Laffitte, and Blount et Cie. Board members included Hottinguer, Laffitte, Adolphe d'Eichthal, Auguste Thurneyssen, Jules Mallet and James, Nathaniel and Lionel de Rothschild.
22 AFP, Emile to James de Rothschild, 18 August 1845, draft.
23 See BNF-A, Fonds Enfantin, 7616/98, Enfantin to Jules Talabot, 16 August 1845, evincing collusion between the three parties, including Rothschild; and 7617/146, to Arlès-Dufour, 18 November 1847.
24 Mirès, *À mes juges*, pp. 88–90.
25 BNF-A, Fonds Enfantin, 7617/71, to Arlès-Dufour, 29 August 1845.
26 I. Pereire, *Chemins de fer*, p.96.
27 *Écrits*, t. 4, fasc., 4, p. xxvii, 6 November 1832.
28 Johnson, 'Revolution of 1830', p. 184, fn. 38.
29 Émile Pereire, 'A MM. les Electeurs du 4me Collège d'Eure-et-Loir' (Paris: 1842), p. 1.
30 Ibid., pp. 2–4.
31 Luna, *French Republic*, pp. 29, 31.
32 Pilbeam, *Republicanism*, p. 146. Twelve of fourteen deputies elected for the Seine were left-wing.
33 McPhee, *Social History*, p. 127.
34 Autin, *Frères Pereire*, Annexe No. 13, pp. 371–2; p. 269.
35 BNF-A, Fonds Enfantin, 7630; Enfantin's correspondence with Arlès-Dufour in 7617, 7664, 7665.
36 Ibid., 7628/55, Enfantin to Holstein, December 1845. Twenty years was closer to the mark.
37 Ibid., 7616/71, Enfantin to Lambert, 16 June 1845; 7616/77, 28 July 1845.
38 Mathieu-Dairnvaell, *Histoire édifiante et curieuse de Rotschild Ier, roi des juifs par Satan* (Paris, 1846), p. 35.
39 Ibid., p. 24 where he claimed 39 deaths. See also Kalman, *Rethinking Antisemitism*, pp. 128–31.
40 *Oeuvres*, s. G, t. 1, p. 376.
41 Caron, *Histoire des chemins de fer*, pp. 85–6.
42 Fargette, *Émile et Isaac Pereire*, pp. 68–9.
43 Ferguson, *World's Banker*, p. 451.
44 Charléty, *Histoire*, p. 250, quoting d'Eichthal's preface to *Lettres sur la race noire et la race blanche* (Paris, 1839), pp. 12–13.

45 Graetz, *Jews in Nineteenth-Century France*, pp. 95, 97–8. See also Jonathan Frankel, *The Damascus Affair: 'Ritual Murder', Politics, and the Jews in 1840* (Cambridge, 1997), p. 237.
46 Barrie M. Ratcliffe, 'Some banking ideas in France in the 1830s', *Revue international d'histoire de la banque* 6 (1973), 33–6 summarises these ideas.
47 Carlisle, *Proffered Crown*, p. 63.
48 Ratcliffe, 'Some Jewish problems', p. 200.
49 I. Pereire, *Chemins de fer*, p. 152–3.
50 *Oeuvres*, s. G, t. 1, ch. VI, p. 474.
51 Ibid., t. 2, p. 1333–4; t. 3, p. 2474.
52 Price, *Economic History*, pp.140–1, who describes the situation as 'the last major crisis of the pre-industrial economy in France'.
53 McPhee, *Social History*, ch. 9.
54 Théophraste, *É. M. Péreire*, p. 25.
55 AFP, *Panthéon des Illustrations Françaises au XIXe Siècle*, Publié sous la direction de Victor Frond (Paris, 1865), p. 3, which noted that Crémieux marched alongside them.
56 A. Pereire, *Je suis dilettante*, p. 21; I. Pereire, *Chemins de fer*, pp. 111–12.
57 GL, Considérant, Vol. 6, Charles Lemonnier, 'Les Saint-Simoniens!!!', 7 June 1832.
58 *Écrits*, t. 1 [fasc., 1], 1900, pp. i–xii.
59 Bibliothèque Thiers-Dosne (hereafter BT), Fonds d'Eichthal, Carton IVR-2. Rodrigues stood unsuccessfully for the Assemblée Nationale on 23 April 1848. Among his works are *Poésies sociales des ouvriers* (1841), *Organisation du travail, association du travail et du capital* (1848), and *Avis aux travailleuses des deux sexes* (1848).
60 [Jules] Vinçard, *Mémoires épisodiques d'un vieux chansonnier saint-simonien* (Paris, 1878), pp. 257–8.
61 Charles E. Freedeman, 'Joint-stock business organizations in France, 1807–1867', *Business History Review* 39 (1965), 199; I. Pereire, *Chemins de fer*, pp. 111–12; Michael Stephen Smith, *The Emergence of Modern Business Enterprise in France, 1800–1930* (Cambridge, MA, 2006), pp. 69–70.
62 Bertrand Gille, *La Banque en France au XIXe siècle: recherches historiques* (Geneva, 1970), p. 126.
63 I. Pereire, *Chemins de fer*, p. 114.
64 Ibid., pp. 121–7.
65 Ibid., p. 111.
66 William H. Sewell, *Work and Revolution in France: The Language of Labor from the Old Regime to 1848* (Cambridge, 1980), pp. 265–73.
67 His mother, Napoléon's adopted daughter Hortense, was daughter of Joséphine and Joséphine's first husband, Alexandre de Beauharnais. His father was possibly Hortense's lover, the comte de Flahaut, and not Hortense's husband, the former King Louis of Holland, Napoléon's brother.
68 Pilbeam, *Republicanism*, p. 225.
69 Éric Anceau, *Napoléon III: Un Saint-Simon à cheval* (Paris, 2012), p. 103, quoting letter to Rothschild, 14 April, AN, 400, AP 41.

70 Morny was the natural son of Hortense and Flahaut.
71 Roger Price, *Napoléon III and the Second Empire* (London, 1997), pp. 14–15, discusses the lack of direction of the various political factions.
72 Anceau, *Napoléon III*, pp. 255, 257.
73 *Extinction du paupérisme par Le prince Napoléon-Louis Bonaparte* (Paris, 1844).
74 Napoléon III, *Napoleonic Ideas: des idées napoléoniennes, par le Prince Napoléon-Louis Bonaparte*, ed. Eugene C. Black, trans. James A. Dorr (New York, 1967), pp. iii, 49.
75 This northern French town was home to the royal château where Napoléon I met his second wife, Marie-Louise of Austria.
76 *Oeuvres*, s. G, t. iv, ch. XVI, pp. 3118–20.
77 Sudhir Hazareesingh, *The Saint-Napoléon: Celebrations of Sovereignty in Nineteenth-century France* (Cambridge, MA, 2004), Chapter 1.
78 Matthew Truesdell, *Spectacular Politics: Louis-Napoléon Bonaparte and the Fête Impériale, 1849–1870* (New York, 1997).
79 Ferguson, *World's Banker*, pp. 500–1.
80 McPhee, *Social History*, pp. 174–82.
81 Pilbeam, *Republicanism*, pp. 236–42.
82 Charles Merruau, *Souvenir de l'Hôtel de Ville de Paris 1848–1852* (Paris, 1875), p. 461. Merruau was senior official in Paris' municipal government and member of the Conseil d'Etat.
83 McPhee, *Social History*, p. 182.
84 Horace Chauvet, *Histoire du parti républicain dans les Pyrénées-Orientales (1830–1877) d'après des documents et des souvenirs inédits* (Perpignan, 1909), pp. 5–6.
85 Anceau, *Napoléon III*, p. 181–93.
86 I. Pereire, *Chemins de fer*, pp. 127, 129.
87 AN/MC VIII/1648, notaire Fould, 'Disposition testamentaire' 18 July 1847, and 'Inventaire', 26 December 1851.
88 Along with Adolphe d'Eichthal, Ernest André, Léon Faucher, the duc de Mouchy, and its President, the comte de Germiny. AN, F12/6775, Crédit Foncier de France, Décrets sur les sociétés de Crédit Foncier et les statuts de la *Société de Crédit Foncier* (Paris, May 1853).
89 I. Pereire, *Chemins de fer*, pp. 149–50.
90 Alain Plessis, *Régents et Gouverneurs de la Banque de France sous le Second Empire* (Geneva, 1985), pp. 228–9, fn. 569. Cibiel had been a deputy for the Aveyron under the July Monarchy and was soon to become President of the Crédit Foncier.
91 Archives Nationales du Monde du Travail (hereafter ANMT), 78 AQ 6, Compagnie des Chemins de Fer du Midi et du Canal Latéral à la Garonne, *Statuts* (Paris, 1852). The act was signed on 5 November 1852.
92 I. Pereire, *Chemins de fer*, p. 151.
93 M. Aycard, *Histoire du Crédit Mobilier, 1852–1867* (Paris, 1867), pp. 31–2.
94 Ferguson, *World's Banker*, Chapter 16, covers this at length.

5

Capitalism and the State

Almost twelve months after the *coup d'état* and a matter of days before he declared himself Emperor, following a plebiscite, Louis-Napoléon Bonaparte issued a decree establishing the Société Générale de Crédit Mobilier.¹ The timing was as symbolic of the direction in which he intended to take his Empire as it was of the speed with which he intended it to travel. The decision was taken boldly, some said rashly, with neither recommendation nor support from the Conseil d'État whose role it was under the Code de Commerce to approve such proposals.² And if the Banque de France had expected either to be consulted or to sight a draft edict, as was customary, its 200 principal shareholders were disappointed.³

The Crédit Mobilier was a powerful instrument in the expansion of French capitalism, the lynch-pin which facilitated a revolution in banking and heavy industry. It provided capital to fuel the needs of a resurgent rail industry which emerged under the Second Empire. It invested in shipping, the heavy demand of which for raw materials, processed metals and manufactures expanded exponentially over the next twenty years. It invested in raw materials essential to these manufactures – coal, iron, lead, zinc and charcoal for coke – and laid the basis for the vertical integration of enterprises which became the hallmark of a twentieth-century economy. The very success of the Crédit Mobilier led to imitation which was pivotal in the growth of large-scale capitalist enterprises in France – the eventual creation of other banks which competed to serve an increasingly sophisticated and demanding market. To a considerable degree, then, the Crédit Mobilier, which differed in so many ways from the bank proposed by the Saint-Simonians, was able to achieve much of the Saint-Simonian project.⁴

While the Pereires had benefited from the rapid rise of sections of the bourgeoisie under Louis-Philippe, they came to typify the economic elite of his successor – influential men having access to privileged information, possessing enormous wealth, politically active in defending their interests, using social networks to forge economic and financial links, paving the way for their businesses through connections if not bribery, cautious of the power which might come to be asserted by the masses. The boundaries between business and government were porous, offering unlimited possibilities. As Jews, they found a generally open society in which their contribution as bankers and financiers was welcomed. But what most characterised these first years of the Second Empire for the Pereires was the elan with which they addressed their many notable enterprises, the sheer breadth of these undertakings, and the extraordinary success they achieved.

Rapport, mutual interests, if not considerable self-interest, were at the core of the Pereires' relationship with Napoléon III, a relationship which was as fundamental to their success as it was to their failure. Their support of his quest for electoral victory had given them a tactical advantage. During the Second Republic after Bonaparte won office, the Pereires, and Emile in particular, were able to capitalise on those good relations. The Crédit Mobilier would not otherwise have come about. The Emperor, whom some – like the Rothschilds – believed to be lazy, disingenuous, impetuous and immoral, was capable of considerable charm and persuasiveness which he displayed towards the Pereires from the outset. For his part, while the support already provided by the Pereires was likely to earn his approval, it was the need of an alternative to the conservative group of elite private bankers, known as the Haute Banque, wealthy, well-established, well-represented on the board of the Banque de France and many of them either Protestant or Jewish, which would prove a more compelling reason to support Emile and Isaac Pereire. This was borne out in March 1852 when, according to Emile, on being consulted about measures which would lead to more vigorous commercial and industrial sectors, his response led to a government decree requiring the Banque de France to lower the discount rate to 3 per cent and to make advances on railway stocks and bonds.[5]

Sudhir Hazareesingh describes the complexity within Bonapartist ideology during the Second Empire as at once 'authoritarian and liberal', 'technocratic and Saint-Simonian', both centralising and decentralising, 'even socialist'.[6] Whatever coherent political views the Pereires entertained, however, they were well suited to Napoléon III's inconsistent policies and programmes. Social stability based on economic prosperity, facilitated, as

Roger Price has described, by 'massive infrastructure investment, urban renewal, and trade treaties' – these were entirely compatible with the Pereires' own recipe for social and economic progress. Less certain was their support for the bloody suppression of republicans which went hand in hand with the regime in its early years, and the use of police spies to maintain control of a more liberal Empire. But 'political liberalisation' achieved through universal manhood suffrage was not a strong element in their political values either.[7]

Napoléon III's ideological flexibility worked, however, and while he experienced difficulties in the later years of his reign his hold on power at this point appeared unshakeable. He in turn rapidly developed a reliance on the Pereires' capacities, in particular their skills as implementers, their malleability and their willingness to cooperate and support his grand plans, for which he rewarded them. Rothschild, with his conservative approach to banking, his strong Orléanist connections, and his private antipathy for the Emperor and his policies was, at least at the beginning, denied the same access.

The Second Empire was a politically fluid period which demanded skilful navigation. The Emperor aside, the Pereires were dealing with political figures whose towering ambitions and subtly diverse political allegiances and agendas created a hazardous path. Most had come lately to the Bonapartist cause and some had been associated with the July Monarchy. Several had ties to Saint-Simonianism. The ministries touching on the Pereires' interests were also sensitive ones and the Finance portfolio in particular was occupied during the early Second Empire by three significant players. Jean-Martial Bineau (1852–55) had links to other Saint-Simonians as a former polytechnician and graduate of the École des Mines. Pierre Magne (1855–61), originally an Orléanist, had rallied to the Bonapartist cause during the Second Republic. Achille Fould (1852) had been a deputy during the July Monarchy and was a major figure during the Second Republic. His initial support of the Pereires waned as the pace of their activities accelerated and eventually he was to withdraw it. Each one of these ministers brought to the table different policy priorities and attitudes towards the Pereires. Railway development initially fell within the remit of Magne in a newly-integrated and expanded Ministry of Agriculture, Commerce amd Public Works. During 1855–63 it came within the ambit of Eugène Rouher as Minister for Agriculture, Commerce and Public Works, a figure with whom the Pereires for much, although not all of the time, were on relatively good terms.

Other personalities came into play and the Pereires chose their connections skilfully. First, there were members of the Emperor's personal staff.

Aside from Auguste Chevalier, Louis-Napoléon's first secretary and director of cabinet, the Pereires' most useful connection by far was Chevalier's successor, Jean-François Mocquard, issue of a family of Bordeaux *négociants*. Recognised as a 'reliable and sensible adviser', Mocquard was, until his death in 1864, Napoléon III's closest collaborator.[8] Through him, Emile found access to the Emperor and the most senior levels of government with relative ease. No doubt there was some degree of bribery or at least personal favour involved in these relationships, an issue which we shall come to more broadly in due course. But some form of corruption was surely at the heart of their relationship with the duc de Morny, Louis Napoléon's half-brother, a key figure in the *coup d'état* of 1851. Morny, whose own business interests and networks were legendary, was an active participant in the Pereires' business circle during the early years of the Second Empire, becoming a foundation board member of the Crédit Mobilier while he was also President of the Corps Législatif, the successor to the Chambre des Députés.

After a long gestation the Crédit Mobilier which emerged in 1852 bore some slight resemblance to the bank envisioned by the Saint-Simonians in the 1820s and 1830s, although over time its nature would change. At the outset the Pereires probably saw a continuum also. But the circumstances in which the bank was created owed something to the well-known advice given to the Prince-President by his then Minister of State Achille Fould: 'It is absolutely essential that you free yourself from the tutelage of Rothschild who reigns in spite of you.'[9] Fould aspired to marshal the pool of middle- and working-class savings, thus creating a substantial financial resource which would generate industrial development. Others close to the Prince-President also claimed credit for creation of the Crédit Mobilier, including the duc de Persigny, Minister for the Interior 1852–54 and again in 1860–63, Ambassador to Britain in the intervening years.[10] Models existed in the Société Générale de Belgique of 1822 and the Banque de Belgique of 1836, both aiming to invest in industry.[11] But it was Achille Fould's brother Benoît, senior partner in B. L. Fould and Fould-Oppenheim, who, so impressed by Jules Mirès' privately-owned Caisse des Actions Réunies (itself influenced by the Belgian banks) with share capital of a mere five million francs, saw in it the prototype for the Crédit Mobilier and the vehicle through which his brother's dictate might be achieved.[12] Benoît Fould understood the potential and the timeliness of the idea: if Mirès could achieve success with only limited resources then others might do even better. He looked for these others and: 'I found nobody ... more suitable for this task than MM. Emile and Isaac Pereire. These gentlemen who, independent of their great qualities in terms of morality and intelligence, had written on the formation of analogous enterprises, had thus a spirit prepared for this objective.'[13]

Emile and Isaac Pereire had earlier proposed to Persigny a bank focused on investment in public works (a 'banque commanditaire des travaux publics'), to provide capital to complete the railway network, add value to associated industries and lower interest rates in the rail industry. This bank would also assist in reducing government expenditure on subsidies to rail companies. It was a direct descendant of the bank described in Saint-Simonian literature. The entity which emerged as the Crédit Mobilier, launched on the Bourse on 23 November 1852, was not formally a bank, however, since it was not entitled to issue money.[14] It was historic, nevertheless. For the first time in France banking shares were placed within the reach of smaller shareholders.[15] While the immediate events leading to its creation are unclear, Benoît Fould's comment indicates there were negotiations between the brothers, Louis-Napoléon and Persigny to discuss their plan.[16] But when Isaac Pereire became Deputy President in 1852, Emile was not even a member of the board. And despite the comparative ease with which the bank came into existence its commercial freedom was restricted from the outset. Government determined board membership and that of the committee of management. Capital was limited to sixty million francs made up of 120,000 shares at 500 francs each.[17] Shares to the value of forty million francs were issued initially, the remainder by 1854. But while the limitation on share capital was to prove an impediment which the Pereires attempted to circumvent in various ways (even so, only the Banque de France's capital was higher), the shares had reached a value of 1,982 francs by 1856.[18] Crédit Mobilier statutes also empowered it to issue interest-bearing bonds ['obligations'], a means to compensate for the limitation on share capital. But the government placed limits on the issue of short-term bonds and on the ratio of bonds issued to total capital, and this became a more serious impediment as the Crédit Mobilier's activities expanded, in the rest of Europe as well as in France.

The Pereires held broad ambitions for the Crédit Mobilier becoming, as Isaac was to say, a 'centre sufficiently powerful to bind together' the great businesses of the country.[19] There were precedents in the Saint-Simonian literature. Isaac himself in 1831 had sketched a plan for the new bank, and Olinde Rodrigues called on bankers to 'focus their attention on the whole of the financial system of industrial peoples'.[20] In 1830, Enfantin had written that 'we find in the bank the germ of a directing institution, of a veritable government of industry'.[21] Over time, according to Isaac, the Crédit Mobilier would facilitate uniformity in the value of railways securities and provide a central source for mounting loans to railway companies.

Other measures laid down in the statutes were essentially facilitative, allowing it to raise loans for private and public enterprises (with the exception of foreign loans which required the approval of government); to exchange loans, commercial bills, shares and bonds for other securities; and to lend against securities.[22]

The Pereires recognised the demand for different levels of banking, which their direct involvement in establishing the Comptoir d'Escompte and the Crédit Foncier confirmed and which the Saint-Simonian literature supported. The Crédit Mobilier was intended as an integral part of these comparatively new institutions, one focused on the financial needs of big business and which would drive the French economy. Thus while government limitations placed a serious brake on their ambition the Pereires were not deterred, pursuing their goal doggedly until the end.

The Crédit Mobilier founders, replete with eminent bankers and financiers, tell us much about the value of the new enterprise to the regime and of the social distance already travelled by the Pereires. They actually included members of the Haute Banque among whom we count the Pereires' long-time supporter Adolphe d'Eichthal; Ernest André of André et Cottier; Benoît Fould of Fould-Oppenheim; the banker and industrialist Baron Achille Seillière; and Charles Mallet of Mallet *frères*.[23] The first Director of the Paris Comptoir d'Escompte, Hippolyte-Guillaume Biesta, was also a founding member, as were Frédéric Grieninger of J.-P. Pescatore et Cie; and representatives of the German banking houses, Salomon Oppenheim of Cologne and Salomon Heine of Hamburg. The widow of a member of the Beauharnais family, Her Imperial Highness the Princesse de Leuchtenberg, the duc de Mouchy, and the duc de Galliera gave symbolic weight and status. Finally, Benoît Fould himself became President, testament to the leading role played by the Fould bank in the exercise.[24] A notable omission was James de Rothschild.

The Pereires were well aware that their future lay in the hands not only of Louis-Napoléon Bonaparte but of their recent mentor. They needed the support of the former while mitigating the opposition of the latter. James de Rothschild had written to Louis-Napoléon just before the Crédit Mobilier's public launch, warning of the folly of such a move: inflation, unbridled speculation, industrial monopoly.[25] This opposition to the Pereires' initiative never wavered. Only a few years later, Persigny, now Ambassador, wrote to the Emperor from London following a meeting there with Rothschild and two of his nephews, including the head of the London house, Lionel. 'On occasion this establishment would compromise the public wealth, at other times it would become so rich and powerful that it would soon be in a position to exert pressure on the government', Rothschild stormed. But James' irritation with the Pereires (and, indeed, with Adolphe d'Eichthal) was also personal, as Lionel pointed out: 'After having made their debut as financiers in his firm, they have been known to have slighted him in several ways', in particular in their purchase of land at Armainvilliers and Crécy, close to the Rothschild château of Ferrières.[26] The intense personal irritation, on this reading, resulted from the effrontery of his former employees in deserting him so publicly.

Whatever the explanation for this fit of bile, however – irritation with upstarts, wounded vanity, professional disdain for what he saw as risky banking policies and practices, fear of serious competition supported by the Emperor, indeed, most likely all of these – the Pereires were looking to create their own great wealth independent of Rothschild. Jules Mirès maintained that the Pereires had at first looked to Rothschild for moral support, even reserving a place on the Crédit Mobilier board for him.[27] Landes also suggested that Rothschild had been offered a 'share [in the Crédit Mobilier] not commensurate with the dignity of his house', and had thus refused.[28] But by 1852 they were already in a position to gather around them an impressive cast without him, indicative of the confidence which they inspired and the perceived importance of their enterprise. The bank was to become their creature, the means by which, over the next fifteen years, they developed a network of alliances placing them at the centre of Parisian business life and beyond.

Emile and Isaac Pereire took 11,446 shares at a total value of 5,723,000 francs. They and the Fould Bank, together with the Fould-Oppenheim Bank, held a commanding 30 per cent of the initial share capital of forty million francs.[29]

Others registered as shareholders from this first day also repay examination, however. They included relatives: their brothers-in-law Charles Sarchi and Henri Baud; Olinde Rodrigues' widow, Euphrasie; and Isaac's former mother-in-law, the widow of their uncle, Jacob Lopès Fonseca. There were the Pereires' long-standing engineering colleagues Eugène Flachat and Emile Clapeyron. And there were Sephardim, Auguste Furtado of Bayonne and Jules Mirès now in Paris. The Pereires also gave twenty-five shares to the Sephardic synagogue in Paris.[30] All their interests and predilections are apparent, in the inclusion of family and friends, of Saint-Simonian colleagues and of Sephardim from the southwest as well as from Paris in an unusual form of *sedaca*. Their own investment demonstrated their confidence in the new enterprise.

Ill-health brought the premature retirement of Benoît Fould before the first annual general meeting early in 1854, and Isaac Pereire stepped into the breach. He was now forty-seven years old, brilliant, impressive, a seasoned board member and a man of considerable vision. He had been Emile's deputy for the better part of twenty years and, given his frustrating experience with the Paris–Lyon–Avignon project, was ready for the task. All his working life to that point prepared him for this role.[31] It was only then, in 1854, that Emile too joined the board. At that first shareholders' meeting Isaac dealt at length with the bank's rationale and its ambitious agenda in terms redolent of Saint-Simonian discourse. The fundamental problem for the French economy, he told the gathering, had been the insufficiency of credit offered to large enterprises. New competitive sources of capital were essential to the development of public and industrial credit. He spoke of the need to centralise the finances and administration of large companies, and especially those of the railways, to ensure maximum potential profitability and shareholder returns. He saw the Crédit Mobilier as a new fiduciary agent which would 'make prosperous the most humble savings as well as the most considerable'. Its first duty was, however, to develop national industry and assist in establishing major companies. While he did not rule out acquiring shares in existing businesses, nor in subscribing to bonds, these were secondary at that stage.[32] Commercial pragmatism had tempered Saint-Simonianism. Reality was to moderate it further.

The Crédit Mobilier advanced credit to and also took equity in start-up organisations and within heavy industries which were at a comparatively early stage. But in many cases guarantees were not provided if they were even demanded. To quarantine the considerable risk inherent in this approach and as a means of monitoring performance, Crédit Mobilier board members became directors of affiliated organisations.[33] The Pereires themselves played a dominant role in all of them. The Crédit Mobilier's statutes also authorised it to fulfil administrative functions on behalf of the companies in which it held an interest. It could maintain current accounts, recover debts, pay interest or dividends on presentation of a coupon and maintain an office for the deposit of securities.[34] Most companies with which the Pereires were associated used the bank in this fashion. But while these means of oversight and control were set in train to alert the bank to possible crises, the vigilance of directors was critical to their success.[35]

The Pereires also bought shares on their own account in all the companies in which the Crédit Mobilier had an interest. Their concern seems to have been for the long haul rather than the short term, to see companies grow and expand rather than to take quick profits. But profits they made nonetheless. Dividends declared in the Crédit Mobilier's first years alone delivered them handsome returns, from almost 12 per cent on investment to more than 40 per cent in 1855.[36]

The Crédit Mobilier was not designed to provide investment capital for small business. Neither was the Comptoir National d'Escompte, founded with Pereire support and involvement in 1848, nor the recently established public mortgage bank, the Crédit Foncier, of which Emile had been one of the principal founders and a board member. Together with Benoît Fould, in May 1853 the Pereires attempted to address this deficiency in a proposal to form a Caisse Centrale des Sociétés de Crédit Mutuel, a bank which would provide the necessary capital through principles of mutuality.[37] They were experimenting with an approach to the organisation of work which had grown in significance during 1848–51 when more than 50,000 workers organised in 300 associations based on trades. This essentially socialist movement, debated by the Saint-Simonians, had been suppressed in the wake of the *coup d*'état.[38] But it provided the two brothers with the kernel of some of their most innovative ideas: 'associations' of workers engaged in related industries.

They claimed that their memory of open confrontation between capital and labour in 1848 had influenced their decision to direct effort towards small-scale entrepreneurs and tradespeople. The 'superior classes' had a responsibility not simply to relieve the misery of the working class, but to 'stimulate their endeavours, to emancipate and ennoble them industrially'.[39] Their submission to the Conseil d'État emphasised the lack of credit available to enterprises employing fewer than ten people: of nearly 65,000 entrepreneurs in Paris, scarcely 2,000 had an account with the Comptoir National d'Escompte.[40]

The submission, probably drafted by Emile Pereire, underscored the proposed bank's social purpose, affirming that: 'a practical experience of twenty-five years has given rise in me, in regard to moral and industrial qualities, [the conviction] that the love of work and of family develops in the most modest workshops'. The Pereires conceived their bank in Saint-Simonian terms, 'to assure the independence of "workers" in respect of "capitalists"'; effectively a reinvention of the corporation 'on a liberal base', accommodating contemporary needs with principles of equality. *Sociétés* would be formed in affinity groups based on trades. A *syndicat* elected by members would manage the affairs of the bank. Measures would be taken to keep interest rates low and to maintain efficiencies commensurate with 'the classic bank'.[41]

The Second Empire was a period of rapid growth in the number of small enterprises, many of which did not long survive, but this did not render the Crédit Mutuel any more appealing to the Conseil d'État. The Emperor's signing off on the Crédit Mobilier only six months previously, without the knowledge or consent of the Conseil, was probably prejudicial to its success. The idea fell by the wayside, to be raised again only when the Pereires launched an attack against the Banque de France in 1864.[42]

The Pereires' support for new financial institutions was matched by the promise of new financial instruments for which they used the Crédit Mobilier as a platform. The Crédit Mobilier attempted unsuccessfully to introduce short-term interest-bearing bonds as a means of extending its capital base.[43] Another of their ideas, a security available in every country in Europe, the *omnium*, had gestated from the 1820s when it was a subject discussed within Saint-Simonian circles. Emile had drafted a paper on a 'Union financière: Omnium Européen-Dette Cosmopolite' with a capital of 100,000 francs based on *rentes*. He saw in it a tool for the maintenance of international peace and harmony.[44] Isaac referred to it again thirty years later at a shareholders' meeting of the Crédit Mobilier, describing it as serving a function similar to those of bonds, commercial bills, bills of exchange, even bank bills, diminishing differences in interest rates and of rates of exchange from place to place, potentially lowering interest rates in the process. He also spoke of a bill of credit circulating throughout Europe, extending and accelerating the application of credit, increasing the pool of available capital and thus its impact on the economy.[45]

The principal objective of the Crédit Mobilier enshrined in its statutes was essentially the development of rail. The first venture in addressing this primary goal concerned the Chemin de Fer du Midi which struck financial trouble almost immediately after the concession had been awarded to the Pereires. In 1853 the Midi formally entered an arrangement with the Crédit Mobilier which took on the railway company's financial functions while extending a loan at interest.[46] The Midi was so personally important to them that in the same year Emile stood for election to the Conseil général of the Gironde department, one of an increasing number of businessmen to enter the regional councils, from which he was able to develop business and personal interests almost as significant as those in Paris.[47] The Midi was to encounter many difficulties throughout its history, not the least of them financial, but it was the vehicle which enabled the Pereires to compete seriously for the hotly contested line through the Pyrenees.

The Midi pressed on with the line from Bordeaux to Bayonne, blessed with the quality of engineering skill available to it. Eugène Flachat was despatched to Bordeaux to oversee construction which had been contracted to a British company advised by Isambard Kingdom Brunel, principally because the rail track was manufactured in England to a Brunel design. 'Succeed [in this project]', Brunel is reputed to have written, 'and the Crystal Palace will be a thing of the past.' But as the English company fell further and further behind its schedule Flachat and Brunel disagreed openly on most matters.[48] As a result of these delays Emile pressured Magne into accepting a lowering of tariffs on iron imports, a significant step in itself towards liberalising trade with Britain.[49] Eventually, however, after the opening in 1855 of the Bordeaux railway station, Saint-Jean, inauguration of the line to Bayonne took place the following year.

The Midi was not their only rail venture in these early years. The PSG and the Paris–Versailles (Rive Droite) together became the cornerstone of a much larger concern which ultimately, in 1855, through integration with lines from Paris to Rouen, to Rennes, and to Calais, led to the new Compagnie de l'Ouest. Achieving an acceptable and workable financial structure for the merger was laboured and difficult, taking over four years for the Pereires, particularly Isaac, to negotiate a solution with the other rail lines and their shareholders, who included English bankers as well as French. As founders and original shareholders of the PSG and of the Paris-Versailles (Rive Droite), the Pereires stood to gain considerable benefit from liquidating the two companies. Their initial investment provided them with substantial dividends as the share price of the new company rose from 500 to 1,800 francs. More importantly, as founders and Emile an original shareholder, they shared in the distribution of 5 per cent on capital and in one-third of the profits.[50] The PSG, for which six million francs had been so difficult to cobble together in the 1830s, was sold for over 60 million francs.[51] The complex transaction completed, Emile remained for the next ten years a director and member of the committee of management of the Ouest, the Crédit Mobilier investing eighteen million francs in bonds.[52] The Crédit Mobilier invested heavily in the Paris–Strasbourg line also, thus becoming the major shareholder in the Compagnie de l'Est and Emile a director.

The Pereires were not always so acute when it came to negotiating their way through the ambitions of others. The case of the Grand Central in which the Crédit Mobilier's investment in April 1853 was to become a saga, unlike the equally unmanageable Paris–Versailles (Rive Droite) ultimately did not turn to their profit. The ambition to link the mining potential of the Massif Central to centres of processing and markets was a task easier said than done: indeed, after an initial feasibility study Emile and Isaac Pereire were lukewarm at best about the proposition, Isaac describing the impossibly mountainous terrain, 'the least populated of central France', and the paucity of industry.[53] The project, entailing 3,000 kilometres of rail at a cost of one billion francs, was as ambitious as it was risky. But when a director of the Crédit Mobilier, the duc de Morny, who was not only a deputy for the region but the long-time President of the Conseil général of Puy-du-Dôme, became President of the Grand Central, there was a more compelling reason to cooperate, and the Pereires did.[54]

Railways with direct links to Paris were obviously the most desirable concessions because the most immediately profitable, but while the Midi held potential benefits it did not have access to the capital city. This forced the Pereires in the first place to seek accommodation with one of their rivals, François Bartholony, and his Paris–Orléans–Bordeaux line which included construction of the iron Saint-Jean Bridge over the Garonne River, Gustave Eiffel's first major commission.

The Credit Mobilier's strategy through the Grand Central was targeted towards securing direct access to Paris and the Mediterranean. It invested carefully in small lines such as the Rhône et Loire railway which potentially would give them these benefits. The Pereires also contemplated an alternative link between Lyon and Paris, the Bourbonnais, which posed a particular threat to the Talabots whose plans for a Paris–Lyon–Méditerranée (PLM) line were in a final stage. Eventually, in 1857, the Pereires were bested in a ruthless game which saw the Grand Central liquidated and parcelled out between Bartholony's Paris–Orléans–Bordeaux and Talabot's PLM. The Midi benefited hardly at all.[55] At Rouher's prompting, Emile Pereire wrote to the Emperor in a very direct way, making his case that the lines attributed to the Grand Central must be annexed by the Midi, complaining of the jealousy, the lies and slander which had been spread against the Crédit Mobilier by hostile competitors and by French and foreign presses.[56] It yielded nothing. There was worse: both Morny and the duc de Galliera, until then supporters of the Pereires, now sought accommodation with the opposition, of Rothschild, Talabot and Bartholony.

Possibly there was some compensatory relation between the loss of the Grand Central and their winning the Pyrenean concession. To complete the task, effectively to extend the line from Bordeaux to Madrid and thus link Paris with the Spanish capital, they needed resources and political support. The Emperor may have interceded with Queen Isabella II of Spain and her ministers on their behalf.[57] The Spanish government, despite the chronic political and economic instability which characterised Isabella's reign, had approved in 1856 the establishment of the Crédit Mobilier Espagnol (Crédito Mobiliario Español), its role to raise loans for the State and to finance railways and other enterprises, to operate in a manner similar to that of the Crédit Mobilier of France.[58] The Empress' brother-in-law, the duc d'Albe, was among the first investors. The Crédit

Mobilier Espagnol in turn sought the concession to construct the rail line between Madrid and Irun, a Spanish town just over the French border and not far from Bayonne, which the Spanish government granted. Two years later, in 1858, the Chemin de Fer du Nord de l'Espagne (Compañía de los Caminos de Hierro del Norte de España) came into being.[59] The Rothschilds' Madrid, Zaragoza & Alicante Railway Company (MZA), servicing southern Spain and linking Madrid, was created the same year.

This was not their only potential entry to Spain, however, and mindful of the possibilities opened by their connection to Perpignan, the Pereires managed to advance the works to Toulouse by August 1856 and to Sète eight months later, with the ambition to open a second line through Perpignan to Barcelona.[60] The line to Toulouse would also facilitate a direct link with Marseille, connecting the Mediterranean with the Atlantic Ocean, and thus competing with the Talabots' PLM which emerged in 1857, with Rothschild support, from an amalgamation of the Paris–Lyon and the Lyon–Avignon–Marseille rail lines.

On 22 April 1857, the Pereires executed their own public relations coup when two trains, one from Bordeaux carrying Emile and the other leaving Sète with Isaac on board, met symbolically in Toulouse to launch the new line. In a spontaneous gesture, the brothers leapt from their respective carriages and flung themselves into each other's arms, happy, as Isaac was to write much later, and probably much relieved, to have completed the task entrusted to them and 'to the achievement of which they had attached the honour of their life'.[61] In recognition of the achievement, Napoléon III promoted Emile to Officier of the Légion d'Honneur.[62] The establishment by the Pereires of a further rail company in Spain that year, to operate between Seville and Cordoba, may have contributed to the honour.

The French railway network had suffered during the Second Republic and languished into the early years of the Second Empire, however: twenty-eight concessions granted by 1852 with no overall plan and with inadequate financing. The Crimean War of 1854–56 imposed a severe brake on railway investment. The Crédit Mobilier committed 250 million francs to the State loan in 1855. The fate of the Grand Central had taught the government salutary lessons about the cost of constructing important but less profitable lines. Gradually, Magne, succeeded by Rouher and supported by the able Director of the Ponts et Chaussées, Alfred de Franqueville, had begun to overhaul the system, encouraging the integration of lines of lesser significance. A convention in 1857 rationalised the number of railway concessions to six main routes which drew the secondary lines within their orbit, and extended the length of concessions to ninety-nine years. The Midi formed one of the six together with the Nord, the Ouest, the Est, the Paris–Lyon–Méditerranée and the Paris–Orléans–Bordeaux. The companies for their part agreed to the construction of a second network of 2,500 kilometres of less important lines, a commitment which imposed considerable financial burden. A further convention in 1859 forced the government to guarantee the interest payable on railway bonds which in turn became repayable by the companies in the future. This solution to railways financing thus drew the State and the entrepreneurs into an insoluble bond which the Pereires attempted subsequently to renegotiate.[63]

While the Midi allowed them to contemplate Spain, the company also directed their attention to profitable opportunities closer to home. Napoléon III had signed legislation in 1854 and in 1857 for the draining and reafforestation of the department of the Landes in southwest France. The Pereires established their own company to undertake this task. The Société Pereire pour la Mise en Valeur des Landes capitalised at eighteen million francs, owed something to pressure exerted by Euryale Cazeaux, the Saint-Simonian from Bordeaux and now a senior hydrographic engineer. The Pereires eventually purchased over 10,000 hectares of the Landes which their company proceeded to drain and desalinate, to restore with pine plantations, to support with agricultural produce and its marketing, and to construct roads. The Midi brought a further 300 kilometres of rail to the area.[64] This venture in the Landes exemplifies in microcosm the Pereires' business strategy: integration of inter-dependent activities, in this case of rail – iron mining and metals for rail construction, pine plantations to provide timber for sleepers, agricultural produce to be transported by rail.

From the outset the Pereires entertained international ambitions and understood that the projects on which they had embarked had immense international ramifications. While the Crédit Mobilier's statutes focused initially on rail investment, they also encouraged broader interests. It was after all a 'Société générale'. Lack of investment capital in shipping and marine infrastructure, ports and harbours, underscored France's exclusion from the profitable sea trade between Europe and America, depending on Liverpool as the intermediary point of departure for French agricultural goods and merchandise and thus presenting a significant commercial opportunity. Early in 1855 an act constituting the Compagnie Générale Maritime (hereafter CGM) was passed with a capital of thirty million francs, its founding shareholders now including Isaac's son Eugène, on the threshold of his own distinguished career. In a pattern reminiscent of the Midi the board included a number of Sephardic friends and acquaintances – Télèphe Astruc, Casimir Salvador and Camille Lopès Dubec – as well as the Avignonais Adolphe Crémieux. Adolphe d'Eichthal became President. While the Crédit Mobilier was the principal investor, François Marie Delessert and Charles Mallet, both prominent Protestant bankers, were also substantial shareholders.

The Pereires saw the CGM as a means to exploit trade with South America, particularly in cod fishing and meat and tallow imports. Ultimately, however, the CGM aimed to secure the lucrative postal contract between France and North America which carried a generous government subsidy, and to compete with English and American shipping companies in providing transatlantic services to the principal ports in North and South America. More immediately profitable, however, was another arrangement with the Minister for the Marine, the transportation of thousands of Chinese and Indian coolies to the colonies of Guadeloupe and Martinique. This trade in 'free' labour lasted into the 1860s, by which time 18,000 Indian, Chinese and African labourers had been transported at considerable profit to the Pereires' company.[65]

The Pereires were fully aware of the nature of the cargoes and it is obvious from their writings and from reports to shareholders that it did not distress them. Neither evinced any moral difficulty, indeed they justified it as economically imperative. They had each written critically about slavery in the past, but now disingenuously defended the introduction of indentured labour to the Antilles as a legitimate means of compensating for shortages resulting from slavery's abolition. The CGM was not simply transporting produce, they argued, but bringing resources and work into a better relation. Labour shortfalls, once addressed 'spontaneously' through colonisation and emigration, must now be regulated by government intervention, and the company must be one of government's principal instruments.[66] The ambivalence within the Bordeaux merchant community – including the Sephardim – in its attitude towards emancipation of slaves in the French colonies may have contributed to this conflicted morality. Hit hard by an international economic crisis in 1857, the company only survived through injections of funds from the Crédit Mobilier, and it was transportation of indentured labour from India and China which saved it.

The CGM's establishment signalled that their ambitions were not confined to France or even to Europe. The propensity to look broadly for business opportunities had much to do with their acculturation in a Sephardic diaspora whose merchants, trading practices and finance had spread across the Atlantic to the Caribbean and as far afield as China. Bordeaux had been a singular node in this trading network, consolidating the city's position over a century or more. The Saint-Simonian ideas the Pereires absorbed, tinged as these ideas were with France's 'civilising mission', reinforced the experience of the Sephardic diaspora. Isaac Pereire certainly saw a greater degree of unity between the countries, telling the shareholders of the Crédit Mobilier in 1856 that solutions to the world's problems may indeed reside in the union of all the principal establishments of Europe,

> in the fusion that they can bring about between apparently opposing interests, in the compensation that they can find, whether through a division of work appropriate to the genius and the needs of the diverse countries, whether through the immense development in general consumption that the lowering of certain barriers produces.[67]

Inexplicably, in view of their success in railways, banking and urban development, the Pereires vastly underestimated the problems involved in running a shipping company, and their efforts to develop trade with France's colonies met with aggressive competition. Initially at least, and indeed for the only time, they failed to gather around them the same technical competence they enjoyed with their railways. Company records show a series of chief executives between 1855 and 1861, only resolved with the appointment in 1861 of Léonce Goyetche, a shipbuilder from Bayonne.[68]

From the outset, all the Crédit Mobilier's excursions beyond the French border owed at least something to the Emperor's view of the bank as an instrument of his foreign policy. While the diplomats at the Quai d'Orsay did not necessarily give the same priority to international commerce as the Emperor, the Second Empire was a period of heightened international economic activity nevertheless.[69] To encourage Austrian neutrality in the face of a possible alliance with Russia, the Pereires in 1855 willingly negotiated contracts with the Austro-Hungarian Imperial Government on behalf of the Crédit Mobilier and the Crédit Foncier, and significant railway ventures as well. The Austrian government took the initiative with Isaac in facilitating establishment of the Société Autrichienne des Chemins de Fer de l'État in partnership with Austrian financiers, capitalised at 200 million francs.[70] This extremely profitable venture ceded to the company railways, both existing and to come, in Austria, Hungary and Bohemia, land and properties, forests, mines, metallurgical works and rolling stock.[71] The Pereires took significant positions in this venture: Isaac Pereire as President of the Paris section, which effectively controlled the enterprise, Emile Pereire on the board, together with d'Eichthal, Casimir Salvador, Victor-Alexandre Bailleux de Marisy (the former prefect and financier), Charles Mallet and Henri Germain (who was to become a founder of the Crédit Lyonnais). When Gustave Pereire wrote of the denouement much later, however, he reflected the residual irritation of the Pereires themselves when, with the Treaty of Paris signed, Napoléon III had no further use for either the commercial interests thus opened nor for Austrian neutrality. His thoughts were already moving towards Italy.[72]

The foray of the Pereires into Austria did provoke the alarm of the Rothschild family who had found threatening enough the establishment in 1853 with considerable Pereire investment of the Darmstädter Bank für Handel und Industrie, along the lines of the Crédit Mobilier and located close to Frankfurt.[73] But while the Pereires had challenged them in Spain and in the Grand Duchy of Hesse-Kassel, Vienna was Rothschild turf. They launched a retaliatory attack, one which led in 1855 to the creation of the investment bank the Creditanstalt of Vienna, a response to the Pereires' incursion and a direct imitation of the Crédit Mobilier.[74] The Rothschilds and Talabots also deprived the Pereires of the Lombard railways. Thus were the Pereires in turn troubled: by the profligacy of Napoléon III and by the growing aggression of some members of the Haute Banque, concerned to protect their interests against the newcomers. There continued to be considerable interchange between members of the banking fraternity, nevertheless. Benoît Fould, Delessert, Mallet and Adolphe d'Eichthal, all of whom were directors in Pereire companies, were also members of the Haute Banque.

The Exposition Universelle which took place in 1855 was hugely popular but financially disastrous, losing over eight million francs during its course. It was the first of Napoléon III's grandiose imperial festivals, designed to emulate the triumph of the British Great Exhibition at the Crystal Palace in 1851. For Emile Pereire, who had been appointed to the Imperial Commission overseeing the Exposition, the role was not merely ceremonial, for the Pereires were awarded in the process, somewhat controversially, contracts to create infrastructure necessary to accommodate the more than five million visitors who flocked to the event, infrastructure which compensated Paris to a degree for the financial loss.[75]

The first of these projects, the Compagnie Générale des Omnibus de Paris, was expected to provide for the public transport needs of Parisians, and to cope with anticipated passenger loads at the Exposition. It drew together eleven existing companies, becoming one year later the Entreprise Générale des Omnibus. In 1855, the company's 347 vehicles carried thirty-six million passengers. The Compagnie Parisienne d'Éclairage et de Chauffage par le Gaz was similarly formed from six existing enterprises, with capital of fifty-five million francs divided into 110,000 shares, of which the Pereires held an advantageous thirty thousand. This company was granted the monopoly for the lighting of Paris and, later, for its heating. Eugène Pereire became a director of this company together with his father Isaac and his uncle. Maintaining tariffs at an economic level for both omnibuses and gas was in each case an important element of the respective agreements but so was the monopoly it gave the companies: for thirty years and fifty years respectively.[76]

Bonapartist symbolism, linking the nephew with his uncle, Napoléon I, continued to underpin the Second Empire. Extension of the colonnaded rue de Rivoli from the Louvre to the Hôtel de Ville, a project begun by Napoléon I, would be completed by Napoléon III and thus contribute to the mystique. There were difficulties gaining interest in developing the land which was mooted early in the tenure of Baron Georges Haussmann who became Prefect of the Seine only in 1853. Through a heavily discounted price negotiated on the land value in exchange for tight construction commitments due to the opening of the Exposition, the Pereires were persuaded to purchase the land to extend the rue de Rivoli and to undertake construction of several significant pieces of tourism infrastructure: a major hotel, the Grand Hôtel du Louvre; a department store, Les Grands Magasins du Louvre; and fine dwellings.[77] For this purpose they established the Société des Immeubles de la Rue de Rivoli, an enterprise which also included Adolphe d'Eichthal, Ernest André and Charles Mallet. The Grand Hôtel du Louvre, in which a final soirée brought the Exposition Universelle to a close, impressed the visitors, particularly British tourists, as the *Illustrated London News* reported of it in October 1855:

> An hotel covering 800 square metres of space, and containing 800 rooms – where the coffee-making needs a separate and distinct department – where machinery lifts dishes and luggage from the ground-floor to the fourth story [sic], and where electric wires govern clocks distributed in every part of the vast building, is a novelty even in this extraordinary time.[78]

The founders of the new company certainly did not see its purpose confined to the rue de Rivoli. It was intended as the cornerstone of building activity throughout Paris when opportunity and necessity allowed. Rental for working-class dwellings was at an all-time high, and housing demand was intense. Nor was the increasing desire for luxury among the wealthy a secondary consideration. Above all, the momentum and prosperity of building activity, fundamental to so many other industries, needed to be sustained. A further consideration was the way in which the company was to be financed: 'We wanted in founding it to put a new form of property within the range of small capitalists and to make profitable the purses of the most humble with benefits that the growth of the Parisian population assures to proprietors of land.' Capital in the rue de Rivoli company, a total of 24 million francs, was therefore to be made up of shares offered at 100 francs, giving small shareholders access to a financial stake.[79] Their entrée into urban development and utilities led to a corresponding interest in insurance. The Confiance dealt with fire and a subsidiary with maritime accidents; another company, the Paternelle, with house insurance.

Napoléon III and Haussmann were not introducing anything new in the way of urban development. To modernise and beautify the city, to clear out and clean up the centre in the interests of its working-class population, to provide clean drinking water and efficient sewerage, all these had long been part of the agenda of the Saint-Simonians, of the July Monarchy, of other 'utopian socialists' Louis Blanc and Charles Fourier. Balzac's *Comédie humaine* is full of references to the deplorable conditions in which Parisians lived in the 1820s and 1830s. The problem had been apparent for decades: only the scale of the solutions under the Second Empire was different.[80]

A Protestant born in Paris of Alsatian heritage, in his roles as Prefect of the departments of the Var and then of the Gironde, Haussmann had been a strong political supporter of the Prince-President. He also had an unassailable and helpful connection to the Bonapartes as Prince Eugène de Beauharnais' godson. Haussmann's vision of the physical changes to Paris was entirely Saint-Simonian in outline, even if this was incidental; moreover, it matched that of the Emperor, translating into a complete renovation of the city – its transport axes, its mix of land uses, its aesthetics, its parks and gardens, its emphasis on health and hygiene, and its dependence on improved infrastructure.[81] These new boulevards and streets certainly fulfilled a strategic defensive military purpose as well, a response to difficulties well-documented from earlier popular uprisings. The boulevards in this reading would thus resist the barricades of 1830 and 1848, providing instead fluid movement of troops and confining militant workers within certain defined areas. They were a means of repression and control. Haussman himself did not deny the importance of straight, wide thoroughfares which would impede the makeshift barricades of previous insurrections.[82] The Pereires for their part, however, were probably not motivated 'to move cavalry and create clear fields of fire against urban insurrectionaries' and certainly did not seek to justify their effort in this way. They owned to have been inspired, rather, by the possibilities of improving markedly the physical and aesthetic qualities of urban life which they expected to achieve at a profit.[83]

All of this rendered the city during much of the Second Empire, as is frequently noted, a gigantic building site which Zola captured so well in *La Curée*, soon after the Empire's demise, and in *L'Assommoir* in 1877. For a considerable period during Haussmann's tenure, 20 per cent of Paris' work force was engaged in the reconstruction of Paris, demolishing 117,000 houses to make way for 215,000 new ones; constructing eighty-five miles of new roads and 700 miles of footpaths; and installing 15,000 gas lamps. Over twenty years from 1850 to 1870, the area of parkland increased nearly a hundred-fold, from forty-seven acres to 4,500 acres.[84] The establishment of what was to be reconstituted in 1856 as the Compagnie Immobilière de Paris was thus a tangible demonstration of the Pereires' support for Napoléon III, the realisation also of their earlier convictions about the imperative to clean up Paris. It was to become the vehicle for redeveloping great swathes of Paris, most evident on the right bank of the Seine.

Meanwhile, the Crédit Mobilier encountered difficulties. Towards the end of 1855 the government refused it authorisation to issue bonds to the value of 120 million francs, twice the sum of its share capital. A few months later, with peace in the Crimea, government issued a note calling a halt to all new enterprises, reflecting fears of inflation in a saturated share market (thirty-three railways and canal companies alone were listed on the Paris Bourse by that year).[85] Both of these measures embarrassed the Pereires in their expansionary plans and to an extent reflected ministerial concerns that the Crédit Mobilier needed to be reined in. Emile Pereire wrote to the Emperor complaining bluntly and bitterly of unfair rivalry, unjustified attacks by the press, and accusations of corruption against them.[86] The bank's difficulties were exacerbated by a general weakness in the economy, brought on by a crisis which started in the United States in August 1857 and spread to England before striking French industry and capital. It exposed deficiencies in the bank's structure and placed in high relief the impact of government control on new capital formation.

Commentators have remarked frequently on the Pereires' capacity to achieve so much through the Crédit Mobilier with so comparatively little.[87] In the space of the first three years in France alone, they brought into being the Midi, invested heavily in the Grand Central, Est and Ouest railways and established the CGM. Mergers leading to the Paris gas lighting and heating company and Paris public transport systems, the rue de Rivoli extension, a tourist hotel, one of the first department stores and two insurance companies, these were all achieved in that brief period. They negotiated public loans to railway companies as well as to the State. But these were the days of major railway development leading to huge profits. The average profit of the Crédit Mobilier in that time was over 14 per cent.[88] Dividends yielded 13.4 per cent (1853), 11.8 per cent (1854) and a massive 40.74 per cent (1855) on investment. In distributing such huge dividends, however, the Pereires were already placing shareholder quiescence before financial prudence and creating major speculative opportunities.

The Rothschilds were not inactive. Concerned about the Pereires' expanding role in European railways and finance and seizing a rare opportunity which found them vulnerable, James de Rothschild sought a more co-ordinated association with other leading houses of the Haute Banque to block the Pereires. The Réunion Financière which emerged, and which included among its number Bartholony, Talabot, the English banker Edward Blount, Galliera and the Belgian Meyer Cahen d'Anvers, was motivated by the desire to compete with the Crédit Mobilier in extending credit to commercial and industrial enterprises, in particular to railways. While Rothschild made efforts to differentiate the new establishment from its rival, he had evidently recanted his earlier negative assessment of the Crédit Mobilier's future and decided that imitation was his best recourse. The Réunion Financière's proposed credit establishment, a Comptoir Impérial des Travaux Publics, du Commerce et de l'Industrie was, however, refused by the Conseil d'État, a response to the government's nervousness about the credit market and excessive speculation, and to its recent agreement to double the capital of the Comptoir National d'Escompte.[89] This was not the end of the matter. In 1857, in a further assault on the Crédit Mobilier, several who had joined with Rothschild, though not Rothschild himself, rallied together British, German and French bankers and industrialists who included Talabot as well as the former Saint-Simonian Arlès-Dufour and erstwhile Pereire supporters in Bischoffsheim and Adrien Delahante.[90] The Minister for Commerce, Eugène Rouher, opposed the proposition vigorously. There was no demonstrable need for it, he argued; it would be rejected by the public (he saw the hand of his rival, Morny); and proposed control mechanisms in its statutes were inadequate. The next year, however, despite the deepening economic crisis, the Conseil d'État did approve the establishment of the Société Générale de Crédit Industriel et Commercial [CIC], an enterprise which included as backers not only Morny, Delahante and associates of the Talabots, but a stalwart of the Pereires, Ernest André.[91]

The Rothschilds had reason for concern as the Crédit Mobilier became the principal source of investment funds for the greater part of the Pereires' enterprises, and for major state loans, the 1850s being a period of vigorous activity when the Crédit Mobilier was responsible for underwriting over half a billion francs to the French government.[92] For his part, Emile Pereire remained on the board of the Nord railway until 1856, presenting himself as a director of the Nord when he took his own place on the board of the Crédit Mobilier. But the Haute Banque in turn was well represented on the Banque de France, and in 1855, James de Rothschild's son Alphonse became a regent, a position hugely influential and capable of inflicting much damage on the Pereires.[93]

The Banque de France had been a target from their Saint-Simonian days. Isaac addressed the role of a central bank in the course of his Lessons at the Athenaeum in 1831 and Emile had written in the *National* in 1834 about the need for reform.[94] In this they were not alone. The Banque de France remained a constant subject of debate among many other writers during the nineteenth century.[95] In 1855, Emile joined its 200 shareholders, attempting to incite from within an offensive against the Banque's statutes which were about to be reviewed. Ernest André and Benoît Fould, original members of the Crédit Mobilier board, had joined the previous year.[96] That the Banque in March 1856 had thwarted an attempt by the Crédit Mobilier to extend its capital beyond the initial sixty million francs capital raising was likely to have lent further urgency to this move. The association was brief, however, and perhaps the intention was all too transparent. While the Emperor, in response to an approach from Emile Pereire, convened a commission to consider his proposals, they were not agreed. Emile's personal loss was heavy. Government renewed the Banque de France's charter until 1897 under much the same terms in which it already operated, though its capital was raised to 100 million francs.

The Pereires' relationship with Napoléon III went through phases, the 1850s being a particularly active and fertile time. Their influence and the profitability of their companies depended on ready access to the Emperor and his ministers. The Fonds Rouher in the French Archives Nationales and the Pereire family archive contain numerous references to a relationship which, despite some spasmodic exasperation on the part of the senior partner, became extremely profitable. The Emperor's visits to his summer residence at Biarritz especially were fortuitous, borne out in a letter of 1858 written to Rouher. He had met Emile Pereire 'and after many lamentations and of figures he presented to me' the Emperor had persuaded him to abandon one of his ideas, that of a particular freight subsidy. On the other hand, he agreed 'to concede to him the extension of [the rail line] from Bayonne to Irun', thus bringing into being a crucial stage of the Paris–Madrid line.[97]

The Pereires' influence had its price and the relationship which came to exist between Emile and the Emperor lends itself to suspicions which were not unfounded. But while reflection on the way the Pereires did business 150 years ago invariably leads to questions of conflict of interest, of poor business ethics, of corruption in one form or another, the historian cannot take the norms of today's business culture as a template for the past. From the seventeenth century, *dirigisme* has been a central factor in French economic progress, demanding a close relationship between the head of State and those directly engaged in commerce and industry. The proximity of Emile and Isaac Pereire to the decision-makers in politics in this context was not unusual. But the extent to which they exceeded the bounds of legality in business practice in their own time is another matter which will be addressed in a later chapter.

This first decade of the Second Empire was, for the Pereires, one of hyper-activity on all fronts. Already, the scope of their businesses was extraordinary: French and international. Underlying the tempo, scale, range and diversity of their enterprises during this establishment phase, however, questions are raised about how they achieved what they did. These businesses were, after all, in the process of becoming multinational companies deploying large sums of French capital. How did they maintain control over them? What was the relationship between the two brothers which underpinned the growth? What were their business ideas? Were these related to the Saint-Simonianism of the past? How did they choose their associates and staff? There are yet more questions and they are as crucial to an understanding of the Pereires' achievements as of their demise. The next chapter, therefore, will address the roles and methods of Emile and Isaac Pereire and of their family in what they treated as 'a family business'.

Notes

1 Louis-Napoléon took the title Emperor and the name Napoléon III on 1 December 1852.
2 Smith, *Modern Business Enterprise*, pp. 71–2, discusses the Conseil d'État's obstruction of joint stock companies in France, as does Freedeman, 'Joint-Stock business organizations'.
3 Gille, *Banque en France*, p. 132.
4 Smith, *Modern Business Enterprise*, Chapter 2, analyses the Crédit Mobilier's role.
5 Emile et Isaac Pereire, *Enquête sur la Banque de France, Dépositions de MM. Emile et Isaac Pereire ... Du système des banques et du système de Law* (Paris, 1866), pp. 11–12.
6 Sudhir Hazareesingh, *From Subject to Citizen: The Second Empire and the Emergence of French Democracy* (Princeton, 1998), Chapter 1.

CAPITALISM AND THE STATE   135

7   Roger Price, *People and Politics in France, 1848–1870* (Cambridge, 2004), pp. 2–3.
8   Anceau, *Napoléon III*, pp. 233–5.
9   Quoted in Pauline Prévost-Marcilhacy, *Les Rothschild* (Paris, 1995), p. 82.
10 Mirès, *À mes juges*, p. 21.
11 Maurice Lévy-Leboyer, *Les Banques européennes et l'industrialisation internationale dans la première moitié du XIXe siècle* (Paris, 1964), ch. XI.
12 Gille, *Banque en France*, p. 128.
13 Frédéric Barbier, *Finance et politique: la dynastie des Fould XVIIIe–XXe siècle* (Paris, 1991), pp. 181–3. A useful analysis of the French banking scene at the time of the Crédit Mobilier remains Landes' *Bankers and Pashas*, especially Chapters 1 and 2.
14 Gille, *Banque en France*, p. 129.
15 Aycard, *Histoire du Crédit Mobilier*, p. 41, for a history of the share price.
16 Stoskopf, *Banquiers et financiers*, p. 275.
17 Smith, *Modern Business Enterprise*, p. 73.
18 Guy P. Palmade, *French Capitalism in the Nineteenth Century*, trans. Graham M. Holmes (Newton Abbot, 1961), p. 143.
19 ANMT, 25AQ 2, Crédit Mobilier Assemblée Générale, *Rapport*, 29 April, 1854. Except where otherwise noted, citations from the ANMT refer to annual general meetings of shareholders.
20 Jacoud, *Political Economy*, p. 151, quoting 'De l'industrie', *Globe*, 24 November 1831.
21 P. Enfantin, 'Lettre à un banquier', *Globe*, 15 July 1830.
22 ANMT, Credit Mobilier, 25AQ 1, Société Générale de Crédit Mobilier, *Décret* and *Statuts* (Paris, Paul Dupont, 1852).
23 An early, influential study on this issue is D. Landes, 'The old bank and the new: the financial revolution of the nineteenth century', in François Crouzet, W. H. Chaloner and W. M. Stern (eds), *Essays in European Economic History, 1789–1914*, trans. Max A. Lehmann (London, 1969), pp. 112–27. See also Nicolas Stoskopf , 'What is the Parisian "Haute Banque" in the nineteenth century', *Journées d'études sur l'histoire de la haute banque France* (Paris, 2000).
24 ANMT, 25AQ 1, Société Générale de Crédit Mobilier, *Décret* (Paris, 18 November 1852); Barbier, *Finance et politique*, p. 182.
25 Autin, *Frères Pereire*, p. 114.
26 Rondo Cameron, 'Une lettre inédite de Persigny (1855) à Napoléon III: à propos de la rivalité Rothschild-Pereire', *Revue historique* 230 (1963), 91–6.
27 Mirès, *À mes juges*, p. 92.
28 Landes, *Bankers and Pashas*, p. 46, fn. 1.
29 AFP, handwritten list of shareholders.
30 Ibid.
31 Isaac was confirmed President, 30 April 1855, when Fould, too ill to continue, became Honorary President. Adolphe d'Eichthal replaced Isaac as Vice-President with Charles Mallet. Emile Pereire replaced the deceased duc de Mouchy. ANMT, 25AQ 2, Crédit Mobilier, *Rapport*, 30 April 1855, p. 37.

32 Ibid., *Proces-Verbaux* 1 (Paris, 1854), 29 April 1854.
33 Ibid., *Rapport*, 30 April 1860.
34 Ibid., 25AQ 1, *Statuts* (Paris, 1852), p. 6.
35 Elisabeth Paulet deals with the risks inherent in the Pereires' approach, employing econometric modelling to demonstrate the impact of their monitoring the Crédit Mobilier's investment in firms. See *The Role of Banks in Monitoring Firms: The Case of the Crédit Mobilier* (London, 1999).
36 Ibid., p. 137, Table A: 1853, 13.4%; 1854, 11.8%; 1855, 40.74%; 1856, 23%.
37 AN, F12/6827. For an account of this proposal and its links to Saint-Simonianism see Franck Yonnet, 'Saint-Simonisme et système bancaire. Utopie et pratique' (PhD dissertation, université de'Évry-Val-d'Essonne, 2000).
38 Harvey, *Paris*, p. 76. Sewell, *Work and Revolution*, ch. 8, deals with this at length.
39 *Écrits*, t. 5, fasc., 2, p. 44, 'Le Crédit Mutuel, en faveur des petits entrepreneurs, tâcherons et ouvriers en chambre, combiné de manière à mettre à leur portée les avantages et l'économie de temps et d'argent dont jouissent les clients de la Banque de France'.
40 Isaac Pereire, *La Banque de France et l'organisation du crédit en France* (Paris, 1864), pp. 164–8.
41 *Écrits*, t. 5, fasc., 2, pp. 36–41. Capital was to be 60 million francs divided into 240,000 shares of 250 francs each.
42 Price, *People and Politics*, p. 134.
43 Ratcliffe, 'Some banking ideas in France in the 1830s'.
44 AFP, two drafts in Emile Pereire's hand among papers of the 1820s.
45 ANMT, 25AQ 2, Crédit Mobilier, *Rapport*, 1855, p, 36.
46 Ibid., 78AQ 6, Midi, *Rapport*, 1854, p. 26.
47 Price, *People and Politics*, p. 22.
48 AFP, letters Eugène Flachat to Emile, June 1854.
49 Girard, *La Politique des travaux publics du Second Empire* (Paris, 1951), p. 145.
50 ANMT, 25AQ 1, *Observations pour les Administrateurs du Crédit Mobilier sur la plaidoirie du Défenseur de M. Tellot* (Paris, [undated, probably 1868]).
51 Théophraste, *É. M. Pereire*, p. 23.
52 ANMT, 25AQ 2, Crédit Mobilier, p. 47. AFP, Isaac's letters to Emile 1851–54 give an account of these negotiations.
53 I. Pereire, *Chemins de fer*, pp. 159–61.
54 Autin, *Frères Pereire*, pp. 134–8; Jacques Jourquin, 'Morny le flamboyant (1811–1865)', *Napoléon III: Le magazine du Second Empire* 16 (2011), 45–7.
55 Girard, *Travaux publics*, pp. 125–35.
56 Autin, *Frères Pereire*, p. 136; AN/AP, 45/3, Fonds Rouher, 21 July 1856.
57 AFP, Emile to Rouher, December, otherwise undated.
58 Teresa Tortella, *A Guide to Sources of Information on Foreign Investment in Spain 1780–1914* (Amsterdam, 2000), pp. 63–4.
59 Ibid., pp. 102–3.
60 ANMT, 78AQ 6, Midi, *Rapport*, 1857, p. 5.
61 I. Pereire, *Chemins de fer*, pp. 151–3.

62 AN-Léonore, 2096/58, 8 April 1857.
63 Smith, *Modern Business Enterprise*, pp. 80–8; I. Pereire, *Chemins de fer*, pp. 156–66.
64 Autin, *Frères Pereire*, pp. 226–31.
65 Marthe Barbance, *Histoire de la Compagnie Générale Transatlantique: un siècle d'exploitation maritime* (Paris, 1955), pp. 36–42.
66 ANMT, 25AQ 2, Crédit Mobilier, *Rapport*, 30 April 1855, pp. 32–3.
67 Ibid., 23 April 1856, p. 64.
68 Barbance, *Compagnie Générale Transatlantique*, pp. 39–40.
69 Yves Bruley, *Le Quai d'Orsay Impérial: histoire du Ministère des Affaires étrangères sous Napoléon III* (Paris, 2012), p. 359.
70 Autin, *Frères Pereire*, p. 261.
71 AFP, Francesco Vigano, Membre de l'Académie de Physique, de Médecine et de Statistique de Milan, 'Hommage à la Mémoire d'Isaac Pereire', 25 December 1880, (Milan, 1880), pp. 7–8.
72 *Écrits*, t. 4, fasc., 4, p. xxix.
73 Ferguson, *World's Banker*, p. 572. Ferguson noted that had the Pereires confined their ambitions to France little harm would have come to them. Once they ventured further afield the whole Rothschild family business felt threatened.
74 AFP, Isaac, Paris, to Emile, September 1858, confirms this, as did Lionel de Rothschild, for which see Cameron, 'Une lettre inédite', p. 94.
75 Brigitte Schroeder-Gudehus and Anne Rasmussen, *Les Fastes du progrès: le guide des Expositions universelles 1851–1992* (Paris, 1992), pp. 64–70. See also *Écrits*, t. 8, pp. 8–10.
76 Autin, *Frères Pereire*, pp. 248–53.
77 Michel Carmona, *Haussmann: His Life and Times and the Making of Modern Paris* (Chicago, 2002), p. 223.
78 *Illustrated London News*, 'The Hôtel du Louvre', 27 October 1855, p. 506.
79 ANMT, Crédit Mobilier 25AQ 2, *Rapport*, 30 April 1855, p. 31.
80 Harvey, *Paris*, pp. 8–10, 37; Bowie, *Modernité avant Haussmann*, esp. pp. 217–30.
81 David P. Jordan, *Transforming Paris: the Life and Labors of Baron Haussmann* (New York, 1995); Carmona, *Haussmann*, Chapter 14.
82 Carmona, *Haussmann*, pp. 143, 153.
83 Jordan, *Transforming Paris*, pp. 185–210.
84 David H. Pinkney, *Napoléon III and the Rebuilding of Paris* (Princeton, 1972), pp. 70–2; Theodore Zeldin, *A History of French Passions, Volume 1, 1848–1945* (Oxford, 1993), p. 554; Fargette, *Émile et Isaac Pereire*, p. 169.
85 Bertrand Gille, *Histoire de la Maison Rothschild*, Tome 2, 1848–1870 (Geneva, 1967), pp. 197–9; E. J. Hobsbawm, *The Age of Capital 1848–1875* (London, 1985), p. 253, quoting P. J. Proudhon, *Manuel du Spéculateur à la Bourse* (Paris, 1857), pp. 429ff.
86 AFP, Emile to Napoléon III, 21 July 1856.
87 'The Pereires did a lot with very little'. Stoskopf, *Banquiers et financiers*, p. 283, quoting Pierre Dupont-Ferrier, *Le Marché financier de Paris sous le Second*

Empire (Paris, 1925), lacking page no.
88 Paulet, *Role of Banks*, Table A2, p. 138.
89 Gille, *Maison Rothschild*, pp. 208–9.
90 Bertrand Gille, 'La Fondation de la Société Générale', *Histoire des Entreprises* 8 (1961), pp.12–20.
91 Ibid.
92 Autin, *Frères Pereire*, Annexe No. 7, p. 365. For details of French government loans see Emile and Isaac Pereire, *Enquête*, p. 120, 'Souscriptions du *Crédit Mobilier* aux Emprunts'.
93 Ferguson, *World's Banker*, p. 571. See also Braudel and Labrousse, *Histoire économique et sociale de la France*, tome 3, p. 353. Of regents sitting on the council of the Banque de France 1800–90, 30 per cent were members of the Haute Banque with the median term of appointment twenty-one years.
94 *Écrits*, t. 4, fasc., 3, 'Réforme de la Banque de France', pp. 1458–76.
95 Alain Plessis, *La Banque de France et ses deux cents actionnaires* (Geneva, 1982), pp. 1–4.
96 Ibid., p. 162, fn. 83. Plessis points out that joint stock companies had little connection with the Banque, with the exception of the Crédit Mobilier which had purchased 194 shares. These it distributed among the three board members.
97 AN/AP 45/3 Fonds Rouher, Napoléon III to Rouher from Biarritz, 21 September 1858.

6

The family business

Emile Pereire was never in doubt that he and Isaac would enter business together. There was a suggestion of inevitability if not of destiny in his remark to Samuel Alexandre in Bordeaux in 1824 that Isaac 'was called to be my partner' and that they were bound to prosper.[1] He held this certainty from his earliest years. As the eldest son in a family whose father had died when Emile was a small boy, he had a particular emotional bond with his younger brother, described by a family member in terms of a deep sense of responsibility towards

> this child born so soon after the death of his father of whom [Emile] became the protector from the age of six years, the affection that they have one for the other which nothing could diminish; each one of them suffering for the other as with a wounded arm or a wounded leg.[2]

This profound reciprocal emotion and affection, the forging of a bond of steel, was the Pereires' *raison d'être* and the core of their success.

The Pereires made their mark at a significant moment in the history of French capitalism and to an extent were agents in its direction. It is thus instructive to consider the nature of the structures they set in place to achieve their ends, how they managed their financial resources, both as a case study in the evolution of capitalism and as another lens with which to observe the workings of the Pereire family. Indeed, in the history of French capitalism the pre-eminence of the family is idiosyncratic. In early modern times that family was usually agrarian, but the large commercial and industrial houses which evolved subsequently depended on a network of extended family members to survive and grow. By the nineteenth century the number of families engaged in large-scale industrial activities in France was remarkable and it remains the case today.³ Families provided long-term security for the business, the injection of funds, and reliable networks.⁴ The incidence of brothers in family business was particularly notable – the Wendels, Talabots, Schneiders, Delesserts and yet others come to mind – sharing the load, providing mutual support, and keeping profits within the family.

The significance of the family is especially relevant to the history of Jewish business and to the 'extraordinary social mobility of Jews' in recent history. With the dynamic growth of capitalism in the nineteenth century, Paula Hyman has described how the family 'stimulated and supported psychologically both the ambition and the self-denial necessary for attaining economic success'.⁵ This, too, is evident in the Pereire family. Here, also, the presence of brothers was remarkable. Rothschild *frères* with their extended, interrelated family businesses in London, Paris, Frankfurt, Vienna and, until 1863, Naples, were the *ne plus ultra*. Family business was the norm also in Sephardic Bordeaux when the Pereires were growing up. The five Raba brothers had established a powerful trading legacy which was still extant in the nineteenth century. The Gradis had become major ship owners and colonial merchants. The Pereires' father and maternal grandfather had been in business together and their uncle Rodrigues, in turn, worked with Fonseca and Pereire from time to time. While there were no openings with other family members when the brothers reached working age, family friends found them employment and gave them their basic training, again a common feature of Sephardic life. And later, when they moved to Paris, Rodrigues *fils* trained them and used his networks to find jobs for both young men. Family and kinship were significant to the Pereires' later success.

It was the advent of rail in the 1830s which changed the business environment forever. Aside from capital on a scale hitherto inconceivable, the magnitude of industrial activity required to project France into the industrial age in the nineteenth century also called for significant change in business structures. Existing forms could scarcely sustain the entities needed to achieve the necessary increase in production. The *société en commandite*, or partnership, favoured by many family businesses, which allowed greater autonomy and flexibility to managers and directors who were frequently one and the same, demanded sufficient family capital to ensure survival and growth. This was often difficult to arrange. The nineteenth-century owners of the Wendel iron works, Charles de Wendel and his family, chose to manage their business in this way so as to protect both family wealth, in particular that of Charles' widowed mother who invested over thirty million francs, and the rights of descendants. Charles, as the younger son whose brother in this case had no direct interest in the ironworks, was also the chief executive. This approach had its problems, although in the case of Wendel raising capital was not among them. Rather, with the passing of primogeniture in 1790, the Wendels encountered problems of intra-family expectations and rivalries as heirs and successors came of age, problems which were not resolved until well after Charles' death in 1870.[6]

It was the *société anonyme*, the joint stock investment company which came into being in 1807, with its appeal to public and dispersed ownership of shares, which better suited the needs of the new capitalist enterprises. But the very virtues of the *société anonyme* were also a cause of concern to governments which feared catastrophic public losses in the case of bad management. The *société anonyme* was thus heavily regulated, requiring legislation carrying the assent of the Conseil d'État and of the Emperor. The number of such companies established after the First Empire was small – only twelve each year from 1817–67 – and the extent of capitalisation cautious. It was not until 1867 that government relinquished its authority to approve establishment of the joint stock company, a decision which led to a very large increase in their number.[7] The Crédit Mobilier was established as a *société anonyme*, and in this case the restriction on finance capital was to curb the Pereires' ambitions, forcing them throughout the Second Empire to seek to increase the initial share capital and to offer alternative sources of investment in the form of bonds. A further dilemma for the Pereires lay in their expectation that they could exert personal control over their company as if it were a partnership and they the partners. A public company, demanding a certain transparency in its affairs and accountable to a large number of often anonymous shareholders, did not provide this degree of latitude.

While in theory the *société anonyme* brought increasing democratisation of ownership and accountability to shareholders, which proved an impediment to the Pereires' need for control of their businesses, they attempted to manage these potential inconveniences through their extensive shareholding and that of their associates. Fifty per cent of Crédit Mobilier shares were controlled by the Pereires and those in the same camp.[8] And while at the beginning Benoît Fould treated his presidency as 'honorific', Isaac in contrast 'sees all, gives impetus to all, directs everything by himself in this immense enterprise'.[9] They thus ensured that the Conseil d'Administration (the board) remained the pre-eminent decision-making body, reporting annually to the Assemblée Générale of the 200 most significant shareholders. Additionally, they took on themselves personal direction of a number of the companies they established.

Until 1852, Emile Pereire had played the major role in almost all of their ventures, all railways, with the exception of the Paris–Lyon. Significantly, it was Isaac who presided over what became the nucleus, the Crédit Mobilier, while Emile was President of the Compagnie Immobilière de Paris, the Midi, La Confiance, the Compagnie des Entrepôts et Magasins Généraux de Paris, the Compagnie Générale des Asphaltes and, later, the Compagnie Générale Transatlantique (hereafter the Transat).

This final sharing of roles may simply give credence to the assertion noted earlier that Emile had always wanted to be a railway concessionaire, that it was his preferred role.[10] Individual preference and ability certainly would have played some part in this division of labour. The economic historian Nicolas Stoskopf suggests an alternative, that Emile held himself apart for the visionary projects, those involving economic development and large-scale planning and organisation. While Emile was a member of the boards of nineteen of his enterprises, Stoskopf claims that he only took the presidency in those companies which involved some significant form of planning, his interest in banking simply the means to an end.[11] The brothers must also have considered a rational sharing of responsibility and effort to be imperative, for there was not a single company in which the Crédit Mobilier invested which did not have a Pereire on the board. As time went on and their enterprises multiplied, the workload, particularly for Emile, exceeded what two men could reasonably support. It was the younger man to whom the long-distance travelling was then largely delegated, Emile increasingly at the mercy of his ailing health. Thus we find Emile's travels confined to the health-giving southwest where, among other commitments, he attended meetings of the Conseil général of the Gironde. Isaac undertook the major negotiations in the Netherlands, Germany, Russia, Spain, Italy and Austria, and presided over the Paris-based committees which effectively gave the foreign enterprises direction and protected French investment. He arranged for French engineers, foremen and workers to undertake construction of railways in these foreign countries. The practice was established early, however, with the construction and launch of their railways the PSG and the Paris–Versailles (Rive Droite), that Emile should take responsibility for dealings with the French head of State as well as the most senior members of his administrations, activities which more frequently occurred in Paris. These contacts needed to be carefully cultivated and maintained, creating their own workload, and this too was a factor in the sharing of their respective roles.

Emile and Isaac shared a strong work ethic until the end, essential to the onerous tasks they had taken on but punishing, nevertheless. For his part, Emile's life-long asthma had a drastic impact on his capacity to sleep easily and he was known to spend his nights sitting upright in an armchair, sleepless, when he worked on his papers until the early hours. Isaac, too, was habituated to working well into the night, his nephew Henry reporting to his father on one occasion that 'my uncle writes every night from 1 o'clock until 3 or 4 o'clock in the morning'.[12]

They also ensured that they were surrounded by people they could trust if not control. That other administrators of the Crédit Mobilier should take on semi-supervisory positions with associated companies became Crédit Mobilier policy. Isaac Pereire was to comment in 1860 that

> our company has never taken out a subscription, never recommended a business without being highly interested in it ourselves, and, just as importantly, our administrators are duty-bound to associate themselves with the new businesses. These are for us matters of high commercial morality ... we hold it an honour to participate actively in their administrations, to help them with our active support and capital advances whenever that has been necessary.[13]

Thus, Adolphe d'Eichthal became President of the CGM and, for a time, of its successor the Transat, and was a director of the Crédit Mobilier and of the Midi; Casimir Salvador, who had begun his career with the Crédit Mobilier as Secretary-General, was a director of the Immobilière, the Midi and the Chemin de Fer du Nord de l'Espagne; and Vincent Cibiel, former deputy and business figure, of the Midi and the Immobilière. Their networks extended beyond this. Emile was a member of the club the Cercle Impérial, as well as the Cercle des Chemins de Fer founded by Morny of which Isaac was also a member.[14] Neither was a member of the Jockey Club of Paris, however, despite the Compagnie Immobilière's ownership of the building in the rue Scribe in which it met. Indeed, Nathaniel [Natty] Rothschild, James' English-born nephew, was one of the few Jews elected to the Jockey Club during the Second Empire.[15]

To consolidate the position of the Crédit Mobilier as the holding company and facilitate the direction of all their companies, since headquarters were invariably centred on Paris (whether or not the companies operated there), they gathered them together under one roof, purchasing in 1854 as headquarters number 15, place Vendôme, an eighteenth-century mansion designed by Jules Hardouin Mansart.[16] Ten years later, Isaac was to purchase another property opposite for office space, and another in the nearby boulevard des Capucines.[17] As the Pereires became more ambitious, extending their influence beyond France to other European countries, their need for effective lines of communication and control became critical. This was especially the case with their rail enterprises. Following their early implementation of the electric telegraph in 1846 to serve the Paris–Versailles (Rive Droite) they embraced the new communications tool, unlike the Rothschilds who distrusted and lamented its impact on their customary ways of doing business.[18] Morny, as Minister for the Interior early in the Second Empire, made extension of the network throughout France a priority and its use spread rapidly to Britain and the rest of Europe.[19] As we know, Isaac also travelled extensively and was absent for long periods of time. Negotiating the Société Autrichienne des Chemins de Fer de l'État saw him in Vienna in September 1854 through to January 1855.[20] Additionally, the committees based in Paris at the place Vendôme which he chaired played a major role in running the businesses. Thus were the Société Autrichienne, the Crédit Mobilier Espagnol, and the Chemin de Fer du Nord de l'Espagne, among others, controlled as part of the Pereire group, eliminating duplication in expenditure on fixed assets.

While business structures were evolving in response to challenges of ownership and investment capital, the new industrial and commercial enterprises required processes to support the variety of functions now brought into play and management skills to ensure these functions were carried out effectively. This was a fertile period in the history of management theory when the ways in which these new enterprises should be managed became the subject of enquiry among economists. In some senses, the intellectual history of Saint-Simonianism itself laid the foundations for some modern theories of management, concentrated as it was on the role of the 'industrial', on the innovative application of technology to industrial processes, on theories of 'association' and on progressive improvement in the condition of the working class.[21] Teachers at the Conservatoire Royal des Arts et Métiers were in the forefront. Charles Dupin, who taught at the Conservatoire from 1819–54, applied mathematical techniques to the problem of determining workloads and time management, but his principal interest was in the good management of the workers and in their well-being. In the year Dupin commenced at the Conservatoire, Jean-Baptiste Say became the first professor of industrial economics there and Adolphe Blanqui succeeded him in 1832. Congruent with Saint-Simonian thought these economists dealt with the moral dimension of management, both in the prevention of fraudulent and corrupt dealings by directors and in the encouragement of 'the collective good' of workers.[22] Emile Pereire was acquainted with these theorists. As early as 1834, Blanqui had invited him to address his students at a regularly held seminar and was moved to add in his letter of invitation: 'I was charmed to make your personal acquaintance and to express all the regard I have for you in person.' The friendship blossomed and in 1837 Emile rewarded him with shares in the PSG.[23] This interplay of Saint-Simonian industrial ideas with theories of workforce management had an influence on the way the Pereires addressed the management of their own businesses.

An element of Saint-Simonian vocabulary which remained constant in Isaac Pereire's rhetoric, for example, was the concept of 'association'. Over time its interpretation had been flexible, employed by radicals and moderate reformers alike.[24] During this early period of growth and development in heavy industry the term was still in common use, a direct legacy of Saint-Simonian engineering practitioners who also were significant figures in training personnel in railway and metals manufacture. The term as it was used by Isaac Pereire thus referred to collective action which might be adopted by industrialists to deal with excessive competition or to share scarce resources.[25] It meant cooperation, collaboration and anti-competitive, anti-individualist behaviour. Isaac used it to describe the rationale of the Crédit Mobilier in its relationships with those companies in which it took a financial stake, one in which 'association' and 'fusion' rather than competition would prevail. He, and Emile also, frequently spoke of the challenges presented by rampant egotism, and by 'the spirit of exclusion or of monopoly' – that is, in unbridled competition, individualism and jealousy, the opposite of 'association'. Thus, Isaac claimed, to introduce rules of order would ensure the best employment of resources and in the interests of both producer and consumer.[26]

Tony Judt has described the divisions and tensions in Second Empire social and political policy and practice – universal male suffrage together with repression of any opposition, an elite of skilled workers' organisations but with strikes of the unorganised industrial proletariat – which he credited 'with having forged that very special sense of internal exile, of deep class resentment combined with political frustration, which has ever since characterised the French working-class movement, even in its rare moments of optimism.'[27] The Pereires recognised this class resentment, finding its depth unfathomable. In contrast, they asserted their belief in 'the genius of association', manifested in the way companies were managed, in their approach to the workforce and in the creation of credit facilities. 'Crédit mobilier institutions are founded on the expression of the spirit of association in contrast to the spirit of isolation', declared Isaac, adding that 'association … is the sentiment of unity which helps us avoid the mistakes of our competitors.'[28] Saint-Simonian socialism, depending on appeals to a model based on Christianity, is far from Marxist or other later nineteenth-century interpretations of socialism. Karl Marx, although influenced by Saint-Simon and his followers at the time of his sojourn in Paris in 1843, went on to denounce them. 'The school of St. Simon', he wrote in a series of articles attacking the Crédit Mobilier in the *New York Tribune*, 'deluded itself with the dream that all the antagonism of classes must disappear before the creation of universal wealth by some new-fangled scheme of public credit'. Later, he and Friedrich Engels castigated the 'utopian socialists' for their inadequate understanding of the class struggle and for their rejection of conflict to emancipate the working class. Marx and Engels understood that the Saint-Simonian emphasis on 'association' did not extend to industrial or revolutionary action.[29]

The Pereires themselves contributed to the developing management theory post-Say and Blanqui. While they did not comprehend the role of chief executive as we know it today and, in fact, probably saw such a role as usurping their own, they began to understand that specialised functions (accounting and finance, personnel management, technology, commercial management) were necessary to differentiate the elements of successful management in large-scale enterprises. The new engineering technology, for example, was critical to the railways and later to the shipping company they founded, and they greatly admired the discipline and innovation of the engineering profession, which accounted for a number of close friends. They did not see it as the core function, however, for in their eyes this was the role of finance. In fact on one occasion an irritated Isaac felt compelled to instruct an associate setting off to inspect the Nord company in Spain that 'we must break up this fraternity of engineers ... and combat the bureaucratic system they have introduced into the railways. We must work energetically to replace it with commercial simplicity'.[30] Later, he instructed his nephew Henry that 'we must re-establish our authority over the Midi railway and show to these messieurs the engineers that we are still something. For that we must go [on inspection] more often'.[31] Railways relied on engineering expertise during the establishment phase, nevertheless, and engineers were thus necessarily to the fore in railway management. Until 1881, the position of chief executive of the Chemin de Fer du Nord de l'Espagne was the fiefdom of a French engineer.[32] While there is no evidence that Isaac acted on the cause of his irritation, installing a chief executive with commercial expertise rather than an engineer in one or other of the Pereire railway businesses, his irritation reflects a gradual recognition shared more generally that other forms of management training and, in particular, of advanced education for commercial managers, was essential to companies in maintaining profits and identifying and exploiting new markets. Isaac's former employer Vital-Roux and J.-B. Say had founded the École

Supérieure de Commerce de Paris in 1819, described as the first business school in the world, but its activities were long constrained by lack of funds. The École des Hautes Études Commerciales, with an ambition to teach commerce as a science, did not open in Paris until 1881.[33]

Luc Marco describes how the Pereires used the finance function to pioneer innovative approaches to company management, maintaining fixed capital at a minimum and circulating capital – raw materials, inventories, other operating expenses – at a constant level. To allow their businesses to expand, external financing was secured through the Crédit Mobilier which injected funds and raised public loans. It was thus a holding company around which clustered complementary businesses. The Pereires achieved a form of vertical integration of these companies in a quasi-supply chain, using the Conseil d'Administration to co-ordinate and manage the employment of funds.[34] In some cases these created markets for the Pereires' own private interests, as well as ample opportunity for conflict of interest. The Midi and the Chemin de Fer du Nord de l'Espagne, for instance, were both supplied with timber for sleepers by the Société Pereire de la Mise en Valeur des Landes (the sleepers manufactured by an old Bordeaux friend, Oxeda). And the Grand Hôtel held a magnificent *cave* of wine from their private vignoble Château Palmer. More legitimately, the hotels and housing constructed by the Compagnie Immobilière were served with laundry services by the Société des Blanchisseries Industrielles, with gas lighting and water heating by the Compagnie Parisienne du Gaz, asphalt for paving by the Société Générale des Asphaltes, insurance through the Compagnie d'Assurance la Confiance, public transport by the Compagnie Générale des Omnibus. The Transat came to rely on the shipyards at Saint-Nazaire. These strategies provided economies of scale and ready access to products and services.

With the increasing complexity and range of their business interests, however, the Pereires' tendency and preference to maintain a hands-on approach became increasingly difficult to sustain. Despite their recognition of the differing processes which contributed to a successful business, they did not understand or differentiate the directorial from the executive role. They appropriated the strategic decisions, seeking advice from other members of the board in whom they trusted rather than from management employees. None of this was unusual; indeed it was typical of mid-nineteenth century French business practice. It was how the Wendels managed their foundries. Among medium-sized companies such as the family luxury goods company Christofle, established in 1830, its founder Charles Christofle was virtually the only manager.[35] There are many other examples which give a similar picture of the nature of management before

6 Eugène Pereire (1890s). Photo © Musée d'art et d'histoire du Judaïsme

the advent of the professional, one in which the originating family took the leadership role in running the business.

If Emile had faith in the inevitability of his partnership with Isaac, they also entertained expectations that a business dynasty would be founded through their heirs. They prepared their sons carefully for the future roles they would assume.[36] While both brothers possessed many talents in areas which underpinned the new business world, neither had received an education of any depth. Isaac had studied accounting for a time with his uncle, Rodrigues, who was then at the forefront of the discipline, but this did not amount to formal education. The Pereires were thus particularly keen to see their own sons provided with the training denied to them. Paradoxically, in view of Isaac's irritation with some of the engineers employed within their companies, they encouraged their male progeny to undertake engineering courses, not at the more prestigious École Polytechnique where the majority of their associates had been trained, but at the École Centrale des Arts et Manufactures. The École Centrale, now one of the *grandes écoles*, had been founded in 1829 by the visionary Alphonse Lavallée whose aim was to provide engineers with the breadth of experience necessary to manage enterprises of the new industrial order. It was thus differentiated from the École Polytechnique whose graduates were destined for the State system. Eugène, who was a very able member of the second generation, graduated as a civil engineer from the École Centrale in 1852, as did Emile II, Henry and Gustave, who studied there in the 1860s.

The Pereires also recognised that education alone was insufficient to prepare their sons for the responsibilities they might assume, and actively encouraged them to augment their studies with practical experience. Upon graduation, the young men were put to work in one of the family businesses before they assumed any more senior role. A study tour taken by Emile II and Henry in 1861 followed an ambitious itinerary designed to introduce them to the heavy industry of the department of the Nord: mines and forges, foundries, collieries, cotton mills and factories manufacturing rolling stock were on the agenda.[37] When, after his graduation, Henry undertook an extended voyage to the Middle East, Egypt and North Africa, Emile chided him, attempting to deflect Henry's obvious enthusiasm for the antiquities he was seeing, concerned that the original purpose of the trip was evolving into a Grand Tour: 'You will do well, independently of your researches, your studies into the antique, not to neglect the industrial, commercial and agricultural point of view', he wrote.[38] Herminie also played a part in the training of her sons, encouraging Emile actively to pass on his knowledge and expertise: 'Every moment [Emile II] spent with you will be of great usefulness.'[39] On a visit to Lyon in 1859, when Emile II was nineteen years of age, she recommended he call on Arlès-Dufour to learn about silk manufacture.[40] In later life when Emile's health curbed his activities, Isaac took a hand in mentoring his nephews Emile II and Henry as well as his son Gustave (Eugène, by then in his forties, was no longer in need of such coaching) in the elements of the family businesses, since they would in time assume the mantles of their father and their uncle. He taught them how to identify staff who would uphold the family interest and those who would not, recognising the weaknesses in existing managers and the

7 Emile Pereire II (1898). Private collection

poor results they achieved. Take advantage of your vacation in Arcachon, he advised Henry, to put our business in the Landes in order and draw from it the best possible results.[41] When disastrous fires in the Landes consumed valuable timber supplies used for sleepers in the Midi and the Nord de l'Espagne he urged them to employ every means possible to avert a repetition. Was the most capable person in control down there? Was he remunerated adequately? Despite a magnificent harvest at Château Palmer in 1870 they would be lucky to make ends meet, he lamented, its management seeming incapable of turning a profit. Henry must go over the accounts with a fine-tooth comb to establish why profits continued to diminish.⁴² To Fanny he wrote: 'Our young people must occupy themselves seriously with our businesses.'⁴³

This education and training was essential, for the Pereires had rapidly come to dominate the boards of French companies during the Second Empire. Within ten years of the Crédit Mobilier's launch the family, including Eugène, held forty-four directorships compared with the Rothschilds' thirty-two.⁴⁴ With their associates they formed a powerful block of further interlocking directorships on the boards of 134 companies.⁴⁵ But no better illustration of this genius for networking can be found than in the marriage in 1859 between Isaac's son Eugène and Juliette Betzi Fould, the daughter of the Pereires' notary Emile Fould, who was thus related to Napoléon III's Minister of State Achille and his brother Benoît, the first President of the Crédit Mobilier. Among witnesses to the marriage were members of the Fould, Furtado, Heine and Oppenheim families; Worms de Romilly; Lalouel de Sourdeval; Fromenthal Halévy; the duc de Valmy; the duc de Glucksberg; and Gustave d'Eichthal.⁴⁶ The Pereires exemplified the maxim that, above all else, 'marriage [among the *grande bourgeoisie*] symbolised an alliance between families' and in this case, between the Pereires and the Foulds, arguably the most influential of their era.⁴⁷

At the most profound level their businesses depended on trust, the core of which lay between Emile and Isaac. The Pereires' trust extended to the immediate family and not simply to the male line. They shared sensitive business information with their wives in whom they confided and, at least in Emile's case, with their daughters.⁴⁸ On completion of their education, each of the sons was taken in to one of the Pereire companies. Eugène, for example, worked initially with the Midi but by 1858, when he was 27 years old, he became secretary to the Transat. Soon after, he was influential in the establishment of the Crédit Mobilier Espagnol, the board of which he joined as he did the Compagnie Générale des Omnibus, the Compagnie du Gaz, the Midi, the Chemin de Fer du Nord de l'Espagne as well as the Transat. Eventually both Gustave and Emile II became administrators of the Nord de l'Espagne while Henry eventually joined the Société Autrichienne des Chemins de Fer and the Midi. Their sons-in-law took positions as well. Charles Rhoné, husband of Fanny's sister Cécile, was favoured with board positions on the Transat, the Compagnie de l'Ouest des Chemins de Fer Suisses, La Confiance and the Compagnie du Gaz, of which he became Vice-President. Georges Thurneyssen who married another sister, Claire, became a director of the Midi and Eugène Mir, deputy for Castelnaudary who married Isaac's daughter Henriette, with the Nord de l'Espagne. Other relatives who had shared the Saint-Simonian

8 Henry Pereire (1890s). Archives de la famille Pereire

experience, Henri Baud, the husband of Mélanie Rodrigues and Charles Sarchi, who married Félicie, both sisters of Herminie, were employed at different times in the PSG and the Crédit Mobilier respectively. Abraham Rodrigues was an administrator of the Compagnie de Chemin de Fer de l'Ouest which had emerged from the PSG and the Paris–Versailles (Rive Droite).[49] The Pereires' nephew Paul Regnault designed and supervised construction of a great number of villas and public buildings at Arcachon, and Félix Laroche, the husband of Emile's granddaughter Marie Rhoné,

9 Gustave Pereire (1880s). Archives de la famille Pereire

became a senior engineer with the Midi and ultimately a director of the Compagnie du Gaz.

Trust extended also to many former Saint-Simonian colleagues who were associated with Pereire businesses. Aside from Adolphe d'Eichthal, who was also a significant investor, Michel Chevalier was on the board of the Transat and became an adviser to the railway companies and – at least at the beginning, for he died in 1854 – Léon Faucher was a director of the Midi. Alfred Armand became the Pereires' chief architect. Henri

Fournel, having been appointed consultant mining engineer to the PSG in 1835, remained close to the Pereires and joined the board of the Nord de l'Espagne in 1864. Emile Clapeyron and Eugène Flachat, both elected to the board of the Transat, were almost as close as the rest of the family, the former having contributed his expertise to all of the railway ventures including the Midi, a long association which Emile Pereire recalled with sadness on Clapeyron's death in 1864. 'Since 1832 he has never left me. I never made an important business [decision] without consulting him; I never found a judgement more sure or more sound.'[50]

Some who were neither family nor old colleagues, commencing careers as employees of the Pereires, proved their loyalty and effectiveness sufficiently to become directors themselves. Ernest Polack, at the age of fifteen, started in 1842 as secretary to Isaac Pereire and rapidly became invaluable, representing Isaac not only in Russia but particularly in Spain where his negotiations with the Spanish government during the Franco-Prussian War and afterwards contributed much to saving the Pereires' interests there. Ultimately he presided over the board of the Crédit Mobilier Espagnol.[51] Casimir Salvador commenced as secretary-general of the Crédit Mobilier, effectively its chief executive, but became a valued director of several Pereire enterprises and confidant of the Pereires.[52] Such promotions could have a negative impact, however, removing effective employees from among the ranks of those close to day-to-day decision-making.

Emile's judgement about employees could sometimes be mistaken. 'L'Affaire Brochon' was the most serious example, a case in which a senior and trusted employee who had been promoted over time to the position of secretary-general of the Compagnie Immobilière at a salary of 15,000 francs per annum, was found guilty of embezzling close to one million francs, a colossal sum. It included the payment in 1863 of the lease by the Jockey Club of Paris, some 100,000 francs which did not find its way into the Immobilière accounts. Clearly, the supervisory and audit processes in place were inadequate; indeed, Emile Pereire himself had been responsible for the lack of oversight on several occasions. The case erupted in 1867 at a time when it was scarcely welcome to the Compagnie Immobilière or to the Pereires, continuing for at least another two years.[53]

Did the Pereires carry Saint-Simonian social policies into their businesses? Were the employment practices they pursued or introduced into their own ventures consistent with raising the living standards of their employees, as the Saint-Simonian maxim demanded? The Pereires certainly did not accept the proposition that workers would take responsibility for arguing and achieving their own rates of pay and conditions of work and regarded industrial action and the right to strike as anathema. Saint-Simonianism had not advanced that far either, even though a few Saint-Simonians, Olinde Rodrigues among them, had later taken up the cause of organised labour. In their earlier writings the Pereires had described with considerable sympathy a class struggle between 'worker' and 'idle', but by the time they acquired a substantial workforce of their own they could not countenance, much less support, struggle between militant workers and industrialists.

The Pereires appear to have remunerated their own staff well, nevertheless, and at a time when the purchasing power of the franc was already strong.[54] They provided company shops ['comptoirs'] for discounted goods – coal, linen, the basics of life – for their work force.[55] Within the Transat a generous system of rewards for loyalty existed – profit-sharing, provision of shares and bonuses, an extra month's salary among them.[56] The Midi was among the first to institute long-service leave, sick leave and salary maintenance for sick railway employees – including recuperation for TB sufferers in a spa town – and relatively generous superannuation provisions. Wives and children also had access to medical care while widows of employees were eligible for a pension.[57] In Morcenx, a small village in the Landes which came into being with the railways, they provided workers' accommodation, a chapel and three schools, largely for the children of Midi railway employees for all of whom tuition and transport were free and, upon completion, employment within the company guaranteed. Free education was not introduced universally to France until the Jules Ferry Laws of 1881. At the Pereire schools, the curriculum for boys was notably modern and included reading and writing, arithmetic and calculus, accounting, history, geography, physics and chemistry, botany and zoology, mechanics and arboriculture. Girls were instructed in more domestic subjects, domestic economy, housekeeping, knitting, sewing and ironing. Physical exercise for all was also an important element at the schools which carried the latest equipment.[58] Emile personally ordered from the publisher Edouard Charton books by Sir Walter Scott, Fenimore Cooper, Georges Sand, Lamartine, Voltaire and Herodotus for a village library.[59] Less successful was the attempt of Emile and Isaac to establish in 1860 an institution for adult education in Bordeaux.[60]

Opportunities were not limited to the children of male employees of the Midi. Wives of signalmen worked as guards at the barriers and at ticket booths in the stations. They made uniforms as well as carrying out certain tasks in the building of carriages. In 1863, nearly 1,100 women were employed by the Midi in these positions.[61] Such rewards and benefits were not entirely uncommon among the largest of the Second Empire industrial enterprises whose proprietors, motivated by Christian virtues of charity and compassion on the one hand, recognised that social stability and political harmony came at some cost. This aspect of industrialisation during the Second Empire has been described as essentially authoritarian and paternalistic, intended to dampen the socialist and revolutionary elements which threatened the Bonapartist regime from the outset.[62] The Pereires were not blind to the effect their generosity had on their own workforce and their prosperity clearly depended on the continued goodwill and political stability of the Emperor. But it is difficult to overlook the tone of their early writing on the conditions of the miners of Anzin and the silk workers of Lyon during the 1830s which showed considerable sensitivity to the degradation and inhumanity of much existing physical labour.[63] Of more long-standing significance, perhaps, was the motivation of *sedaca*, the requirement of all Jews that they commit to acts of beneficence towards their fellows, among which the greatest was to help others stand on their own two feet through providing a job or a loan. The Pereires' employment practices could be interpreted as guided equally by religious strictures engrained through their childhood and by the lessons learned within the Saint-Simonian movement as by calculated effort to obtain the quiescence of their work force.

Aside from the profits earned from their investments in associated companies, Emile and Isaac Pereire pursued opportunities on their own account, building and increasing wealth through every means at their disposal. Such significant wealth required protection and in 1857 they formed a family trust to accommodate their combined assets at that point and all the gains they were to make together thereafter, the *Société Universelle Pereire*. This was to exclude 'all the real or personal property they owned currently and every one of the objects, furnishings, clothing, household linen, silver, jewellery, paintings, objets d'art etc, which can and will be able to be found in their respective apartments'. Through this vehicle Emile and Isaac held extensive power over their joint estates without the need to consult each other. On their death the *Société Pereire* was to continue in law among their heirs.[64]

Real estate was the nucleus of their private fortune. They had been purchasing land neighbouring their rail interests over many years – initially in the vicinity of the Gare Saint-Lazare and at Saint-Germain-en-Laye, in Armainvilliers and Crécy and, later, in the Landes and at Arcachon – but the most lucrative deal they closed was that of the plaine Monceau which Emile bought from the city of Paris in 1861 after lengthy negotiation with the Orléans family which had owned it. As Emile wrote to Herminie,

I have finished with the Parc Monceaux [sic] business. We are owners of the entirety except of course for the public gardens and public highways. We paid a high price, but it has helped us to get a good deal for the whole and we are receiving interesting offers. I will put a start to the negotiations.⁶⁵

The price was over eight million francs for seven large parcels of land surrounding a proposed new public park, what was to become the parc Monceau, and which were to include provision for streets and roads at the Pereires' expense. They retained many choice parcels of land – in the boulevards Pereire, Courcelles, Malesherbes, Neuilly among others – in which they built houses, shops, apartments and stables, drawing by 1870 rentals of over seven hundred thousand francs per annum.⁶⁶ Emile had kept the area in his sights for thirty years, from the early 1830s in fact when he worked on securing the first *entrepôt*. Now, however, with Haussmann's decision in 1859–60 to double the size of the city to incorporate eleven entire communes, including Monceau-Batignolles, it became the centre of luxurious housing development. Symbolically, it was to be here that Zola located the mansion of his corrupt developer Aristide Saccard, in *La Curée*.⁶⁷

In addition to the loans they advanced to friends and acquaintances, on a most generous scale and for a variety of purposes, they invested in the projects of others. In 1860, under the chairmanship of Michel Chevalier, Emile and Isaac participated with Eugène Pereire in a plan to publish an *Encyclopédie: Exposition universelle des progrès des sciences, des arts et des lettres au XIXe siècle*. Directed towards workers who supported peaceful rather than conflictual resolution of industrial and political questions, its purpose was to promote Saint-Simonian ideas about the centrality of industry and applied science to the economy. Only twelve trial chapters saw the light of day.⁶⁸

Their wealth was a magnet for fortune-seekers needing investment capital, and they seem to have been remarkably forbearing in their consideration of proposals of varying degrees of seriousness. They certainly supported works of innovation, anticipating, for instance, the direction in which photography was leading, towards an art form with potential for mass reproduction and for recording places and people as they were. Emile had become a patron of the painter Paul Delaroche, who was among the first to recognise the significance of the daguerreotype when it appeared in 1839. From the 1850s the Pereires invested in this new technology, their interest in the work of Nadar particularly eliciting much gratitude from the recipient.⁶⁹ This active interest in photography exemplified their support for technological advances and an aesthetic appreciation of all its forms. In 1860 they became shareholders in the Société

Générale Félix Tournachon dit Nadar et Cie, and financed Nadar's studio in the boulevard des Capucines.[70] He repaid them 'eighty-seven francs 56 centimes for each 100 francs invested', as well as in kind, taking many photographic portraits of them and their family. Eugène Pereire was also one of Nadar's backers and Gustave Pereire continued to advance Nadar loans for well over a decade.[71]

What has been described here as the Pereire family business was widespread and increasingly unwieldy, given the resources with which they had to manage it. They disposed of enormous capital investments in a spectrum of industries as well as through their own private family trust. The demands here were in some senses equally challenging, incorporating real estate developments of different magnitudes, innovative enterprises such as Nadar's, agricultural produce, sardine preservation, the manufacture of *confiture*, to name a few. Their interests were insatiable. To control their activities and garner support for their projects, the Pereires relied on a network of family members, close friends and colleagues who approved their decisions. Even then the capacity to juggle all the balls in the air became ever more difficult to the point of disaster. Shareholders, lulled into a false sense of security through the handsome dividends and increasingly inadequate reporting they were receiving, were shocked into action with the collapse of first one then the other of the Pereire flagships. How this came about will be addressed in a later chapter. But first, having considered how the Pereires attempted to manage their businesses as family concerns, we shall now turn to the wider family itself, particularly to the Pereire wives and daughters, and examine its meaning to the private and public lives of '*les frères Pereire*'.

Notes

1 AFP, Emile to Samuel Alexandre, 24 June 1824.
2 Sarchi, *Lettres*, t. I, p. 469, letter 309, Félicie to Hélène, Paris, 18 August 1868.
3 Harold James, *Family Capitalism: Wendels, Haniels, Falcks, and the Continental European Model* (Cambridge, MA, 2006), p. 4. In 2013, 15 per cent of the top 40 listed companies were family businesses, including PSA Peugeot Citroën, Auchan, Leclerc and Bouygues. Of French businesses, 83 per cent are family businesses. See Christopher Bernard, 'Leading French family businesses', www.kpmgfamilybusiness.com/leading-french-family-business, 5 March 2013.
4 James, *Family Capitalism*, p. 16.
5 Paula E. Hyman, 'Afterword' in Steven M. Cohen and Paula E. Hyman (eds), *The Jewish Family: Myths and Reality* (New York, 1986), pp. 233.
6 James, *Family Capitalism*, pp. 41–71.
7 Freedeman, 'Joint stock business organizations'.

8 Le Bret, *Frères d'Eichthal*, p. 384. Elisabeth Paulet makes the same point in 'The Péreire Brothers: bankers or speculators? An interpretation through agency theory paradigm', *Journal of European Economic History* 35 (2006), 476.
9 *Panthéon des Illustrations Françaises au XIXe Siècle*.
10 *Oeuvres*, s. G, t. 1, p. 3.
11 Stoskopf, *Banquiers et financiers*, p. 276.
12 AFP, Henry Pereire, Paris, to Emile, Arcachon, 22 November 1871.
13 ANMT, 25AQ 2, Crédit Mobilier, Rapport, 30 April 1860.
14 Eric Anceau, *Dictionnaire des députés du Second Empire* (Rennes, 1999), p. 426, fn. 97; p. 428, fn. 104.
15 Joseph-Antoine Roy, *Histoire du Jockey Club de Paris* (Paris, 1985), p. 73.
16 From 1898 the Hotel Ritz.
17 Diane de Saint-André, '35-37 Hôtel Pereire', in Béatrice de Andia and Dominique Fernandès (eds), *Rue du Faubourg-Saint-Honoré* (Paris, 1994), p. 132.
18 Ferguson, *World's Banker*, pp. 573-4.
19 Girard, *Travaux publics*, pp. 157-8.
20 AFP, Isaac, Vienna, to Emile.
21 Philippe Fontaine and Luc Marco, 'La gestion d'entreprise dans la pensée économique française aux XVIIIe et XIXe siècles', *Revue d'économie politique* 4 (1993), 591-2.
22 Luc Marco, 'From the dynamics of the entrepreneur to the analysis of the firm: *la science des affaires*, 1819-1855', in Gilbert Faccarello (ed.), *Studies in the History of French Political Economy: From Bodin to Walras* (London, 1998).
23 AFP, Blanqui to Emile, 10 February 1834, 7 April 1837.
24 Lynn Hunt and George Sheridan, 'Corporatism, association, and the language of labor in France, 1750-1850', *Journal of Modern History* 58 (1986), 813-14.
25 Peter N. Stearns, 'Individualism and association in French industry, 1820-1848', *Business History* 40 (1966), 310-12.
26 ANMT, 25AQ 2, Crédit Mobilier, Rapport, 30 April 1855, p. 30.
27 Tony Judt, *Marxism and the French Left: Studies on Labour and Politics in France, 1830-1981* (New York, 2011), pp. 86-91, 96-7.
28 ANMT, 25AQ 2, Crédit Mobilier, *Procès-verbaux*, 23 April 1856, pp. 60-3.
29 Karl Marx, *Dispatches for the New York Tribune: Selected Journalism of ...*, James Ledbetter (ed.) (London, 2007), 24 June, 1856, p. 178; Karl Marx and Friedrich Engels, *Manifesto of the Communist Party* (London, 1888).
30 AFP, Isaac to Casimir Salvador, 18 August 1860.
31 Ibid., Isaac to Henry, 3 June 1871.
32 Javier Vidal Olivares and Pedro Pablo Ortúñez, 'The internationalisation of ownership of the Spanish railway companies, 1858-1936', *Business History* 44 (2002), 29-55.
33 Marc Meuleau, 'From inheritors to managers: the École des hautes études commerciales and business firms', in Youssef Cassis, François Crouzet and Terry Gourvish (eds), *Management and Business in Britain and France: The Age of the Corporate Economy* (Oxford, 1995), pp. 128-46.
34 Marco, '*Science des affaires*', pp. 306-8.

35 Marc de Ferrière le Vayer, 'Christofle: a family firm', in Cassis et al., *Management and Business*, Chapter 4.
36 Adeline Daumard discusses the formation of the nineteenth century business dynasty in *Les Bourgeois et la bourgeoisie en France depuis 1815* ([Paris], 1987), pp. 172–9.
37 AFP, 'Plan de voyage de mes fils, 1861'.
38 Ibid., Emile to Henry, within a letter Herminie to Henry, 8 January 1865.
39 Ibid., Herminie, Armainvilliers, to Emile, 18 January 1863.
40 Ibid., Herminie, Paris, to Emile II, 18 May 1859.
41 Ibid., Isaac, Paris, to Henry, Arcachon, 22 March 1871.
42 Ibid., letters Isaac to Henry, March 1871.
43 Ibid., Isaac, Paris, to Fanny, Arcachon, 25 March 1871.
44 Plessis, *Banque de France*, p. 80.
45 Robert R. Locke, 'A method for identifying French corporate businessmen (the Second Empire)', *French Historical Studies* 10 (1977), 261–92.
46 Frédéric Barbier, 'Les origines de la maison Fould: Berr Léon et Bénedict Fould (vers 1740–1864)', *Revue historique* I, 1989, 188.
47 Price, *People and Politics*, p. 41.
48 There are no letters extant between Isaac and his daughters Henriette and Jeanne.
49 AN, MC VIII/1682, notaire Fould, 21 March 1857.
50 *Livre du centenaire (École polytechnique), 1794–1894* (Paris, 1897), pp. 194 ff.
51 Gustave Pereire paid tribute to Polack in *Ecrits*, t. 3, fasc., 2, pp. 2, 764.
52 Aycard, *Histoire du Crédit mobilier*, p. 84.
53 AFP, 'Affaire Brochon'.
54 Barbance, *Compagnie Générale Transatlantique*, p. 99. The Chief of Traffic earned 11,000 francs p.a., the deputy 4,300 francs.
55 Louis M. Clot, *Emile Pereire* (Paris, 1858), p. 16.
56 Barbance, *Compagnie Générale Transatlantique*, p. 99.
57 ANMT, 78AQ 6,7, Midi, *Rapports*, 1856, 1864, 1865.
58 *Écrits*, t. 4, fasc., 4, 'Écoles de Morcenx', pp. 2225–30.
59 AFP, undated letter to Charton, who founded a public library in Versailles in the 1860s.
60 Autin, *Frères Pereire*, p. 322.
61 ANMT, 78AQ 6, Midi, Conseil d'Administration, *Rapport* (Paris, 1864), pp. 46–8.
62 Price, *People and Politics*, pp. 52–60.
63 Addressed in Chapter 3 above.
64 AN/MC VIII 1682, 29 March 1857.
65 AFP, Emile, Arcachon, to Herminie, 11 September 1860.
66 Autin, *Frères Pereire*, Annexe No. 15, p. 374.
67 AFP, notarial contract between the City of Paris and Emile Pereire, 6 January 1861. The *banlieues* entirely absorbed into Paris were: Auteuil, Passy, Batignolles, Montmartre, La Chapelle, La Villette, Belleville, Charonne, Bercy, Grenelle, Vaugirard. Hazan, *Invention of Paris*, p. 175, fn. 4.
68 BNF-A, Fonds Enfantin, 7860/1–21; Jean Bonnerot, 'Sainte-Beuve et l'encyclo-

pédie Pereire (notes inédites)', *Revue des sciences humaines* 109 (1963), 39–57.
69 Elizabeth Anne McCauley, *Industrial Madness: Commercial Photography in Paris, 1848–1871* (New Haven, 1994). Nadar, *A terre et en l'air ... Mémoires du Géant* (Paris, 1865), pp. 199–200, expressed enormous gratitude to the Pereires.
70 McCauley, *Industrial Madness*, pp. 61–2.
71 Ibid. Nadar's debt to Gustave by 1875 amounted to 24,000 francs in loans and interest.

7

Private lives of public men

Within a half century the Pereires had gone from poverty in the Jewish quarter of Bordeaux to enormous wealth and luxury among the *grande bourgeoisie* of Paris. The capital in companies of which Emile Pereire was a director in 1863 was estimated at just under four billion francs. From a quarter to one-third of all business treated on the Bourse was carried out under their aegis.[1] Their personal fortunes had grown commensurately. While in the past they had need to borrow, not only from Adolphe d'Eichthal and Auguste Thurneyssen but from their uncle Isaac Rodrigues, within five years of the PSG launch the Pereire brothers had been in a position to repay their debts. Over the next thirty years they amassed a huge portfolio of real estate, frequently associated with land around their railways and which was then expropriated from them by the State to their profit. They were major shareholders in their own right in all their companies, attracting generous dividends. An estimate of their combined wealth from this source alone comes close to 100 million francs. Stoskopf has estimated with some justification that in 1859 Emile Pereire's fortune was in the order of 200 million francs, to which could be added Isaac's portfolio, often mirroring Emile's in value, to give a conservative 300 million.[2]

What was the quality of their private life? What lay behind this enormous wealth? And how did they spend it? Family correspondence tells us much about both the Pereires' public and private lives, and while business – more particularly money – was a recurring topic it is the significance of the family itself which emerges just as clearly from their letters. Emile and Isaac wrote constantly to each other, to their families and to their colleagues, as also did family members write to them and to each other. Family news sustained them all. And since business took the family to most parts of Europe and they owned properties in various parts of France, there were ample opportunities for letter writing.

But first let us examine the position they had reached in relation to Judaism by the time their great wealth arrived. In 1861 there were 11,000 Jews living in the capital. By 1872, there were more than 25,000 in Paris, principally Ashkenazim, searching economic opportunity or fleeing Alsace-Lorraine to escape the annexation by a unified Germany. Other eastern European Jews also began to seek a better life in the 'land of liberty'. A great number lived in poverty in the third and fourth *arrondissements*, some 16 per cent of whom were totally indigent.[3] In comparison, the Sephardim scarcely grew in number at all, although their significance in other ways remained strong. In 1819 they had built their own synagogue in the rue de Notre-Dame-de-Nazareth and later, in 1877, an imposing edifice in the rue Buffault. Sephardim were regarded, and in this they connived, as 'the patricians of Jewry ... from which they drew a pretension of supremacy'.[4] This notion of superiority may have been mythical, but perhaps it was the self-confidence which emerged from it, allied to their history of successful accommodation and integration with Catholic mercantile interests, which enabled the Sephardim to grasp the more easily the opportunity of equality in French citizenship.[5] While the Pereires gave to Sephardic causes, however, they did not play an active role within the practising Sephardic circle in Paris. After Emile's death, Isaac was not among the subscribers to the 'Société Civile du Temple Israëlite suivant le Rite Espagnol-Portugais' which constructed the temple in the rue Buffault, although ironically this did not discourage the leader of that enterprise, the Bordelais Daniel Iffla, from including the names of both Pereires on the plaque situated to the left of the sanctuary and dedicated 'to the illustrious children of Israel'.[6]

Recent studies of the d'Eichthals and of the Rothschilds provide vivid examples of Jewish success among families of the *grande bourgeoisie* in France.[7] They also illustrate the differing means adopted by Jews to consolidate their success. The d'Eichthals converted to Catholicism (in 1817) to ensure their banking enterprise took root in a Catholic country in which they were newcomers. The Rothschilds, on the other hand, remained observant. Indeed, when a niece in London decided to marry a non-Jew, James de Rothschild declared furiously that 'nothing could be more disastrous for our family, for our continued well-being, for our good name and for our honour ... [than to renounce] the religion which, thank God, made us great'.[8]

The Pereires did not share this devotion nor did they convert to Christianity, either to Protestantism like the politician Achille Fould or to Catholicism like the d'Eichthal family. They always identified publicly as Jews and were in turn identified as Jews. Despite Isaac's apparent lack of interest in Daniel Iffla's synagogue they contributed handsomely to Jewish causes and played some role in Jewish organisational life, making a major contribution to reconstruction of the synagogue of Bordeaux after its destruction by fire in 1873 and each providing in his will 25,000 francs to the poor of the 'Israélite' constituency of both Bordeaux and Paris.[9] Their belief in and practice of Judaism was increasingly perfunctory, however, limited so far as Emile was concerned to attendance at the synagogue on holy days and not even thus far for Isaac although, having written in his youth with some diffidence of Jewish religious practices, he was to write in later life with approval of Jewish accomplishments.

Emile, in contrast, lukewarm as he was towards Judaism in reality, was recognised and treated as a senior member of the Jewish community. He had assisted the efforts of James de Rothschild and Adolphe Crémieux to mediate in what came to be known as the Damascus Affair in 1840 and, later, he was called upon to intervene between the Consistoire Central of France and the Prefect of the Seine concerning the salary of the Chief Rabbi.[10] But his attachment to Judaism had by now become social and cultural rather than religious or spiritual. He was wont to use Jewish references on particular occasions, reciting the *Shema Israel* upon the arrival of the first Bordeaux–Madrid train in Spain, the land from which his ancestors had been banished.[11] Emile's identification with Judaism is also captured in other more domestic ways, for instance when, as tradition expected, he named his sons after his own father (Isaac Emile), and his own grandfather (Jacob Henry). Isaac did not.

Isaac, while inherently the more spiritual of the two and continuing to affirm his attachment to Saint-Simonianism until the end, gave no semblance of being a religious Jew at all, and there are no indications that he attended the synagogue for any reason, save one: three of his children, unlike Emile's, married Jews. Eugène, whose marriage to Juliette Fould took place in a synagogue, went on to become secretary of the Consistoire Central of Paris. Gustave also married within the faith (he wed Amélie Emerique) as did his sister Jeanne, who married the Florentine architect Edmond Philipson. Indeed, one could argue that it was Fanny herself who may have brought influence to bear on her own family, including her stepson, impressing upon them the need to reclaim fidelity to their religious antecedents which her husband had long abandoned. Upon her death the Chief Rabbi of France, Alfred Lévy, presiding at the memorial service in Paris, extolled her virtues as the perfect wife and mother, 'the faithful companion who becomes the joy, the pride, the support of the husband', Isaac's 'guardian angel whom God sends to man on the path of life to render the crossing happy and easy'.[12]

Emile's children, on the other hand, with the single exception of Fanny, married sons or daughters of prominent non-Jewish business or political figures who frequently became associated in some way or other with the family businesses. Thus Cécile married the engineer Charles Rhoné, a Catholic; Claire married a Protestant, Georges Thurneyssen, son of the Pereires' associate the banker Auguste Thurneyssen who was a director of the Midi; and Emile II married Suzanne Chevalier, daughter of Auguste Chevalier, also a Catholic, a member of the board of the Crédit Mobilier, and brother of Michel. Henry at the age of thirty-six married Léontine de Stoppani, a young woman born in Brazil who had been adopted by French parents.

Marriages between Emile's children and Christians were not necessarily simple to arrange, however. Recognition by prospective parents-in-law of the Pereires' Jewish background also required clarification of religious preferences. In 1853, when Georges Thurneyssen asked for the hand in marriage of Claire, Emile responded with obvious pleasure since the Thurneyssens were friends of long standing. But Georges' parents had at least some concern on the subject of religion, wishing discretely to establish the expectations of Claire's parents. 'Your wishes concerning religion will be satisfied', replied Emile,

> My daughter is not a Catholic. Not wanting to raise her in the religion in which I was born, we educated her from the start in the knowledge of the most advanced religions without forcing her to practice any of them. Her wedding will be celebrated according to the customs of her husband's faith, which will also be her children's.[13]

Thus were the Thurneyssens' Protestant sensibilities relieved and the religious position of the Pereires' crystallised.

Another of Emile and Herminie's children, Emile II, actually created a controversy with his marriage in April 1864 to Suzanne Chevalier. They married in the Mairie of the VIIIth *arrondissement* followed by a mass in the parish church attended by a large crowd of well-wishers. But the happiness issuing from the friends and relatives of the young couple was not reflected by the Church which quickly denounced the insidiousness of an increasing number of mixed marriages, the papal nuncio writing specifically about this marriage to the Vatican's Secretary of State, in May. As we know, Emile II was not raised within the Jewish religion and the description of this marriage as 'mixed' was not entirely accurate – only common knowledge that the Pereires were Jews called the occasion into question. The Pereire-Chevalier marriage thus summed up tension over the breach of previously impermeable barriers, of a lapse in strict Catholic standards which was perceived to hold dangers of becoming widespread.[14] Emile II's sister Cécile Rhoné, in contrast, had converted on her marriage and become a devout Catholic, counting Catholic clerics among her close friends.

The experience of the Pereire family, privileged and wealthy, inconsistent in its religious devotion or affiliation, sheds light on the rapid changes in Jewish community life which occurred in nineteenth-century Western Europe. These changes were a product both of emancipation and of industrial development, the former removing barriers to geographic and financial mobility, the latter promising dazzling opportunities for those inspired by the new innovations and preparedness for hard work.[15] But while at one level the historical Jewish emphasis on family life could be seen to epitomise bourgeois virtues – indeed, the Jewish family was promoted by Jewish leaders in this way – on another level entirely, community regulation which had once sustained and guided the family in its rectitude and religious adherence had been dissolved, leaving a vacuum which needed to be filled, and thrusting the very question of Jewish identity to the fore. Sex roles which had seen some permeability after the Revolution had now become more circumscribed in bourgeois Jewish homes: men inherited the public sphere, women the private. Men moved in the world, making their way in new commercial and financial endeavours. The domestic sphere – the home, care of the children, religious devotion and the maintenance of religious standards – was the preserve of women. The Jewish family was also an extended one, however, ensuring that if relatives did not share the same establishment they lived as neighbours. Help, support and advice were thus at hand for husband and wife alike. The Second Empire was a period of heightened family significance in any case, when the intimacy of the home provided tangible shelter from the pressures of an ever-changing economic and social environment. Children were an accepted and important presence in this bourgeois home with a separate identity from its adult occupants. 'The child-centred family with the mother at its heart was increasingly promoted as the ideal during the nineteenth century', as one historian has commented, and the Jewish family in particular is cited by historians as especially devoted to children.[16] In all its aspects, then, the Pereires' family life typifies patterns of behaviour among the highest social stratum during the Second Empire while maintaining certain Jewish traditions, customs and values, displaying enormous wealth while claiming modesty and an egalitarian spirit.

As leaders of industry, the Jewish Saint-Simonians had attracted anti-Semitic vitriol from an early time and the Pereires' prominence reinforced and invigorated prejudice. Subjected to attack in the 1840s by Mathieu-Dairnvaell, their family now offered even more obvious targets. Passages in the Goncourts' journal recording Jules Goncourt's encounters with Eugène Pereire defy belief. Even Herminie Pereire's charitable works incited the Goncourts to their virulent extreme.[17] The very closeness of the family encouraged unwelcome attention, as the recollections of Ernest Feydeau attest. In his *Mémoires d'un coulissier*, describing Bordeaux as 'the great nursery which fed the Bourse with the sons of Israel', as much a diatribe against the Pereires to the advantage of James de Rothschild as a true memoire of a trainee banker, he described the Pereires, surrounded by friends, thus: 'Men sharply polite, ulcerated with hatred, always concentrated, hard and tense as bars of iron, inflexible in their ideas, penetrated with admiration of themselves'.[18] The entry of the Pereires into politics in 1863 was to give full rein to anti-Semitism targeted against them, and particularly from the Catholic Church.

The ambiguity which characterised the lives of French women and their families for most of the nineteenth century was even more marked within families of the *grande bourgeoisie*. Women enjoyed great wealth and luxury but suffered inequality before the law. Lacking the right to vote, their inferior status enshrined in the Code Civil, the family was nevertheless the core of Second Empire society. The central roles played by Herminie and Fanny within the family were thus circumscribed. Certainly, both marriages appear to have been love matches, brought about by personal choice, and relations between Emile and Herminie on the one hand and between Isaac and Fanny on the other remained secure throughout the many years of their marriages, the better part of fifty years and forty years respectively. But divorce had been abolished in any case in 1816 and was not reinstated for another sixty-eight years. Given the particular and endogamous circumstances of both marriages it is unlikely that they would have been anything other than enduring.[19]

Nevertheless, when Emile and Herminie were apart they wrote to each other constantly, letters filled with news and gossip, avid for information about family members. There is no doubt of their close relationship, epitomised so poignantly when Herminie, late in her life and almost blind, her dependence on Emile evident, wrote: 'I feel myself incomplete, I need to feel myself close to you, to hear your voice when I cannot see you; otherwise I am sad, as I start to be at present.'[20] Yet there are instances

10 Rachel Herminie Rodrigues Henriques (Herminie), Mme Emile Pereire
Private collection

in the correspondence between them when silences are also noted and hurt feelings seem to be expressed. 'In spite of the silence that you are observing towards me my dear Emile I do not want to stay long without giving you our news', wrote Herminie in 1851. 'I do not understand your silence nor that of my sons', wrote Emile to Herminie in 1858, continuing that: 'I think that the silence you are keeping with regard to me is not motivated by the illness of anyone of ours.'[21]

One can only speculate about the correspondence between Isaac and Fanny as few letters have survived, but these few are redolent of a warm intimacy, addressed invariably by Isaac to 'Ma chère amie' and concluding with tender endearments: 'Je t'embrasse comme je t'aime.' Whether the concern for women, which Isaac had articulated so passionately during his later Saint-Simonian days, endured beyond that early time is not clear from these documents. But during the Third Republic, when he purchased a newspaper to express his opinions, he argued that in matters of succession the wife be treated as equal in the ménage.[22] He reprimanded Léon Gambetta for failing to mention women in a wide-ranging speech which covered the needs of children, adult men, France, citizens and everybody else.[23] Within the marriage, he confided in Fanny and valued her opinions. Both she and her sister Cécile took on the role of secretary when he became a newspaper proprietor, a position of trust, of shared knowledge and of competence. Thus Isaac's feminism may have had a longer, albeit a less passionate, life than in its first manifestation.

Emile Pereire was not immune from innuendo of infidelity. It is difficult to make anything else of the story which appeared in *Le Figaro* in 1857 in which he was accused of being in the habit each day of visiting the same address in the rue Saint-Georges, the inference being that there was something untoward here. This street, in an area known as Breda, was notable as a quarter where there lived a large number of kept women.[24] Emile's reply was ambiguous but he insisted it be published: 'My morality and the respect of the family are the most precious heritage I can leave to my children [he wrote] and I do not admit to anyone the right to undermine it.' His response was puzzling, as Mme Jules Baroche was to note in her diary. 'Instead of wrapping himself in his innocence and observing a prudent silence' the 'irascible capitalist's' highly ambiguous response did not address the accusation at all but seemed tacitly to confirm it.[25] Adultery was common among men of the bourgeoisie in nineteenth-century France and although there is no proof of infidelity one should not be surprised to hear that the exceedingly wealthy Pereires kept mistresses.[26] It was as the lecher that the Paris correspondent for the *Boston Daily Advertiser* described Emile Pereire at a reception given by the Prince Napoléon:

'This little old man in knee-breeches, examining with an eye-glass the beautiful shoulders of the ladies of the court as if they were marble statues. He had something of a Mephistopheles about him.'[27] The description is reminiscent of Zola's account in *La Curée* of Napoléon III's lascivious appraisal of Renée Saccard at a reception at the Tuileries.[28]

Over thirty years or so there were many pregnancies. Herminie and Emile had five surviving children: Fanny (1825), their eldest, was followed by Cécile (1829) and Claire (1834), and then by two boys, Emile II (1840) and Henry (1841). Isaac had fathered two sons with Laurence, his first wife – Eugène (1831) and Georges (1836) – and Isaac and Fanny had three surviving children of their marriage, Gustave (1846), Henriette (1853) and Jeanne (1856).[29] There were certainly more pregnancies on each side, but infant mortality was high in the community: between 1825 and 1856, when Herminie and then Fanny were producing children, one in six to one in five infants in France did not live beyond one year. The reasons associated with this high rate of infant mortality – poverty, industrialisation, overcrowding, a low level of obstetric care – scarcely explain why the Pereire women experienced an even higher rate of loss than the community, however, and one must ask whether consanguinity was not a cause.[30] The years between Herminie's six children (her first child was born in 1825, her last in 1841) suggest there were other births. A daughter born in August 1837, Marie, died at fourteen months. The first two children of the marriage of Fanny and Isaac, Jules (1843) and Lucien (1845), also died in infancy, and the seven-year gap between the births of Gustave and Henriette may be accounted for in the same way. Disability also touched the family. We know very little of yet another son, Edouard, save that he suffered from severe intellectual or physical disabilities ('this creature who is so imperfect', wrote Félicie Sarchi) and died in 1876 at the age of twenty-one, a death which was regarded as a merciful release for both Fanny and her son.[31]

It has been said of bourgeois families in the department of the Nord that their increasing size 'could often satisfy any desire for a varied social life ... [providing] an abundance of playmates'.[32] The surviving offspring of Emile and Herminie and of Isaac and Fanny were all friends in one way or another, though there were complexities to negotiate. In the mansion which was to be their final home, the *hôtel Pereire*, their living arrangements encouraged intimacy and it seems to have helped that Fanny was not only the aunt of four other siblings but also their sister (she was also a first cousin of her own children and sister-in-law to her own parents!). Eugène, son of Isaac and his first wife Laurence, nine years older than his nearest male cousin and fifteen years the elder of his brother

11 Fanny Rebecca Rodrigues Pereire, Mme Isaac Pereire, with her daughters Jeanne and Henriette. Photo © Musée d'art et d'histoire du Judaïsme

12 Cécile Rodrigues Pereire, Mme Charles Rhoné
Photo © Musée d'art et d'histoire du Judaïsme

Gustave, was thus almost in a position of adult authority in relation to his younger contemporaries. Female children of the Pereires were even further distanced by age, Emile and Herminie's daughters having reached adulthood by the time their female cousins were born. It was the children of Cécile and of Claire who befriended their second cousins Henriette and Jeanne.

There are no surviving letters from Henriette or Jeanne but for the most part the younger Pereire women were intelligent and sophisticated, well-read and cultivated. Letters written by Emile and Herminie's daughters Fanny, Cécile Rhoné and Claire Thurneyssen are lucid and express strong opinions on subjects of public interest. While the details of their schooling are sketchy, Herminie and her sisters all had received tutoring at home in history and geography among other subjects as well as music lessons. While the boys were educated at *lycées*, one can only imagine that the Pereire daughters, infinitely more favoured financially than the Rodrigues family, would have been educated at home by a governess. A schoolroom in Emile and Herminie's living quarters in the *hôtel Pereire* gives some clues.[33] They were strong-willed, Michel Chevalier writing caustically that 'the women share the sceptre with the men', springing immediately to the defence of Emile and Isaac, contesting or rejecting vigorously any accusation or action brought against them. This comment of Chevalier was written after his famous falling out with the Pereires, which we shall come to, and any malice on his part may need to be interpreted in this light.[34]

The picture of family life built up from the family correspondence is striking in its affection. When, during the events of 1870–71, members were separated for some time their parting was a source of genuine pain. Isaac in particular was said to radiate happiness on reading aloud letters from Fanny and his children who were in Pau, greeting his family with much delight and great relief at their reconciliation in Paris. Playing games with the grandchildren, billiards and dominoes, was a source of considerable pleasure to Emile. Newcomers to the Pereire family were also made welcome quickly. Marie Rhoné's suitor Félix Laroche, who hesitated to ask for her hand for fear that her grandfather Emile might refuse, was rapidly reassured. Ironically, it was Emile who coached Emile II in the niceties of his son's initial approach to the young woman he was later to marry, Suzanne Chevalier, and her family.[35]

While Herminie and Fanny maintained separate kitchens and dining rooms in the *hôtel Pereire* their families regularly dined together, Wednesday night often given over to a convivial gathering which might also include close friends. Each family also maintained a music room in their apartments.[36] Profiting from lessons, members of the family were accomplished pianists, and family concerts were regular pastimes. Cécile Rhoné, Emile II and Fanny's and Isaac's younger daughter Henriette were particularly gifted. Within the Pereire archive a large stack of sheet music consists principally of works by Jewish composers Halévy and Meyerbeer.[37] There were outdoor activities as well: swimming at Arcachon in summer and skating in Paris in winter – Claire Thurneyssen's three small boys were taught by their uncles Emile II and Henry. All the males in the family were keen horse riders also and *la chasse* at Armainvilliers was a regularly scheduled event. Emile at least was adamant that their properties outside Paris should be used as much as possible and not treated merely as investments. He was thus to write with approval of his young granddaughter Marguerite Rhoné pitching in with everybody else to help with the grape harvest at their *vignoble*, Château Palmer.

The health of children thus was a frequent topic, although it often consisted of a comment on their *good* health. When Henriette was temporarily paralysed during the Franco-Prussian War, however (the nature of her illness is not clear but may have had its origins in some psychiatric disturbance), Isaac in Paris expressed considerable anguish, weeping on receiving a letter outlining her condition.[38] But it was the health of the patriarch Emile whose asthma elicited the most disquiet and which was a constant item of news discussed by all the family members.

Both families expressed satisfaction with their children's progress in life. Emile and Herminie were especially proud of the results obtained by Emile II and Henry when they concluded their engineering studies. And although Emile had died before Henry's marriage, they were extremely satisfied with the marriages their other son Emile II and their daughters contracted. Henry's probably brief interest in radical politics was greeted with paternal forgiveness: 'He is young and does not realise sufficiently the dangers that revolutionary ideas present to society.' While we lack similar information from Isaac and Fanny, we do know of Isaac's pride in Eugène's entry into the family business.

Like other women of their class, Herminie and Fanny devoted themselves to charity. Susan K. Foley has emphasised that this activity, undertaken 'to the benefit of the less fortunate', contributed to 'the task of preserving social order by easing suffering, teaching self-improvement and instilling resignation in the poor'.[39] It was an expected element in the lives of elite society women. It was also a means through which to secure 'civic status and influence' in the face of their own legally construed inferiority, to make their mark as individuals in the public sphere.[40] From Herminie's perspective at least, her charity work was no doubt

13 Suzanne Chevalier, Mme Emile Pereire II. Private collection

14 Juliette Betzi Fould, Mme Eugène Pereire
Photo © Musée d'art et d'histoire du Judaïsme

prompted by maternal values and her great wealth, but it had a slightly different aspect. She had been a Saint-Simonian and thus her instinct to do good for the working class and the indigent had its philosophical core in her past. Both her husband and brother-in-law referred consistently in their writings and in their actions to the central problem of poverty and to the importance of raising living standards of 'the most numerous class'. Herminie's social conscience was thus sustained by the household over which she presided. There is little Christian 'resignation' in Saint-Simonianism which emphasised, rather, the individual self-reliance needed by the working class and the considered collective action necessary from those who wished to aid them. Foley's assertion that the usual rationale for such charity was 'the inevitability of poverty', the belief among elite women that poverty could only be addressed through 'moral reform' rather than through 'social reform', thus does not truly describe the Pereire family's *raison d'être*. Fanny, too, saw charitable works as a way of contributing materially to eliminating the problems of poverty. Their philanthropic gestures were probably no more effective in addressing the causes of poverty than those of other wealthy female benefactors, however, and, certainly, differed little in nature. Only the Saint-Simonian rationale distinguished them. Fanny worked within the constraints of the achievable, setting up a 'fourneau' which provided daily meals for 2,000

15 Château Palmer. Archives de la famille Pereire

of the poor and encouraging others to deposit goods and toys for their children.[41] Later in her life, after the death of Isaac, she established and maintained two local hospitals, both providing free consultations and aimed to manage the medical needs of residents in particular *arrondissements*, a means of relieving the strain on large general hospitals.[42]

Despite Emile's capacity to alienate people and possibly because of Isaac's capacity to draw them in, the Pereire family valued friendship and seems to have had a talent for making and keeping friends. Their generosity towards old Saint-Simonian colleagues in particular and their concern for the general welfare of their friends was legendary. The devotion to the composer Félicien David, for example, which continued throughout his life, was one shared by the whole Pereire family. Indeed, the family collectively cared for David over a long period, commissioning music and giving money for sure, but attending also to his state of health (he had rheumatic heart disease) and, given his largely solitary life (he never married), making certain he looked after himself.[43] After he returned to France from exile in 1860 and despite his earlier anti-Jewish pronouncements, Pierre Leroux received their financial support to write *La Grève de Samarez* and the drama *Job*. Another Saint-Simonian, the Guyanese, Ismayl Urbain, spoke with particular warmth of the 'irreproachable' tolerance shown by the Pereire women towards him and his Algerian wife whom he had married according to Islamic rite, this at a time when Catholics had shunned the couple for the same reason. The Pereires provided him with a parcel of shares worth 12,000 francs. Later, Isaac invited Urbain to advise and contribute articles on Algeria for the newspaper the *Liberté*, which he had purchased, and gave Urbain a further 12,000 francs for the education of his son. After Isaac's death, Fanny went out of her way to ensure an annual pension of 2,000 francs was provided and then more funds to help with his son's education.[44] Together with Henri Fournel as President, Enfantin, the Chevalier brothers, Henri Baud, Charles Duveyrier, Arlès-Dufour and others, they also supported and contributed to a 'Société de secours mutuels: les amis de la famille', to care for the increasingly frail, elderly and impoverished former Saint-Simonians, and to provide benefits in case of unemployment or illness.[45]

Aside from the extended Pereire family – the Bauds, the Sarchis, the Regnaults, Olinde's widow Euphrasie and Herminie's widowed sister Amélie Levy – there was a nucleus of very close friends. Among these were a senior professor of mathematics at the École Polytechnique, Jean-Marie Constant Duhamel, and his wife Virginie Bertrand, friends of long-standing associated through the Saint-Simonians. Duhamel and his wife were frequent guests at the *hôtel Pereire* and at Armainvilliers, as were Henri Fournel and his wife Cécile. The Michel Chevaliers were also on friendly terms up to the time of the Crédit Mobilier fall, although there seem to have been certain difficulties from time to time even before that. Chevalier, sensitive to the merest slight, expressed pique when Isaac and Fanny were unable to spend time at his family château at Lodève. Gustave d'Eichthal and his wife Cécile Rodrigues-Henriques were certainly friends as were Adolphe and his wife Louisa de la Rue.[46] And the letters of the publisher Edouard Charton to his wife Hortense are filled with accounts of sumptuous dinners, concerts and balls at the *hôtel Pereire* or at Armainvilliers. Herminie took a particular shine to his son Jules, whom she treated as a member of the family.[47]

They became ever more identified with the capital and had a close circle in Paris but they did not shed their friends from Bordeaux and Bayonne – their Sephardic roots in the southwest remained deep. Late into their lives they continued to entertain Bordeaux and Bayonne friends at the *hôtel Pereire* and at their château outside of Paris, Armainvilliers, and there are many letters recording debts of gratitude for the numerous courtesies extended to visitors. But the Pereires passed time in Bordeaux themselves and, rather less frequently, in Bayonne, where they owned property. They also often visited Château Palmer, the *vignoble* in the Médoc which they acquired in 1853, and Arcachon, the seaside resort on the Atlantic coast near Bordeaux which Emile developed. On these visits, particularly by Emile, they made a point of spending time with the Léons, the Alexandres, the Lopès Dubecs, the Oxedas, reciprocating with invitations to stay at Arcachon or at Château Palmer.

Isaac's several early and precipitate returns to Bordeaux notwithstanding, the Pereire brothers rarely lived apart, sharing rented accommodation from their arrival in Paris.[48] Even after Emile and Herminie had married, they continued to live with Isaac and Sara-Sophie Rodrigues, first in the rue de l'Échiquier, in what is now the tenth arrondissement, then in the rue des Petites Écuries and then in the rue Montholon in the ninth, where the Halévy brothers Fromenthal and Léon also lived.[49] All of these addresses on Paris' right bank were within a short distance of each other. It was not until the Pereires went into business and achieved greater financial independence that they left the Rodrigues ménage. Emile and Herminie, who initially rented an apartment at number 16 rue de Tivoli with Isaac and his first wife Laurence, took up residence in a house in the 'route Royale' at Saint-Cloud in 1837. After several more years they all rejoined at 5 rue d'Amsterdam.[50]

While they had profited from handsome returns on real estate investments from the 1830s, their first major purchase of property on their own account, in 1853, was Château Palmer, an estate of 177 hectares for which they paid 413,000 francs. Substantially enhanced and expanded in the wake of Napoléon I's demise by an Englishman, General Charles Palmer, who had fallen on hard times in the 1840s, the estate was sold to the Caisse Hypothécaire de Paris from which the Pereires bought it. Several years later they commissioned the Bordeaux architect Charles Burguet to design the château.[51] The carving on either side of the façade of the initials 'EP' and 'IP' symbolised both the importance Palmer came to hold for each of them as a place of leisure and productivity, and of their indissoluble partnership. Unfortunately, when in 1855 Napoléon III ordered the best Bordeaux producers to be ranked in order, the Pereires had insufficient time to bring the estate up to the mark and Château Palmer has been forever a *Troisième Cru*, third growth, unlike Château Lafite Rothschild which was awarded a *Premier Cru* at the same time.

As much as other members of the *grande bourgeoisie* in the Second Empire, the Pereires now spent their immense fortune in order to demonstrate, to display, how much of it they had. It was expected, a necessary element in the social circles within which they moved, but it was also partly an antidote to recollected poverty in their childhood and youth. The vicissitudes of their early experiences in Bordeaux heightened their appreciation of a comfortable and stable home, free from financial pressures. Not that either forgot the efforts made by their mother to give them a secure environment and a solid start, a fact to which they returned in their letters, their gratitude tinged with some guilt about the sacrifices she had made and the rewards she did not live to enjoy.

Modesty and simplicity were said to have characterised their private lives and manners, but the Pereires' public face was impressive. It was not long after acquiring the Château Palmer that they became serious property-owners in Paris, purchasing in 1855 for 1,600,000 francs an existing, somewhat neglected, mansion at 35-37 rue du Faubourg Saint-Honoré in the eighth *arrondissement*.[52] Built in 1713 by Louis Chevalier, Chief Justice of the Parlement of Paris, to a design by Pierre Grandhomme, it eventually passed to the lawyer Anne-Élie Pierre Jean Commaille and thence to the Pereires. Their peripatetic life finally at an end, this *hôtel Pereire* remained, from 1858 when they moved into it, the principal place of residence for most of the family for the better part of a century.[53] It was also located conveniently near to the place Vendôme, providing a virtual extension of the offices there. They commissioned Alfred Armand, the architect of the Gare Saint-Lazare, the Grand Hôtel du Louvre and the Grand Hôtel, to redesign the building substantially, giving it in the process a new façade, an imposing, monumental new entrance hall and staircase, and a wide terrace onto the formal garden at the rear, the cost of all these renovations exceeding that of the original building.⁵⁴ The total property with courtyards, gardens and stables amounted to 60,000 square metres, extending a city block to the avenue Gabriel beyond.⁵⁵

More important than the architecture, perhaps, was the extent of the embellishments to it. No expense was spared on art works and artistic decoration or on marble and sculptures. Emile had become a friend and patron of the history painter Paul Delaroche, whose pupils – Auguste Gendron, Charles Jalabert and Henri Picou – were commissioned to paint largely allegorical panels and frescoes in the apartments. The sculptors Jules Klagmann and Amboise Choiselat ornamented the *hôtel* with sculptural figures. Alexandre Cabanel, Ary Scheffer and William Bouguereau, academic painters and prominent members of the Paris salon, also received commissions. Five of the painters commissioned had won the Prix de Rome. So sumptuous was the quantity of gilt and gold leaf they employed that Emile felt compelled to defend himself, admitting: 'there is too much gold here'.⁵⁶ Isaac, however, delighted with the results of the work to his quarters in the *hôtel Pereire*, commissioned Cabanel to paint five portraits of family members. These certainly included those of Fanny, his daughters Jeanne and Henriette and his son Gustave. Cabanel also painted a portrait of Herminie. Sometime later, in 1878, Léon Bonnat, the society portrait painter from Bayonne, executed a portrait of Isaac.

The Pereires also became serious collectors. They had started to collect works of art in 1834, but it was twenty-one years later with the spaciousness promised by a mansion and their now considerable wealth which accelerated their collecting. Each had a gallery of paintings in the *hôtel Pereire* and paintings also came to be spread across their other properties, notably at Armainvilliers.⁵⁷ Their purchases were eclectic. Delaroche was a significant influence, painting a fine portrait of Emile in 1853 which won first prize for portraiture in the Great Exhibition of 1862 in London.⁵⁸ After Delaroche's death in 1855, when Emile organised a retrospective exhibition of his work, the art critic Théophile Thoré (also known as William Bürger) played a part particularly in Emile's purchase of Old Masters. But as the Pereires gradually became more confident in their tastes they exerted their own preferences, purchasing directly from the salons and from individual artists whose ateliers they patronised. Contemporary painters – Ingres (from whom Emile in 1864 commissioned the second rendering of Oedipus and the Sphinx), Delacroix, Tissot, Gérôme, Chassériau, Meissonnier and Ary Scheffer, and members of the Barbizon School, Théodore Rousseau and Narcisse Diaz – were favourites. Neither brother became a patron of the Impressionists, however, ironic when one considers that it was Claude Monet and Camille Pissarro among others who captured the essential modernity introduced to urban life by the Pereires. Among the Old Masters in their collection there were works by Botticelli, Fra Angelico, Carpaccio and Tintoretto; by the seventeenth-century French painters Lorrain and Poussin; the eighteenth-century French artists Boucher and Fragonard; and notably by representatives of the Dutch and Flemish schools, Rembrandt, Van Dyck, Rubens, Vermeer, Hobbema, Hals and Ruisdael, which the *grande bourgeoisie* had helped to bring into vogue.

There was also a large number of the Spanish masters, Goya, El Greco, Velasquez, Murillo, many having been part of the Spanish collection of Louis-Philippe which came onto the market in England in 1853. Purchased by Isaac, the collection was considered to have been first rate and unique.[59] 'There is my real treasure', Emile said of his picture gallery.[60] When in 1866 the Empress Eugénie expressed a wish to organise public exhibitions to display parts of her personal collection and those of other French collectors, the Pereires readily agreed to loan some of their paintings.[61]

Much has been made of the competitive spirit which characterised the relationship between the Pereires and the Rothschilds, usually to the detriment of the Pereires and employed to portray them as parvenus, upstarts, motivated by envy and a rather childish desire to imitate, if not outdo, their rivals. But both families engaged in these practices, becoming locked equally into a struggle that was as serious as it was juvenile. The comment by Alphonse de Rothschild about the Pereire art collection, that it contained 'no work of great renown, simply a few honorable mediocrities', is cited frequently, used as a final comment on the Pereires themselves.[62] But whatever the respective merits of the rival collections, there are enough examples from which we can judge the quality of the Pereires', and there must surely be something to say for the presence in their gallery of Vermeer's *Le Géologue* and *L'Astrologue*. Ironically, it was Alphonse de Rothschild's purchase of *L'Astrologue* sometime later which won him accolades as a connoisseur.[63]

Isaac, together with Fanny, became equally assiduous in the pursuit of sculpture, bronzes, jewellery and silver, fine cabinet-making, and *objets de vertu*. Even in 1867 when their financial empire was collapsing around them, Fanny Pereire continued to purchase expensive items of jewellery, sculpture and fine cabinet-making at the Exposition Universelle in Paris. 'M. and Mme Isaac Pereire' are listed among those buying or commissioning work by the silversmith and jeweller Emile Froment Maurice; the renowned sculptor and bronze-maker Antoine-Louis Barye; and from the cabinet-makers Fourdinois and Chéret. At the same time, both brothers purchased antique furnishings which appeared on the market

16 Amélie Emerique, Mme Gustave Pereire
Photo © Musée d'art et d'histoire du Judaïsme

from the time of the French Revolution, especially pieces from the eras of Louis XV and Louis XVI. This need to be counted as connoisseurs was an accepted and expected part of high bourgeois life under Napoléon III and the Empress, the trend-setter Eugénie creating a style of decoration combining modern with antique pieces which was much copied, including by the Pereires.[64]

17 Léontine de Stoppani, Mme Henry Pereire. Archives de la famille Pereire

The *hôtel Pereire* house-warming in February 1859 was a splendid affair, the three lines of carriages creating a traffic jam the length of the rue du Faubourg Saint-Honoré and extending down the rue Royale, the kind of congestion almost unheard of to that time. Once inside, the formal presentation of guests took half an hour.[65] Since the Pereires were now close neighbours of members of the Rothschild family (Nathaniel Rothschild had purchased the adjoining 33 rue du Faubourg Saint-Honoré in 1856) any inconvenience to their former associates would have heightened their pleasure. Charles Sarchi later commented that the *fêtes* mounted at the *hôtel Pereire* gave Emile a foretaste of paradise![66]

The census of 1860 showed the disposition of the family thus: Emile and Herminie with their sons Emile II and Henry, occupying the ground and second floors; Isaac and Fanny and their children the first; and Eugène and his wife Juliette the third floor. Each of the brothers' apartments contained staircases leading to upper or lower areas. Emile and Herminie's other daughters, Cécile Rhoné and Claire Thurneyssen, lived with their husbands and families on the first and second floors respectively of another part of the *hôtel* facing onto the street.[67] There were seventeen servants.[68] No greater contrast can have existed than that between the extravagant *hôtel Pereire* in Paris' eighth *arrondissement* and their childhood home in the rue Bouhaut, Bordeaux.

The building of Armainvilliers in the Seine-et-Marne was certainly a riposte to the Rothschilds whose château Ferrières was only a stone's throw distant.[69] The Pereires who together with Adolphe d'Eichthal had purchased nearly 4,000 hectares at Armainvilliers/Crécy in 1852, commissioned Alfred Armand ten years later to design a château on part of this estate.[70] Isaac's grandson Alfred Pereire described the château's style as 'jolie laide', with a central core and two wings, one accommodating Emile and his family and the other Isaac and his. A large salon in the centre brought them together. To the right and left of the central cupola two large decorative motifs in stone, a locomotive and a ship, symbolised their principal transport companies.[71] Armainvilliers was another repository for their art works and was furnished with great care.[72] The château and domain, the initial cost of which was 3,500,000 francs, were to remain in the family until a mishap during the Second World War rendered the building uninhabitable: bombarded mistakenly but with great accuracy by the US Air Force, it was eventually demolished and the property sold for a golf course, which it remains.

There are, however, a few surviving fragments which recall the life lived at Armainvilliers, a *maison de gardien*, remnants of a large kitchen garden, a long brick wall among them. Most arresting are the vestiges of a wood of oak through which visitors, alighting at a railway siding on the route of the Est rail line, strolled to the *calèche* conveying them to the château. Designed by Jean-Pierre Barillet-Deschamps, a foremost landscape architect of the Second Empire, a natural reservoir provided the focal point and the source around which grottoes, stalactites, a Chinese pagoda, a Jules Verne bridge delighted the eye and cleansed the mind of the stresses of Parisian life.[73] Isaac was most at home here and it was where he spent most of his later years.

Emile, in contrast, found the micro-climate exacerbated his chronic asthma and, with advancing age, retreated with increasing frequency to the seaside resort he had developed, Arcachon. As early as 1853, Emile and Herminie had rented a house in the area for the summer holidays, arranged for them by Aristide Pereyra (who may not have been related).[74] But the desire to build a seaside resort at Arcachon had its origins in Saint-Simonianism, an idea conceived when in 1832 the disciples confronted cholera in the city of Paris and considered ways of prevention through more healthful forms of living. Spas and mountain resorts offering health benefits had long existed, and there were even fashionable seaside retreats to be contemplated as models, such as the duc de Morny's Deauville and, earlier, Isidore Bloch's Dieppe.[75] Not too far from Arcachon was Biarritz, the Empress' own favourite, and Arcachon was itself also close to Bordeaux.

In her study of Arcachon, Alice Garner is sceptical of this view of what after all became a prime real estate development, arguing the profit motive as the driver for the Pereires' interest in Arcachon, their desire to recoup what they had outlaid on the rail line from Bordeaux by promoting Arcachon as a place of convalescence and of refuge in winter, a veritable Ville d'Hiver.[76] The Pereires obviously expected a return on their considerable investment in the town, amounting by 1861 to a purchase of some 10,000 hectares and large sums expended on later developments.[77] Their nephew Paul Regnault designed and built the exotic Villa Pereire for them there in 1864, which Napoléon III visited briefly, and managed construction of a further sixteen private villas. Eventually there was also a Casino Mauresque. But Emile's poor health cannot be underestimated as a driver to this investment.[78] His asthma was as severe in later years as it had been in his youth. Dubbed 'the king of asthmatics' by Prosper Mérimée, a fellow sufferer, much of Emile's journeying away from Paris on business dovetailed with his search for relief, if not a cure, from a pitiless malady.[79] From Cauterets in the Pyrénées he wrote to Herminie of his delight in having slept well on three consecutive nights without recourse to the camphor cigarettes on which he would normally have relied.[80]

The Pereire women were clearly significant figures, formidable, indeed, to outsiders: adorning their husbands and spending as conspicuously as other members of their class. Their residence in Paris and the château at Armainvilliers allowed them to entertain in a lavish fashion, to mount events of great sumptuousness. In summer, Armainvilliers received large numbers of the extended Pereire family and friends who enjoyed hunting and riding and the pleasures of a good table with good conversation. When not at Armainvilliers or Arcachon (during January–April), both Herminie and Fanny were at home in Paris to guests, Herminie every second Tuesday evening and Fanny every Friday. One of Fanny's concerts, at which Adelina Patti performed – one of the highest-paid singers in Europe and James de Rothschild's personal favourite – attracted 800 people.[81] Herminie's soirées were preceded by dinner for a number of intimates and followed usually by a concert of leading singers of the Théâtre Lyrique or the Opéra de Paris. Two hundred arrived to a reception held on 27 February 1865 when Mme Tardière and Christina Nilsson, who had just made her highly-acclaimed début at the Théâtre Lyrique, and M. Varo of the Opéra entertained the guests, an event over which Herminie agonised.[82]

The concerts mounted by Herminie and Fanny, while typical among the Second Empire *grande bourgeoisie*, demonstrated the family's genuine interest in music and musicians. Félicien David dedicated his opera in two acts, *Lalla-Roukh*, to Emile in recognition of his patronage. On the first performance at the Opéra-Comique in May 1862, when it was an immediate success, Emile was the guest of honour. Fromenthal Halévy, composer of the grand opera *La Juive* (1835), the most popular opera of the era, remained a close friend. But Emile and Herminie also sought out young singers with talent. They arranged for singing lessons for the daughter of a friend in Bayonne, and an acquaintance introduced Emile, to his great delight, to a young illiterate cooper with a magnificent voice who sang for his small audience the aria 'Rachel, quand du seigneur' from Halévy's opera.[83]

Despite the social circumstances and living style with which they were surrounded, there was some ambivalence about the sumptuous and extravagant houses, the accoutrements, furnishings and precious objects, and their entertainment. Emile at least seemed to experience discomfort in the disparity between the luxury in which they lived and the deprivation of their childhood and youth, his contemporary biographer Adolphe Guéroult highlighting this dichotomy. Immensely wealthy as he was, according to Guéroult, Emile Pereire always maintained a very simple and unaffected lifestyle and the assiduity towards work of a man who still had his fortune to make. His life, filled by work, embellished by an intelligent wealth of research, was almost entirely spent in the midst of his family and a small group of friends whose fortunes were more or less linked to his.[84]

Herminie shared this ambivalence. Indeed, it was said that she actually suffered from the effects of such wealth. Letters concerning the regular soirées she was expected to arrange and over which she presided show a woman anxious, nervous, about this aspect of her role as the wife of Emile Pereire. According to her sister Félicie,

> [h]er wealth never dazzled her, nor was she charmed by it. She may even have suffered from it more than she enjoyed it. If she had followed the natural bent of her taste and temperament, she would have been much happier with a more ordinary life. This duty to associate with people for whom she had no great esteem was very hard on her. She was made for the intimate ties of family life.[85]

Félicie's husband, Charles Sarchi, agreed with this view, describing Herminie as a woman of high intelligence but, interestingly, one whose natural abilities Emile had done nothing to foster. This comment smacks of the assumption, common among certain men at the time, that the husband had a responsibility to educate his wife, to consolidate his authority over her, a view which seems at odds with what we know of Herminie.[86] What Herminie had achieved, Charles went on to tell his married daughter Hélène Van Tieghem, was to inspire in her children the sense of obedience, respect and love for the family. Great wealth had occurred unexpectedly for her after years of more modest fortune but it had altered neither her tastes nor her habits. Fanny, on the other hand, he continued, had only known luxury and thus had done nothing to raise her children with any expectations other than those money could provide.[87] From other evidence, including from the same correspondents, this is a little unfair on Fanny who had her share of tragedy with which she coped courageously.

There is one particularly subdued picture of Emile, rattling around alone in his quarters in the *hôtel Pereire* during Herminie's absence, she having taken their two sons away from the capital on a holiday. He had had meetings from 7 am, he wrote to her, all of which 'keeps me busy and makes me forget a little the silence and the isolation in which I find myself and which is made more acute by the great spaces I have to walk through to get to my bedroom'.[88]

The private sphere they built around them thus sustained Emile and Isaac Pereire, the family providing them with the social and emotional space and support necessary to maintain their considerable enterprises. While the Pereires moved away from their Jewish faith, their family life continued in many respects to be Jewish, based on endogamy and the construction of a tight-knit circle of family members. Their friends also were frequently Jewish, often Sephardic from Bordeaux or Bayonne. Through education, marriage and sociability, however, the circle opened up a wider network of potential allies. It demonstrated to Napoléon III and his government that the Pereires were people of substance, reliability, members of the *grande bourgeoisie* and in step. The role of the Pereire women in this social milieu was thus pre-eminent. They behaved as they were expected as members of their class, epitomising the upper echelons of bourgeois society – consuming, entertaining, adorning, despite Herminie Pereire's sometime reluctance – but they were also in some senses an integral and necessary part of the businesses, partners, even, in a shared enterprise: '*les frères Pereire*'. In their manner of ordering the properties over which they ruled, of managing their staff, large domestic budgets and the day-to-day running of their properties, their roles were significant. Their intelligence and intellectual curiosity added a further dimension to the ideal of the bourgeois wife. More important still, however, they were confidants; they had an intimate knowledge of the Pereire businesses, their successes, the competition and the importance of the network, which rendered them essential to continuing success.

Notes

1 J.-B. Vergeot, *Le Crédit comme stimulant et régulateur de l'industrie: la conception saint-simonienne, ses réalisations et son application au problème bancaire d'après-guerre* (Paris, 1918), p. 166; Franck Yonnet, 'La Structuration de l'économie et de la banque sous le Second Empire: le rôle du Crédit mobilier des frères Pereire', in Nathalie Coilly and Philippe Régnier (eds) *Le Siècle des saint-simoniens: du Nouveau christianisme au canal de Suez* (Paris, 2007), p. 128; Stoskopf, *Banquiers et financiers*, p. 277.
2 Stoskopf, *Banquiers et financiers*, p. 281; ANMT, company annual reports; AFP, *Statuts* and other documents; and Aycard, *Crédit Mobilier*. This does not take into account any trading they carried out subsequently.
3 Béatrice Philippe, *Les Juifs à Paris à la belle époque* (Paris, 1992), ch. III.
4 Piette, *Juifs de Paris*, p. 109.
5 See for instance Todd Endelmann, 'Disraeli and the myth of Sephardi superiority', *Jewish History* 10 (1996), 21–35.
6 AN, MC VIII, 1796, 'Statuts de la Société Civile du Temple Israélite selon le Rite Sephardi', 22 May 1875; Dominic Jarrassé, *Osiris: Mécène juif nationaliste français* (Brussels, 2008), pp. 160–1.

7 Ferguson, *World's Banker*; Le Bret, *Frères d'Eichthal*.
8 Stanley Weintraub, *Charlotte and Lionel, A Rothschild Love Story* (London, 2003), p. 70.
9 AFP, 'Dispositions testamentaires de mon [Henry's] père, 21 décembre 1874'.
10 Ibid., letters to both Pereires from Lazare Isidor, Chief Rabbi, Consistoire Central des Israélites de France, 1866–7.
11 'Nécrologie [Emile Pereire]', *Univers israélite*, xxx (1875), 310.
12 AFP, *En Souvenir de Madame Isaac Pereire, discours prononcé par Monsieur Alfred Lévy Grand Rabbin de France à la Mémoire de Madame Isaac Pereire, le 5 Juin 1910* (Paris, 1910).
13 AFP, Emile to Auguste Thurneyssen, 20 July 1853.
14 Vincent Gourdon, 'L'union d'Émile Pereire II et Suzanne Chevalier. À propos des mariages mixtes sous le Second Empire', *Archives Juives* 42 (2009), 33–50.
15 Hyman, 'Afterword', pp. 230–5; Paula Hyman, 'The modern Jewish family: image and reality', in David Kraemer (ed.), *The Jewish Family: Metaphor and Memory* (New York, 1989), pp. 179–93.
16 Susan K. Foley, *Women in France since 1789: The Meanings of Difference* (Basingstoke, 2004), p. 46; Hyman, 'Afterword', pp. 231–3.
17 Edmond et Jules de Goncourt, *Journal: mémoires de la vie littéraire* (Paris, 1956), t. 1, pp. 1155–7; t. 2, pp. 278, 19. Jules de Goncourt attended the Collège Royal de Bourbon (later known as the Lycée Condorcet) with Eugène.
18 Feydeau, *Mémoires*, pp. 165–6, 158. He also mimicked cruelly James de Rothschild's pronunciation of French.
19 Jennifer Ngaire Heuer, *The Family and the Nation: Gender and Citizenship in Revolutionary France, 1789–1830* (Ithaca, 2005), Chapter 1.
20 AFP, Herminie, Paris, to Emile, Arcachon, 23 February 1872.
21 Ibid., Herminie, Paris, to Emile, 5 September 1851; Emile, Bordeaux, to Herminie, 27 August 1858.
22 *Écrits*, t. III, fasc., 2, p. 766 where Gustave reflected on some of his father's favourite subjects.
23 Ibid., fasc. 3, p. 1832, 30 January 1878.
24 Hazan, *Invention of Paris*, pp. 142–4.
25 Mme Jules Baroche, *Second Empire: notes et souvenirs* (Paris, 1921), pp. 49–50, 20 December 1857.
26 Fargette, *Émile et Isaac Pereire*, p. 203, concluded, however, that his subjects were 'too absorbed by their professional occupations and too attached to their family life', to have engaged in extra-marital affairs.
27 *Boston Daily Advertiser* 40, 17 February 1875.
28 Emile Zola, *La Curée* (Paris, 1996), pp. 167–8.
29 AP, État Civil de Paris, V3E/N 1768, 'Acte de naissance' of Fanny Rebecca, Eugène, Marie Henriette and Jeanne Sophie Rodrigues Pereire.
30 J.-P. Bassino and J.-P. Dormois (2011). 'Is industrialization alone to blame for damaging their life prospects? Determinants of infant mortality variations across France in the 19th century', *Economic History Society Annual Conference*, Robinson College, University of Cambridge.

31 Sarchi, *Lettres*, t. 1, pp. 129–3, letter 74, Félicie to Hélène, 22 January 1866; t. III, pp. 42–3, letter 722, Charles to Hélène, 3 December 1876.
32 Bonnie G. Smith, *Ladies of the Leisure Class: The Bourgeoises of Northern France in the Nineteenth Century* (Princeton, 1981), p.127.
33 Saint-André, 'Hôtel Pereire', p. 133.
34 Letter sold by auction through Vente Piasa, Paris, 2009, Chevalier to his lawyer, 1877.
35 AFP, Laroche to Henry, 25 May 1870, and letters to Henry from Rhoné family, 1870.
36 Saint-André, 'Hôtel Pereire', p. 133.
37 AFP, letters particularly between Emile and Herminie, and to Henry from his parents, his sisters and brother.
38 AFP, 'Journal d'une Femme de Chambre pendant le siège de Paris' and 'Lettres de Camille, 21 mai–27 mai 1871', pp. 37–8. A chambermaid at the *hôtel Pereire*, Camille Desrochers kept a diary during the Franco-Prussian War, the siege of Paris, the insurgency and the Commune, and wrote letters to her sister Georgine, chambermaid to the Pereire daughters in Arcachon.
39 Foley, *Women in France*, p. 51. Betty de Rothschild was the pre-eminent figure in charitable activities, including construction of hospitals and other medical facilities bearing the Rothschild name and directed principally towards the Jewish community. See Claude Collard and Melanie Aspey (eds), *Les Rothschild en France au XIXe siècle* (Paris, 2012), pp. 149–61.
40 Christine Adams' *Poverty, Charity and Motherhood* (Urbana, 2010), pp. 3–11, makes interesting observations about the role of charity work in facilitating women's participation in 'the socio-political sphere'.
41 *Écrits*, t. III, fasc., 3, p. 1951, fn. 1.
42 AFP, Fondation Isaac Pereire, *Quatre Années de Fonctionnement (1887–1890)*. Hospitals in Levallois-Perret and Tournan-en-Brie catered for female maladies among other illnesses.
43 Ibid., letters Cécile Rhoné and Isaac to Henry, 1865, 1871.
44 Anne Levallois, *Les Écrits autobiographiques d'Ismayl Urbain: Homme de couleur, saint-simonien et musulman (1812–1884)* (Paris, 2005), pp. 113, 125–9.
45 BNF-A, Fonds Enfantin, 7860/22–33, 1861–65.
46 Gustave d'Eichthal's wife Cécile was the daughter of Edouard Rodrigues. They met at the wedding party of Isaac and Fanny Pereire.
47 Edouard Charton, *Correspondance générale (1824–1890)*, ed. Marie-Laure Aurenche (Paris, 2008), vol. II, letters 1862–63.
48 Pauline Prévost-Marcilhacy shared with me her research on the Pereires' art collection which included *inter alia* information on their various domiciles from 1841.
49 ACCP, GG1, 'Mariages célébrés', p. 4; Halévy, *F. Halévy*, pp. 16–22.
50 AFP, notes taken by Colette Pereire from records of the Mairie de Saint-Cloud on the death of Isaac Rodrigues in 1846 showing Rodrigues' place of death as 5 rue d'Amsterdam, 'chez le Sieur Pereire', who was in turn domiciled at Saint-Cloud.

51 www.château-palmer.com
52 AFP, Guyonie, agent, to Emile, 20 April 1855.
53 Vacant during the German occupation of Paris in the Second World War and purchased from the Pereire family by the British Government in 1947, it is now the Chancellery of the British Embassy and the immediate neighbour of the British Ambassador's residence.
54 AFP, 'Payements faits pour construction de l'hôtel Faubourg St. Honoré jusqu'au 29 février 1860'.
55 Saint-André, 'Hôtel Pereire', pp. 132–6. Surviving interior decoration is in excellent state of preservation. Ceilings on the ground floor have been covered for protection, but those on the first floor – Isaac's apartments – can still be seen and are in pristine condition. Art works and artistic decoration cost 260,000 francs, and marble and sculptures a further 320,000 francs.
56 Castille, *Frères Pereire*, p. 41.
57 Constance Cain Hungerford, *Ernest Meissonier: Master in his Genre* (Cambridge, 1999), p. 109.
58 Albert Boime, 'Entrepreneurial patronage in nineteenth-century France', in Edward C. Carter III, Robert Forster and Joseph N. Moody (eds), *Enterprise and Entrepreneurs in Nineteenth- and Twentieth-Century France* (Baltimore, 1976), p. 193, fn. 33.
59 *Galerie de MM. Pereire, catalogue des tableaux anciens & modernes des diverses écoles dont la vente aura lieu Boulevard des Italiens, no.26, les 6. 7. 8 et 9 mars 1872* (Paris, 1872), p. iii. See also Boime, 'Entrepreneurial patronage', pp. 140–5.
60 Castille, *Frères Pereire*, p. 41.
61 Alison McQueen, *Empress Eugenie and the Arts: Politics and Visual Culture in the Nineteenth Century* (Farnham, 2011), pp. 184–5.
62 Ferguson, *World's Banker*, p. 674.
63 *L'Astrologue* was presented to the Louvre in 1950. Four other paintings from the Pereire collection are now in the National Gallery in Washington.
64 *The Second Empire, 1852–1870: Art in France under Napoleon III* (Philadelphia, 1978), pp. 75, 99–136.
65 Saint-André, 'Hôtel Pereire', p. 133.
66 Sarchi, *Lettres*, t. 1, p. 250, letter 156, Charles to Hélène, 20 December 1866.
67 Saint-André, 'Hôtel Pereire', p. 133.
68 David Cohen, *La Promotion des juifs en France à l'époque du Second Empire* (Aix-en-Provence, 1980), t. 2, pp. 545–6.
69 Ferrières was designed by Joseph Paxton, creator of the Crystal Palace, the venue for the Great Exhibition of 1851.
70 Hervé Le Bret, 'Les Frères d'Eichthal: Gustave, penseur saint-simonien, et Adolphe, homme d'action' (PhD dissertation, Paris-Sorbonne [Paris IV], 2007).
71 A. Pereire, *Je suis dilettante*, pp. 14–15.
72 AFP, lists of purchases for Armainvilliers.
73 Luisa Limido, *L'Art des jardins sous le Second Empire, Jean-Pierre Barillet-Deschamps (1824–1873)* (Mayenne, 2002).

74 AFP, Aristide Pereyra to Emile, 1853. Aristide's brother was a doctor who believed in the efficacy of sea bathing for treating tuberculosis.
75 Pierre Assouline, *Le dernier des Camondo* (Paris, 1999), p. 224. Many resorts were financed by Jewish financiers: the Rothschilds at Megève, the Bischoffsheims at Bordighera, Cornelius Herz at Bussang and Salomon Alphen at Vittel.
76 Alice Garner, *A Shifting Shore: Locals, Outsiders, and the Transformation of a French Fishing Town, 1823-2000* (Ithaca, 2005), pp. 120-3.
77 Stoskopf, *Banquiers et financiers,* p. 38, Tableau 2.
78 Garner, *Shifting Shore,* pp. 121-2. By 1859, Emile Pereire had undertaken to invest 300,000 francs in the development. Garner also notes that treatises were published during the 1840s and 1850s on the beneficial effects of ozone on diseases of the lungs and heart, and these influenced the Pereires.
79 Prosper Mérimée, *Correspondance générale,* ed. Maurice Parturier (Toulouse, 1956), t. X, p. 79.
80 AFP, Emile to Herminie, 22 August 1859.
81 Ibid., 7 February 1865 and Gustave to Henry Pereire, 18 January 1865.
82 Ibid., Herminie, Paris, to Henry, 15 January 1865.
83 Ibid., Emile to Herminie, 14 September 1871.
84 Théophraste, *É.M. Péreire,* p. 31.
85 Sarchi, *Lettres,* t. I, pp. 320-1, letter 212, Félicie to Hélène from Florence, 16 January 1867.
86 Foley, *Women in France,* p. 39, referring to Jules Michelet's *La Femme.*
87 Sarchi, *Lettres,* t. I, pp. 320-1, letter 212, Félicie to Hélène, 16 January 1867; t. III, pp. 185-6, letter 869, Charles to Hélène, 3 May 1877.
88 AFP, Emile to Herminie, 18 April 1858.

8

Boom and bust

On the Crédit Mobilier's tenth anniversary in 1862, Isaac Pereire recalled to shareholders the vicissitudes they had overcome during their first decade, including wars, bad weather, poor harvests, financial and commercial crises. They had achieved impressive results, nevertheless. Powerful credit institutions now existed. Over 5,000 kilometres of rail threaded throughout Europe. Paris had become a new city, enlarged, embellished, furnished with modern infrastructure and services. All these accomplishments, Isaac went on,

> are not the chance result of improvisation and luck ... they are simply serious ideas applied and elaborated over time. We have played a large role in all these great creations, all these institutions, all these improvements to credit ... realised thanks to the two modern forces of association and credit.[1]

The Crédit Mobilier's triumphs were laid at the feet of Saint-Simonianism.

If the 1850s had been a period of growth and success for Emile and Isaac Pereire, this next decade tested them. Notwithstanding soaring international trade and industrial expansion, they were to encounter more economic crises and political setbacks. Competitors gathered their forces to fight the Pereires on their own turf. Political decisions did not go their way. And they began to overreach themselves, to make mistakes, the sheer range, scale and geographic spread of their ventures outgrowing their capacity to control them personally. This was a period also when the demands of the Emperor became a drain on their resources, when the penalties far exceeded the rewards.

Trade treaties were to come having significant impact on worker and proprietor alike. Certain activities, including the production of basic

18 Emile Pereire (1863). Collection Serge Kakou, Paris

foodstuffs such as bread, became subject to broader deregulation. New communications and manufacturing technology brought raw materials and finished goods closer to the consumer while demanding entrepreneurial skills, flexibility and capital on the part of business leaders to progress in a changing market, none of which was acquired easily. The effects of these major shifts were compounded by particular events: the loss of cotton imports as a result of the American Civil War of 1861–65; a poor grain harvest in 1863, another in 1867, the second leading to food-price escalation; French military defeat in Mexico and military victory for Prussia against Austria at Sadowa in 1866. Financial crises in 1863–64 and again in 1867 resulted. By 1866, when the Pereires' companies were starting to feel the pinch anyway, their customary capacity to respond quickly to events was impaired and the fragility of their own personal resources to maintain the grasp on their businesses became apparent.

The return of Achille Fould to the Finance Ministry in November 1861 did nothing to help them, even though his brother Benoît had been the inaugural President of the Crédit Mobilier. Fould, a fiscal conservative, had resigned from the government the previous year as a result of the publication by the Emperor of an article reaffirming his faith in public works to stimulate the flagging economy, an article which had all the hallmarks of the Saint-Simonians. It is thus ironic that Fould, who had advised Napoléon III to detach himself from the Rothschilds, by implication in favour of the Pereires, and whose family banking company was crucial to the establishment of the Crédit Mobilier, should now appear to advocate the opposite. His own approach to economic recovery, which he outlined in a letter to the Emperor late in 1861, was more stringent and conservative and it was the Emperor's positive response to this approach which saw him return to the ministry.[2] While Emile Pereire personally placed at Fould's disposal a sum of ten million francs to balance the books of the Banque de France in February 1862, in December Napoléon III was for the first time guest of honour at Ferrières, the estate of James de Rothschild near Armainvilliers.[3] A sumptuous repast there was followed by the planting of a commemorative tree; a hunt, at which 800 game were shot; and the performance by a chorus of the Opéra de Paris of a specially written piece by Rossini which concluded with the words: 'Friends! The stag is taken!' This extravagant but magnificently stage-managed event bore the fingerprints of the Minister of Finance.[4]

They were not helped either by the appointment in 1863 to the Ministry of Agriculture, Commerce and Public Works of the former Saint-Simonian Armand Béhic, whose commercial and personal ties were with Talabot and Rothschild. On Béhic's acceptance of this portfolio, the Saint-

Simonian industrialist from Lyon, Arlès-Dufour, percipiently described his elevation as being 'as disagreeable for Pereire as it is agreeable for Talabot'.[5]

Napoléon III continued to favour the Pereires, nevertheless. One of the most prestigious forms of recognition paid to their subjects by the imperial couple was through an invitation to 'les "Séries" de Compiègne', a command received by some one hundred guests at a time, together with their retinue, to pass seven days at the château of Compiègne during the months of October–November. Emile joined the Séries for the first time in 1862 alone and again in 1865 with Herminie when Eugène and Juliette Betzi Pereire were lodged in an adjoining suite.[6]

He was also invited to receptions, balls and dinners at Saint-Cloud and the Tuileries, where the Emperor took the opportunity to discuss business projects with him and Emile put forward ambitious propositions. Relations with the Empress were possibly more ambiguous than either brother realised, however. Despite the Rothschild family's private contempt for Louis-Napoléon, they had publicly supported Eugénia de Montijo, Comtesse de Teba, as a suitable wife for him and thus won her continuing approval and that of her mother.[7] The Pereires nevertheless seemed to be on relatively good terms with Eugénie – whom Michel Chevalier titled sarcastically 'la plus belle partie du gouvernement' – almost certainly resulting from her interest in their businesses in Spain.[8] Elements of the 'fête impériale', the marking of rail inaugurations and significant stages of construction, presented fine opportunities to press a particular cause with her. That the Empress' favourite summer residence at Biarritz was close to Arcachon and to Bordeaux made this easier.

The Pereires were closer to the imperial household than mere lobbying suggests. They loaned considerable sums to people in a position to further their interests, from the Emperor down. In 1860 he borrowed over one million francs for the acquisition of prime land in the rue d'Albe and the rue de l'Elysée, as well as for the hôtel Wittgenstein. Two repayments of 50,000 francs in favour of the Pereires are listed in the Emperor's household accounts of 1865. In 1869, after the collapse of the Crédit Mobilier, repayments of 100,000 francs were made for each of the first six months of the year for the loans extended by the Pereires to purchase properties in the rue François 1er as well as the rue d'Albe.[9] Aside from these repayments, arrangements seem to have been loose if not quite irregular. An undated note from Mocquard advised Emile Pereire that 'the Emperor prefers the payment in cash – 780,000 francs – The other conditions ... present no difficulties'. The purpose of this large cash payment is unknown but the bald demanding of it is revealing.[10] On another occasion the Pereires loaned half a million francs to the Empress' brother-in-law, the duc d'Albe, one of the first investors in the Chemin de Fer du Nord de l'Espagne.[11] Why this loan should have been necessary is unclear since the duc d'Albe was extremely wealthy. The Rothschilds also extended loans to Napoléon III, to invest in *rentes*, but although the sums were large (one million francs at a time) there seems, by contrast, to have been an underlying agreement about repayments which were tightly scheduled and maintained.[12]

The relatively frequent meetings which Emile Pereire engineered with Napoléon III through Jean-François Mocquard in Paris, Bordeaux, Bayonne, in Biarritz, in Vichy and in Tarbes, were not used solely to promote business propositions or to discuss money, however. He also grasped the opportunity to promote ideas, pre-eminently the introduction of free trade between France and Great Britain. In his earlier career as a journalist, he had written extensively about the impact of taxes and import duties. He was to claim later that from the first encounter with Louis-Napoléon, in 1849, free trade was the subject he raised most often, that in each meeting which occurred in 1859 he was to spend three or four hours exploring 'liberty of commerce'.[13] Ideas about tariff reform were not new but the subject was divisive, especially among those members of the social elite, the industrialists and large landowners producing wool and corn, fearing that they had much to lose. His persistence was rewarded, nevertheless. While Michel Chevalier played the pivotal role in dealing with the British free-traders Richard Cobden and John Bright, Emile Pereire provided material for a letter signed by the Emperor and published in the *Moniteur universel* early in January 1860, announcing a far-reaching programme of measures to ensure France's competitiveness and arguing the case for a loosening of trade barriers.[14] An engraving in the *Illustrated London News* of 1 March 1862 shows Emile Pereire standing among French (Baroche, Chevalier, Dollfuss, Arlès-Dufour, Fould, Persigny, Rouher, Villiers) and English figures who had contributed to the successful conclusion of the Treaty. But the decision to enter into a free trade agreement, taken without broad consultation, shocked many of the Emperor's intimates and forced him into the first of those concessions which later translated into the 'liberal Empire'. His trustworthiness was in question, his action a catalyst for cohesion among his opposition.[15]

The Compagnie Générale Maritime had struggled in its first years, some shareholders even writing to the Minister in 1858 calling on the Emperor to liquidate the company.[16] In the eighteen months to June 1859, the Crédit Mobilier was forced to advance close to thirty million francs. While the transport of 'free' labourers was the source of its survival in

19 Isaac Pereire (1860s). Collection of the author

the short term, winning the transatlantic postal contract became imperative for long-term security. Isaac Pereire, his son Eugène, both directors, and the vice-presidents Mathieu Dollfus and Vincent Cibiel together vigorously pursued the contract, putting to the test all the technical and financial knowhow they had acquired through railway development and mastering every element in running a postal service. To this end and to augment the engineering expertise which until then had been missing from the company, Eugène Flachat and Clapeyron joined the board. The effort was rewarded. In 1861, with the backing of the Crédit Mobilier, Adolphe de Forcade Laroquette, briefly Minister for Finance, agreed a treaty with the shipping company for the delivery of transatlantic passenger and postal services between Le Havre and New York and between Saint-Nazaire and Aspinwall on the Isthmus of Panama.[17] The company changed its name to the Compagnie Génerale Transatlantique (the Transat) to reflect its overriding new purpose. A generous annual subsidy of 9,300,000 francs was significant in view of the company's shaky financial history, together with a long-term interest-free advance of 18,600,000 francs.[18]

As *quid pro quo* the State demanded that at least half the new ships required – initially eight – were built in France. Marine technology was changing rapidly and fulfilling the order was challenging. The first three ships were constructed by a Scottish shipbuilder, but the remainder was consigned to a new shipyard at Penhoët, close to Saint-Nazaire, which the Transat soon took over. The first launched under the new company banner, the 1,000-horse-powered *Impératrice Eugénie*, was followed by the equally impressive *Napoléon III* and the more modest (850-horse-powered) *Pereire*. Through manufacture of sheet metal in Commentry, steam engines at Le Creusot, hulls at Saint-Nazaire and the assembly of the whole at Penhoët, aside from the profitability of regular passenger and freight shipping to the new world, the Transat contributed significantly to Second Empire trade and the economy.[19] Winning the postal contract also laid the foundation for the emergence of the iconic French passenger ships the following century – the *Paris*, the *Île de France*, the *Normandie* and the *France*.

Regular services to Vera Cruz in Mexico formed part of the new contract at a time when France and Mexico were on the verge of hostilities. In 1861 the Emperor declared war on the Mexican republican government, ostensibly as a reaction to the President Juarez' foreclosing on all foreign debt, but with an eye to the rich silver mines of Mexico. He intended to install the Archduke Maximilien of Austria as Emperor and extend French hegemony over Mexico at a time when the United States of

America was preoccupied with Civil War. Maximilien and his wife Charlotte arrived in Vera Cruz in May 1864 and were crowned in Mexico City the following month.

The Pereires had little choice but to accede to the Emperor's demand for assistance – the Transat became a troop transport – although taking an interest in the Banque Nationale de Mexique, licensed to issue its own banknotes, had been in prospect as had a stake in the Mexican railways.[20] But profits made from troop transportation (some 6,000–8,000 soldiers at a time were repatriated at 250 francs per soldier) did not compensate for the losses as the war turned to disaster.[21] The French, forced to fight alone after the withdrawal of British and Spanish troops, withdrew ignominiously over 1866–67 leaving Maximilien to face execution by firing squad. The directors of the Crédit Mobilier, who had underwritten a loan of eight million pounds sterling to support Maximilien, washed their hands of any further financial involvement.[22] The war in Mexico, prolonged for five years, had a significant impact on the French economy. It distracted the attention of the Emperor and his government, it was costly, adding 300 million francs to the floating debt, and it thus tied up capital at a time when investment finance was in any case in short supply.

Despite the prominent role Emile and Isaac Pereire had played in the early days of rail in France, by the 1860s in a number of cases they had come off second best. Emile remained until 1865 a director of the Ouest line and had an interest in the Est from Strasbourg to Paris, and both Pereires were firmly in control of the Midi and of the Nord de l'Espagne. But the Talabots, with Rothschild support, had reaffirmed their dominance of the PLM; Rothschild maintained the pre-eminence of the Nord; and François Bartholony's Paris–Orléans–Bordeaux and Tours–Nantes lines effectively blocked the Pereires from any direct entry into Paris. The Pereires were forced increasingly to look outside France altogether for business opportunity. They had mixed fortunes.

On the conclusion of the Crimean War, Isaac Pereire and others approached the Russian government to extend the Russian rail system by 4,000 kilometres. The Russians agreed to the proposal, but it met with a marked lack of enthusiasm from the French government. This vast project, initially capitalised at 300 million francs but with a target of over one billion, gave promise of major French investment opportunity in skill, exports of manufactured goods and capital. In a comparatively short period, however, by 1861, with a depression in Russia, hopes crumbled. Russian government apathy was only matched by that of the French and the Crédit Mobilier disengaged itself slowly at a loss.[23]

The delayed completion of the Chemin de Fer du Nord de l'Espagne served to confirm further the obstacles against which the Pereires were pitted. Mastering the terrain of the sierra of Guadarrama and the Pyrénées was beset with problems; so too was the Spanish political landscape, the necessarily incremental acquisition of rail concessions and stages to add to the line, compounded by financial hurdles – the total cost of construction escalated to over 339 million francs. In April 1863, Isaac Pereire reported to Crédit Mobilier shareholders that there were now 25,000 workers employed to complete the project. Finally, on 15 August 1864, the line was inaugurated at San Sebastian near the Franco-Spanish border with a lavish banquet in the presence of Napoléon III, at which Emile and Isaac Pereire sat on either side of the King of Spain. Several days earlier the Emperor had promoted Emile to Commandeur of the Légion d'Honneur and conferred the rank of Officier on Isaac.[24] The banquet provided the opportunity for much badinage on the theme of Louis XIV's pronouncement: 'the Pyrénées no longer exist'. But the share price of the Nord de l'Espagne languished and the value of its bonds fell on the Paris Bourse.[25]

To meet the requirement for finance increasingly demanded of international rail ventures, the Pereires needed to replicate the Crédit Mobilier in other countries in Europe, demanding a network of financial associates. The complexity of this undertaking was exacerbated by shifting alliances in the European financial world and fluidity in financial affairs. Banks and bankers allied to the Pereires showed the same agility in their allegiance as did allies of the Rothschilds. While in the 1850s the Crédit Mobilier had commanded a virtual monopoly of the French investment banking scene, competitors now circled. Former Saint-Simonian colleagues drifted into and out of competitive coalitions.

Arlès-Dufour, for instance, an early proponent of the CIC, the investment bank established in 1858 in Paris, sought a banking facility focused on his native city to provide deposit services for local businesses and longer-term investment capital for Lyonnais industry, services from which the CIC was excluded. The Crédit Lyonnais came into being in 1863, founded by Henri Germain, son-in-law of Adolphe Vuitry (a deputy, regent of the Bank of France and president of the PLM); and by Arlès-Dufour. Enfantin, Talabot and Chevalier were also directors. The Société Générale which was approved in 1864, a product of Rothschild's Réunion Financière but with which Rothschild was not involved, included a number of PLM associates behind it: Talabot, Bartholony and the English financier Edward Blount, an original director of the Pereires' Midi. Consortia of British and Dutch bankers, the latter of which included Bischoffsheim, were also significant investors in the Société Générale.[26]

The years 1862–4 thus made heavy demands on the Pereires, years in which they launched a herculean offensive against the dominance of the Rothschilds who remained implacably opposed to any and all of the Pereire enterprises. Other banking figures could be more accommodating. Aside from the French Mallet *frères* and André et Cottier, Benoît Fould had introduced them to the significant German firms of Oppenheim and Heine and to the Luxembourgeois J.-P. Pescatore. Adolphe d'Eichthal used his family connections with other German bankers. When the Pereires looked further afield, to Russia, they formed an alliance, albeit temporary, with the bankers Stieglitz and Mendelsohn; and in the Austro-Hungarian Empire with Sina, Eskelès, Pereira and Wodianer. Many of these new banking associates were Ashkenazi Jews, underscoring an increasing rapprochement between previously divided elements in European Jewry, Sephardim and Ashkenazim, drawn together by the wider Jewish diaspora and the new demands and opportunities of big business.

The international Rothschild network was formidable, however, and had been for almost fifty years. Gille commented that the focus of the Réunion Financière was not on France but on foreign interests, and in this it had the advantage over the Pereires.[27] Incessant, ruthless, competition within and outside France thus characterised these years for the Pereires.

Several of their international ventures turned out well for them, nevertheless. The Caisse du Commerce et de l'Industrie de Turin had emerged from the carve-up of northern Italy following war with the Austro-Hungarian Empire. A Rothschild initiative which had failed, the Pereires took control in 1862 through the French and Spanish crédit mobiliers. The Crédit Mobilier Italien saw the return of the Genoan Raffaele de Ferrari, duc de Galliera, who had defected to the Rothschild camp.[28] Similarly, in the wake of the Crimean War, the Ottomans needed desperately to instil rigour and stability into national financial and monetary policies. In 1863, after negotiation with Crédit Mobilier directors Alfred André and Charles Mallet, the Sultan of the Ottoman Empire, Abdul Aziz, awarded the state bank, the Banque Impériale Ottomane, to a combination of French and English interests in which the Pereires were prominent. These banks, in Turin and Istanbul, were significant enterprises with capital of 50,000,000 and 67,500,000 francs respectively. The Banque Ottomane in particular negotiated foreign loans including the significant state loan of 1865.[29]

Other ventures were not so rewarding. The Société Générale de Commerce et d'Industrie of Amsterdam which also emerged in 1863 saw its principal supporter and proponent Alexandre Mendel take flight the year following its establishment. The Crédit Mobilier had invested 25 per cent of capital, ten million florins, but the venture was not a success.[30] In the same year, the Pereires were bested by the English when confronting them on their own ground. They contributed half the capital to a Société Financière Internationale through the crédit mobiliers of France, Spain, Italy and the Netherlands, but the bank was only marginally successful.[31]

The reappearance of Fould had had an immediate impact on the affairs of the Pereire group. He blocked an attempt by the Compagnie Immobilière de Paris to launch a bond issue and rejected Isaac's call to establish the *omnium* as a new financial instrument. In addition, 'money was rare and dear': the Banque de France discount rate was high (up to 8 per cent in 1864).[32] The Pereires were in need of a vehicle for railway financing to counter the difficulties incurred through Fould's inflexibility and the Banque de France's monopoly.

Conclusion of the war against Austria in Northern Italy in 1860 which had led to the establishment of the Crédit Mobilier Italien also brought Savoy into France and with it the central Banque de Savoie. Established in 1851, the Banque was a modest affair, the initial share capital of 800,000 francs having been increased to only four millions subsequently, but it had certain advantages: it could raise capital by direct approach to the market, as it had done in 1856; it had a licence to issue its own banknotes; and it was empowered to establish branches. But while the Treaty of Turin (1860) which concluded the war explicitly defended the Banque de Savoie's sovereignty in this respect, the French government established a commission to consider its integration with the Banque de France.[33] The Savoyards wished to maintain their independence, however, and directors thus approached Emile Pereire with a proposal effectively to launch a takeover.

In October 1863, following a proposal put to the shareholders by Emile Pereire, the Banque de Savoie resolved to raise its share capital to forty million francs and to exercise its right to establish branches in France. The additional shares were to be purchased by the Pereires. Over 1863–64, Emile waited on the Emperor at various locations to press his case and to gain approval for this gamble, as his letters to Herminie confirm.[34] At first he was gratified with his reception.[35] But by July 1864, his confidence in the Emperor's support was less assured.[36] It was the Banque's capacity to issue its own banknotes in opposition to the Banque de France which as much as any other problem raised alarm about the Pereires' intentions.[37] Achille Fould's eventual response was a rebuff. Only a matter of days after a further discussion between Emile, the Emperor and Fould, in April 1865 the Banque de Savoie was merged with and became a branch of the Banque de France.[38]

Repercussions were serious. While some associates, Chevalier included, supported the Pereires, others were mortified to have their names linked.[39]

For Adolphe d'Eichthal (a former regent of the Banque de France) the affair was disastrous, a matter of bad faith, unpatriotic even. The possibility of two rival currencies in circulation was treachery that would only attract public odium, yet another example of Emile's headstrong nature, of his intransigence and lack of judgement, and a painful repudiation of their long friendship. D'Eichthal had resigned from the board of the Crédit Mobilier in late 1862 and as Vice-President of the Compagnie Immobilière a year later.[40] The Banque de Savoie affair strengthened the resolve of the Haute Banque to oppose the Pereires at every stage: it also frightened senior political figures, including Rouher and the Emperor himself.[41]

The Pereires renewed their efforts to bring about change in the Banque de France and its modus operandi, badgering the Emperor and his ministers on every occasion which presented. Isaac published a treatise on *Les Principes de la constitution des banques et de l'organisation du crédit* which went into a second edition. The further raising of interest rates brought forth a number of petitions against the Banque de France, and critical articles appeared in the press, many engineered by the Pereires. In January 1865, before the Banque de Savoie was finally merged, Napoléon III was persuaded to launch an inquest into the Banque de France – *Enquête sur les principes et les faits généraux qui régissons la circulation monétaire et fiduciaire* – to be carried out by the Conseil Supérieur du Commerce, de l'Agriculture et de l'Industrie and chaired by Rouher, now Minister of State.[42] Both Emile and Isaac Pereire appeared before this Conseil, on 7 November and 26 December respectively, during which one of their toughest interlocutors was Adolphe d'Eichthal, a member of the Conseil.

The Banque de France came very reluctantly to defend its case before the Conseil. That the inquest had been called at all and that the Pereires, when they appeared before it, used it as a platform to attack, these did nothing to foster amicable relations. Emile laid the cause of the crisis of 1863–64 squarely at its feet, claiming that its capital was 'immobilised' by exposure to *rentes*, that credit was too expensive and discount rates subject to wild fluctuations – they had been adjusted thirty-four times in six years. His attempt to take over the Banque de Savoie had been in the public interest rather than for his own profit, he claimed, as he outlined a proposed transformation of the Banque de Savoie into a financial entity put to the service of all railway companies, issuing bank bills and bonds, extending credit, under direction of representatives of all the railway companies and banks, and regulated by government.[43] But this attack was no more successful for the Pereires than its predecessors. The inquest was still in progress several years later and eventually, on its winding up, ratified the Banque de France's central role in the French financial and monetary system.

The Pereires were forced to consider their options in promoting and defending their business interests. The republican deputy Emile Ollivier was on the public record in questioning the high level of government subsidy paid to the Midi, claiming that the Pereires used the subsidy to prop up the Midi's dividend and that financial information provided to shareholders was insufficient to help in their decision-making.[44] Both accusations probably had some truth. To influence the direction of policy and to defend themselves against commercial attack, the Pereires stood for election to the Corps Législatif. This step was bound also to witness the satisfying culmination of their careers as public figures and as Jews. Indeed, Herminie, in a letter to her son Henry, was to write that 'I rejoice and take my part with pride in the welcome made in all the departments to the name *of Pereire* [sic].'[45]

The Anglo-French Commercial Treaty in particular continued to be contested, and there were many who had come to believe that Napoléon III's propensity for unilateral decisions should be tempered, if not curbed altogether. The Corps Législatif had been toothless for the first eight years of its life and certainly restrained from introducing legislation. Forced to countenance more liberal political measures to accommodate an increasingly critical electorate, in November 1860 the Emperor had introduced reforms which gave the Corps Législatif more influence in the political process. Spokesmen now presented and defended government legislation before the Corps which had also gained more control over expenditure and the budget. He created the position of Minister of State. Deputies now debated the Emperor's address from the throne and the *Moniteur universel* published these debates verbatim rather than the officially sanctioned extracts as they had previously.[46] The national election of 1863 was thus to be a watershed for the Emperor, his allies and the republican opposition.

Emile and Isaac, together with Eugène Pereire, all stood for seats having some strategic commercial association with railway development in the southwest and southeast: Emile in the Gironde, Isaac in the Pyrénées-Orientales and Eugène, now thirty-two years old, in the department of Gers. All three won but at a personal cost. Eugène, the officially sanctioned candidate in his electorate, was attacked by anti-Semites as a 'Jewish foreigner'.[47] Isaac too had a struggle against the official candidate, the incumbent and mayor of Perpignan, Justin Durand, whose father had also held the seat. Isaac was the target of a vicious anti-Jewish campaign orchestrated as much by the Catholic Church as by his opponent. Accusations of Jewish involvement in blood rituals, notably the Damascus Affair, were revived as well, and the expulsion of the Jews from Spain in 1492 lauded. While Isaac Pereire easily won the popular vote the Corps Législatif declared his election invalid, agreeing with his opponent Durand that he had employed 'seduction, intimidation, corruption' to secure the outcome, a charge for which there was clear evidence. Forced to another ballot, Isaac won by 6,000 votes.[48]

As deputies the Pereires did not distinguish themselves. Other than on the occasions when they were forced to protect their commercial interests or their reputation, they appear on the record infrequently. Contemporary commentators noted that Emile's capacity for public speaking was limited, that he spoke only rarely and was easily bested in robust debate.[49] This may have been the case. He did speak on the subject of the Transat and in 1866 on the free trade issue.[50] His influence emerged more clearly as a member of the group commissioned to frame a response to the Emperor's opening speech to the Corps. The *Projet d'adresse* of January 1864 which was read by Morny expressed the hope that the current emphasis given to public works would be sustained with the construction of railways, improvements in ports, in rivers, in canals, and in roads.[51] The Conseil d'État also appointed Emile a member of the council examining the international monetary convention.[52] Isaac had no such trouble in addressing a crowd but his presence was even less conspicuous. Although his appointment to the Conseil général of the Pyrénées-Orientales department after the 1863 election occupied his time, the historian of the Corps Législatif wrote of him that 'he sat rather discretely within the majority'.[53] Nothing was heard from Eugène at all.

Particularly noticeable, however, was the abstention of all three from the vote in 1864 on the abolition of the law against coalitions, one which legislated the right to strike, permitting workers to organise in defence of conditions of work and rates of pay, and which was approved by a large majority.[54]

Their entry into politics had at least one specific goal and that was Marseille. They had never yielded the idea of a toehold in the Mediterranean city despite the pre-eminence of the Talabots there and the inescapable fact that the PLM railway had arrived there already. The Midi railway had advanced as far as Sète, only 136 kilometres away. Invoking the law of 1842 which sanctioned a rail line from Bordeaux to Marseille through Toulouse, Emile argued to his shareholders that the Midi's work would not be finished until this was achieved.[55] The city was now France's second largest and by 1860 work on the Suez Canal was under way in Egypt. Marseille would become a crucial link in the new international trade routes. The Pereires in 1862 thus proposed to establish the Chemin de Fer du Littoral de Cette [the former spelling] à Marseille, a project which would see the line extended further and a railway station constructed in the port city for passengers and freight, linking the Mediterranean with the Atlantic Ocean at Bordeaux: a variation on Chevalier's 'Mediterranean system'.

While the Pereires converted a number of departmental notables to the cause, Paulin Talabot opposed them vigorously, countering with a proposal to extend the PLM from Marseille to Sète. More importantly, the Pereires failed to win over Rouher, then Minister responsible for Public Works.[56] Ultimately, while a new rail convention in 1863 accorded the Midi ten new branch lines together with state subsidies and guarantees for the work to be undertaken, the sole benefit they achieved in Marseille was a concession to build a station for freight destined for their own network.[57] As Emile wrote to Mocquard in April 1863: 'After having been encouraged [by the Emperor] to hope for much I have been reduced to contenting myself with very little.'[58] Even this they conceded finally was not worth the effort and they abandoned the proposed Chemin de Fer du Littoral altogether in 1869.

Meanwhile, the Compagnie Immobilière de Paris had undertaken significant developments in central Paris during the 1850s, contributing in a major way to Haussmann's first network – the rue de Rivoli, the Champs-Élysées and the boulevard des Capucines – work which was to be extended with the decision in 1858 to construct a new opera house in an area delineated by what is now the rues Scribe, Auber, Halévy and Gluck. Haussmann's department of the Seine had expropriated land to the west on the boulevard Malesherbes and east to the boulevard Prince-Eugène (now the boulevard Voltaire) which the Compagnie Immobilière purchased in 1863. With soaring employment an increase in the working population put pressure on accommodation. High rents and massive demolition of old housing stock created social problems needing redress which the inclusion of eleven outlying communes within the municipalities of the capital was intended to relieve. Not that displacement of working people from the centre of the city to its periphery caused the Pereires any qualms, Isaac Pereire telling Crédit Mobilier shareholders in 1861 that

> there is no other means to combat this increase [in rents] than to deliver new spaces for construction and to facilitate the successive shifting of the population of the centre towards diverse points of the circumference, through opening new roads, through the creation of new districts, through improvement to and lower cost in transport.[59]

The following year, with construction of the Grand Hôtel adjacent to the site of the new Paris Opéra completed – the Empress Eugénie who inaugurated it was reported to have said that: 'It is absolutely like my home, I believed myself at Compiègne or at Fontainebleau'[60] – the Compagnie Immobilière introduced a combination of rental accommodation which included 'social housing'. Almost one-third of the apartments constructed along the lengthy boulevard du Prince-Eugène, ceremoniously inaugurated by the Emperor on 7 December 1862, carried a rental of less than 500 francs per annum; the remaining two-thirds were rented at between 500 and 1,000 francs per annum. This had been the site of the insurrections of the Faubourg Saint-Antoine in 1830 and 1848, and many have seen the move as politically motivated, calculated to confine militants within 'an islet of stability resting on the most favoured elements of the laboring population'.[61]

The Compagnie Immobilière was a time bomb, however, dependent on loans from the public mortgage lender the Crédit Foncier and the Crédit Mobilier. With Emile Pereire on the boards of each, neither of these institutions demanded security to the degree they might have and the extent of supervision, despite the much vaunted policy of oversight by Crédit Mobilier directors, was lax. Liquidity of the Compagnie Immobilière was in any case by nature uncertain, demanding long lead-times to realise urban development projects while consuming massive amounts of capital in the process. Capital gain on land and buildings reported in the company's annual reports was frequently designed to mislead. The Pereires maintained generous dividends instead of directing financial reserves to the service of the longer-term viability of their companies. By 1862, over 100 million francs had been poured into the Compagnie Immobilière.[62]

As a corollary to their attempt to gain entry into the Marseille rail market and to exercise more traction, the Pereires had persevered with other enterprises in Marseille which ultimately proved catastrophic. The Emperor wished to re-create in Marseille as in other large provincial cities the modern metropolis which Paris was becoming, and there had been some activity in this direction during the 1850s, notably from one of Jules Mirès' companies, the Société des Ports de Marseille, to which Paulin Talabot was linked. In September 1860, Napoléon III visited the city for the opening of the new Marseille Bourse and reiterated a wish to see the construction of a major transport artery, to be known as the rue Impériale, to link the new port extensions directly with La Joliette, the city centre.[63] It was no small matter, requiring the removal of a large hill among other challenges. Local developers were notably reluctant to respond to the imperial decree and the Pereires themselves were not quick off the mark. The Compagnie Immobilière de Paris was, in any case, constrained by its statutes to work within Paris. But the Emperor persisted and in 1862 Emile Pereire himself bought the 500,000 metres of land required for the project. The attendant difficulties which then confronted him, both organisational and financial, were enormous. If the Immobilière was prohibited from executing the work, some other body was necessary to achieve it. And the manner in which the financing was to be structured needed to be carefully evaluated: Marseille was not Paris. The city of Marseille required of Emile Pereire that he build the road and its accompanying infrastructure ('walls, sewerage, steps, pavements, water and gas') within eighteen months, and within a further two years to construct the buildings which would form the façade to the rue Impériale, to a Haussmannian pattern similar to those in Paris.

The charter of the Société des Ports de Marseille made it the perfect vehicle to undertake the project, but it was scarcely in a fit state to do so. Jules Mirès in 1861 had been arrested for fraud and swindling associated with another of his ventures and was facing a term in jail. His company had already defaulted on a project to develop a considerable area of land for port use and for a railway station to serve the port.[64] Its share price languished; the Credit Foncier refused it a loan.

Official documents claimed that the initiative for a merger with the Compagnie Immobilière de Paris had issued from the Ports de Marseille as a last ditch attempt to save itself. Litigation initiated by shareholders in the Ports de Marseille claimed that it was effectively the victim of a hostile takeover. Further actions were brought against Mirès and former members of the Ports de Marseille administration for embezzlement.

Nevertheless, work at Marseille began in October 1862, and in June 1863 Napoléon III finally issued a decree which permitted the fusion of the Compagnie Immobilière de Paris and the Société des Ports de Marseille as the Compagnie Immobilière with a capital of eighty million francs.[65] Expropriation of 935 houses and the displacement of 16,000 residents made way for a building site in which 1,200,000 square metres of rubble was poured into the sea using four locomotives, 250 excavators and twelve kilometres of rail track. The city, which had found itself in conflict with all the stakeholders, including the Emperor's personal representative, congratulated itself on attracting such an eminent personage prepared to commit his time and capital, with the expectation that this was just the beginning. When completed in 1864 the rue Impériale was the largest building site of its kind in any French city to that time.[66] But having been forced to undertake construction through local entrepre-

20 Commencement of construction, rue Impériale, Marseille
Archives de la famille Pereire

neurs, the Compagnie Immobilière had made numerous costly compromises to encourage completion of the work and recoup its investment.

The company's report to shareholders of 1864 alluded to some difficulties with the project but painted glowing images of the future. Much was made of the adverse impact of the current economic crisis. All would be well, however, when, with the scaffolding removed to reveal the magnificent dwellings, a current of life and movement would be created between the old city and the new. With the Suez Canal opened, Marseille would become a second Liverpool.[67] But the seventeen million francs in bonds issued to the public to underwrite the development were perforce largely absorbed by the Crédit Mobilier.[68]

The report to the Compagnie Immobilière shareholders in 1865 was as lengthy as it was unforthcoming, but it continued to strike a confident albeit misleading note. Eighty-seven houses in Marseille were yet to be completed. There were problems offloading the properties through either sale or rent as the rue Impériale failed to attract buyers. To recoup their outlay, local entrepreneurs were forced to demand higher prices of potential purchasers. They defaulted on generous loans extended them by the Compagnie Immobilière. Despite these shortcomings, however, and to lend weight to the claim that a brighter future lay ahead, the dividend was raised to thirty-seven francs fifty centimes.

The Compagnie Immobilière's balance sheet included an impressive portfolio of properties in Paris. Aside from the Grand Hôtel and the Grand Hôtel du Louvre, the combined values of which were calculated at 50,000,000 francs, there was an industrial laundry at Boulogne-sur-Seine, and housing developments on the boulevards des Capucines, Prince-Eugène and Malesherbes, on the Champs Elysées and in the quartier Monceau. The company held land in the plaine Monceau, the boulevards du Prince-Eugène and Malesherbes and the chaussée d'Antin as well as in Marseille. Altogether these were valued at almost 127,000,000 francs. Mortgagees and 'diverse debtors' for both Paris and Marseille properties added a further 56,000,000 francs to the Immobilière's assets. On the other side of the ledger, however, there was a debt owing to the Crédit Foncier of 44 million. There was no reference to a debt to the Crédit Mobilier, submerged amid the 'balance of construction and land, current account' of sixty-eight million francs.[69]

Only a year after the Pereires' attack on the Banque de France, Isaac was forced to go cap in hand for agreement to double the Crédit Mobilier's capital, to 120,000,000 francs. In January 1866, after the Emperor intervened on their behalf before a council of ministers, the Banque de France agreed.[70]

In October that year, Emile wrote to Herminie of an audience with Napoléon III which lasted one hour. He gave no details.[71] But both brothers knew well before December that the situation of the Compagnie Immobilière was irretrievable. Indebtedness to the Crédit Foncier had climbed to 72,500,000 francs, including a mortgage loan of 30 million extended in mid-1866, while the Crédit Mobilier was owed over 63 million. Provision for redemption of bonds accounted for a further 70 million francs.[72] It would only worsen. Emile met with the Emperor again and also with Rouher to discuss the possibility of a merger between the Compagnie Immobilière and the Crédit Foncier, meetings of no avail. The Pereires contrived various possible share exchange combinations which might make a merger more palatable. A merger of the Crédit Mobilier with the Compagnie Immobilière was considered.[73]

With the onset of the new year, however, Emile was forced to concede to Rouher that they had nowhere to turn and were likely to be severely embarrassed before the looming annual general meeting of shareholders. He begged for some indication of moral support from the government.[74]

On 1 April 1867, the Exposition Universelle was launched by the Emperor at the Champs de Mars. All the sovereigns of Europe attended – the Emperors of Austria and Russia, the Kings of Prussia, Holland, Belgium, and the Sultan and Vice-Roy of Egypt – giving Napoléon III belated legitimacy with which neither his coronation nor his marriage had been favoured. It was considered 'the splendid apotheosis of the Second Empire'.[75] But there was a sense of gloom, nevertheless, which Prosper Mérimée captured in his letter to Madame de Montijo, the Empress' mother: 'They speak of financial crisis and among others they say that the Pereires are very much threatened. If the Exposition Universelle succeeds, perhaps it will make a diversion from the anxiety and the general unease.'[76]

In his report to Crédit Mobilier shareholders that same month Isaac had referred to financial problems caused by the Compagnie Immobilière which were now too obvious to conceal.[77] In May, Emile attempted desperately and futilely a rescue of the Immobilière by raising a loan of 200,000,000 francs in mortgage bonds on the London Stock Exchange, to be secured by the Crédit Mobilier. Some 'palpable indication' of support from Napoléon III might help, it was suggested.[78] The Emperor charged Rouher to look for ways in which the Pereires might be saved, but the cause was hopeless.[79] No amount of obfuscation could conceal the staggering debts under which the Crédit Mobilier now reeled.[80]

The Pereires returned to the Banque de France, seeking to limit the damage by raising more capital. The Banque de France agreed to a loan, conditional on the Pereires' resignation. On 14 September 1867, Emile wrote a letter to his son Henry, surprisingly matter-of-fact given its significance:

> Yesterday we terminated our arrangements with the Banque for a sum of 37 million and a half – that was not without pain. We shall retire, my brother, Salvador & me from the Crédit Mobilier, – Michel Chevalier has tendered his resignation in advance. Other administrators want to retire also, we shall try to urge them to stay.[81]

The Crédit Mobilier share price had fallen to 280 francs, dragging with it the Pereires and the finances of thousands of small investors.

Isaac became ill and took to his bed. Herminie described her usually even-tempered brother-in-law in a letter as 'much changed'. Emile, who surprisingly remained in good health, felt the disaster cruelly nevertheless, doodling on a piece of paper: 'To start again at my age', then, 'ostracism, draw up an inventory of the houses in Paris', haunted inevitably by the bankruptcy of his own father.[82] The family closed ranks. A few days after the fateful decision, Herminie urged her children Cécile and Henry to return quickly to Paris:

> We all need more than ever to reunite so that we can consult each other on the line to take in the present circumstances. Your father is going well. Thank God, he is not lacking in courage, but he is very sad …. We all have need of you soon.[83]

By November 1867, the comte de Germiny, who had been sent in by the government to sort out the mess of the Crédit Mobilier, uncovered a total loss of 47,542,000 francs in a balance sheet which held as assets 58,000,000 francs in advances to the Compagnie Immobilière. Falls in the share prices of all the companies in which the Compagnie Mobilier had invested exacerbated the situation.[84] Germiny also chaired the shareholders meeting of the Compagnie Immobilière in December 1867, outlining the catastrophe which afflicted the company – over 70,000,000 francs owed to the Crédit Foncier, and now almost 80,000,000 francs to the Crédit Mobilier; assets on paper valued at 321,751,747 francs in large part unrealisable; and shareholders' funds vanishing under a mountain of debt.[85] Paris presented its share of problems, but in Marseille they were a nightmare, the rent from properties there contributing only 600,000 francs.

The Compagnie Immobilière was not liquidated finally for a further fourteen years, in 1881, by which time almost all of its building stock had been sold and funds set aside for any lingering litigation.

It was not until the end of 1868, that Germiny and both Pereires signed a formal agreement which committed them to pay 12 million francs in tranches of two million francs over the better part of six years. The total of 36 million was to be paid in unequal proportions to the two companies. The Pereires, Galliera, Seillière, Charles Mallet and Frédéric Grieninger, all of whom except Galliera had been directors of the Crédit Mobilier for fifteen years, were required to pay over 1.5 million francs each per annum until 1874. The remaining administrators – Cibiel, Darblay, Edouard Rodrigues, Dollfus, Lebey and Auguste Thurneyssen, all board members of the Compagnie Immobilière – were committed to paying lesser, though still significant, sums.[86] Shareholders in the Crédit Mobilier and Compagnie Immobilière, for their part, were called upon to renounce 'all appeals and all actions for whatever reason having a social character, against each one of the administrators who contributed to the subsidy'.[87] The two Assemblées agreed to take responsibility for all convictions registered or about to be registered against the administrators and any costs awarded against them.[88]

While Emile and Isaac Pereire were not without resources they were themselves major shareholders in the Crédit Mobilier and the Compagnie Immobilière, as well as their other companies, and shared the losses with everyone else. Some of the most valuable assets held by the Société Pereire trust which might have been brought into play to expunge their debt were in property and were thus difficult to liquidate rapidly. Preparing to put even Armainvilliers and the *hôtel Pereire* on the market, they requested that the Emperor be apprised of this move despite the uncertainty that this would lead to a sufficiently speedy resolution to the problem posed by payment of the reparations.[89]

For James de Rothschild the drama was a triumph, a resounding victory for himself and for his family. But it came at a cost. He died the year following the fall of the Crédit Mobilier, on 15 November 1868.

Litigation was rife. Jules Mirès had launched a defamatory attack on the Pereires in 1867 in the *Presse* which led to a prolonged court case. As early as January 1868, shareholders in the Compagnie Immobilière took action against the former administrators,[90] enraged on hearing that the deal with the Pereires had been concluded through secret meetings between the new administrators (including Germiny), and senior members of the government Rouher, Vuitry and Magne.[91]

Despite Herminie's pleas for unity it is not surprising to read of differences between Emile and Isaac at this time, given the nature of the collapse of the two companies, each presided over by one or other of them. Félicie Sarchi spoke to her daughter of the painful situation in which Fanny now found herself, caught between her father's family, 'marching in concert', while Isaac was suffering from 'self-deception, believing too much in himself ... marching always with his head lowered against the cannons, you know him, it's his nature'. Thus, wrote Félicie, did the Pereire family present at that time 'a touching spectacle of a complete opposition of views, of opinions, of characters, which clash [but] without shaking the most real and the most deep tenderness [of Emile towards his brother]'.[92] This may have been the time of Isaac's long (undated) letter to Emile, one filled with anger and reproach towards those who continued to hound them, refusing to continue to find a path through the morass:

I consider I have worked enough. I want to rest. I do not want to accumulate money for indifferent or ungrateful people. Alone you [Emile] can do nothing. Your age and your health will not permit it. You have no choice but to rely on me and I absolutely refuse to step in, to re-engage anew in a business world which has rejected us, where we can hold only an infinitesimal role, to plunge into this abyss again ... I want my revenge on the abuse of the egotists who surround us.[93]

The seriousness of this rift and its resolution are equally unclear, for while subsequent correspondence between them exists it is not helpful. And soon after, Emile was to leave Paris for the southwest from which he never returned for any length of time. Emile and Isaac were thus separated by geography if not by residual anger.

The collapse of the Crédit Mobilier also brought a schism with other board members who, running for cover, argued the relative responsibilities for the calamity between themselves, the Pereires and Salvador. Michel Chevalier, having lost half a million francs through his shareholding in the Immobilière, attacked the Pereires publicly and demanded they be removed from all their companies, particularly from the Transat. Arlès-Dufour and other Saint-Simonians attempted unsuccessfully to persuade him out of a violent outpouring against those who had been close to him for forty years.[94] In July 1870, as a result of the case brought by shareholders in the Crédit Mobilier against the doubling of the company's capital, the Pereires, Salvador, Galliera and Thurneyssen were ordered to pay an indemnity of 100 francs per new share issued at the time of the doubling of the share capital.[95]

While the Crédit Mobilier and the Compagnie Immobilière were in difficulties, the other Pereire companies were not immune either. No governmental influence was brought to bear on the Pereires to resign from these but they were at the mercy of their shareholders. The Midi remained shaky, though they stayed the course as active members of its board. The Transat was a different story, however, and in 1868 Emile, Isaac and Eugène were all voted out when shareholders attacked the accounts as misleading and probably fraudulent, demanding a commission be set up to examine the situation. But the Transat did include among its shareholders many members of the Pereire family, giving a base from which to fight back and lending Isaac the confidence to set about reconstructing the family legacy.[96]

It was their international interests which saved them. Not that the Crédit Mobilier Espagnol and the Chemin de Fer du Nord de l'Espagne were rock solid, but since they were incorporated in Spain the companies had a certain immunity which the others lacked. They were fortunate in their loyal employee Ernest Polack, whose services became essential and who was the agent of their survival.[97]

As politicians, the Pereires defied their critics, remaining deputies and with Isaac and Eugène standing for re-election in 1869 in what historians have called 'the freest elections for twenty years'.[98] Emile was fearful about the effects on his brother of renewed vilification. 'I am very gloomy and would want to get out of this brawl sooner', he wrote to Henry.[99] Eugène lost his seat. Isaac, after suffering and surviving an extraordinary anti-Semitic campaign against him, even more ferocious than the election six years earlier, was forced to yet another poll. This time he lost. The result hardly mattered, for within a year, Napoléon III led France into a disastrous war against Prussia which drew the Empire to a sudden and bloody end. With the French Army's wretched defeat at Sedan in September 1870 a small group of republicans and the monarchist General Trochu declared a republican Government of National Defence at the Paris Hôtel de Ville.

Notes

1 ANMT, 25AQ 2, Crédit Mobilier, Procès-Verbaux [handwritten], *Rapport*, pp. 164–5, 30 April 1862.
2 Frédéric Barbier, '"Achille Fould": Principal ministre de Napoléon III'. *Le Souvenir Napoléon*, 56ème année (1993), 19–27.
3 AFP, 'Acte entre Emile Pereire et Achille Fould (Ministre des Finances)', 16 February 1862.
4 Weintraub, *Lionel and Charlotte*, pp. 175–6. Lionel's son 'Natty' reported to his mother that the shooters who should have bagged 1,500 game were too drunk to aim accurately.
5 BNF-A, Fonds Enfantin, 7687, Arlès-Dufour to Enfantin, 26 June 1863.
6 I thank Sandrine Grignon Dumoulin, Musées et Domaine Nationaux du Château de Compiègne, for this information.
7 Ferguson, *World's Banker*, p. 564.
8 AFP, Chevalier to Emile, 15 September 1865.
9 A[uguste] Poulet-Malassis (ed.), *Papiers secrets et correspondance du Second Empire* (Paris, 1877), pp. 50, 331, 358.
10 AFP, Mocquard to Emile Pereire.
11 Poulet-Malassis, *Papiers secrets*, p. 331.
12 Ibid., pp. 361–2.
13 AFP, 'Note d'Emile au sujet de ses rapports avec l'Empereur', undated.
14 Bruley, *Quai d'Orsay*, p. 365, quoting Rouher to Baroche.
15 Price, *People and Politics*, pp. 79–81.
16 AN, F12/6772, Bordeaux shareholders to Rouher, 14 February 1858.
17 Barbance, *Compagnie Générale Transatlantique*, pp. 42–7.
18 ANMT, 9AQ 3, fo. M7, CGM, 9 April 1861.
19 Ibid., fos M7–12, Rapports, 1861, 1862, 1863, 1866.
20 Bertrand Gille, 'La Fondation de la Société Générale', *Histoire des entreprises* 8 (1961), pp. 37–8.
21 AFP. Convention passed between Emile Pereire and the Minister of War, 18 June 1866.
22 Rondo E. Cameron, 'The Crédit Mobilier and the economic development of Europe', *Journal of Political Economy* LXI (1953), pp. 482–3.

23 ANMT, 25AQ 2, Crédit Mobilier, *Rapports*, 1858-61; Cameron, 'Crédit Mobilier', pp. 476-8.
24 AN-Léonore, LH/2096/57 and /58.
25 Gustave Pereire, *Historique du Chemin de Fer du Nord de l'Espagne* (Paris, 1901), pp. 1-11.
26 Gille, 'Fondation de la Société Générale', pp. 5-64.
27 Gille, *Maison Rothschild*, t. 2, p. 191.
28 Christophe Bouneau, 'The Pereires' international strategy for railway construction in the 1850s and 1860s', in R. Roth and G. Dinhobl (eds), *Across the Borders: Financing the World's Railways in the Nineteenth and Twentieth Centuries* (Aldershot, 2008); Gille, 'Fondation de la Société Générale', pp. 27-8.
29 ANMT, 207AQ, Banque Ottomane, Geneviève Drouhet, 'Historique de la Banque Ottomane', 1991. A further investment in Rumania led to the establishment in 1864 of the Casa Economii și Consemnațiuni (CEC) bank.
30 Sarchi, *Lettres*, t. I, p. 343, fn. 3, letter 226, Charles to Hélène, 24 January 1867. Sarchi lost heavily from his investment in the bank.
31 Gille, 'Fondation de la Société Générale', pp. 33-4.
32 Girard, *Travaux publics*, pp. 278-80.
33 AFP, copy of a letter sent by the commission to Baron de Ruphy, President, Banque de Savoie Conseil, 16 August 1861.
34 Ibid., from Biarritz, Vichy and Paris.
35 Ibid., to Herminie from Bayonne, 15 September 1863, after one such meeting in Biarritz: 'I am not only very satisfied with the form, but above all with the depth [of the discussions].'
36 Ibid., to Herminie from Vichy, 28 July 1864.
37 Ambroise Rendu, *Consultation pour la Banque de Savoie* (Paris, 1864). The relevant documents are included as annexes to the consultation paper, prepared on behalf of the Pereires by their lawyer.
38 Banque de France, *Décret portant suppression du privilège de la Banque de Savoie*, 8 April 1865.
39 AFP, Chevalier to Emile, 2 June 1864.
40 Ibid., six letters d'Eichthal to Emile in October 1863 alone.
41 Ibid., Chevalier to Emile, 2 June 1864.
42 Ibid., Emile to his son Henry, 3 January 1965; Gustave Pereire to his cousin Henry, 18 January 1865.
43 Émile and Isaac Pereire, *Enquête*, pp. 1-107.
44 ANMT, 78AQ 6, Midi, *Rapport*, 16 May 1863, pp. 52, 72, where reference was made to these allegations.
45 AFP, to Henry, Paris, 22 May 1863.
46 Roger Price, *The French Second Empire: An Anatomy of Political Power* (Cambridge, 2001), pp. 69-71.
47 Anceau, *Dictionnaire*, p. 287.
48 Helen M. Davies, '"Séduction, intimidation, corruption" et antisémitisme: l'élection de 1863 dans les Pyrénées-Orientales', *Domitia: Revue du Centre de Recherches Historiques sur les Sociétés méditerranéennes* 12 (2011), 183-94.

49 *Grande Dictionnaire universel du XIXe siècle*, t. 12 (Paris, 1874), p. 598. The entry on the Pereires was written by their republican opponent Clément Laurier.
50 AFP, notes for a lengthy speech.
51 AN/AP, Fonds Rouher, 45 AP/9–10, File 2, Corps Législatif Session 1864, No. 70.
52 AFP, Vice-President, Conseil d'État, to Emile, 28 May 1866.
53 Anceau, *Dictionnaire*, p. 286.
54 Jean Sagnes, *Napoléon III: le parcours d'un saint-simonien* (Sète, 2008), p. 385.
55 ANMT, 78AQ 6, Midi, *Rapport*, 1862, p. 39.
56 Ibid., 78AQ 98 (6), Midi, *Note sur l'Enquête des Chemins de Fer du Midi* (Paris, 1862).
57 Ibid., 78AQ 6, Midi, *Rapport* (Paris, 1863).
58 AFP, Emile to Mocquard, 9 April 1863.
59 ANMT,, 25AQ 2, Crédit Mobilier, *Rapport*, 30 April 1861.
60 Quoted in Georges Poisson, 'La naissance des palaces', *Napoléon III: Le magazine du Second Empire* 7 (2009), p. 54.
61 Michel Lescure, *Les Sociétés immobilières en France au XIX siècle: contribution à l'histoire en valeur du sol urbain en économie capitaliste* (Paris, 1980), p. 47.
62 Paulet, *Role of Banks*; Stoskopf, *Banquiers et financiers*, p. 278; Le Bret, 'Frères d'Eichthal' [dissertation], pp. 579–81.
63 Now the rue République.
64 AFP, 'Dépêche Ministérielle du 19 juillet 1859, Société des Ports de Marseille, demande de conversion en Société anonyme'. 400,000 metres of land had been ceded to Mirès by the city.
65 Girard, *Travaux publics*, pp. 243–8.
66 Claude Jasmin, 'Marseille', in P. de Moncan and C. Heurteux (eds), *Villes Haussmanniennes: Bordeaux, Lille, Lyon, Marseille* (Rennes, 2003), pp.178–225.
67 AN, F12/6782, Compagnie Immobilière, *Rapport*, 27 April 1865 (Paris, 1865), pp. 13–15.
68 Girard, *Travaux publics*, p. 344.
69 AN, F12/6782, Compagnie Immobilière, *Rapport*, 28 April 1866, pp. 5–6, 27.
70 Girard, *Travaux publics*, p. 346 and fn. 333.
71 AFP, Emile to Herminie, 4 October 1864.
72 AN, F12/6783, Compagnie Immobilière, *Rapport*, 30 April 1867, p. 19.
73 AFP, containing numerous letters, calculations, reports etc concerning the proposed merger.
74 Ibid., Emile to Rouher, 9 January 1867.
75 Charles Adrien Gustave Conegliano, *Le Second Empire: la maison de l'Empereur* (Paris, 1897 [reprint 2005]), p. 296.
76 Mérimée, *Correspondance générale*, t. 13, p. 482.
77 ANMT, 25AQ 1, 'Avances faites'. This appears to be the only document extant relating to the final meeting over which Isaac Pereire presided.
78 AFP, correspondence Emile and F. Eber, May–August 1867.
79 Girard, *Travaux publics*, p. 348 fn. 340.

80 AFP, Crédit Mobilier Assemblée Générale Extraordinaire du 30 Novembre 1867, *Rapport*, p. 17.
81 Ibid., to Henry, 15 September 1867.
82 Ibid., note undated in Emile's hand.
83 Ibid., to Cécile and to Henry, 18 September 1867.
84 Ibid., Crédit Mobilier, Assemblée Générale Extraordinaire du 30 novembre 1867, *Rapport ... présenté par ... de Germiny* (Paris, 1867).
85 AN, F12/6781, Compagnie Immobilière, Assemblée Générale Extraordinaire des Actionnaires du 21 Décembre 1867, *Rapport du Conseil d'Administration présenté par ... de Germiny, Sénateur, Résolutions de l'Assemblée Générale* (Paris, 1867).
86 AFP, 'Compte de Subvention de 36,075,000 francs: Situation au 5 Septembre 1871 des sommes restant à recevoir sur les différentes échéances'.
87 Ibid., agreement signed Paris, 23 December 1868. 16 million francs was to be attributed to the Crédit Mobilier, 20 million to the Compagnie Immobilière, the whole directed towards reducing the Immobilière's debt to the Crédit Mobilier.
88 Ibid. See also records of Assemblée meetings in *Journal officiel de l'Empire français*, 2 and 27 February 1869, in AN, F12/6781, Compagnie Immobilière.
89 AN/AP, Fonds Rouher, 45/3. Mocquard notaire to Rouher, 30 October 1867; and AFP, letters de Villiers to Emile, 1868–72, re estimates of prices and potential sales for various of their properties.
90 BNF-F-M [Factum. Pereire, Isaac. 1880] 'Conclusions pour M. Isaac Pereire et les Héritiers de M. Emile Pereire ... contre la Société du Crédit Mobilier, 1880'.
91 AN, F12/6782, *Le Moniteur des Valeurs Mobiliers et Immobiliers: Bulletin Général des Tirages*, 10 January 1869.
92 Sarchi, *Lettres*, t. I, p. 469, Letter 309, 18 August 1868.
93 AFP, Isaac to Emile, undated.
94 Jean Walch, *Michel Chevalier: Economiste Saint-Simonien 1806–1879* (PhD dissertation, l'Université de Paris IV, 1974), p. 527.
95 AN/MC VIII, 1875, Cours d'Appel de Paris, 28 June and 5 July 1870.
96 ANMT, 9AQ 2, 3, 4, 5, 6, Compagnie Générale Transatlantique, *Rapports*, 1868–71. These shareholders included Eugène, Emile II and Henry Pereire, and members of the Rhoné, Andrade, Lévy, Rodrigues and Baud families.
97 AFP, letters Polack to Emile, 1868–73. See also G. Pereire, *Nord de l'Espagne*, Chapter 2.
98 McPhee, *Social History*, p. 202.
99 AFP, Emile, Arcachon, to Henry, Paris, 25 October 1869.

9

Epilogue

The siege of Paris, which began soon after the Emperor's surrender at Sedan and the declaration of a republican government, brought great disruption to daily life. Business was impossible to transact in normal terms and Emile and Isaac Pereire thus found themselves confounded in their various attempts to find solutions to the problems of the Crédit Mobilier and Compagnie Immobilière. Emile's immediate response to the collapses had been stoic but the aftermath was punishing. He spent increasing periods of time in Arcachon, seeking relief from chronic asthma, living there semi-permanently from 1869 even before the onset of the Franco-Prussian War and remaining until well after the demise of the Paris Commune. Indeed, he now spent considerably more time in Arcachon than in Paris and scarcely any time at all in Armainvilliers, a place which exacerbated his asthma even more than did Paris.

More importantly, the war and the siege, followed in turn by the Paris Commune and massive instability in government throughout France, saw Emile and Isaac parted. Léon Gambetta, who had become Minister of the Interior in the Government of National Defence, had issued a proclamation threatening retribution to those who had played a role under the Second Empire, a threat which Emile took to heart. He fled to Bayonne, where he stayed with the Léons for several months, returning then to Arcachon where he remained throughout the hostilities.[1] Herminie, her daughters Fanny, Claire and Cécile and their children, were also in Arcachon with Emile where they were to remain for almost twelve months. Communications with Paris, and especially with Isaac who had stayed at the *hôtel Pereire* to defend their financial and material interests, were thus erratic; the extended Pereire family, so intimately domestic in Paris, was torn apart by this cataclysm. Aside from Isaac only Emile II, Henry, Georges Thurneyssen (each of whom had joined the Garde Nationale) and Charles Rhoné remained in Paris, Eugène and Gustave managing usefully to evade the troubles and concentrate on business activities in Spain.[2]

By 1871, Emile's ill-health had forced his resignation or retirement from all the directorships he had once held, leaving his place on the Nord de l'Espagne to Emile II and on the Midi to Henry. Isaac retired from none, remaining on the boards of the Austrian railway and both Spanish companies, his sons Eugène (in 1870) and Gustave (in 1875) also joining the Nord de l'Espagne. It is instructive in view of Emile's long residency in Arcachon to find Isaac confiding in Fanny in March 1871 that the family's business interests in the southwest had been 'badly neglected'.[3]

Isaac's energy and initiative had received a new lease, however. He retained the position of Vice-President of the Crédit Mobilier Espagnol and of the Nord de l'Espagne, using the resources of the former to rehabilitate the family's financial interests. In a time of war and civil unrest and in view of the declining health of his brother, he saw urgency in involving the next generation in the process of re-building their future. As he told Fanny, if measures were not taken rapidly all their ventures would self-destruct.[4] The letters he wrote to his nephew Henry, the new board member of the Midi, over 1871 and into 1872, are the best exemplars we have for this. Isaac several times a week coached his nephew in how to analyse and deal with their current problems.

> I am expecting you any day [he wrote to Henry], because we must seriously get back to work. Each of us will have to take part in the management of our affairs to re-establish, as much as possible, a situation which the war has gravely compromised ... methodically, with perseverance and without becoming unduly discouraged.[5]

The Pereires' major shareholding in the Austrian railway was another useful tool in restoring the family's position. Indeed, Isaac set out for Vienna at the very time Thiers withdrew the government to Versailles and elections which would install the Paris Commune were being called. This visit was fortuitous for he negotiated with senior officials the extension of the railway to Belgrade and the possibility of an expression of interest for a line along the Danube. Their interests in Spain were also being managed efficiently by Polack, who negotiated a temporary advance to the Nord de l'Espagne from the Spanish government. Henri Germain through the Crédit Lyonnais provided additional relief also to the Crédit Mobilier Espagnol and the Nord de l'Espagne, to the extent of 28 million francs.[6]

While Isaac was attempting to keep the family businesses afloat throughout this difficult time, ordinary life in Paris was challenging. The initial insouciance of the Parisians towards the siege had ebbed as reality took hold. By January 1871, many were dying from starvation. Supplies of bread were running out. Rationing had been instituted. The bitter cold of early January – it reached minus eight degrees – could not be ameliorated because there was no fuel of any kind for heating, all commandeered by the army.[7] The Pereire establishment did not experience the terrible hardship of the poor, however, and while famine affected everyone in some way the wealthy survived in a little more comfort. The *hôtel Pereire* appeared to have sufficient food, if not a surfeit, eating its way through all the horses in the Pereire stables and capable of putting on dinners for up to eighteen guests at a sitting. A little produce from Armainvilliers helped from time to time. While they were not immune from the freezing cold, aside from the possibility of a stray cannon shot they were in no immediate personal danger. But with the advent of the Commune, Isaac was forced to leave the *hôtel Pereire* for a safer refuge. Members of the Garde Nationale soon after invaded the mansion on 11 April, breaking into the *cave* in which were stored well over a thousand bottles of Château Palmer and sampling the contents. In the days following, guardsmen spirited away five carriages laden with wine, fortunately leaving five hundred bottles behind. The ringleader was discovered subsequently to have been a trainee *sommelier* with the Pereires' Grand Hôtel![8]

The Commune entered its last days and Thiers' troops fought their way into the city from Versailles. With peace restored, however, Emile's health became increasingly fragile. He remained at Arcachon. He and Isaac were now shunned by a number of their former associates and he had little appetite to re-enter Parisian society. He and Herminie too were thus separated more often than they had been in the past, the remaining family now all re-settled in Paris where she joined them in February 1872. It was only the sale of their collection of paintings which drew him back also the following month. He had developed a close relationship with the art dealer Jean-Baptiste Marie Guillermoz, who was acting on behalf of the brothers in this important sale taking place in the boulevard des Italiens. It attracted considerable interest, the results exceeding expectations: 181 paintings sold for over one and a half million francs, a profit of almost 100 per cent as Guillermoz informed Emile with satisfaction.[9]

Late in 1872, however, with Emile back in Arcachon, he wrote to Herminie of his sadness in not being able to spend his birthday with her, the first absence in forty-eight years: 'May we be able to count on some birthdays less tormented than those of recent times, that is the wish that I form in my solitude just as it is the hope which sustains me.'[10]

Herminie's own health deteriorated. From 1871 her waning eyesight increasingly caused concern and it also impeded her mobility. Now more or less confined to the *hôtel Pereire* in Paris, her daughter Cécile Rhoné, whose own husband Charles had died suddenly in 1873, became her companion, writing letters to Emile on her behalf. Herminie clearly hated having the intimacy of her thoughts channeled through the pen of another. The last extant letter Emile himself wrote to her was from Arcachon and dated 19 October 1873, bordered in black to mark the passing of his son-in-law. It was full of domestic detail. The weather in Arcachon was magnificent, he wrote, drawing him onto the terrace to take his coffee until the heat drove him inside again. The trees in the park were laden with fruit and flowers. He had ordered the pruning of the border along a path to the dune they had opened together, affording a view of the ocean. He recounted progress with others of their projects, promising to return to Paris as soon as the weather changed.[11] We do not know whether they shared his seventy-third birthday just over six weeks later, nor whether he was with her when she died, on 25 January 1874.

Herminie's death overwhelmed him. He stayed in Paris from that time, his health worsening over the months which followed. During the last two weeks of his life it was reported that he regulated his accounts and put his affairs in order while the city awaited news of his death. Occasionally, it was said, though this was by no means authenticated, that he repeated Louis XIV's reflection: 'Perhaps you thought me immortal.'[12] On New Year's Day 1875, *l'Univers israélite* advised that prayers for his health would be recited the following Sabbath.[13] But almost a year after Herminie's passing, at 10.40 pm on 6 January 1875, Emile too died, in the presence of his son-in-law Georges Thurneyssen and his friend Guillermoz, who each signed the death certificate.[14]

Emile's death was reported widely, its significance noted well beyond France. The *Univers israélite* recorded that 'today a great Jew has fallen'. And a journalist with the *Liberté*, Edouard Drumont, later to become the face of virulent anti-Semitism, wrote a lengthy obituary for the *Avenir d'Arcachon* which, ironically, was re-printed in the *Univers israélite*:

> He pushed the century in the direction he wanted it to take [he wrote]; he did not meddle with events like so many politicians; he created a world, utterly modifying social environments and shifting the levels on which society moved before him.[15]

Not all were as respectful, the *Boston Daily Advertiser* reporting that Emile 'left this world as a banker leaving home to look after a distant branch establishment'.[16] His estate was valued at sixteen million francs.[17]

Despite the ignominy in which they had been held at the collapse of the Crédit Mobilier, almost every notable in Paris, it seemed, came to the rue du Faubourg Saint-Honoré to sign the books of condolence. On the morning of the funeral, 8 January 1875, Isaac, Emile II and Henry received at the *hôtel Pereire* those who had come to offer their sympathy personally. A large and distinguished number from across the spectrum of French society attended Emile's funeral: members of the Rothschild, Fould, Halphen, Cahen and Hottinguer families, the ducs Decazes and d'Abrantès, the comtes Jules Delaborde and de Berthois, the vicomte Aguado, Generals Changarnier and Fleury, members of the Assemblée Nationale – Carnot, Crémieux, Naquet included – and finally, as the *Bulletin français* noted, 'all the high financial world of Paris and the principal notabilities of journalism'.[18]

Several thousand lined the path taken by the cortège of some 200 carriages which set out at 11.15 am, progressing along the rue du Faubourg Saint-Honoré, the rues Royale, Tronchet, du Havre, and the boulevard de Clichy before arriving at the gate of Montmartre cemetery. Emile had requested a simple funeral and refused the escort due to him as a member of the order of the Légion d'Honneur. Six workers from the Midi and of the Ouest instead marched on either side of the hearse and a deputation of 500 workers from the same railway companies brought up the rear. A concession in perpetuity to build a family tomb had been granted in 1874 to receive the mortal remains of Pereire family members and unfortunately, when the cortège reached the graveside in the Jewish section, monumental masons were still at work on the tomb, disrupting the proceedings. Finally, the Chief Rabbi of Paris, Zadoc Kahn, surrounded by twelve children clothed in white with blue sashes, was able to begin the simple ceremony, reciting the Hebrew prayers for the dead. Lazard Isidor, the Chief Rabbi of France, then spoke of Emile's life, and so did Emile's old friend and colleague Adolphe d'Eichthal. When the lead-lined oak coffin was lowered into the tomb, mourners cast earth upon it.[19] Several days later, Herminie's remains were also re-interred there from Père Lachaise.

With the death of Emile the extraordinary partnership with Isaac was severed, one which had been at the forefront of every major French innovation in banking, in transport, in urban development and utilities, in retailing, in tourism and more, and which had spread its benefits throughout Europe. There is no record of Isaac's emotion on the death of his brother: it can only be imagined. They had traversed almost the whole century together, sharing triumphs and disappointments. They had come to be as one in their ideas, their ambitions, their predilections, their aversions. The circumstances of Emile's last years – the collapse of their cherished enterprises, the frantic search for solutions which would reinstate them, Emile's increasingly poor health, the separations – these had been a tragedy for them both, the aftermath of which Isaac was now left to deal with alone.

Before Emile's death, in November 1871 Isaac had purchased the controversial newspaper the *Liberté* from Emile de Girardin. His influence on its direction was immediate as columns on finance appeared for the first time signed by Louis de Bourgneuf, Isaac's nom-de-plume, which he later changed to Anglet, the name of a commune near Bayonne.[20] The initial collaboration with Girardin ceased in 1872 and Isaac then used the journal to attack the authors of his and Emile's distress, mounting a vigorous rearguard action against the Talabots and their Marseille interests and weighing in against the Crédit Foncier and the Compagnie Immobilière's new board who were attempting to sell the assets of the Immobilière at rock bottom prices. The year following Emile's death, by which time Isaac's differences with the editor Léonce Detroyat had become acute, he took over the journal outright, Gustave recalling that what was not actually written by him was influenced strongly: 'the *Liberté* was his work from 1876 to 1880'.[21] Each day, Gustave received a letter dictated to his mother Fanny, to Cécile Rhoné or to Ernest Polack, whom Gustave described as Isaac's 'private secretary'. Gustave was asked especially to research the articles written by Emile and Isaac during their Saint-Simonian days between 1826 and 1833, particularly those dealing with tax reform. For, as Gustave wrote, they always maintained their ideas and their friendships with constancy, perseverance and generosity of heart. Gustave suggested that his father's reasons for taking on the *Liberté* were to use it as a vehicle for ideas on taxation and 'conversion of the rente'.[22] But politics more likely influenced Isaac's decision to buy the paper in the first place; the evolution of events under the Third Republic goading him to re-engage in political life as he had not done since 1848.

The pivotal year for the Republic was 1875, when a republican constitution was accepted by the Assemblée and organs of government assumed a shape which was to change little over succeeding years. The year following, republicans finally won a majority in an Assemblée which had previously been dominated by monarchists. Government was now firmly in their hands. Nevertheless, while Isaac supported the monarchist Marshall MacMahon in the important election of 1877, he later publicly announced his disappointment with MacMahon's policies, claiming to have been 'duped'.[23]

Isaac's ideas were presented to the public in an aggressive manner, for he used the *Liberté* to influence the new government from the outset, publishing on 14 May 1876 a political programme: 'The raison d'être of governments'.²⁴ 'Monarchy, empire or republic [he wrote], what power can justify itself and call itself legitimate, if it is not the paternal power and fraternal love, extended to the whole of the national family?'²⁵ His credo was not new: while he accepted universal [male] suffrage as the 'law of gravitation of modern societies', the underlying constitution was key.²⁶ Revolution and poverty went hand in hand. Political unrest could be addressed only by eliminating poverty. He was opposed to organised labour, nevertheless, seeing no reason for strikes which were only caused by lack of foresight on the part of government and owners. Strike leaders generally were interested solely in stirring up 'bad passions', 'to poison' the debate between workers and proprietors. The issue lay not in the strike but in its cause.²⁷ Isaac used pieces written for the *Liberté* as the basis for *La Question religieuse*, published in 1878.

Aside from his newspaper interest, he remained actively engaged throughout in winning back the Transat which had evicted him and Emile from its board in 1868. Playing a patient game with tremendous guile over the next five years he called on the resources of long-time associates and investors Galliera, the Bischoffsheims of Paris and Bischoffsheim Goldschmidt of London, who had been original investors in the Midi and the Crédit Mobilier Espagnol. The reports of shareholders' meetings make fascinating reading. The year of Emile's death, through the agency of the Crédit Mobilier Espagnol which had increased its holding to 5,700 shares, the Pereires, Isaac and Eugène, made their move. It was Isaac, who now owned 4,500 shares, and Eugène, who held over 700 – majority shareholders – who took on the challenge. Eugène was voted onto the board in April 1875, and Isaac re-joined the following September. Within two years when the Crédit Mobilier Espagnol and the Pereire family between them owned a total of 17,357 shares, their hold was secure.²⁸

Meanwhile, an earlier enthusiasm for and interest in the development of the Suez Canal led to a more direct involvement in moves by Ferdinand de Lesseps to build an interoceanic canal through the Isthmus of Panama. Lesseps' Saint-Simonian sympathies had drawn him to the Pereires and he remained on friendly terms with the family throughout. Isaac, through his network, was able to attract finance to the initial stages of the project from 1869 when the Suez was opened. He was one of a consortium formed to offer support to de Lesseps and a member of subsequent interest groups also, the Société Civile Internationale du Canal Interocéanique de Darien being one, which included Jacques de Reinach, Oppenheim and Abraham Camondo. When, in 1880, the first attempt was made to construct the canal, its financial backers included the Crédit Mobilier Espagnol, the Banque Franco-Égyptienne and the

Banque Heine.²⁹ Paradoxically, this marked the commencement of a horrendous ten years during which the project brought devastation to its workforce, totally unaccustomed to the harsh physical environment in which their labour was concentrated. Finally brought to a halt, work on the Canal was only taken up again in 1935 by an American company.

Belying the energy with which he had dealt the family back into the market, or perhaps as a result of it, Isaac's own health became increasingly problematic. His sight deteriorated and his movement impeded by severe vascular problems, incidental perhaps to an underlying arterial disease. His employee Edouard Drumont provided the most poignant picture of Isaac at this sombre period of his life, describing his 'beautiful patriarchal head, his manners at once supple and dignified, he had the air of a true descendant of David'. Only Isaac's hands, he went on, 'clawed like a bird of prey betrayed his race'. Drumont's portrait, betraying his anti-Semitism, is nevertheless sensitive in its portrayal of Isaac's blindness, describing his inability to see the works of art in his possession, knowing his sculptures only by touch.³⁰ When Gustave in 1877 became engaged to marry Amélie Emerique, on the first meeting (after the announcement) at the *hôtel Pereire* her parents were taken aback to be greeted by Fanny alone and received by Isaac only when dinner was announced, finding him already seated at the dining table. Nor was the dinner itself an occasion of much social interchange as he was constantly interrupted by assistants carrying bank bills, papers to sign and news of the Bourse. Amélie claimed fifty years afterwards that in the years she knew Isaac they met only a dozen or so times.³¹

He scarcely moved from this room although, in the last years of his life, he exchanged it for his study at Armainvilliers. Increasingly reliant on Gustave and Polack to bring his ideas before the public, he remained engaged to the end despite his disabilities. His working day remained long and his approach unrelenting, continuing, as the Emeriques found, through lunch and dinner when letters or reports were read to him, or in the garden when newspapers were read aloud. He continued to write for the *Liberté*, bringing to fruition projects which had long been put to one side. He promoted cooperative societies through a fund providing credit and consumables to members, managed by workers. He established a series of prizes, the Concours Pereire, worth in total 100,000 francs for essays on subjects familiar to the Pereires' interests: 'practical socialism', free public instruction, tax reform, the most effective organisation of banks, credit, the organisation of labour and the extinction of poverty. Competitors were encouraged to read Talleyrand, Vauban, Quesnoy and Turgot.³² Perhaps the most significant project on which he embarked was the establishment of the Société J. R. Pereire, his final attempt to draw the attention of the public to the work and achievements of his grandfather. He had met a Swiss teacher of deaf-mutes, Marius Magnat, whose methods were similar to those pioneered by Jacob Rodrigues Pereire – that is, he taught through an approach which came to be known as 'oralism', in contrast to sign language. Isaac established Magnat in a school in the avenue de Villiers. He also financed several major public events designed to promote the legacy of his grandfather, to give his work a new lease of life. Eugène was to take up this project vigorously in the coming years, one of the major events which he supported financially being a controversial conference in Milan in 1880 which established oralism as the preeminent method of teaching deaf-mutes.[33]

At Armainvilliers, however, Isaac suffered a cerebral haemorrhage from which he did not recover, dying soon after on 12 July 1880. This time the respectful words of the *Univers israélite* towards his brother were more restrained about Isaac. However remarkable his personality, however solemn the death of a man who held such a high position in finance, his life and death did not offer the same interest to the 'Jewish world', it commented.

Isaac's sons Eugène and Gustave and son-in-law Eugène Mir, his nephews Emile II and Henry, and Georges Thurneyssen received those tendering condolences at the rue du Faubourg Saint-Honoré. Three thousand people accompanied the cortège which was flanked by officers, masters and 80 sailors of the Transat together with boys from all the other companies presided over by Isaac. A deputation of 'sourds-muets' from the École Pereire also marched. At the family gravesite at Montmartre Cemetery, two of three rabbis attending pronounced a short eulogy after prayers of rite. It was all Isaac had asked for.[34]

Four years previously the mortal remains of his grandfather Jacob Rodrigues Pereire, and of one of Jacob's young sons, Samuel, who died at eight years, had been removed from a Sephardic cemetery in the avenue de Flandres and reinterred in Montmartre.[35] The names of the Pereires' father Isaac and their brother Télèphe were later also engraved on the tomb.

Isaac' death elicited, as had Emile's, a wide variety of opinion in its reporting. The *Boston Daily Advertiser*, under a heading 'A French Speculator', summed up both Pereires when it wrote that 'they were a novel mixture of good hearts and egregious business habits which made them rich while it impoverished others'.[36] Others, however, mourned the loss of a brilliant and generous man, a 'distinguished benefactor of humanity, glory of philanthropy, whose helping hand was always held out to those who are in trouble and who suffer because of social injustice which still makes the shame of our century'.[37] He left just under thirty-three million francs.[38]

Despite the collapse of the Crédit Mobilier and the eventual demise of the Compagnie Immobilière, the Pereires had left a considerable legacy in public infrastructure and iconic companies. Many of the remaining Pereire businesses stayed afloat until well into the twentieth century. The Transat continued to operate independently until 1977 when it merged with Messageries Maritimes to become the present-day Compagnie Générale Maritime. The Grands Magasins du Louvre became the Société du Louvre in 1889 with the remit to own and operate hotels, relinquishing its interest in department stores. The Compagnie Parisienne du Gaz survived until the expiry of its concession in 1905. The Compagnie des Entrepôts et Magasins Généraux has seen its building assume an integral role in the new developments in Paris' north, the parc du Millénaire, La Villette, the Cité des Sciences et de l'Industrie. Finally, the family retained Château Palmer until 1938 when they sold it to a consortium, two members of which, the Sichel and Mähler-Besse families, still manage the *vignoble*.

The cost and significance to the State of efficient transport infrastructure was recognised in France and in the rest of Europe by the time of the Second World War. All the Pereires' railway enterprises became national assets. The Midi, which had already merged with the Paris–Orléans, became a component in the Société nationale des chemins de fer français (SNCF) in 1938. The Compagnie Générale des Omnibus was integrated with another company in 1921 and, eventually, this too was taken over by the State (in 1948) to become the Régie autonome des transports parisiens (the RATP Group), providing transport services to the Paris region. Of the European railways, the Chemin de Fer du Nord de l'Espagne was the last to be taken over by the State, in 1941.

The Pereire family continued to play a role in French commercial circles. Eugène Pereire became President of the Transat from 1875 to 1904. He founded in 1881 and presided over the Banque Transatlantique, and presided over the Banque de Tunisie, founded in 1884. The latter two still exist, the first as a subsidiary of the CIC Crédit Mutuel which also has a stake in the second. Emile and Herminie's son Emile II was to have a major falling out with Eugène which led to the son's resignation from the Transat board. He, together with his brother Henry, remained directors of the Magasins du Louvre, however, Emile II becoming President in 1888, and Henry from 1913 to 1929. Until his death in 1913, Emile II also continued a director of the Midi, as did Henry until his election as vice-president, a position he held from 1911 to 1926.[39]

It was their Spanish interests which saved a considerable portion of the family fortune. Both Gustave and Emile II remained directors of the Chemin de Fer du Nord de l'Espagne, a legacy handed on to their sons. Emile II and Suzanne's son Maurice, born in 1867, became one of three Vice-Presidents from 1901 until 1941. Gustave's son Jacques was also a director of the Nord de l'Espagne up to the same date.[40] In turn, Jacques' son and Isaac's great-grandson François was from 1967 a director of the Spanish insurance company the Fénix, which the Pereires had established in 1864, and President of its Paris committee from 1971.

The social standing the family had enjoyed during much of the Second Empire was lost to them in the years immediately following the failure of the Crédit Mobilier. They were not counted within high society under the Third Republic. The financial loss incurred by shareholders may also have contributed to the growing anti-Semitism in France and, certainly, the family suffered during the years of the Dreyfus Affair, forcing Gustave to sell the *Liberté* which he had taken over from his father. More happily, from 1875 there developed a rapprochement of sorts with the Rothschilds with the friendly takeover of the Pereires' Seville–Cordoba rail line by the Rothschilds' MZA, according benefits to the Nord de l'Espagne. The rivalry was further dissipated with the marriage in 1909 of Eugène's granddaughter Noémi to Maurice de Rothschild, and then with the establishment in 1953 of the Compagnie Financière, a private bank, by Edmond de Rothschild and François Pereire, over which François presided until 1975. This bank still operates as an affiliate of the Compagnie Financière Edmond de Rothschild.

Notes

1 AFP, Polack to Emile in Bayonne, 4 November 1870.
2 Ibid. Henry managed to leave Paris during the first six months of 1871, even though he was in the Garde Nationale. About six domestic staff remained in Paris to support the male members of the Pereire family.
3 Ibid., to Fanny, 25 March 1871.
4 Ibid.
5 Ibid., to Henry, 3 June 1871; Stoskopf, *Banquiers et financiers*, p. 288.
6 AFP, Isaac to Henry, 5 June 1871.
7 Robert Tombs, *The Paris Commune, 1871* (London, 1999).
8 AFP, 'Journal d'une Femme de Chambre', pp. 41–4.
9 Galerie de MM. Pereire, *Catalogue des tableaux anciens et modernes*. See also AFP, Guillermoz to Emile, 'Dimanche'.
10 AFP, to Herminie, 2 December 1872.
11 Ibid., to Herminie, 19 October 1873.

12 'Pereire, the French Banker', *Boston Daily Advertiser*, 17 February 1875.
13 *L'Univers israélite*, XXXe, 9, 1 January 1875, 287.
14 AN/MC VIII 1793, 19 January 1875, registered Paris 20 January 1875, 'Notoriété après le décès de M. Jacob Emile Pereire'.
15 *L'Univers israélite*, XXXe, 10, 15 January 1875, 309–10. Drumont's obituary appeared in *l'Avenir d'Arcachon*, Tuesday, 12 January 1875.
16 *Boston Daily Advertiser*, 17 February 1875, quoting the Paris correspondent of the *Gazzetta d'Italia*.
17 Stoskopf, *Banquiers et financiers*, p. 281.
18 'Obsèques de M. Émile Pereire', *Le Bulletin français*, 9 January 1875.
19 Ibid.
20 *Écrits*, t. 3, fasc., 1, pp. 605–6, for a brief history of the *Liberté*.
21 Ibid., t. 3, fasc., 2, p. 49, 'Avis Préliminaire'.
22 Ibid., p. 763.
23 Ibid., t. 3, fasc. 3, p. 1575.
24 Ibid., fasc. 2, 'Première Partie: Programmes', p. 788.
25 Ibid., p. 828.
26 Ibid., 789.
27 Ibid., fasc. 3, pp. 1885–86, 18 May 1880.
28 ANMT, 9AQ 4–7, CGT shareholders' meetings, 1872–77.
29 Ghislain de Diesbach, *Ferdinand de Lesseps* (Paris, 1998).
30 Edouard Drumont, *La France juive* (Paris, [1912]), pp. 354–5.
31 Autin, *Frères Pereire*, pp. 335–6.
32 AFP, Vigano, 'Hommage à … Isaac Pereire'.
33 The controversy continues. See Lasne, 'Jacob Rodrigues Pereire et l'abbé de l'Épée'.
34 *L'Univers israélite*, XXXVe, 22, 1 August 1880, p. 698, quoting *XIXe Siècle*, 16–17 July 1880.
35 La Rochelle, *Jacob Rodrigues Pereire*, p. 459, fn. 1.
36 *Boston Daily Advertiser*, 28 July 1880.
37 AFP, Vigano, 'Hommage à … Isaac Pereire'.
38 Stoskopf, *Banquiers et financiers*, p. 187.
39 AFP, and AN-Léonore, notices dealing with the award of Légion d'Honneur to Pereire family members.
40 *Bradshaw's Railway Manual, Shareholders' Guide and Directory, 1910* (London, 1910); *Universal Directory of Railway Officials, 1930* (London, 1930); *Universal Directory of Railway Officials and Railway Year Book, 1942–43* (London, 1943).

10

Conclusion

Emile and Isaac Pereire were controversial figures in their own time and they remain so. In their relationship to Judaism, in their Saint-Simonianism, their socialism, their partnership, the broad scope of their businesses, their business practices, their political allegiance, they have been subjects of criticism, comment and analysis by historians and others for over 150 years. How can we now assess them and the complex fields of history they inhabit? Let us examine first their continuing relationship to Saint-Simonianism and, in particular, the coherence of their later actions and enterprises with their earlier beliefs, elements which have been questioned by some and affirmed by others.

While the emotional responses of the two brothers to Saint-Simonianism differed as the organised movement was coming to an end, fundamentally they agreed on the economic and financial direction necessary for France to enter the industrialised world. These ideas probably changed little over time, though the means of achieving them did. It is clear, for instance, that the Pereires' considerable influence on banking in France had its roots in Saint-Simonian writings. Four pillars conceived as essential to banking reform were achieved either with the Pereires' direct intervention or attempted by them: day-to-day banking for small merchants (the Comptoir d'Escompte de Paris of 1848), for mortgage finance (the Crédit Foncier of 1852), for large-scale investment (the Crédit Mobilier of 1852), and for investment finance for small business (the Caisse Centrale des Sociétés de Crédit Mutual of 1853, which failed to obtain approval).[1] In the context of reform, their attacks against the Banque de France which commenced during Saint-Simonian days continued to their last breath. The view of rail as the wave of the future was first promoted through

Michel Chevalier's 'Mediterranean system' and by Saint-Simonian engineers. The Pereires' PSG flowed directly from Saint-Simonian discourse. Aside from these early triumphs, they never relinquished their bid to fulfil Chevalier's concept through a link between the Atlantic at Bordeaux and the Mediterranean at Marseille. The broad urban developments undertaken in the capital by the Compagnie Immobilière, with their emphasis on hygiene, accessibility and open space, were at least foreshadowed in Saint-Simonian literature. These continuing Saint-Simonian influences on their lives and careers thus cannot be dismissed, for it was the Pereires who brought a significant number of the most important Saint-Simonian ideas to fruition. And despite the collapse of the Crédit Mobilier and its ultimate failure to achieve the goals Isaac Pereire had set out, at times it came close. With the exception of the Immobilière, the companies in which it invested in France and elsewhere in Europe survived, and continued to make a contribution to national economies long after the bank's demise.

If it is relatively easy to point to practical achievements of Saint-Simonian origin, what then did Saint-Simonian 'socialism' mean to them? That Isaac was still using the term 'practical socialism' until the end must have signified something. Marx had adopted certain Saint-Simonian ideas and expressions from his move to Paris in 1843, but we can be certain that neither Pereire used the term in the same sense as Marx and Engels eventually did, nor that militancy was an ingredient in its use. They employed and promoted the term synonymously with the Saint-Simonian maxim: 'All social institutions must have for their goal improvement in the moral, physical and intellectual condition of the most numerous and the poorest class. All the privileges of birth, without exception, will be abolished. To each according to his capacity, to each according to his works.'[2] This daunting agenda was to be achieved through credit, through employment and through education. It was a significant point of agreement with Napoléon III who declared that he 'would rather face a hostile army of 200,000 than the threat of insurrection founded on unemployment'.[3] Through their bank the Pereires certainly provided employment on a massive scale. By 1865, the building industry in Paris – which owed much to the Pereires' urban development company and was critical to the Emperor's interests – employed over 20 per cent of the work force.[4] Railway workers and those employed in engineering and metal manufactures accounted for many of the more than one million industrial workers in Paris in 1860.[5] The Pereires' shipbuilding works at Penhoët employed 2,000 workers. For whatever reason – Saint-Simonian philosophy, Bonapartist exigency, or both – the Pereires made it their mission to mobilise the French workforce into jobs.

Nevertheless, the radical ideas promoted by Isaac Pereire in his 'Lessons on Industry and Finance' of 1831 and which foreshadowed Marx's critique of value were revisited by him and Emile only in part.[6] They did attempt, albeit unsuccessfully, to introduce a savings and loan bank in 1830 and were instrumental in introducing a similar institution in 1848, as Isaac had recommended in his early work. But the necessity for a 'universal association' of workers canvassed in his lectures he later appropriated to serve capitalism, to consolidate industrial rather than trades associations. A world without buying and selling, in which workers had at their disposal the tools they needed, and in which all the instruments of production – land, factories, machinery – were in the hands of those best able to employ them, thus transferring the right to property from the 'idle' to the workers: these ideas did not underlie the Pereires' later enterprises. Thus the Saint-Simonianism socialism of which Isaac at least was a leading proponent in 1831 was considerably watered down in its application from the moment they became employers and business owners themselves.

This does not mean that they did nothing of any consequence for the working class. They brought education to the region where they had made significant investment and participated in reforms to technical and professional education. They attempted to balance the impact of economic downturns on workers with generous acts of public charity. When food was scarce during the Crimean War they used the CGM to import cattle, wheat, rice and sugar and funded farms and factories, attempting to make produce available to workers at low prices.[7] With a bad harvest in 1863 they placed 30,000 kilos of bread at the disposal of the poor of Paris.[8] Isaac Pereire provided 50,000 francs for distribution to the poor during a punishing winter in 1879–80.[9] Indeed, he was said to have exhorted his fellow entrepreneurs: 'Give, give without counting, have your wealth forgiven through your munificence.'[10] Obviously, these acts of charity did not amount to socialism, and they would be better described today as paternalistic. But the Pereires' social welfare concerns, consistent with the Jewish command of *sedaca* we have noted, mirrored Saint-Simonian actions and ideology directed to the 'proletarian'.

It would have been difficult for the Pereires in later life to stay a clear course, however, to remain the true believers they had been, especially when the enterprises on which they embarked were large and entering uncharted waters, where the political and economic environments were treacherous. The Pereires compromised and were compromised. And while they always claimed, in true Saint-Simonian fashion, that their ceaseless activity was all in the public interest, the huge amounts of money they made from it give one pause. For one, the development of the Crédit Mobilier was restricted by forces that were as much external as internal, as Isaac Pereire claimed with some justification. Members of the Haute Banque gave no quarter in the battle against the Pereires, and the Banque de France placed impediments in their way at every turn. From its inception, Isaac wrote, the Crédit Mobilier had been 'paralysed in its means of credit, as much through the jealousy of which it was the object and through the abuse of speculation as through the arbitrariness and weaknesses of power'.[11] The grand plans he laid out to its shareholders in 1854 were constrained from the outset.[12] Again, the very secretiveness with which the Pereires stood accused, one could argue, as they did, was born as much from early disillusionment, a sense that they had been 'exploited by some, combated by others; instructed by a sad experience', that they had only each other to count on in pursuing their great projects.[13] This was all accurate, but in it lay the seeds of corruption.

Saint-Simonian ideology was filled with references to morality and high principles, at variance with the recurring criticism of the Pereires' financial rectitude which appears in some of the literature. What illegal or suspect means might they have used to influence or pervert business decisions, if indeed they did? Certainly, in their own lifetime the Pereires' business dealings became increasingly a matter of conjecture and suspicion and ultimately of legal action against them. The collapse of the Crédit Mobilier and the Compagnie Immobilière which took with them the savings of investors large and small generated much of the anger. But there were earlier claims of fraudulence and corruption and frequent lawsuits during the 1860s and 1870s. The evidence of bribery noted in Chapter 8 emerged from the commission charged with compiling and publishing imperial household documents seized at the Tuileries in 1870 – described in notes from the Civil List to be a work of 'calming ['apaisement', presumably for the Emperor] and seduction'.[14]

The Pereires also provided gifts. Press proprietors, whom the Saint-Simonians with their customary foresight recognised as crucial moulders of favourable public opinion, were among the recipients of parcels of shares: Jean-Baptiste Paulin, founder of *L'Illustration*, for one; Jules Mirès, as founding editor of the *Journal des Chemins de Fer des Mines et des Travaux Publics*, was another, although Mirès, in picaresque fashion, returned his 500 shares in the Bordeaux–Sète railway, claiming conflict of interest. He did accept 300 shares in the Crédit Mobilier![15] But these kinds of gift were fairly common among large business houses, a practice which the Rothschilds mastered early and employed frequently, described as 'spreading the sugar about'. Indeed, the Rothschild family's most recent biographer has dwelt at length on the variety of lavish gifts presented by family members to senior politicians, members of royalty and other business leaders.[16]

The Pereires' lack of business transparency was also apparent. They were notoriously private in their business dealings, playing their cards close to their chest, especially when the Crédit Mobilier encountered severe cash-flow problems. The accounts for the Credit Mobilier for April 1867, the last under Isaac Pereire's presidency, are lacunate. Complete records in either public or private repositories are not available. This is at least curious. During the Crédit Mobilier's fall one critic declared the information they provided to shareholders lamentably inadequate.[17] Accusations of bribery on a colossal scale were made against them from 1855 when the contract for the Paris gas companies was being determined.[18] Similar accusations were made about the means they employed to acquire the concession for the Paris omnibus company in the same year, accusations which may have been accurate but which cannot now be proven. But if they were advancing money to the Emperor one might suppose with some justification they were also bribing municipal officials. The handsome monopolies which accompanied these contracts were in any case bound to create controversy.

The legal morass within which they were ensnarled from 1867 needs also to be considered as another dimension to their business practices. Some of the actions brought against the Pereires were consequential upon business decisions they took, such as the doubling of capital in 1866 which diluted the value of shareholdings. The court demanded that the Pereires repay the complainants to the extent of one hundred francs per share. Eventually this ruling was struck out.[19] Later, bondholders attempted to gain compensation for losses in the value of bonds. This action too finally was considered to be unsound.[20] Some actions related to the legality of the agreement the Pereires reached with Germiny which saw them pay reparations in exchange for (an illusory) immunity. Again, this case did not succeed ultimately and the agreement was found to be legally sound.[21] The newly constituted Crédit Mobilier attempted in 1871, through its new president, Haussmann, to recover losses through applying mortgages to Pereire properties, a move which was initially aproved but eventually delared nul and void.[22] None of these actions carried criminal implications or accusations of criminal intent.

There were other legal actions brought against the Pereires for misrepresentation, however, especially in their reporting of the true situation of the project in Marseille. The Pereires had known of the Immobilière's situation well in advance of any announcement about it. As late as April

1866, Emile Pereire continued to present a confident assessment even though the picture was dire. Shareholders who purchased stocks under the misapprehension that the Compagnie Immobilière was profitable sued them for the substantial losses they sustained.[23] The Paris Cour de Cassation ruled in favour of the Pereires, to discourage speculation! It emerged also that Isaac Pereire had loaned the Immobilière fifty million francs from Crédit Mobilier funds without collateral and without much discussion.[24] Earlier accounts of the Marseille development were shown to be at least questionable, with long-term credits needing to be repaid in the future counted as assets to mislead investors.[25] These are clear cases of fraud, even though the Pereires largely escaped punishment.

To the extent that Emile and Isaac Pereire were known to use bribery and acted without transparency in relation to shareholders, that they manipulated the accounts ('cooking the books') when their businesses were in trouble, this gives them few points for financial rectitude. The picture of dishonest dealings is compounded by the knowledge that they made a fortune through their companies and that they managed to retain a reasonable portion of it.

Obviously their commercial behaviour fell far short of currently accepted norms for company directors. But standards of business morality change, together with the legal and regulatory apparatus which keeps it in check. In hindsight, few nineteenth-century businessmen would escape the courts today if standards of contemporary corporate law were applied to them. Jules Mirès, jailed in 1862 for swindling, was one of the few found guilty in his own day, and that conviction was soon quashed by the Cour de Cassation. It is neither legitimate nor useful to project our standards on the past. One cannot ignore or defend the Pereires' shortcomings, however, but nor can one conclude from them that their primary ambition was to defraud shareholders for their own enrichment, as was suggested in their own time and which more recent commentators have used to dismiss them.[26]

Everything in their history points to a scenario different from mere profit-taking, one in which their purpose was more complex, their manner of achieving it constrained by external and internal factors, and their later business decisions flawed as they attempted to rescue their enterprises. Certainly they sought profit in their various undertakings, but these had a wider significance. That they fulfilled so much of the Saint-Simonian agenda signified a broadly-based economic and social vision at work. And while shareholders and others suffered in the aftermath of the Crédit Mobilier bankruptcy, many more had profited directly and indirectly from its successes and that of its affiliates, not the least being in the employment generated by their businesses, the flow-on effects of rail and shipbuilding to large-scale mining and metal manufactures, and the major contribution of French capital and technology transfer to other European countries through their banks and railways. Roger Price notes that the introduction during the Second Empire of a more co-ordinated and aggressive policy on railway development, which owed much to the Pereires' early leadership, increased the volume of trade to the order of 101 per cent between 1851 and 1863 and 248 per cent over the period 1851–82.[27] While exports of manufactured goods remained well over 50 per cent of total exports during the Second Empire, the market for capital goods in those countries where French railway technology was introduced expanded appreciably.[28] French heavy manufacturing companies, Schneider and Greffenstaden, constructed 72 locomotives between 1859 and 1864 for the Nord de l'Espagne, to a value of 12 million francs.[29] An estimate made by Emile Pereire in 1865 showed orders placed with French companies like Ernest Goüin et Cie for locomotives, bridges and viaducts in Austria, Russia and Spain worth in excess of 44 million francs in heavy engineering exports from France.[30]

What then can we make of the Pereires? If luck is simply the capacity to recognise and grasp opportunity the Pereires' history is one of great foresight, steel and enormous courage. But their story also tells of personal gifts: high intelligence, organisational skill and energy. These qualities, honed in a disadvantaged Sephardic household in Bordeaux, found expression in the enterprises they founded and the successes they achieved. They seized and exploited every opportunity presented and for the most part they made every post a winner.

Innovation was the spur to their imagination and there was scarcely an element of modernity the Pereire brothers did not touch. One recent historian has gone so far as to place them firmly in the context of the twenty-first century along with the inventors of the internet, 'start-up' companies and globalisation![31] But the sheer sweep of their activities, even though ultimately it constrained their capacity to manage them well and was to bring them undone, all these represented a clear break with the past.

In 1879, the year before his death at the age of 73, Isaac Pereire reflected upon the history of the Crédit Mobilier. In a publication entitled *La Question des chemins de fer*, which was as close as he came to an autobiography, his reflections settled on the expulsion of the Jews from Spain and the Protestants from France. He drew attention to the harsh consequences for national economies of the withdrawal of intelligent, productive and hard-working contributors. State finances and the affairs of industry, both, were deprived of all direction as a result, he wrote. And it was out of these circumstances that the Crédit Mobilier was born.[32] This reading of the origins of the Crédit Mobilier as an outcome of religious persecution and, by implication, of the emancipation of Jews and Protestants by the French Revolution, was telling. For emancipation shaped the Pereires and gave rein to their ambition. It opened citizenship and opportunity to them. It gave them confidence and it gave them access to resources. Without it their achievements are unthinkable. Paradoxically, emancipation also loosened their attachment to Judaism while attracting them inexorably to a national identity as Frenchmen.

Their story with all its nuances thus illustrates the dilemmas confronting the Jews of France in the nineteenth century, their responses to anti-Jewish behaviour and anti-Semitism and their evolution in the process of becoming both Frenchmen *and* Jews. Their lives and careers also demonstrate the dynamism of nineteenth-century France in the ideological ferment which followed the Revolution, the enormous changes which altered the face of industry and commerce, and the transformation in society and politics – from the Consulate of Napoléon Bonaparte to the Third French Republic.

Notes

1 Yonnet, 'La Structuration de l'économie et de la banque sous le Second Empire', pp. 128–9; Stoskopf, *Banquiers et financiers*, pp. 274–5.
2 *L'Organisateur*, IIe année. From 2 August 1830 every issue carried the *devise* on its masthead.
3 Quoted in Harvey, *Paris*, p. 144.
4 Ibid.
5 Louis Girard, *Nouvelle Histoire de Paris: la Deuxième République et le Second Empire 1848–1870* (Paris, 1981), p. 214.
6 Briscoe, 'Saint-Simonism', p. 209–25.
7 Barbance, *Compagnie Générale Transatlantique*, pp. 40–1. They lost heavily when, as conditions rapidly improved on conclusion of the peace treaty, Russian wheat flooded the market.
8 *L'Univers israélite*, 1863, p. 285.
9 *Écrits*, t. 3, fasc., 3, p. 1909.
10 Autin, *Frères Pereire*, p. 324.
11 I. Pereire, *Chemins de fer*, pp. 146–7.
12 ANMT, 25AQ1, Crédit Mobilier, *Rapport*, 29 April 1854.
13 I. Pereire, *Chemins de fer*, p. 140.
14 Poulet-Malassis, *Papiers secrets*, pp. 50, 331, 358.
15 AFP, Paulin to Emile, 3 May 1853; Mirès to Emile, 10 September 1853.
16 Ferguson, *World's Banker*, pp. 162–73, 305–6.

17 Aycard, *Crédit Mobilier*, pp. 111.
18 Lenard R. Berlanstein, *Big Business and Industrial Conflict in Nineteenth-Century France: A Social History of the Parisian Gas Company* (Berkeley, 1991), Chapter 9. An accusation was made in 1892 that Emile Pereire had spent three million francs in bribes to officials to make sure the project was realised.
19 BNF-F-M, FM-8260, 'Société Générale de Crédit Mobilier (Doublement du capital social, en 1866), Jugements & Arrêts sur Demandes en Responsabilités et en Dommages contre les Anciens Administrateurs de la Société Générale de Crédit Mobilier'.
20 Ibid., FM-8251, 'Cour de Cassation, Chambre de Requêtes, Mémoire ampliatif pour M. Isaac Pereire ... Mme Fanny-Rebecca Pereire'.
21 Ibid., FM-25482, 'Cour d'Appel de Paris (1ère Chambre): Affaire de MM Emile et Isaac Pereire contre le Crédit Mobilier'.
22 Ibid., FM-8251, 'Mémoire ampliatif'.
23 Ibid.
24 Ibid., FM-8254, 'Note pour le Crédit Mobilier sur la convention du 23 décembre 1868' (Paris, 1874).
25 Ibid., Factum Pereire, Isaac/Pereire, Emile/Salvador, Gabriel/Société de Credit Mobilier/Compagnie Immobilière Liquidation/Boulard, Albert/Paul Blavet et Cie/ etc, 1-137, from 1864 to 1878.
26 For instance, Christopher Prendergast refers to 'the shady Pereire brothers, the whiz-kids of modern Parisian finance who launched the Crédit Immobilier' [sic] spreading the 'stench of corruption'. Review of Carmona's biography of Haussmann in *London Review of Books* 24 (2002), 29-30.
27 Price, *French Second Empire*, pp. 215-16.
28 Lévy-Leboyer and Bourguignon, *French Economy*, pp. 48-9.
29 Nicolas Stoskopf, *Le Train: une passion alsacienne (1839-2012)* (Strasbourg, 2012), p. 99.
30 AFP, 'Etat approximatif des commandes faites en France ... pour les chemins de fer étrangers au 14 octobre 1865'.
31 Berthon, *Émile et Isaac Pereire*, p. 10.
32 I. Pereire, *Chemins de fer*, p. 146.

Appendix
Pereire companies

Between 1835 and 1867, Emile and Isaac Pereire were involved in a large number and diversity of businesses, within France and elsewhere. Aside from holding equity, in many cases they, singly or together, also held directorships in the enterprises. The list below shows the more significant of these.[1]

France

Compagnie du Chemin de Fer de Paris à Saint-Germain-en-Laye
Compagnie du Chemin der Fer de Paris à Versailles (Rive Droite)
Compagnie du Chemin de Fer du Nord
Compagnie du Chemin de Fer de Paris à Lyon
Société de Construction des Batignolles
Comptoir National d'Escompte de Paris
Compagnie des Chemins de Fer du Midi et du Canal Latéral à la Garonne
Compagnie du Chemin de Fer du Grand-Central de France
Compagnie des Chemins de Fer de l'Est
Compagnie des Chemins de Fer de l'Ouest
Chemins de Fer du Dauphiné
Société Générale de Crédit Mobilier
Compagnie Immobilière
Crédit Agricole
Société des Blanchisseries Industrielles
Compagnie Générale Transatlantique
Compagnie Parisienne de l'Éclairage et de Chauffage par le Gaz
Compagnie Générale des Omnibus

Compagnie Impériale des Petites Voitures
Compagnie des Entrepôts et des Magasins Généraux de Paris
Compagnie des Salins du Midi
Société Générale des Asphaltes de Paris
Compagnie des Assurances La Confiance
Compagnie des Assurances La Paternelle
Société du Mise en Valeur des Landes
Château Palmer
Conserveries Palmer

Foreign

Banque Darmstädter für Handel und Industrie
Société Autrichienne des Chemins de Fer de l'État
Grande Compagnie des Chemins de Fer Russes
Chemin de Fer Central Suisse
Compagnie de l'Ouest des Chemins de Fer Suisses
Compagnie des Chemins de Fer François-Joseph
Chemin de Fer du Nord de l'Espagne
Chemin de Fer de Cordoue à Seville
Compagnie du Gaz de Madrid
Compagnie d'Assurances l'Union et Phénix Espagnol
Real Compañía de la Canalización del Ebro
Crédit Mobilier Italien
Crédit Mobilier Espagnol
Société Générale de Commerce et d'Industrie à Amsterdam
Banque Ottomane
International Financial Society
Banque Impériale Romane

Note

1 This list is adapted from several documents in the AFP, including *Note sur les Travaux de MM. Emile et Isaac Pereire* (Paris, [1868]); *Statuts* of companies in which they held directorships, collected by Gustave Pereire; and 'Notices biographiques de mon père et de mon oncle pour le Panthéon de la Légion d'Honneur', handwritten by Henry Pereire.

Select bibliography

Archival sources

ARCHIVES NATIONALES
Minutier central des notaires de Paris, MC/VIII/notaire Fould/1586/1595/1648/1655/1682/1793.
AP 45, Fonds Rouher, 1–19.
181 AQ 87/15; 89/17; 93/258, 'Archives et histoire de la maison Gradis (1551–1980)'.
BB/15/322–329, 'Dispensation pour marriage – clause 164 Code Civil, Années 1840–44'.
F12, Ministre du Commerce, banques.
F12/1793–97, F12/6471, F12/6772, F12/6773, F12/6775, F12/6781-2, F12/6827, F12/6831.
F14, Travaux publics.
F14/9146–9152, F14/8536–8540, F14/9240–9269, F14/15001–15012.

ARCHIVES NATIONALES DU MONDE DU TRAVAIL, ROUBAIX
9AQ 2–10, Compagnie Générale Transatlantique, shareholders' annual general meetings [AGM].
25AQ 1-2, Crédit Mobilier, AGM, 1854–.
25AQ 3, Crédit Mobilier, Conseil d'Administration, 1871–75.
78AQ 6, Chemin de Fer du Midi, AGM, 1852–66.
78AQ 7, Midi, AGM to 1866–70.
78AQ 27, Midi, Procès-Verbaux, Conseil d'Administration 1861.
78AQ 98 (5) and (6), Chemin de Fer du Littoral de Sète à Marseille, 1862.

ARCHIVES DÉPARTEMENTALES DE LA GIRONDE, BORDEAUX
D110, 'Registre contenant 187 feuilles Délibérations du Conseil Général 21 Messidor l'an 2', f.35, 1 Thermidor l'an 2.

3E 24125 (liasse), notaire Mathieu, 'Fonseca neveu Inventaire'.
3E 24127 (liasse), notaire Mathieu, 'Isaac Rodrigues Pereire, Inventaire, 10 12 1806', 'Procuration, 3 12 06'.
12L 6, Séances de Section 9, dite 'La Loi'.
12L 9, Séances de Section 18, 'Dix-Août'.
12L 10, Séances de Section 19, 'Bon Accord'.
6M I, 'Recensement de la Population 1.1.06'.
8M 1, 'Chambre de Commerce au Préfet de la Gironde 1811–26'.
4L 116, 'Etat de disboursements, par communes des citoyens en état de porte les armes'.
3Q 1017, 'Registre des Actes Commencé le 7 Ventose an 12 et fini le 12 prairial même année', fo. 144.
7V 14–19, 'Cultes 1800–1940', Construction des synagogues, comptabilité, indemnités et traitements du personnel, secours, correspondance.

Archives communales de Bayonne

FF209 (liasse), fo. 39–42.
GG229 (liasse), 1600–1786, 'Les Juifs de Saint-Esprit', fo. 4–69.
GG275 (liasse), 1776–1789: Correspondance (Lettres Originales), fo. 49.
2D 2, [St Esprit] 'Registre de proclamations, procès-verbaux, requisitions et arrêtes de la municipalité de Jean-Jacques Rousseau'.
2D 3, [St Esprit] 'Registre de publication des certificats de résidence, des procès-verbaux, adjudications & autres objets'.
2I 24, [St Esprit] 'Lettre de la Société Populaire de Bidache à la Société Populaire de J.-J. Rousseau, accompagnant l'envoi d'une affiche relative à l'abandon par les Juifs de leur synagogue, 1er Ventose l'an 2e [1794]'.
2I 32, [St Esprit] 'Lettre de la Société régénérée et épurée des Amis de la Constitution de 1793 de Dax, à la Société Populaire de J.-J. Rousseau, relative à l'épuration de ladite société et à son changement de nom, le 28 Germinal an 2 [1794]'.
2I 36, [St Esprit] 'Lettre de la Société Populaire montagnarde régénérée des Amis de la Constitution de 1793 de Cap-Brutus, à la Société régénérée de J.-J. Rousseau, relative à la prière à l'Être suprême, 22 prairial, an 2me [1794]'.
Archives départementales des Pyrénées-Atlantiques, Pau
IIIE 3484, notaire Paul Duhalde, fos 86–9.
IIIE 4594, Maître Forgues 1793–An II (et début 1794).
IIIE 4672 (1) and (2), notaire Pierre Cazenave.
C171 Liasse, 'Rolle de la Capitation & Extraordinaire de la Nation Portugaise ... 1783', fo. 24, fo. 31.

Archives municipales de Bordeaux

GG 842–51 (micro), 'Culte israélite Portugais: Registres de circoncisions, naissances et sépultures, 1706–1792'.
2 MI D 4/3 Mariage Isaac Rodrigues Henriques et Sara-Sophie Lopès Fonseca, 1794.

IE 19-21, 'Culte israélite: Naissances, Mariages, Décès, 1706-1792'. [Photocopies of registers in one volume].
IE 27 (microfiche), acte de naissance 361, 'Jacob Emile Rgues. Pereire'.
IE 33 (microfiche), acte de naissance 952, 'Mardochée Télèphe Rodrigues Pereyre'.
IE 45 (microfiche), acte de naissance 1717, 'Isaac Rodrigues Pereire'.
30 E I 'Régistre de Déliberations des Israélites'.
IF 4, (micro) 'Recensement 1822'.

ARCHIVES DU CONSISTOIRE CENTRAL DE PARIS
CC, 21-VII-1824, 8-VII-1831, 'Correspondance Registre'.
GG1, 'Mariages célébrés dans le Temple israélite de la N. D. de Nazareth à Paris depuis le 24 novembre 1822 jusqu'au 31 Xbre 1841'.
MM10, 'Recensement de 1872 Population Juive 8ème Arrondissement'.

ARCHIVES DE LA FAMILLE PEREIRE, PARIS

BIBLIOTHÈQUE NATIONALE DE FRANCE, PARIS

Site l'Arsenal
Fonds Enfantin
7601/7602/7606/7613/7616/7617/7620/7621/7622/7628/7622/7630/7643/7664/7665/ 7728/7769/7774/7861/7819/7820/7822/7828/7848/7849/7860/7861.

Fonds d'Eichthal
13728-30/13754-55/14804/15031(t.1)-32.

Site François-Mitterand
Factum [legal, statement of case]: 4 - FN 2287, 2291, 2578-9, 3855, 3891-2, 8243-4, 8247, 8251, 8254, 8260, 8920, 25476-82.

Site Richelieu
Fonds Alfred Pereire, NAF/24605-24611.
Collection Joly de Fleury, 425, fo. 306.
585 (MICRO 17309), fos 288-9, 293-4.

BIBLIOTHÈQUE THIERS-DOSNE, PARIS, FONDS D'EICHTHAL
Mss. Cartons I, IIa, III, IV N-Q, IV Q3, IV R-R2, IV R8, V A-B.

ROTHSCHILD ARCHIVE, LONDON
Correspondence, much of it in *judendeutsch*, translated into English.

Printed primary sources, Emile and Isaac Pereire

Écrits de Emile et Isaac Pereire and *Oeuvres de Emile et Isaac Pereire*.

Gustave Pereire gathered together the *Écrits de Emile et Isaac Pereire* over the first decade of the twentieth century for private printing for the family. The *Écrits* cover broad subjects, such as the Pereires' railway ventures, and draw together writings for particular journals.

Gustave took control of the *Liberté* on the death of his father Isaac, where his editor was Laurent de Villedeuil. Alfred Pereire tells of his father, 'having given up the *Liberté* at the time of the Dreyfus Affair'. Wishing to provide Villedeuil with employment, he retained Villedeuil to undertake a more comprehensive approach to the documents than he, Gustave, was able to do with the *Écrits*; hence the *Oeuvres de Emile et Isaac Pereire*, advertised for publication in 1912. The *Oeuvres* contain an extensive commentary by Villedeuil on the documents. Divided into ten volumes, the *Oeuvres* were to have been sub-divided into 28 'fascicules', of which the railways alone was to have contributed twelve. There are only six volumes of the *Oeuvres* in the BNF-F-M and in the AFP. Whether any other volumes saw the light of day is unclear, although an original advertisement suggested that one volume, 'Série A – Vie et Travaux d'Emile et Isaac Pereire – Leçons et Doctrines' which I have been unable to locate, had already appeared.

Pereire, Emile et Isaac, *Écrits de Emile et Isaac Pereire* (Paris, 1900–9).

Tome I: [lacking fascicule number] 'Emile et Isaac Pereire, Collaboration au journal *Le Globe*, 1830–1832'; Isaac Pereire, 'Leçons lues à l'Athénée; Collaboration au *Journal des Débats*, 1838', 1900. Deuxième fascicule: 'Emile Pereire, Contributions à la *Revue encyclopédique*, 1832', 1902.

Tome II: Premier fasc. 'Contributions à la *Revue de la Bourse*, 1838, 1839, 1840, 1841, 1842', 1900. Deuxième fasc., parties 1–2, 'Isaac Pereire Contributions au *Journal des Débats*, 1838–1846', 1901.

Tome III: Premier fasc. 'Isaac Pereire, Correspondance Saint-Simonienne et Oeuvres Diverses', 1902. Deuxième fasc., première partie à troisième partie, 'Isaac Pereire, Direction Supérieure de *la Liberté* (1876–1877)', 1904. Troisième-quatrième fasc., quatrième à neuvième partie, 'Écrits Diverses, Direction Supérieure de *la Liberté*', 1905, 1906.

Tome IV: Fascicules 1–4, 'Emile Pereire, Contributions au *National*', 1831–35, 1900, 1901.

Tome V: Deuxième fasc. 'Emile et Isaac Pereire, Questions de Banque et de Crédit', 1902.

Tome VI: 'Compagnie Parisienne d'Eclairage et de Chauffage par le Gaz', Paris, 1909.

Tome VII: Fascicules 1–11, 'Chemins de fer (1832–1864)', 1902–9.

Tome VIII: 'Expositions Universelles de 1855 et 1867', 1905.

Oeuvres de Emile & Isaac Pereire, Pierre-Charles Laurent de Villedeuil (ed.), Paris, 1913–23.
Série D, 'Le Crédit public moderne et la politique française (1831–1835)', t. 2, 1913.
Série G: t. 1 t. 2, t. 3, t. 4, t. 5, 'Documents sur l'origine et le développement des chemins de fer (1832–1851)', 1920–23.

Published works by the Pereires and family

Pereire, Alfred. *Je suis dilletante, mon métier* (Paris, 1955).
——. *Autour de Saint-Simon: documents originaux* (Paris, 1912).
——. *Des premiers rapports entre Saint-Simon et Auguste Comte, d'après des documents originaux (1816–1819)* (Paris, 1906).
Pereire, Emile. *Du Système des banques et du système de Law* (Paris, 1866).
——. 'Note Adressée à Son Excéllence le Ministre des Travaux Publics par la Compagnie des Chemins de Fer du Midi à l'appui du projet d'Établissement de la Gare à la Grave' (Bordeaux, 1853).
——. 'A Messieurs les Electeurs du 4me Collège d'Eure et Loire' (Paris, 1842).
[Pereire, Emile]. *De la Suppression des octrois en France*: Rapport présenté au Conseil général de la Gironde au nom de la Commission des Finances, 4 septembre 1869 (Paris, 1869).
——. 'Moyens de supprimer immédiatement tous les impôts des boissons, l'impôt sur le sel, et la loterie'. *Globe* (1831).
Pereire, Gustave. *Historique du Chemin de Fer du Nord de l'Espagne* (Paris, 1901).
Pereire, Isaac. *La Question des chemins de fer* (Paris, 1879).
——. *Politique financière, La conversion et l'amortissement* (Paris, 1879).
——. *La Question religieuse* (Paris, 1878).
——. *Budget de 1877: questions financières* (Paris, 1876).
——. *Politique industrielle et commerciale: budget de réformes* (Paris, 1874).
——. *Principes de la constitution des banques et de l'organisation du crédit*, par M. (Isaac Pereire, Paris), 1865.
——. *La Banque de France et l'organisation du crédit en France* (Paris, 1864).
——. *Discours prononcé ... au Comice Agricole de Beynat (Corrèze), 23 October 1864* (Paris, 1864).
——. *Discours ... le 13 Août 1865, à l'occasion de l'inauguration de la statue de François Arago à Estagel* (Paris, 1864).
Emile and Isaac Pereire. 'A Monsieur le rédacteur en chef du journal la *Presse*' (Paris, 1868).
——. *Enquête sur la Banque de France, Dépositions de MM. Emile et Isaac Pereire* (Paris, 1866).
[Emile and Isaac Pereire]. *Considérations sur la crise monétaire et la banque de France* (Paris, 1871).
——. *Réorganisation des banques: légalité et urgence d'une réforme* (Paris, 1864).
——. *Réorganisation du système des banques, Banque de France-Banque de Savoie* (Paris, 1863).

Other published primary sources

Edited collections

Jacoud, Gilles (ed.). *Political Economy and Industrialism: Banks in Saint-Simonian Economic Thought* (London, New York, 2010).
Nahon, Gérard (ed.). *Les 'Nations' juives portugaises du sud-ouest de la France (1684–1791): Documents*, Vol. 15 (Paris, 1981).
Schwarzfuchs, Simon (ed.), *Le Registre des délibérations de la Nation juive portugaise de Bordeaux (1711–1787)* (Paris, 1981).

Other

Aycard, M. *Histoire du Crédit Mobilier* (Paris, 1867).
Castille, Hippolyte. *Les Frères Pereire* (Paris, 1861).
Clot, Louis M. *Emile Pereire* (Paris, 1858).
de Goncourt, Edmond and Jules. *Journal: mémoires de la vie littéraire*, 4 vols (Paris, 1956).
Doctrine de Saint-Simon: première année, exposition 1829 (Paris, 1830).
Drumont, Edouard. *La France juive*, 2 vols (Paris, [1912]).
du Camp, Maxime, *Souvenirs d'un demi-siècle: Au temps de Louis-Philippe et de Napoléon III 1830–1870* (Paris, 1949).
Feydeau, Ernest. *Mémoires d'un Coulissier* (Paris, 1873).
Fournel, Henri. *Bibliographie saint-simonienne* (Paris, 1833).
Halévy, Léon. *F. Halévy: sa vie et ses oeuvres* (Paris, 1863).
———. *Résumé de l'histoire des juifs anciens* (Paris, 1825).
Hubbard, G. *Saint-Simon: sa vie et ses travaux* (Paris, 1857).
La Rochelle, Ernest. *Jacob Rodrigues Pereire: premier instituteur des sourds-muets ... sa vie et ses travaux* (Paris, 1882).
Lauzac, Henry. *Isaac Pereire* (Paris, 1864).
Marx, Karl. *The Eighteenth Brumaire of Louis Bonaparte*, trans. Karl Marx ([based on 2nd edn 1869] New York, 1991).
Mérimée, Prosper. *Correspondance générale*, ed. Maurice Parturier, Deuxième Série (Toulouse, 1956).
Mirès, Jules. *A mes juges: ma vie et mes affaires* (Paris, 1861).
L'Organisateur; gazette des saint-simoniens, 2 vols (Reprint, New York, 1973), 1–2 année; 15 août 1831.
Poulet-Malassis, A[uguste] (ed.). *Papiers secrets et correspondance du Second Empire* (Paris, 1877).
Rodrigues, Eugène. *Lettres sur la religion et la politique, 1829: suivies de l'Éducation du genre humain de Lessing, traduit de l'Allemand* (Paris, 1831).
Sarchi, Charles et Félicie. *Lettres à Hélène: Correspondance de Charles et Félicie Sarchi à leur fille Mme. Van Tieghem*, Louis Bachy (ed.) (Montpellier, 2006), Vol. 1 (1862–1868), 2 (1869–1875), 3 (1876–1878).
Saint-Simon, Henri. *Oeuvres Complètes*, Introduction, notes et commentaires par Juliette Grange, Pierre Musso, Philippe Régnier and Franck Yonnet, 4 vols (Paris, 2012).

Saint-Simon, Henri and Prosper Enfantin, *Œuvres de Saint-Simon et d'Enfantin*, 2nd edn (Paris, 1865–1877).
Séguin, Edouard. *Jacob-Rodrigues Pereire ... notice sur sa vie et ses travaux, Précédés de l'Eloge de Cette Méthode par Buffon* (Paris, 1847).
Théophraste, [Adolphe Guéroult]. *É. M. Péreire* (Paris, 1856).
Vinçard, [Jules]. *Mémoires épisodiques d'un vieux chansonnier saint-simonien* (Paris, 1878).

Secondary sources

Albert, Phyllis Cohen. 'Ethnicity and Jewish solidarity in nineteenth-century France', in Jehuda Reinharz and Daniel Swetschinski (eds), *Mystics, Philosophers and Politicians: Essays in Jewish Intellectual History in Honor of Alexander Altmann*, pp. 249–74 (Durham, NC, 1982).
———. *The Modernization of French Jewry: Consistory and Community in the Nineteenth Century* (Hanover, NH, 1977).
Alem, Jean-Pierre [J.P. Callot]. *Enfantin: le prophète aux sept visages* ([Paris], 1963).
Altmann, Simon and Edouardo L Ortiz (eds), *Mathematics and Social Utopias in France: Olinde Rodrigues and His Times* (Providence, 2005).
Anceau, Éric. *Napoléon III: un Saint-Simon à cheval* (Paris, 2012).
———. *Les Députés du Second Empire: prosopographie d'une élite du XIXe siècle* (Paris, 2000).
———. *Dictionnaire des députés du Second Empire* (Rennes, 1999).
Autin, Jean. *Les Frères Pereire: le bonheur d'entreprendre* (Paris, 1984).
Barbance, Marthe. *Histoire de la Compagnie Générale Transatlantique: un siècle d'exploitation maritime* (Paris, 1955).
Barbier, Frédéric. *Finance et politique: la dynastie des Fould XVIIIe–XXe siècle* (Paris, 1991).
Benbassa, Esther. *The Jews of France: A History from Antiquity to the Present*, trans. M. B. De Bevoise (Princeton, NJ, 1999).
Benjamin, Walter. *The Arcades Project*, trans. Howard Eiland and Kevin McLaughlin (Cambridge, MA, 1999).
Berkovitz, Jay. *The Shaping of Jewish Identity in Nineteenth-Century France* (Detroit, 1989).
Berlanstein, Lenard R. *Big Business and Industrial Conflict in Nineteenth-Century France: A Social History of the Parisian Gas Company* (Berkeley, 1991).
Berthommé, Dominique (ed.). *Les Juifs de Bayonne 1492–1992* (Bayonne, 1992).
Berthon, Maurice-Edouard. *Emile et Isaac Pereire: la passion d'entreprendre* (Paris, 2007).
Bezucha, Robert J. *The Lyon Uprising of 1834: Social and Political Conflict in the Early July Monarchy* (Cambridge, MA, 1974).
Boime, Albert. 'Entrepreneurial patronage in nineteenth-century France', in Edward C. Carter III, Robert Forster and Joseph N. Moody (eds), *Enterprise*

and Entrepreneurs in Nineteenth- and Twentieth-Century France (Baltimore, 1976), pp. 137–207.
Bonin, Hubert. 'Les Pereire et Lesseps: gloire, opprobre et valorisation, ou les cycles de la perception historique', Actes du Congrès du Comité des Travaux Historiques et Scientifiques (Bordeaux, 24 April 2009).
Bouneau, Christophe. 'The Pereires' international strategy for railway construction in the 1850s and 1860s', in R. Roth and G. Dinhobl (eds), *Across the Borders: Financing the World's Railways in the Nineteenth and Twentieth Centuries* (Aldershot, 2008).
——. 'Chemins de fer et développement régional en France de 1852 à 1937: la contribution de la compagnie du Midi'. *Histoire économie et société* 9, 1 (1990), 95–112.
Bourillon, Florence. 'La rénovation de Paris sous le Second Empire: étude d'un quartier'. *Revue historique* 278, 1 (1987), 135–60.
Bouvier, Jean. *Un Siècle de banque française* (Paris, 1973).
Bowie, Karen (ed.). *La Modernité avant Haussmann: formes de l'espace urbain à Paris 1801–1853* (Paris, 2001).
——. 'Les grandes gares parisiennes: historique', in Karen Bowie (ed.), *Les Grandes Gares parisiennes au XIXe siècle* (Paris, 1987), pp. 53–67.
Bresler, Fenton. *Napoleon III: A Life* (London, 2000).
Briscoe, James Bland. 'Saint-Simonism and the Origins of Socialism in France, 1816–1832' (PhD dissertation, Columbia University, 1980).
Cameron, Rondo. *La France et le développement économique de l'Europe (1800/1914)*, trans. Marianne Berthod (Paris, 1971).
——. (ed.). *Essays in French Economic History* (Homewood, 1970).
——. 'The Crédit Mobilier and the economic development of Europe', *Journal of Political Economy* 61 (1953).
Cameron, Rondo, Olga Crisp, Hugh T. Patrick, and Richard Tilly (eds), *Banking in the Early Stages of Industrialization: A Comparative Study* (London, 1967).
Carlisle, Robert B. *The Proffered Crown: Saint-Simonianism and the Doctrine of Hope* (Baltimore, 1987).
Caron, François. *Histoire des chemins de fer en France. Vol. premier, 1740–1883* (Paris, 1997).
——. (ed.). *Paris et ses réseaux: naissance d'un mode de vie urbain XIXe–XXe siècles.* (Paris, 1990).
——. *An Economic History of France*, trans. Barbara Bray (New York, 1979).
Cassis, Youssef, Francois Crouzet, and Terry Gourvish (eds), *Management and Business in Britain and France: The Age of the Corporate Economy* (Oxford, 1995).
Cavignac, Jean. *Les Israélites bordelais de 1780 à 1850: autour de l'émancipation* (Paris, 1991).
——. *Dictionnaire du judaïsme bordelais aux XVIIIe et XIXe siècles: biographies, généalogies, professions, institutions* (Bordeaux, 1987).
Charléty, Sébastien. *Histoire du Saint-Simonisme (1825–1864)* (Paris, 1931).

Cohen, David. *La Promotion des juifs en France à l'époque du Second Empire (1852–1870)*. 2 vols (Aix-en-Provence, 1980).
Cohen, Steven M., and Paula E. Hyman (eds). *The Jewish Family: Myths and Reality*. (New York, 1986).
Collard, Claude and Melanie Aspey (eds). *Les Rothschild en France au XIXe siècle* (Paris, 2012).
d'Allemagne, Henry-René. *Les Saint-Simoniens 1827–1837* (Paris, 1930).
Daumard, Adeline. *Les Bourgeois et la bourgeoisie en France* (Paris, 1987).
———. *Maisons de Paris et propriétaires parisiens au XIXe siècle (1808–1880)* (Paris, 1965).
———. (ed.). *Les Fortunes françaises au XIXe siècle, civilisations et sociétés* (Paris, 1973).
Davies, Helen M. 'Jewish Identity, Social Justice, and Capitalism: the making of the Pereire brothers' (PhD dissertation, University of Melbourne, 2005).
———. 'Les Frères Pereire', in Rémy Cazals (ed.), *Le Mouvement saint-simonien: de Sorèze à l'Égypte, Actes du Colloque Abbaye-École de Sorèze*, 30 septembre–1er octobre 2011 (Quercy, 2012).
de Andia, Béatrice, and Dominique Fernandès (eds). *Rue du Faubourg-Saint-Honoré* (Paris, [1994]).
de Bertier de Sauvigny, Guillaume. *The Bourbon Restoration*, trans. Lynn M. Case (Philadelphia, 1966).
des Cars, Jean, and Pierre Pinon. *Paris-Haussmann: le pari d'Haussmann* (Paris, 1991).
Draï, Raphael-Pierre. 'Saint-simonisme et judaïsme', *Saint-Simonisme et pari pour l'industrie*, No. de *Économies et sociétés* 2 (1970), 1109–19.
Fargette, Guy. *Émile et Isaac Pereire: l'esprit d'entreprise au XIXe siècle* (Paris, 2001).
Ferguson, Niall. *The World's Banker: The History of the House of Rothschild* (London, 1998).
Foley, Susan K. *Women in France since 1789: The Meaning of Difference* (Basingstoke, 2004).
Forrest, Alan. *The Revolution in Provincial France: Aquitaine 1789–1799* (Oxford, 1996).
———. *Society and Politics in Revolutionary Bordeaux* (London, 1975).
Garner, Alice. *A Shifting Shore: Locals, Outsiders, and the Transformation of a French Fishing Town, 1823–2000* (Ithaca, 2005).
Gille, Bertrand. *La Banque en France au XIXe siècle: recherches historiques* (Geneva, 1970).
———. 'Les Saint-Simoniens et le crédit'. *Saint-Simonisme et pari pour l'industrie*, No. de *Économies et sociétés* 2 (1970), 1173–98.
———. *Histoire de la Maison Rothschild*, Tome II, 1848–1870 (Geneva, 1967).
———. 'La Fondation de la Société Générale'. *Histoire des entreprises* 8 (1961), 5–64.
———. *Recherches sur la formation de la grande entreprise capitaliste (1815–1848)* (Paris, 1959).

Girard, Louis. 'Valeur et permanence des thèmes saint-simoniens'. *Saint-Simonisme et pari pour l'industrie*, No. de *Économies et sociétés* 2, 4 (1970), 773–92.
——. *La Politique des travaux publics du Second Empire* (Paris, 1951).
Graetz, Michael. *The Jews in Nineteenth-Century France: From the French Revolution to the Alliance Israélite Universelle*, trans. Jane Marie Todd (Stanford, 1996).
Harvey, David. *Paris, Capital of Modernity* (New York, 2003).
Hazan, Eric. *The Invention of Paris: A History in Footsteps*, trans. David Fernbach (London, 2011).
Hazareesingh, Sudhir. *The Saint-Napoléon: Celebrations of Sovereignty in Nineteenth-Century France* (Cambridge, MA, 2004).
——. *From Subject to Citizen: The Second Empire and the Emergence of Modern French Democracy* (Princeton, 1998).
Hourmat, Pierre. *Histoire de Bayonne: la Révolution 1789–1799*. Vol. 2 (Bayonne, 1992).
Hyman, Paula E. *The Jews of Modern France* (Berkeley, 1998).
——. 'The modern Jewish family: image and reality', in David Kraemer (ed.), *The Jewish Family: Metaphor and Memory* (New York, 1989), 179–93.
——. 'Afterword', in Steven M. Cohen and Paula E. Hyman (eds), *The Jewish Family: Myths and Reality* (New York, 1986), 230–5.
James, Harold. *Family Capitalism: Wendels, Haniels, Falcks, and the Continental European Model* (Cambridge, MA, 2006).
Johnson, Christopher H. 'The revolution of 1830 in French economic history', in John M. Merriman (ed.), *1830 in France* (New York, 1975).
Jordan, David P. *Transforming Paris: The Life and Labors of Baron Haussmann* (New York, 1995).
Judt, Tony. *Marxism and the French Left: Studies on Labour and Politics in France, 1830–1981* (New York, 2011).
Kalman, Julie. *Rethinking Antisemitism in Nineteenth-Century France* (New York, 2010).
Kroen, Sheryl. *Politics and Theater: The Crisis of Legitimacy in Restoration France, 1815–1830* (Berkeley, 2000).
Kudlick, Catherine J. *Cholera in Post-Revolutionary Paris: A Cultural History* (Berkeley, 1996).
Landes, David S. *The Unbound Prometheus: Technological Change and Industrial Development in Western Europe from 1750 to the Present* (Cambridge, 1972).
——. 'The old bank and the new: the financial revolution of the 19th century', in F. Crouzet, W. H. Chaloner and W. M. Stern (eds), *Essays in European Economic History, 1789–1914*, trans. Max A. Lehmann (London, 1969).
——. *Bankers and Pashas: International Finance and Economic Imperialism in Egypt* (London, 1958).
Le Bret, Hervé. *Les Frères d'Eichthal* (Paris, 2012).
Leff, Lisa Moses. *Sacred Bonds of Solidarity: The Rise of Jewish Internationalism in Nineteenth-Century France* (Stanford, 2006).

Lenoble, Jean. *Les Frères Talabot: une grande famille d'entrepreneurs au 19e siècle* (Limoges, 1989).
León, Henri. *Histoire des juifs de Bayonne* (Marseille, 1976) [Reprint, original publication, Paris, 1893].
Lévy-Leboyer, Maurice. *Les Banques européennes et l'industrialisation internationale dans la première moitié du XIXe siècle* (Paris, 1964).
Magraw, Roger. *A History of the French Working Class*, Vol. 1, *The Age of Artisan Revolution* (Oxford, 1992).
——. *France 1815–1914: The Bourgeois Century* (London, 1985).
Malino, Frances. *The Sephardic Jews of Bordeaux: Assimilation and Emancipation in Revolutionary and Napoleonic France* (Tuscaloosa, 1978).
Manuel, Frank E. *The Prophets of Paris* (New York, 1965).
Marco, Luc. 'From the dynamics of the entrepreneur to the analysis of the firm: *la science des affaires*, 1819–1855', in Gilbert Faccarello (ed.), *Studies in the History of French Political Economy: From Bodin to Walras* (London, 1998).
McPhee, Peter. *A Social History of France, 1789–1914* (Basingstoke, 2004).
——. *The French Revolution 1789–1799* (Oxford, 2002).
Merriman, John M. *The Margins of City Life: Explorations on the French Urban Frontier, 1815–1851* (New York, 1991).
Muhlstein, Anka. *Baron James: The Rise of the French Rothschilds* (New York, 1984).
Nahon, Gérard. *Juifs et judaïsme à Bordeaux* (Bordeaux, 2003).
Neher-Bernheim, Renée. 'Un savant juif engagé: Jacob Rodrigues-Pereire (1717–1780)', *Revue des études juives* 142 (1983), 373–451.
Palmade, Guy P. *French Capitalism in the Nineteenth Century*, trans. Graeme M. Holmes (Newton Abbot, 1961).
Papayanis, Nicholas. *Planning Paris before Haussmann* (Baltimore, 2004).
Paulet, Elisabeth. 'The Péreire Brothers: bankers or speculators? An interpretation through agency theory paradigm', *Journal of European Economic History* 35 (2006), 463–93.
——. 'Financing industry: the Crédit Mobilier in France, 1860–1875', *Journal of European Economic History* 31 (2002), 89–112.
——. *The Role of Banks in Monitoring Firms: The Case of the Crédit Mobilier* (London, 1999).
Picon, Antoine. *Les Saint-Simoniens: raison, imaginaire et utopie* (Paris, 2002).
——. *Les Polytechniciens au XIXe siècle* (Paris, 1994).
Piette, Christine. *Les Juifs de Paris (1808–1840): la marche vers l'assimilation* (Québec, 1983).
Pilbeam, Pamela. *The Saint-Simonians in Nineteenth-Century France: From Free Love to Algeria* (Basingstoke, 2014).
Pilbeam, Pamela M. *Republicanism in Nineteenth-Century France, 1814–1871* (London, 1995).
Pilbeam, P.M. *The 1830 Revolution in France* (London, 1991).
Pinkney, David H. *Napoleon III and the Rebuilding of Paris* (Princeton, 1972).

Plessis, Alain. *Régents et gouverneurs de la Banque de France sous le Second Empire* (Geneva, 1985).
——. *La politique de la Banque de France de 1851 à 1870* (Geneva, 1985).
——. *La Banque de France et ses deux cents actionnaires sous le Second Empire* (Geneva, 1982).
Prévost-Marcilhacy, Pauline. *Les Rothschild: bâtisseurs et mécènes* (Paris, 1995).
Price, Roger. *People and Politics in France, 1848–1870* (Cambridge, 2004).
——. *The French Second Empire: An Anatomy of Political Power* (Cambridge, 2001).
——. *Napoleon III and the Second Empire* (London, 1997).
——. *An Economic History of France, 1730–1914* (London, 1981).
Ratcliffe, Barrie M. 'Some banking ideas in France in the 1830s: the writings of Emile and Isaac Pereire, 1830–1835', *Revue internationale d'histoire de la banque* 6 (1973), 23–46.
——. 'The origins of the Paris–Saint-Germain railway'. *Journal of Transport History* 1 (1972), 197–219.
——. 'Some Jewish problems in the early careers of Emile and Isaac Pereire', *Jewish Social Studies* 34 (1972), 189–206.
——. 'Les Péreire et le Saint-Simonisme'. Saint-Simonisme et pari pour l'industrie, No. de *Économies et sociétés* 5 (1971), 1215–56.
Reuveni, Gideon and Sarah Wobick-Segev (eds), *The Economy in Jewish History: New Perspectives on the Interrelationship between Ethnicity and Economic Life* (New York, 2011), especially Helen M. Davies, 'Socialists, bankers and Sephardic Jews: The Pereire Brothers and the Crédit Mobilier', pp. 94–114.
Rouart, Jean-Marie. *Morny, un voluptueux au pouvoir* (Paris, 1997).
Sewell, William H. *Work and Revolution in France: The Language of Labor from the Old Regime to 1848* (Cambridge, 1980).
Smith, Michael Stephen. *The Emergence of Modern Business Enterprise in France, 1800–1930* (Cambridge, MA, 2006).
Sowerwine, Charles. *France since 1870: Culture, Society and the Making of the Republic* (Basingstoke, 2009).
Spitzer, Alan B. *The French Generation of 1820* (Princeton, 1987).
Stanziani, Alessandro. *Rules of Exchange: French Capitalism in Comparative Perspective, Eighteenth to Early Twentieth Centuries* (Cambridge, 2012).
Stein, Margot B. *The Social Origins of a Labor Elite: French Engine-Drivers, 1837–1917* (New York, 1987).
Stoskopf, Nicolas. *Banquiers et financiers parisiens* (Paris, 2002).
Szajkowski, Zosa. *Jews and the French Revolutions of 1789, 1830 and 1848* (New York, 1970).
——. 'The Jewish Saint-Simonians and socialist anti-semites in France', *Jewish Social Studies* 9 (1947), 33–60.
Truesdell, Matthew. *Spectacular Politics: Louis-Napoleon Bonaparte and the Fête Impériale, 1849–1870* (New York, 1997).
Tulard, Jean. (ed.). *Dictionnaire du Second Empire* (Paris, 1995).
Vergeot, J.-B. *Le Crédit comme stimulant et régulateur de l'industrie: la conception*

saint-simonienne, ses réalisations et son application au problème bancaire d'après-guerre (Paris, 1918).

Walch, Jean. *Michel Chevalier: Économiste Saint-Simonien 1806–1879* (PhD dissertation, l'Université de Paris IV, 1974).

Wallon, Maurice. *Les Saint-simoniens et les chemins de fer* (Paris, 1908).

Weill, Georges. 'Les Juifs et le saint-simonisme'. *Revue des études juives* 31, 62 (1896), 260–73.

——. *L'École saint-simonienne: son histoire, son influence jusqu'à nos jours* (Paris, 1896).

Weintraub, Stanley. *Charlotte and Lionel: A Rothschild Love Story* (London, 2003).

Williot, Jean-Pierre. 'Un monde à part au coeur de la grande entreprise: le cas des employés du gaz à Paris dans la seconde moitié du XIXe siècle', *Histoire économie et société* 17 (1998), 119–38.

Williot, J.-P. 'Naissance d'un réseau gazier à Paris au XIXème siècle: distribution gazière et éclairage', *Histoire économie et société* 8 (1989), 569–91.

Yonnet, Franck. 'La Structuration de l'économie et de la banque sous le Second Empire: le rôle du Crédit mobilier des frères Pereire', in Nathalie Coilly and Philippe Régnier (eds), *Le Siècle des saint-simoniens: du Nouveau christianisme au canal de Suez* (Paris, 2006).

——. 'Saint-Simonisme et système bancaire: utopie et pratique' (Doctorat ès Sciences Économiques dissertation, d'Evry-Val D'Essonne, 2000).

——. 'La Banque saint-simonienne, les "travailleurs" et les "capitalistes": le projet des sociétés mutuelles de crédit de 1853 des frères Pereire'. 27, 1998.

Index

Note: 'n' after a page reference indicates the number of a note on that page.
Page numbers in italics refer to illustrations.

Alexandre, Samuel (Alexandre *fils*) 14, 17, 19, 22, 40, 139
Andrade, Abraham, Chief Rabbi Bordeaux 22–3, 40
André, Ernest 101, 107, 111n.88, 117, 129, 132, 133
Anglo-French Commercial Treaty and free trade 21, 70, 198, 207
Arcachon 3, 107, 152, 156, 186–8, 222
Arlès-Dufour, François 50, 95–6, 132, 149, 178, 197, 198, 202, 216
Armainvilliers 118, 156, 174, 179, 181, 185–6, 187, 215, 221
Armand, Alfred 153, 180, 185

banks and banking
    Banque de Belgique 115
    Banque Darmstädter für Handel und Industrie 128
    Banque de France 51, 62, 112, 113, 133, 138n.93, 204, 205, 212–13, 236
    Banque Impériale Ottomane 203
    Banque de Savoie 204–5
    Caisse des Actions Réunies 115
    Comptoir National d'Escompte 101, 117, 120, 132, 233
    Crédit Foncier de France 106, 111n.88, 120, 127, 212, 233
    Crédit Industriel et Commercial (CIC) 132, 202
    Crédit Lyonnais 128, 202
    Crédit Mobilier Espagnol 123–4, 144, 154, 216, 222, 227
    Crédit Mobilier Italien 203, 204
    Crédit Mutuel, Caisse Centrale des Sociétés de 120–1
    Réunion Financière 132–3, 202
    Société Financière Internationale (International Financial Society) 204
    Société Générale (French) 202
    Société Générale de Belgique 115
    Société Générale de Commerce et d'Industrie à Amsterdam 203
    see also Crédit Mobilier (French); Haute Banque; Pereire, Emile; Pereire, Isaac; Rothschild, James de; Saint-Simonianism
Bartholony, François 91, 123, 132, 201, 202
Baud, Henri 46, 67, 97, 118, 152, 178, 220n.96

Bayonne 1, 11–12, 20, 107
  see also Jews: Sephardim; railways
Bazard, Claire 49, 65
Bazard, St.-Amand 45, 50–1, 53, 55, 64, 65
Béhic, Louis Henri Armand 196
Bineau, Jean-Martial 114
Blanchisseries Industrielles, Société des 3, 147
Blanqui, Adolphe 79, 102, 144
Blount, Sir Edward 109n.21, 132, 202
Bonaparte, Louis-Napoléon see Napoléon III
Bordeaux
  British blockades of 10, 13, 14, 18, 20
  economy and trade 13–14, 16, 18, 19, 20, 25, 27, 55
  French Revolution and 13–14, 16
  loss of political dominance 13, 20–1
  slavery 13, 14, 18, 25
  transport 73–4, 81, 90–1, 106–7
  see also Jews: Sephardim; railways
Bourbon Restoration
  Bordeaux, effects of 25
  Catholic resurgence 38–9, 41
  Charles X 41, 46–7, 51, 54
  Louis XVIII 38–9, 41
Brunel, Isambard Kingdom 121–2
Buchez, Philippe 45, 53, 64, 100

Cabanel, Alexandre 181
capitalism
  1848 Revolution and 101
  family capitalism 139–42, 235
  July Monarchy and 68
  role of Crédit Mobilier 112
  Saint-Simonianism on 4
Carrel, Armand 55, 66
Cazeaux, Euryale 125
Cazeaux, Georges 66
Charles X see Bourbon Restoration
Charton, Edouard 155, 160n.59, 179
Château Palmer 177, 180, 230

Chevalier, Auguste 50, 107, 115, 165, 178
Chevalier, Michel
  falling out with Pereires 173, 179, 213, 216
  'Mediterranean system' 73, 81, 95, 101, 234
  Saint-Simonianism 45, 49, 73–4, 88
  see also Anglo-French Commercial Treaty and free trade
Chevalier, Suzanne see Pereire, Suzanne
Clapeyron, Emile 50, 72, 75, 78, 154, 200
Compagnies des Assurances La Confiance and La Paternelle 130, 142, 147, 151
Compagnie des Entrepôts et des Magasins Généraux de Paris 142, 230
Compagnie Générale Maritime 125–7, 198–9
Compagnie Générale Transatlantique
  board members 151, 153, 154, 230
  employee rewards 155
  establishment of 200
  Messageries Maritimes merger 230
  Penhoët shipyard established 147, 200, 234
  Pereire family fall out over 230
  Pereires regain control 220n.96, 227, 229
  Pereires voted out 216
Compagnie d'Assurances l'Union et Phénix Espagnol 231
Compagnie Immobilière (and de Paris)
  'L'Affaire Brochon' 154
  attempted rescues of 213, 221
  demise 213–16, 226
  establishment 131, 142
  financial difficulties 209, 212
  Fould blocks bond issue 204

INDEX 259

shareholders take action 215, 237–8
significant developments Paris 147,
    208–9, 212, 234
Société des Ports de Marseille and
    210–12
Crédit Foncier de France *see* banks
    and banking
Crédit Mobilier, Société Générale de
    (French)
  antecedents 115–16
  competitors 132
  directors 117, 143, 151
  emprunts 124, 132–3
  failure of 214, 216
  financial instruments 121, 204
  financial returns 120, 132, 162
  foundation 112, 117
  Marx on 146
  modus operandi 119, 147
  problems with 131, 141, 196, 211–13,
    236–7, 238
  shareholders 118, 141
  statuts 116–17, 119
Crémieux, Adolphe 96, 99, 100,
    110n.55, 164

David, Félicien César 178, 187
Delaroche, Paul 157, 181
Drumont, Georges *see* Jews: anti-
    Semitism
Durand, Justin *see* elections: Corps
    Législatif (1863)
Duveyrier, Charles 67, 178

education
  École Polytechnique 44, 50, 149
  of Pereire daughters 173
  Pereire, Isaac views on 146
  of Pereire sons 148–51
  professional 146–9
  Saint-Simonianism on 47, 50, 234
Eichthal, Adolphe d'
  Armainvilliers/Crécy 118, 185
  Compagnie Générale Maritime

(*and* Transatlantique) President
    126, 143
Crédit Mobilier founder of 117,
    135n.31
falling out Emile Pereire 204–5
Haute Banque member 128
Midi director 107, 109n.21
Société des Immeubles de la rue de
    Rivoli director 129–30
speaks at Emile Pereire funeral 225
support of Pereires 75, 153, 179, 203
Eichthal, Gustave d' 49, 64, 78, 97, 151,
    179, 191n.46
elections
  Chambre des Députés (1842) 93–4
  Chambre des Députés (1846) 95
  Corps Législatif (1863) 206–7
  Corps Législatif (1869) 216–17
Emerique, Amélie *see* Pereire, Amélie
Enfantin, Prosper
  antagonism towards Pereires 78,
    92–3, 95–6
  break up Saint-Simonianism and
    trial 66, 67
  Crédit Lyonnais director 202
  leader Saint-Simonianism 43, 44,
    46, 47–8, 51, 64, 178
  new direction Saint-Simonianism
    53
  see also banks and banking;
    Pereire, Emile; Pereire, Isaac;
    Saint-Simonianism
Eugénie de Montijo, 9th comtesse de
    Teba, Empress of Napoléon III
    182, 183, 197, 200, 209
Expositions universelle
  (1855) 128–9
  (1867) 182, 213

Faucher, Léonard (Léon) Joseph 78,
    100, 102, 107, 153
Flachat, Eugène 50, 72, 75–6, 81, 121–2,
    200
Flachat, Stéphane 50, 72, 78

Fonseca *neveu see* Lopès Fonseca, Mardochée
Fould, Achille
   Finance Ministry return to 196
   Protestant convert 96, 164
   rejects Banque de Savoie proposal 204
   supports Emile Pereire 101, 115
   support wanes 114–15
Fould, Benoît 37, 56, 96, 106, 115–16, 117, 119, 120, 128, 133, 135n.31, 203
Fould, Emile 151
Fould, Juliette Betzi *see* Pereire, Juliette Betzi
Fournel, Henri 7, 50, 154, 178, 179
free trade *see* Anglo-French Commercial Treaty and
French Revolution *see* individual headings

Galliera, Raffaele de Ferrari, duc de 101, 107, 117, 123, 132, 203, 214, 216, 227
Germain, Henri 127, 202
Gironde, department of 121, 130
   see also Bordeaux; elections: 1863 Corps Législatif (1863)
Girondins 13–14, 30n.35
Globe (journal) 46, 52, 60n.88, 62, 64, 66, 69, 71, 73, 83n.28
Gradis family 11, 25, 27, 140
Grieninger, Frédéric 117, 214

Halévy, Fromenthal 67, 151, 179, 187
Halévy, Léon 42, 49, 67, 179
Haussmann, Baron Georges
   Crédit Mobilier (1871) President of 237
   Seine Prefect of 129, 130, 131, 208
   Var and Gironde Prefect of 130
   vision of Paris 130
   see also Compagnie Immobilière (*and* de Paris); Napoléon III; Paris

Haute Banque 113, 117, 128, 138n.93, 236

Iffla, Daniel 163

Jewish emancipation 4, 10, 12–13, 15, 21, 30n.31, 38, 166, 240
Jewish regeneration 39, 48
Jews
   anti-Jewish sentiment
      Damascus Affair 97, 164, 206–7
      Leroux, Pierre 96
      Mathieu-Dairnvaell, Georges-Marie 96, 98
      philosophes 13
      targeting Ashkenazim 12
      targeting Sephardim 11
      working class 91
      see also Bourbon Restoration
   anti-Semitism
      Catholic Church 206
      Drumont, Georges 224, 228
      targeting Pereires 167, 240
      see also elections: Corps Législatif (1863), (1869)
   Ashkenazim
      citizenship 92
      population Alsace-Lorraine 12
      population Paris 38, 163
      Sephardim claims to superiority over 4, 12–13
      usury 21
      see also Rothschild, James de
   Sephardim
      antagonism towards Ashkenazim 92, 163
      Assemblée des Notables 21
      Census 1808 21–2
      citizenship 26, 163
      Consistoire Bordeaux 22–3, 27
      Corporation Bordeaux 11
      French Revolution and 12, 14, 29n.22
      history of 1–2, 4
      letters patent 10, 12

population Bordeaux 11, 22
population Paris 163
rapprochement with Ashkenazim 203
sedaca 10–11, 43, 118, 156, 235
slavery and 13, 126
synagogues 23, 40, 163
see also Bayonne; Bordeaux; Rodrigues Pereire, Jacob
Judaism
  Amsterdam influence on 11–12
  French Revolution and 15
  Saint-Simonianism on 48–9, 50–1
  see also Pereire, Emile; Pereire, Isaac; Jews: anti-Jewish sentiment, anti-Semitism
July Monarchy 55, 68–9, 70, 88, 99

Laffitte, Jacques 37, 43, 51, 54–6, 66, 69, 101
Landes, department of 125, 147, 155
Legrand, Baptiste Alexis Victor 68–9, 74, 90
Leroux, Pierre 52, 69, 100, 178
  see also Jews: anti-Jewish sentiment
Lopès Dias, Miriam (grandmother) 9–10, 13, 17
Lopès Fonseca, Jacob 21, 41, 63
Lopès Fonseca, Mardochée 11, 14, 15, 17, 18, 19, 23
Lopès Fonseca, Rachel Laurence *see* Pereire, Laurence
Lopès Fonseca, Rebecca Henriette *see* Rodrigues Pereire, Henriette
Lopès Fonseca, Sara-Sophie *see* Rodrigues, Sara-Sophie
Louis XVIII *see* Bourbon Restoration
Louis-Philippe, King of the French *see* July Monarchy

Magne, Pierre 114, 122, 124
Mallet, Charles *including* Mallet *frères* 56, 117, 126, 127, 128, 129, 135n.31, 203, 214

Mérimée, Prosper 186, 213
Mirès, Adolphe 22, 28, 39, 43, 57n.28, 71
Mirès, Jules 23, 32n.83, 115, 118, 209–10, 219n.64, 236, 238
Mocquard, Jean-François 105, 115, 197–8, 208
Morny, Charles Auguste Louis Joseph, duc de 102, 115, 207

Nadar 3, 157–8, 161n.69, n.71
Napoléon I, Emperor of the French
  fall of 25
  regulation of Jewish community/ Consistoire system 21
  slavery and 18
  visits Bordeaux 20
Napoléon III, Emperor of the French
  coup d'état 105–6
  failure of Pereire companies 212–13
  heir to Napoléon I 102, 129
  'Liberal Empire' 198, 206–7
  Mexico 200–1
  Pereires extend loans to 197–8
  Prince-President 102–3, *104*, 105
  Saint-Simonian influences 102–3
  Spanish railways 124, 202
  speech Bordeaux (1852) 107–8
  urban development
    Marseille 209–10
    Paris 129–31
National (journal) 66–7, 72, 74, 78

Ollivier, Emile 206

Paris
  building activity 131, 234
  cholera 71–2
  development of 36–7, 73–4
  gas, Compagnie de l'Éclairage et de Chauffage par le Gaz 128–9, 147, 153, 230
  infrastructure 128–9
  Omnibus, Compagnie (*also*

Entreprise) Générale des 128–9, 147, 151, 230, 237
population growth 36–7, 72, 157
see also Compagnie Immobilière (*also* de Paris), Crédit Mobilier; Haussmann, Baron Georges; Pereire, Emile
Pereire, Alfred 34, 36, 55, 185, 247
Pereire, Amélie 164, *183*, 228
Pereire, Cécile *see* Rhoné, Cécile
Pereire, Claire *see* Thurneyssen, Claire
Pereire, Emile
  appearance 33, *34*, *195*
  asthma 25, 26, 71–2, 143, 174, 186, 221
  attitude towards Judaism 38–9, 40–2, 97–8, 163–4, 240
  banking ideas 55–6, 115–17, 120–2, 233
  childhood 17, 22, 23
  Conseil général of Gironde department 121, 142
  death of 224–5
  deputy *see* elections
  early working life 25, 27, 39, 48
  education 23–4
  hôtel Pereire 180–3, 185, 187
  impact of father's death on 36, 139, 214
  journalism 52–3, 66–7, 69–70, 73
  plaine Monceau 74, 156–7, 212
  political opinions 4, 55, 93–4, 95, 99–100, 103, 113–14
  relations with Isaac 26, 35–6, 43–4, 68, 89–90, 97, 151, 215–16, 225–6
  relationship with Napoléon III 113–15, 128, 133–4, 189, 196–8
  role-sharing with Isaac Pereire 56n.7, 142
  Saint-Simonianism
    industrial action 154–5, 207
    in later life 178
    involvement in and resignation from 43, 48, 53, 64, 65, 66
  meets Saint-Simon 42
  temperament 35–6
  vision of Paris 74
  writing style 52–3
  see also Arcachon; banks and banking; education; Exposition Universelle (1855); Exposition Universelle (1867); Napoléon III; Pereire, Isaac; Pereire, Isaac (father); Pereire, Herminie; railways
Pereire, Emile II 89, 149, *150*, 151, 165–6, 170, 173, 174, 185, 220n.96, 222, 230–1
Pereire, Eugène 67, 89, 125, 129, *148*, 149, 151, 157–8, 164, 170, 185, 190n.17, 200, 216, 220n.96, 222, 227, 229, 230
Pereire, Fanny Rebecca
  at home 187
  birth 48
  Cabanel portrait 181
  charitable work 174, 177–8
  children 170, *171*, 188
  collector 182
  Judaism 164–5
  marriage with Isaac Pereire 89–90, 167
  role in the *Liberté* 226
Pereire, François 231
Pereire, Gustave 6, 60n.88, 149, 151, *153*, 158, 161n.71, 164, 170, 181, 222, 226, 228, 231, 247
Pereire, Herminie (Rachel Herminie)
  ambivalence about wealth 188
  at home 187
  Cabanel portrait *168*, 181
  charitable work 174, 177
  children and pregnancies 88, 89, 170
  correspondence with Emile 167, 169
  educating sons, role in 149
  health deteriorates 223–4

marriage with Emile Pereire 39–40
music 187
Saint-Simonianism 49
Pereire, Henry 149, 151, 152, 165, 170, 220n.96, 222, 230
Pereire, Isaac (father)
  bankruptcy and death 19–20, 229
  business with Mardochée Lopès Fonseca and Isaac Rodrigues 14, 17, 18–19
  childhood and training 13
  French Revolution and revolutionary club 16
  Judaism 15
  position in Sephardic community 14
  see also Pereire, Emile; Pereire, Isaac
Pereire, Isaac
  appearance 34, 35, 199
  attitude towards Judaism 43–4, 63, 70–1, 96–7, 98, 163–4, 240
  banking ideas 55–6, 62–3, 70, 233
  childhood 23
  death of 229–30
  early working life 25, 39, 64
  education 23–4, 53
  father's death 36, 51
  journalism 78, 88–9
  political opinions 4, 55, 62–3, 99–100, 113–14, 226–7
  proprietor of the *Liberté* (journal) 226–7, 228, 231
  restores family interests 222, 227
  role Pereire companies 56n.7, 127, 142–4
  Saint-Simonianism
    in later life 178
    'Lessons on Industry and Finance' 62–3
    letters to Jacques Rességuier 47–8
    relationship with Enfantin 47–8, 51, 65, 66, 85n.87

writings 70, 73
temperament 36, 141
wealth 162
see also banks and banking; education; Pereire, Emile; Pereire, Fanny Rebecca; Pereire, Isaac (father); Pereire, Rebecca Henriette (mother); railways; socialism; Third Republic
Pereire, Léontine 165, 184
Pereire, Juliette Betzi 151, 164, 176
Pereire, Mardochée Télèphe (Télèphe) 18, 23–4, 26, 229
Pereire, Rachel Laurence (Laurence)
  children 67, 170
  death of 87–8
  marriage with Isaac Pereire 63–4
Pereire, Rebecca Henriette (mother) 6, 17, 20, 21, 22, 23–4, 26, 37, 40, 43–4, 45–6
Pereire, Suzanne 165–6, 175
Pereire family 151–2, 158, 162, 165–6, 167, 169, 170, 173–4, 178–9, 180, 182, 185, 189
Persigny, Jean Gilbert Victor Fialin, duc de 115–16, 117–18, 198

Raba *frères* 11, 20, 31n.69, 140
railways
  French
    Cette (Sète) à Marseille, Chemin de Fer du Littoral de 207–8
    l'Est, Compagnie des Chemins de Fer de 122
    Grand Central de France, Compagnie du Chemin de Fer du 122–3, 124
    Midi et du Canal Latéral à la Garonne, Compagnie des Chemins de Fer du 107, 121–2, 123, 124–5, 146, 154, 155, 206, 207, 208, 216, 230

Nord, Compagnie du Chemin
de Fer du 91–2, 93, 95, 108,
133
Orléans à Bordeaux, Compagnie du Chemin de Fer de
90–1, 123, 230
l'Ouest, Compagnie des
Chemins de Fer de 122, 201
Paris à Lyon (1846), Compagnie
de Chemin de Fer de 95
Paris à Lyon et à la Méditerranée, Compagnie des
Chemins de Fer de 95–6,
123, 124, 201, 207
see also Talabot, Paulin
Paris à Orléans, Compagnie du
Chemin de Fer de 90–1, 123,
230
see also Bartholony, François
Paris à Saint-Germain-en-Laye,
Compagnie du Chemin de
Fer de 74–5, 78, 79, 80, 81,
84n.72, n. 73, 98, 99, 109n.21,
122
Paris à Versailles (Rive Droite),
Compagnie du Chemin de
Fer de 81, 88, 93, 98, 122,
144, 152
Other
Autrichienne (Austrian),
Société des Chemins de Fer
de l'État 127–8, 144, 222, 239
Cordoue à Seville, Chemin de
Fer de 124, 231
Madrid–Zaragosa–Alicante,
Ferrocarriles 124, 231
Nord de l'Espagne, Chemin de
Fer du 124, 144, 146, 151, 198,
201–2, 216, 222, 230, 231, 239
Russes, Grande Compagnie des
Chemins de Fer 201
Pereire competitors see Bartholony,
François; Rothschild, James
de; Talabot, Paulin

railways policy 68–9, 72, 90–1,
124–5, 208
railway stations 80, 81
Regnault, Paul 152, 178, 186
Rhoné, Cécile 67, 151, 165, 166, *172*, 173,
174, 224, 226
Rhoné, Charles 151, 165, 222, 224
Rodrigues Henriques see Rodrigues
Rodrigues, Eugène 39, 44, 48–9, 53,
54, 65, 67
Rodrigues family 38–9, 40, 46, 54,
83n.35, 97, 106, 173, 220n.96
Rodrigues, Isaac (Rodrigues *fils*) 14,
15, 16–17, 21, 24, 37, 38, 40, 97,
140, 148, 162, 179, 191–2n.50
Rodrigues, Mélanie 43, 46, 49, 97
Rodrigues, Olinde
attitude towards Judaism 38
birth of 16
death of 106
education 24
friendship with Emile Pereire 39,
48, 67, 97
political views 55, 100, 155
secretary to Saint-Simon 42–3
Saint-Simonianism 43–5, 46, 49, 53,
64, 66, 67, 116
Rodrigues, Sara-Sophie 16, 37, 97, 179
Rodrigues Pereire, Jacob (grandfather)
legacy to Pereire brothers 6, 9, 17,
23–4, 36, 44, 229
marriage with Miriam Lopès Dias
9–10, 13, 17
represents Sephardim of southwest
6, 12–13
secretary and pensioner at court 6
teacher of deaf-mutes 6
Rodrigues Pereire *otherwise see*
Pereire
Rothschild, Alphonse de 133, 182
Rothschild, Anselm von 91, 97
Rothschild, Betty de 89, 191n.39
Rothschild, James de
Austria 128

Bordeaux concession and Midi 91, 107
Crédit Mobilier opponent 117–18
death of, 215
leader Jewish community 77, 97, 163–4
Napoléon III rapprochement 118, 185, 196, 197, 198
Orléanism 76, 103–5, 114
Pereire family rapprochement 231
relations Emile Pereire 48, 76, 102, 108
Réunion Financière 132–3, 202
Rothschild, Lionel de 109n.21, 117–18
Rothschild, Nathaniel (Natty) 109n.21, 143, 185, 217n.4
Rothschild, Salomon Mayer von 76, 108n.6
Rothschild family 76, 89, 92, 128, 140, 182, 203, 236–7
Rouher, Eugène
  Banque de France *Enquête* 205
  Banque de Savoie 205
  Crédit Mobilier rescue attempts 212–13
  railways and 114, 123, 124, 208

Saint-Simon, Claude Henri de Rouvroy, comte de 42–5, 54
Saint-Simonianism
  on banking 50, 55–6, 116
  Encyclopédie: Exposition universelle des progrès des sciences, des arts et des lettres au XIXe siècle 157
  Enseignements 65
  on Judaism 48–9, 50–1
  lectures 50–1, 61–2, 65
  religion 48, 53, 61, 65
  women 49, 50, 61, 65
  see also individual names; socialism: 'association', Saint-Simonian socialism
Salvador, Casimir
  Compagnie Générale Maritime, director 125
  Crédit Mobilier, secretary-general and director 143, 154, 213, 216
  Société Autrichienne des Chemins de Fer de l'État, director 127
Salvador, Joseph 39
Sarchi, Charles
  comments on Pereires 185, 188
  Crédit Mobilier investor 118
  employed by Pereires 97, 152
  Saint-Simonian 48, 49
Sarchi, Félicie
  comments on Pereires 170, 215
  marriage 46
Second Empire
  collapse of and retribution 217, 221
  economy and trade 112, 124, 127, 144, 200, 239
  family life under 166–7
  grande bourgeoisie 180, 187
  ministries 114
  paternalism under 155–6
  political ideology 113, 114, 129, 145
  small business under 120–1
  see also Fould, Achille; Napoléon III; individual names
Second Republic 99, 100–2
Socialism
  'association', concept of 42, 45, 47, 50, 51, 62, 69, 120, 144, 145, 194, 235
  Marxism 69, 145–6, 234, 235
  'practical socialism' 100, 228, 233, 235
  Saint-Simonian socialism 4, 61, 63, 100, 130, 145–6, 228
Société Générale des Asphaltes de Paris 142, 147
Société des Immeubles de la rue de Rivoli (precursor to Compagnie Immobilière de Paris) 129–30
Société Universelle Pereire 156–7
Stoppani, Léontine de *see* Pereire, Léontine

Talabot, Paulin
   banking interests 132, 202
   Marseille 209, 226
   Paris à Lyon et à la Méditerranée and (PLM) 101, 128, 196–7, 208
   Saint-Simonianism 49, 72
   see also railways
Third Republic 169, 223, 226, 231
Thurneyssen, Auguste 75, 109n.21, 214, 216
Thurneyssen, Claire 88, 170
Thurneyssen, Georges 151, 165, 222
Tournachon, Gaspar-Félix *see* Nadar
Transat *see* Compagnie Générale Transatlantique

Urbain, Ismayl 90, 108n.9, 178, 191n.44

EU authorised representative for GPSR:
Easy Access System Europe, Mustamäe tee 50,
10621 Tallinn, Estonia
gpsr.requests@easproject.com

www.ingramcontent.com/pod-product-compliance
Lightning Source LLC
Chambersburg PA
CBHW021852230426
43671CB00006B/354